The Flowe

Maryland ꞏ ꞏꞏꞏꞏꞏꞏꞏꞏꞏ

An intimate and objective history of the Province of Maryland to the overthrow of Proprietary Rule in 1654, with accounts of Lord Baltimore's settlement at Avalon.

by

HARRY WRIGHT NEWMAN

CLEARFIELD

Reprinted for
Clearfield Company, Inc. by
Genealogical Publishing Co., Inc.
Baltimore, Maryland
1998, 2001

Originally published: Washington, D.C., 1961
Reprinted: Genealogical Publishing Co., Inc.
Baltimore, 1984, 1985
Library of Congress Catalogue Card Number 83-82451
International Standard Book Number 0-8063-1051-0
Made in the United States of America

Dedicated to the Memory of
GOVERNOR THOMAS GREENE, ESQ.
and MISTRESS ANNE COX, *my ancestors,*
who braved the Atlantic in 1633
to aid in the establishment of
another part of England in America.

TABLE OF CONTENTS

PART III

PREFACE

In offering this treatise to the public as an objective contribution to Marlandiana, I have endeavored to give a personal, intimate yet documentary history of that flowering of the Palatinate of Maryland before the deflowering temporarily by the Virginia Puritans. The character of those Adventurers to Maryland from Old England and the ideals they held and inculcated into the everyday life society lay a foundation for the rôle which Maryland was to play and has played as an integral part of the struggles and destiny of a young Nation to ultimate greatness. For it was in those early formative years when the Adventurers had to combat unfriendly Indians, the intrigue, jealousy, and envy of the Virginia Colony, and the hardships of a primitive land that stalwart and Christian men and women with a fear of God and his Son were born.

Not a few historians have treated this early phase of Maryland's history, but it is not believed that any has handled the subject matter of the first fifteen years or to the Puritan Revolution as objectively as I have attempted, or has gone into the personal history of each Adventurer—examining all extant known records and seeking truth with concrete factual reasoning. I do not contend that my work on Maryland's beginnings is final and absolute. Often after a lifetime of toil, writers believe that their work is ultimate, but during the intervening years, they look backward and recognize as already their work is obsolete, for new conclusions become drawn not so much from fresh stand-points, as from new discoveries.

In writing early Maryland history of the past, we of the present peer at the scenes and personalities through telescopes of research across a gulf of 350 years. We attempt to project ourselves into the lives, experiences, and feelings of our ancestors through the records which have been preserved and have been left behind. As in most historical research one comes across evidence that is contradictory or reaches a period where records are lost, but then it is the duty of the introspective historian to analyze the visible elements by projecting his thoughts and mind into that missing period and to come out with logical conclusions, though they may sometimes be inferential or implicative.

To the viewpoint of the present-day history student, new sources are accumulating much faster than they can be assimilated or absorbed. It has been true to a certain limited extent in this research, for I have had the benefit of sources heretofore unknown or unobtainable to the past historian, yet there has been a craving for the unobtainable. In spite of ever new discoveries, we always have that desire for that which has been obliterated. We feel squelched and stagnated in our eager pursuit of truth by a lost or destroyed record or made to realize in our unfinished conquest that nothing is so silent as an unmarked grave.

Maryland is no exception in the category of missing or destroyed records, but when one reviews the meagre material of that very early period and compares it with Maryland's sister Colonies, the Maryland historian is indeed fortunate, for Maryland records were recorded more meticulously than any other Southern Colony.

When the antiquarian attempts, however, to reconstruct that period and is anxious to know more about the way-of-life and thoughts of those early Adventurers, he wishes most earnestly for the libers of the years 1633-1637—four years of vital happenings lost to the researchers—reputedly destroyed by the Puritan ruffians. And the loss by fire of the early deeds for the mother county of St. Mary's is another irreparable loss.

These missing elements are also an impediment in the work of the historian-genealogist who knows well the mass of material that he has to collate and dreading lest that he may make a slip through overlooking some obscure or newly discovered source. The historian-genealogist must therefore draw conclusions on what he has found, but never draw conclusions until examination has been completed of every extant known source. Yet time limitation often prevents stirring beyond the boundary of the subject during the short period allotted to the research. We print what we know and believe at the time, for to wait too long before publication, we may come to that ultimate passing into the beyond without giving our contributions to posterity.

Personal visits to England and individual research there have aided in accomplishing materially this work, but the sources in London were limited. Perhaps some material is hidden among the public archives of England waiting to be discovered. We regret the loss of many of the Calvert Papers which were once examined by Dr. John Henry Alexander, of Maryland, in 1839 and which were missing when the State of Maryland purchased them from the English Calvert heirs some years later, now deposited in the Maryland Historical Society and the Land Office at Annapolis.

I am particularly grateful to Mr. Fred Shelley, one-time librarian of the Maryland Historical Society, when about five years ago he brought the Calvert Papers at the society to my attention and actually advised that much material from them had been published in the so-called Fund Publication. Furthermore, he permitted me to examine personally many of the previous documents. A gold mine had been revealed and placed at my disposal, for over a period of 30 years or more I had made repeated enquiries about the Calvert Papers at the Maryland Historical Society, but I was encountered with only casual and evasive replies, received no cooperation and was ultimately advised that they were not for public dissimulation. In other words I was denied their use. The original papers and the printed matter in the Fund Publications would have aided me materially in the preparation of "Seigniory in Early Maryland" and would have made that publication more authoritative and complete.

I also wish to extend sincere appreciation to the staffs at the Hall of Records and the Land Office at Annapolis, the former under the direction of Dr. Morris Radoff which during the research for my ten opuses have been most courteous, helpful, and cooperative, especially the late Mr. Roger Thomas and his earnest successor, Mr. Guy Weatherly.

My appreciation is also extended to Crolian Edelen, Esq., of New Jersey, who painstakingly went over portions of my manuscript and offered many valuable suggestions, for a different pair of eyes can see discrepancies in copy which the author's eyes never see.

Written at The St. Albans Apartments, Washington, D. C., on Maryland Day, March 25, 1959.

THE AUTHOR.

PART I

PROLOGUE

The morning was rather cloudy and somewhat bleak, so characteristic of coastal England in the late autumn. The day was Friday, November 22d or the Feast of St. Cecilia, according to the religious calendar to be more exact, and the year was 1633, when the Ark and her pinnace the Dove were moored restlessly in the harbour of Cowes on the Isle of Wight. The two ships had remained in the harbour now for several weeks arousing not undue suspicion and mistrust among the town folks. It was fully ten o'clock in the morning, but that small village on the northern coast of the Isle was wide awake, for Englishmen rose early for their labour in that day.

The two ships were rather crowded, with nearly two hundred passengers or Adventurers destined for that new, unseen, and untamed land in Virginia* north of the Potomac River now given the name of "Merrie Land". These two hundred or less Englishmen were leaving their ancestral homes to establish with high hopes and expectations a permanent settlement as another link in that once mighty British Empire yet unborn.

There were not many friends and relatives at the dock to bid farewell. The silent leave-takings of the family and present sweethearts, with some visible tears, had already been shed at London several weeks previously and to those Adventurers the sailing from Cowes on that sunless morning was just another anti-climax. For the delaying of the ships by designing enemies, provoked somewhat by hostile agents from the Virginia Colony then in London and a none-too-friendly Parliament to Lord Baltimore, had taken all that first-moment thrill and excitement of departing Englishmen to an unknown land and the fascination of a perilous sea voyage. But there were the usual sprinkling of curious housewives and idle urchins who always come down to witness the sailing of a vessel as well as the inevitable wenches and town trollops who, from time immemorial, had discovered the fascination of sea-going men. A few farewells, however, between them and the sailors were apparent, for the two ships had been at Cowes sufficiently long for that casual familiarity experienced among those classes.

Captain Robert Wintour, the Commander of the Ark, was proud of his charge, for the ship was superior to the average sea-going vessel of that epoch. Leonard Calvert and his two commissioners, Captain Thomas

---

* To the Britisher of the 17th century, Virginia was a geographic term given to that vast and undefined portion of North America which John and Sebastian Cabot discovered and claimed for the Kingdom of England. The name came into popular use before 1580 and is credited to Sir Walter Ralegh, Knt. who named it after the unwed Elizabeth Tudor. Virginia in a broad sense and the Colony of Virginia were therefore two different and separate entities.

Cornwalys and Jerome Hawley, were on the forward deck of the Ark surrounded by the other gentlemen Adventurers, as the heavy iron anchors were lifted from the brownish waters of the two straits known as the Solent and the Spithead, actually inlets from the English Channel which separate the Isle from the mainland. The ships then sailed slowly away from their moorings. They had been blessed with a brief Roman Catholic ceremony before sailing, for Father Andrew White, a Jesuit, had joined the Adventurers at Cowes, with his assistant, Father Altham, and two lay brothers. Within a short time the Ark followed by the Dove was well out from the shore heading for the Needles, as the rocks at the western extremities of the Isle were known.

Father White and Father Altham assembled the pious on deck and on bended knees they asked God for protection and safety and offered prayers and supplications to the Holy Mother, to St. Ignatius, who had been made the patron saint of the infant colony, and to St. Michael. No Anglican priest had joined the adventure and those Anglicans, called in that day Protestant Catholics, were not an irreligious group, so they joined with reservations or watched silently the prayers and supplications of the Roman Catholics.

Within a few minutes the two ships were passing slowly between the shore of the Isle and the mainland of Old England, some distance away but visible on a clear day.

BEFORE THE ARK AND THE DOVE

In one sense the sailing of those two small but significant ships may be said to be the genesis of Maryland, once a small but very mighty integral part of Great Britain—now just one of the fifty units which compose the United States of America, but one which has maintained an individuality even in this twentieth century of regimentation.

The genesis of Maryland, however, did not commence actually on that dull morning in November 1633. It went back to the year 1579 when a son was born to Leonard Calvert, a prosperous commoner, at Kipling in the Chapelry of Bolton, Yorkshire, who, at the baptism in the Established Church, was given the Christian name of George. The Calvert family, as some authentic sources reveal, had its origin in Flanders, but the family name has more the flavour of the Walloons rather than the Flemings.*
It was perhaps in the fourteen-hundreds that the English progenitor crossed the channel and settled in County York and became a breeder of sheep—no doubt sending the wool back to his kinsmen in Flanders to be made into cloth—for Flanders in that day was the principal center of the textile-weaving industry.

The senior members prospered and their land holdings increased until the family was rated among the lesser county gentry, though it had never proved itself capable of using armorial trappings. The personal charm and integrity of the younger generations contracted marriages with heiresses of the county squirarchy and eventually the family took its place among the recognized gentry of York. It was not until 1622 that the armorial bearings of the family were exemplified, the charges taken from an ancient Flemish family and for that reason the family does not appear in any of the Visitations of York taken during the fifteen and sixteen hundreds. After George Calvert was knighted in 1617 Sir Richard St. George, Knight, Norroy King of Arms of the North parts of the Realme of England from the River of Trent Northward, by patent of 1622 granted Sir George permission to quarter his arms with that of his mother's family, the Crossland—his mother being Alicia, the daughter and sole-heiress of John Crossland, of Crossland, Gent., an ancient family.

What dreams were early planted in young George, is a matter of mental conjecture, but they were ambitious ones interposed with righteous visions

---

* When the Calvert arms were exemplified in 1622, it was stated by an Antwerp antiquarian, Richard Verstegan that the family was "a Noble and auntient familie ... in the Earldom of Flanders", the principal seat being at Warvickoe. See, the Exemplication of the Arms of Sir George Calvert, printed in Fund Publication no. 28, pp. 38-40, Md. Hist. Soc.

1

of personal eminence and position, and the possible existence of a British State beyond Island Britain. While the early English explorers did much to claim new territory for the upcoming kingdom, England owes much to her subject born in Yorkshire for paving the foundation of the British Empire which flourished for more than 300 years until its demise in the nineteen forties after her ruthless politicians fought two wars to destroy a rising great power of their own blood, but in the end spelled doom to her greatness and ushered in a new order of events. Our story, however, is not concerned with the disintegration of the British Empire or the future of Great Britain and her diminishing possessions beyond the seas, but with the founding of the Province of Maryland on the banks of the Potomac separated by the mighty Chesapeake Bay into the Eastern and Western Shores—two sections which have ever been attuned in race, culture, heritage, and the pursuit of individual happiness.

Like the sons of the prosperous Yorkshiremen, George Calvert was destined to be sent to one of the two great historic universities, and at the age of 14 his parents entered him at Trinity College, Oxford, from which he was graduated in February 1597. Then extensive travels on the Continent opened his eyes to a greater world beyond his Island Britain, and upon his return he established his seat at Danbywiske in his native county of York. But not wishing to remain a provincial figure, he engaged himself in 1605 as a clerk to the Privy Council in London which brought him in contact with current political forces of the day. In 1611 he conducted a special diplomatic mission to France and in 1615 a similar mission to the Elector Palatinate. He served in the House of Commons from 1606 to 1624, where he was distrusted by many of his colleagues for his fervent advocacy of the then proposed Spanish marriage of the Prince of Wales, later Charles I, with Infanta Maria, the daughter of Philip III of Spain, scions of the Catholic House of Hapsburg. For this ardent support of the Spanish alliance which did not materialize and other worthy deeds, Calvert won the esteem of James I who made him a Knight Bachelor of the Realm on September 29, 1617.

In February 1618, Sir George was appointed Secretary of State and in 1620 High Lord of the Treasury. During these formative years at court and in the pursuit of statemanship, he thus saw the righteousness of the conservative or court party and from his own convictions he became a leader against the rising power of the Puritans led by a few ambitious or dissatisfied demagogues from the gentry, but drawing most of the support from the yeomanry and burgers of the cities, or the radical lower classes.

While Sir George was becoming a power at court, his thoughts were continually wandering to the possibilities of settlements in the New World. Raleigh's Colony at Roanoke Island had failed and the settlement of Captain Sir Richard Whitbourne in 1615 on New Found Land [orthography of the times], had not been too great a success. After many ups and downs the London Company was making somewhat success of its commercial adventure in the Colony of Virginia, and of course the Pilgrims of New England wanted to establish a separate State with allegiance only to themselves, but their jealous and selfish ambitions to found a State divorced from England royal allegiance was early thwarted. Some success was also being made at Barbadoes in the West Indies, but nevertheless England had lagged in the development of her new possessions, and at that time Spain, Portugal, and France all had been successful, with the results that their colonial empires were bringing much wealth to the mother countries. Furthermore, France, Spain, and the Netherlands were encroaching upon English claims of the fifteen hundreds and unless the English people strengthened their ownership, their rights would be lost.

Sir George approached King James and other interested members in court circles as to a scheme of colonization and his willingness to finance a colony in America. In that day when distances were great, the nearest land to the mother country naturally held a psychological effect, besides the economic advances of the fishery industry were being fully realized.

Fishing fleets were going farther into the North Atlantic and the discovery of the great beds proved a material asset on the economy of nations at that time, especially with a growing European population and more fast days in the religious calendar than at present. Besides salted fish was a staple product during the long winter months for the British Isles as well as all Northern European countries.

When the Cabots discovered an island in the North Atlantic in 1497 which they called New Found Land, they claimed it for the Crown of England. In 1500 the Portuguese explored and named some of the bays and inlets. Nothing was attempted by England until 1583 when Sir Humphrey Gilbert planted a colony there, but it had more the features of a fishing outpost rather than a prominent English settlement. Then on May 11, 1615, Captain Sir Richard Whitbourne, who had visited New Found Land as early as 1579, sailed from Exeter to establish courts of justice there, and in 1617 he sailed again from England with a second detachment of colonists, mostly Welshmen. Although by 1620 some settlers remained, it could not be called a success.*

In 1608 France planted a colony at Quebec and was becoming more audacious in her rights in that area, with an accelerated monopolistic control of the fishery. The French from the very beginning had resented the English attempts at settlement on an island which strategically controlled the gateway to her Province of New France, and as the French settlements increased in strength, France was asserting herself more and more and

---

* Captain Whitbourne published an enthusiastic book in which he recorded his memories of June days in New Found Land with their delicious wild strawberries and cherries, "the solf air redolent with the fragance of red and white roses, the woods vocal with thrushes and other songsters that rivalled the nightingale; of wild beasts there were none that were harmful and that in St. John's harbour he once saw a mermaid". Ref.: Browne's Calverts, p. 17.

foresaw the competition of the English in the great fishing areas of the North Atlantic. In fact France contested English sovereignty on New Found Land and did not acknowledge British rights until the Peace of Utrecht in 1713.

The King of England was well aware of the situation, and as Sir George at his own expense was anxious to establish a permanent part of Great Britain in the oversea possessions, he or his advisers centered their attention on New Found Land.

As early as 1621 Sir George dispatched Captain Edward Wynne to New Found Land to establish a fishing post with the ultimate idea of a permanent settlement. Wynne established the colony some 40 miles south as the crow flies from the present harbour of St. John's on a bleak promontory which they called Ferryland, a name still retained today.* In 1622 another ship financed by Sir George was sent under Captain Daniel Powell to carry on the work and to augment the small colony with fresh settlers. The reports which came back to Calvert were in some manner extremely favourable which encouraged him to push certain legal claims and rights for colonization.[1]

Sir George wrote to Sir William Alexander saying ". . . hath planted a colony at Ferryland which both for building and making trial of the ground have done more than was ever performed of any in so short a time, having on hand a brood of horses, cows, and other bestials".

Captain Sir Richard Whitbourne who in 1588 had commanded an English ship in action against the Spanish Armada visited New Found Land and in 1622 printed in London most favourable aspects as to its climate and vegetation.† He stated "in the winter season it is as pleasant and healthfull as England is".

He furthermore wrote of Sir George's colony at Ferryland:

> "The Right Honourable Sir George Calvert Knight principall Secretarie unto the Kings most excellent Majesty also undertakes to plant a large Circuit of that Country who hath already sent thither this yeare and the former yeare a great number of men and women, with all necessarie provisions fit for them; where they live pleasantly building of houses, cleansing of land for Corne, and meddowes, Cabage, Carrets, Turnips and such like, as also for Wood and Tobacco. Likewise they are there preparing to make Salt for the preserving of fish another yeare and for divers other services. And his house is likewise well pleased to entertaine such as will adventure with him therein upon very fit conditions".

---

* Ferryland is now a small fishing village clustered around the Roman Catholic Church which contains in the vestibule the coat-of-arms of the barony of Baltimore. The foundations of the mansion house of Sir George are still visible and some archaeological work had been accomplished when the author visited Ferryland in the summer of 1939.

[1] Letters of Wynne and Powell, printed in Oldmixon's British Empire in America.

† A Discourse and Discovery of New Found Land", by Captain Richard Whitbourne of Exmouth in the County of Devon.

The colony was well underway by July 1622, when Captain Edward Wynne who styled himself "Governor of the Colony of Ferryland within the Province of Avalon in New Found Land" addressed a communication to the "Rt. Hon. Sir George Calvert Knight his Maiesties Principall Secretary", dated 28 July 1622.

The husbandmen had planted barley, oates, pease and beanes. The carpenters had constructed a building 44 by 15 feet with a hall of 18 feet long and an entry of six feet. The ceiling was eight feet. Underneath was a cellar of 20 feet in length. It was a story and a half high and contained four chambers, with a chimney of stonework in the hall. The kitchen was 18 by 12 with a ceiling of eight feet and a large chimney. "Over the kitchen I fitted another chamber with stair case and finished a hen house all before Christmas".†

Governor Wynne also advised that the new supply of men which Captain Daniel Powell conducted arrived in the spring, and that most of the goats which were sent died en route. He also submitted a list of "Men which remained [with him] this yeare" 1622.‡

On April 7, 1623, the Royal Charter was granted by James I which conferred on Sir George a lordship over the entire southern promontory of New Found Land between Trinity and Placenta Bays to be held by him

---

† This could be a communal home for all the colonists, although some believe it to be the residence constructed for Sir George of which the foundations still remain at Ferryland.

‡ See appendix. None of the names can be identified as those who sailed on the Ark and the Dove, but the family names of Wynne, Hoskins, Prater, Hatch, Higgins were identified with Maryland at a later period.

§ Patent dated April 7, 1623. ". . . inflamed with a laudable & pious desire of propagating the Xpian religion . . . and withall of enlarging the Territorys of our Empire purchased the land commonly called Newfoundland thereafore assigned to him and his heirs forever . . . with certaine Privileges and Jurisdiction for the better Government & welfare of his said Colony and country . . . being towards ye South from the Middlemost pointe of a Certaine Promontary lying between two bays that of fformosi and Aquafort including Portio Port and which bounds the Colony of St. Johns on the South and was adjacent to the lands of John Guy, a Citizen of Bristol ‘. . . all fisheries in the Sea or Rivers . . . mines, precious metals and stones . . . all patronages and Adowsons of and all structures of Worshipp and Religion built in the country . . . rights Jurisdictions privileges, Prerogatives Royalty Liberty Immunity and Royall Rights and ffranchises same as any Bishopp of Durham within the Bishopprishe or County Palatine of Durham . . . (to be) the absolute Lord Proprietary to be held by Knights Service . . ." The rent was to be one white horse, and the Crown was to receive one-fifth of all gold and silver as "from time to time shall happen to be found in the Country". Sir George had power to ordain judges and justices, magistrates and all officers, and all persons going there with their families and all children born there were to have all rights and privileges as subjects of the Kingdom of England. He was furthermore given power to muster men and make war on savages, robber pyrates, and other emenies by land and sea, and had power "to bestow any Titles and Dignitys at his Pleasure provided they be not such as are used in the Realme of England". He could erect ports, parishes into townships and townships into cities, and all Englishmen were to have the free and equal use of fishing in sea, rivers, and ports. Ref.: Calvert papers, no. 178.

and his heirs forever, with all fishing rights in the surrounding waters. The charter granted him contained perhaps the most extensive powers ever bestowed by the English Crown on a single subject. It virtually created him the absolute lord of a proposed state with all the prerogatives of a sovereign subject only to the crown.§ Sir George gave the name of Avalon to his new domain.‡

Accelerated plans for the colonization of Avalon were immediately put into effect. Sir William Vaughan, Knt., had already been given certain inalienable rights on New Found Land and in order that the Royal Charter be valid Sir George Calvert paid Sir William a handsome sum.

James I, though only 58 years of age, perhaps realized that his days were numbered, but still holding fast to his royal prerogatives and wishing to reward another loyal favorite, on February 16, 1624/5, actually a month before his death, created Sir George, a peer of the Realm with an Irish barony. He had already received large grants in Ireland and four days before his elevation to the peerage he received or had confirmed certain grants in County Longford, Ireland.*

About this time, Baltimore became deeply introspective of his continued adherence to the Church of England, but whether he was converted to the Roman Catholic Church by some over-jealous proselyte, or simply made public profession of a faith long nourished in secret, is a matter of conjecture. A contemporary wrote, "It is said that Lord Baltimore is now a professed Papish".

He apparently had nourished it for some time. The most potent factor was perhaps his early instructions presumably surreptitiously within the portals of his boyhood home. Furthermore, it has been said that the Crosslands, his mother's family had strong Roman Catholic propensities. His father, Leonard Calvert, had some doubts about his allegiance to the Established Church and from 1580 to 1594 was summoned frequently before the Yorkshire High Commissioner to answer why he had not communed at the usual feasts of the Church. In 1580 he submitted a certificate to the authorities of his conforming in accordance with the State Church.[1a]

---

* Hamill Kenny threw new light on the Irish estates of Lord Baltimore and corrected the oft quoted statement that his Irish estates were the fishing village of Baltimore, in County Cork. See, his article in Md. Hist. Magazine, 1954. The Complete Peerage, vol. 2, p. 393, states "There was not and is not any place of that name [Baltimore] in Co. Longford, which is the county generally assigned to this creation [Barony of Baltimore]".

[1a] Yorkshire High Commission Act Book 3 (1580-1585), p. 18.

---

‡ The ancient Isle of Avalon in Somersetshire on which the abbey of Glastonbury was built is reputed to be the site where in 61 A.D. St. Joseph of Arimathaea and his eleven companions first preached the Christian doctrine in Britain. In the abbey now in ruins were buried the remains of King Arthur, Edmund the Elder crowned in 940 A.D., Edgar the Peaceful crowned in 973 A.D., and Edmund Ironside crowned in 1016 A.D.

On October 9, 1592, "Leonard Calvert de Kipling, gent. and Grace† his wife" appeared before the authorities and gave word that he would conform to the Established Church. Furthermore, he gave bond that he would maintain no Catholic servants or Catholic schoolmaster for his children and would buy within a month a Book of Common Prayer, a Bible in English and a catechism, all to lie open in his house. All Popish books or other trumpery or reliques of Popery were to be dispensed with. His children were to be placed in school in York and not to leave without license from the Archbishop of York.[1b] Madam Calvert was definitely more obstinate, for she appeared in court by summons on April 23, 1592, and revealed that she had not received the Holy Eucharist of the Church of England and refused to do so.[1c]

It is therefore quite evident that young George, who was born in 1679/80, came under the influence at home of the Roman Church, though his father conformed at certain intervals perhaps half-heartedly to the Church of England to satisfy the local authorities. Throughout George Calvert's life there is evidence of vacillation or uncertainty in his religious faith, and all factors indicate that ultimately before his death he returned to the Church of England and died an Anglican.

By swearing spiritually in 1625 to a foreign ecclesiastic with far-reaching political power, the conscience of George, Lord Baltimore, could no longer permit him to maintain the portfolio of State—in truth it was unlawful to do so at that time. He resigned his preferments and as an Irish Peer, he retired to his newly acquired estate north of Cloonagechir, County Longford.

After a retirement of a year or thereabouts, he became restless and anxious to inspect his colony at Ferryland, so early in 1627 he engaged two ships the "Ark of Avalon" of 160 tons[2] and the "George" of 140 tons for the contemplated sea journey. On April 27, 1627, the two ships embarked for Avalon with Lord Baltimore and a fresh contingent of colonists, arriving safely in July of that year. Lord Baltimore remained only a short time, so returned to England, thence to his family in Ireland. The next spring of 1628 he made a second voyage to Avalon, this time bringing Joan, his

---

† Recent research reveals that Leonard Calvert had two wives, both members of the Crosland family and which accounts for the confusion of some writers giving the Christian name of the mother of George, Lord Baltimore, as Alice and others Grace. The Complete Peerage states Alice, sole-heiress of John Crosland, of Crosland. The second wife was Grace Crosland, baptized Feb. 8, 1573, the daughter of Thomas Crosland, of Crosland Hill, near Almondbury, Yorks, and only a few years older than her step-son.

[1b] *Ibid.*, Book 3 (1591-1595), p. 83.

[1c] *Ibid.*, p. 110.

[2] Tonnage expressed in letter to Edward Nichlas, Apr. 7, 1627, Public Record Office.

second wife,* and family, except his eldest son, and also his sons-in-law, Sir Robert Talbot, Knt., and William Peasley, Esq.

In August 1628, he wrote to His Grace, the Duke of Buckingham, saying that he had arrived at his plantation with the intentions to "build, set, and sow but is fallen to fighting the Frenchmen who greatly interfer with fishing trade" and requested that two men of war be sent to guard the coast.[3]

Difficulties were therefore many. The French in Canada did everything conceivable to annoy and drive the English out of New Found Land with incessant attacks. At one time Baltimore successfully repulsed the attacks of some French privateers and took six prizes. Two ships from His Majesty's Navy were sent, as requested, one being the "St. Claude".[4] Several sea battles resulted in which figured the "Ark of Avalon". Besides the weather was far from what the colonists expected, in spite of the alluring description of Capt. Sir Richard Whitbourne. They were accustomed to the more or less mild climate of England and as a consequence suffered greatly in health. The rocky soil was unfavourable to agriculture as a means of supplying local needs, but fishing was the principal economic objective and became the staple diet.

Whether Lord Baltimore began the construction of his mansion house on his first or second trip, it is not known, but the foundation which is still visible indicates a house of considerable proportions. He, however, ordered immediately the construction of numerous ships and smaller fishing crafts and a number of sheds for the drying of fish. The boat which he built for his own private use was given the name of "Anne" after Lady Calvert his first wife. At his own expense he fortified the harbour to resist the troublesome French.

In the autumn of 1628 Leonard Calvert, the second son, and William Peasley returned to England in the interest of the colony, and thus escaped the severe winter which followed. Much sickness occurred with many deaths, and Lord Baltimore writing to England stated that Lady Baltimore was ill and his mansion had become a veritable hospital caring for the sick. When spring arrived he realized that his adventure was unsuccessful and he had sustained heavy financial losses to the value of £25,000.[5]

A party of militant Puritans came to Avalon, and these unbidden and unwelcomed guests were horrified at what they saw. The Rev. Erasmus Stourton returned to England with a shocking story of how Lord Baltimore

---

* The family name of his second wife is unknown. James I questioned Calvert closely concerning Lady Calvert warning him of the example made by Sir Thomas whose wife and daughter he compared respectively to Eve and the serpent. Ref: Hall's The Lords Baltimore and the Maryland Palatinate.

[3] Public Record Office, London.

[4] Public Record Office, London.

[5] The Complete Peerage, vol. 2, p. 393.

not only had mass performed every Sunday, but had even permitted a Presbyterian child to be baptized by a Romist priest.[6]

In August 1629, Lord Baltimore wrote to Charles I, as follows:[7] "Have met with difficulties and encumbrances here which in this place are no longer to be resisted, but enforce me presently to quit my residence and to shift to some other warmer climate of this New World, where the winteres be shorter and less rigorous. For here your Majesty may please to understand that I have found by too dear-bought experience, which other men for their private interests always concealed from me, that from the middle of October to the middle of May there is a sad fare of winter upon all this land; both sea and land so frozen for the greater part of the time as they are not penetrable, no plant or vegetable thing appearing out of the earth until the beginning of May, nor fish in the sea, beside the air so intolerable cold as it is hardly to be endure. By means whereof, and of much salt meat, my house hath been an hospital all this winter; of a hundred persons fifty sick at a time, myself being one, and nine or ten of them died. Hereupon I have had strong temptations to leave all proceedings in plantations, and being much decayed in my strength, to retire myself to my former quiet; but my inclination carrying me naturally to these kind of works, and not knowing how better to employ the poor remainder of my days than . . . to further, the best I may, the enlarging of your Majesty's empire in this part of the world, I am determined to commit this place to fishermen that are able to encounter storms and hard weather, and to remove myself with some forty persons to your Majesty's dominion Virginia; where, if your Majesty will please to grant me a precinct of land, with such privileges as the king your father. . . . was pleased to grant me here, I shall endeavour to the utmost of my power, to deserve it".

In the late summer of 1629 Lord Baltimore and a number of his followers sailed from Avalon for the Colony of Virginia with the expectations of establishing a province in a more conducive climate. A few colonists, however, remained behind under a Governor or agent whom Baltimore appointed. The Calverts continued to claim their Province of Avalon and for many years thereafter the Lord Proprietary styled himself "Charles Absolute Lord & Proprietary of the Province of Maryland & Avalon in America & Baron of Baltimore in the Kingdom of Ireland".

In 1637, with characteristic recklessness, King Charles I granted Avalon to James, Marquis of Hamilton, and other noblemen on the ground that the charter had been forfeited by disuse. Then on November 13, 1638, believing that the other proprietors, namely: Francis Bacon, Lord St. Albans; James, Marquis of Hamilton; and Philip, Earl of Pembroke; on certain portions of New Found Land displayed no interest, he Charles I

---

[6] Fiske's Old Virginia and Her Neighbors, vol. 1, p. 248.

[7] Browne's Calvert, p. 25.

granted the whole island to Sir David Kirke, Knt., one of the gentlemen of the Privy Council.*

On October 1, 1629, George, Lord Baltimore, arrived at Jamestown in Virginia. The reception was anything but cordial. Anglican Virginia with a good sprinkling of Puritans had no love for the Popish Calverts and

---

* Ultimately, Cecilius made formal protests of the family's hereditary rights which were propitious for the following depositions which throw a number of side lights on Lord Baltimore's settlement at Ferryland. Ref: Calvert Papers, no. 193.

On August 31, 1652, Annie Lowe, of Ferryland, aged 50 and upwards, swore that George Calvert came to Ferryland at his own proper charge and was lawfully possessed of the Province of Avalon and provided ships and boats. That Lord Baltimore built a ship called "Anne" and divers boats and also constructed stages for drying fish. She was there in 1638 or 1639 when Captain Hill was in possession of Lord Baltimore's mansion. That Sir David Kirke upon his arrival took possession of the mansion. "Shee knowes Sr David Kirke well, but shee loves the Lord Baltimore better".

On August 24, 1652, John Steephans, an inhabitant of Ferryland, stated that Lord Baltimore had seizure of Ferryland and fortified the harbour, and that a "considerable quantity and number of boates were kept in the harbour of ferryland and houses for drying of fish". That he knew Sir David Kirke took possession of the mansion house as an agent of Lord Baltimore after Lord Baltimore departed and knew that Kirke took one boat of Lord Baltimore and made use of it. He did not know Lord Baltimore, but he knew Sir David for about 13 years, "but as far as hee knowes my Lord Baltimore may be as bad as Sir David Kirke". Steephans was in Avalon in 1638 and 1639, but never saw Lord Baltimore in his life. He remembered furniture that was left in the house "a table board and an ould chaire and an oulde boate left on the beach in possession of Captain Hill".

Ann Taylor, aged 51 years, of Ferryland, on August 24, 1652, deposed that Lord Baltimore built about 100 fishing boats and divers stages for drying fish. Captain Hill was left in possession of the mansion and Sir David Kirke took all the goods that Lord Baltimore had left behind upon his departure. She did not know Lord Baltimore, but she remembered when Sir David arrived.

William Poole, aged 60 years, stated that Lord Baltimore left an agent at Ferryland, one Hoyle and afterwards Ralph Morley, and that two years after the departure of Morley, Captain William Hyll arrived and took possession of the mansion house until Sir David Kirke dispossessed him.

Philip Davies also made a deposition as well as one Slaughter who knew that Lord Baltimore kept 32 boats at Ferryland and Sir David Kirke came in 1638 with a patent from King Charles.

James Pratt on March 11, 1651/2, of County Surrey, Mariner, aged about 32, deposed that in April 1638 he sailed "from London to Newfoundland as servant to Captain Cylliar, an agent for Sir David Kirke, and arriving at Ferryland about June following, he found one Captain William Hyll residing in the dwelling in the whole mansion house at fferryland which did keepe and possess thereof for and in behalfe of Lord Baltimore as his agent and deputy there and that after arrival of Sir David Kirke he demanded possession of the mansion and Captain Hyll refused, but not finding himself able to resist Sir David Kirke's power was thereafter forced to yield. He was forced to go to the north side of the said harbour and dyed there some years ago".

More or less controversy went on until 1663, when in consequence of a judgment in courts pronouncing the Hamilton grant void as well as the Kirke, Avalon was surrendered to the Calverts. The subsequent Lords Baltimore neglected it, and in 1754 the charter was again declared forfeited, and the Crown resumed its rights over the entire island.

immediately became suspicious. He was forbidden to land and tarry unless
he subscribed to the Oaths of Allegiance and Supremacy by which he
would recognize the English sovereign as the only supreme authority
throughout the British dominions in all matters ecclesiastical and spiritual.
No Roman Catholic could take such an oath. On November 30, 1629, the
Commissioners of Virginia wrote to the Lords of the Council that Lord
Baltimore "wish to settle with all his family, to the Southward" and that
he refused to take the Oath of Allegiance and Supremacy, but offered to
take a different oath, a copy of which they enclosed and asked for
instructions and advice.[8]

On the records of the Virginia Assembly, for March 25, 1630, is found
"Thomas Tindall to be pilloried two hours, for giving my Lord Baltimore
the lie and threatening to knock him down". A very light punishment,
however, for a member of the Virginia Company who assisted in financing
the possibility of the Virginia commercial adventure and the first Peer of
the Realm to honour the Colony with a visit.

Wishing to establish a colony in a more desirable climate and after a
residence of a few months in hostile Virginia, Lord Baltimore realized
fully that he could not count on any sympathetic assistance from his compatriots along the James. He left Lady Baltimore and some of the younger
children in Virginia, and returned to England where he had expected to
receive permission from the King to found a colony south of the James
River. At court he was confronted with many obstacles despite the fact
that he had been one of the faithful supporters of the King's father and
mother, but at that time the Puritans were gradually weaving their way
into positions of formidable power in court circles. Realizing that he could
not reasonably return to Virginia any time soon, he sent for his wife and
family. According to some authorities, Lady Baltimore died on the return
voyage.

William Clayborne, Secretary of the Virginia Colony and aligned with
the Puritans, who, when hearing of Lord Baltimore's intentions, took the
first available boat to England and there are reasons to believe that Clayborne could not get there fast enough, with much pacing of the deck in
anticipation.

Lord Baltimore proposed a settlement between the James River and
Albemarle Sound to be named Carolina in honour of Charles I, the reign-
ing monarch, but his plan was rejected, inasmuch as Clayborne and others
were already entertaining schemes for founding in that area a sugar-
planting colony. Lord Baltimore then proposed a colony north of the
Potomac, but again Clayborne politically ambitious and envious objected
because he had already established trading posts on Kent Isle and Palmer's
Island all north of the Potomac.

At that time the English Privy Council was somewhat concerned over

[8] Public Record Office, London.

the settlement of the Dutch on the Hudson and in the Jerseys, as well as
the Swedes on the Delaware. The aims and visions of Lord Baltimore
were brought to the attention of the council which, after some forethought,
conceived the desirability of a colony north of the Potomac. Such a settlement would form a buffer state to the encroachments of the Dutch and the
Swedes and therefore would further strengthen English claims to a greater
portion of the Atlantic Coast.

Baltimore accepted the proposals of the Privy Council. A charter was
drawn granting him more or less an indefinite area of land north of the
Potomac with himself as Lord Proprietary with rights and privileges
somewhat similar to his Province of Avalon. It is not known who wrote
the charter, but Lord Baltimore left a blank space for the insertion of the
name which he had hoped to be "Crescentia" or Land of Crescence. Lord
Baltimore stated that he had hoped to call the new settlement by a name
in honour of His Majesty, but the newly organized colony of Carolina
had already been named in his honour. The King, therefore, replied that
it be named after Her Majesty, the Queen, and proposed Marianna.
Baltimore dissented as it was the name of a Jesuit who had condemned the
monarchy, whereupon Charles I suggested the latin Terra Marieae, which
in English became Mary Land. The King therefore wrote Maryland in
the blank space.

As Sir George Calvert, when Lord Baltimore first planned his colony at
Avalon, he had not openly professed his allegiance to the Roman Church,
but in the intervening years after his public announcement he became
conscious of the restrictions of the English Government against those who
accepted the dogma of Rome. He therefore visualized his second colonization to be a haven for Roman Catholics where they could worship according
to their conscience. It then became common knowledge around London
that Maryland was to be a solely Papist settlement. Often premature
publicity to a project acts adversely, consequently his proposed Roman
Catholic colony created many vicious enemies in Parliament, in spite of
the fact that the Privy Council was anxious to develop a buffer state north
of Virginia to reinforce English claims. By direct opposition to his scheme
and subtle unfavourable publicity Lord Baltimore realized that he should
remain at home and dismissed all hopes of joining the Adventurers on
their initial sailing.

At the same time that he was planning a Catholic colony, his conserva-
tiveness visualized the creation of an aristocratic, feudal state where Roman
Catholic families, who were feeling more and more the pressure on their
belief from Parliament, might live as in Britain under English institutions
and traditions. Charles I favoured such a state; but, in the meantime,
Baltimore became more conscious of the continued hostility of the strong
Puritan influence in court circles and their objections to a solid Roman
Catholic state. Through the advice of friends he requested a modification
on the exigency of the situation and sound policy, as a result complete

religious toleration was to be granted to all who believed in the Christian faith. As a result Maryland was the first English colony in America to offer complete religious freedom to all Christians.

To outfit a permanent colony with all the trappings of a feudal state was no minor task and required the utmost sagacity and tact. Fortunately, he had a group of aristocrats interested in the colonization who were willing to assist in a limited degree to certain financial responsibilities. They were trying days, however, and after the hardships experienced on Avalon, the insults and disappointments received at the hands of Parliament, and aggressive opposition from Clayborne and his ilk, George, Lord Baltimore, realized that his health was failing.

Before the charter received the royal seal, George, First Baron of Baltimore, died on April 15, 1632, in his London lodgings at Lincoln's Inn Fields. The direct cause of his premature death in the fifty-third year was believed to have resulted from the physical hardships which he sustained during the years in New Found Land. He was buried with solemn rites in the chancel of St. Dunstan's in the West, Fleet Street, London, an Anglican parish church, but the rebuilding of the church has made some changes in his final resting place and the exact spot at present is not known. By his being interred within the sacred shrine of the ancient English Church, it is prima facie evidence that Lord Baltimore had returned to the Established Church of Britain.*

In June the charter was issued to his son and heir, Cecilius, 2d Baron

---

* The entry of his interment recorded in the parish register of St. Dunstan-in-the-West reads as follows: "[1632] Aprill 16. The right honble George Lord Baltemore was buried from the backside of the Bell".

A. H. Hall, Esq., the librarian of the Guildhall Library where the parish registers of St. Dunstan are deposited, under date of October 12, 1960, stated that "the interpretation of this somewhat curious wording [backside of the Bell] would be that Lord Baltimore was buried from an Inn or Hostelry, or messuage or tenement, in or about Fleet Street, where the Guild Church of St. Dunstan-in-the-West still is. The parish clerk recording the burials carefully noted the places from which the funeral took place and 'backside of the Bell' occurs several times in the interment entries of the year 1632. In the present case 'The Bell' could mean either the tavern 'The Bell within Temple Bar' or the site of a house and grounds known as 'The Bell' belonging to the Knights Hospitallers, over which runs Bell yard, all within the parish of St. Dunstan".

The Anglican clergy consulted agree that if George, Lord Baltimore, had not returned to the Anglican faith, he would not have been buried under the consecrated chancel of the Established Church of England. Furthermore, the Established Church would not have permitted the clergy of the Roman Catholic Faith to perform the sacred rites of burial within the Anglican Church, and the Roman Church priesthood would not have performed their ritual within an Anglican Church. It is therefore evident that George, Lord Baltimore, died an Episcopalian.

Father W. C. Repetti, of the Jesuit Order, Archivist of Georgetown University, writing under date of August 16, 1960, could cast no light upon the matter, but he did state that "it would be very peculiar for a Catholic priest to perform burial rites in a church of another sect".

of Baltimore, with all the investiture, title and responsibility of his deceased father's visions.

Much of the work and detailed planning fell to the second son, Leonard, who had been selected as the titular underlord of the new Province aided by the interests of Thomas Cornwalys, a Norfolk gentleman, and Jerome Hawley of an excellent family of Middlesex, who invested quite heavily in the undertaking. Hawley, who in his youth had been seduced by the notorious Countess of Somerset, had shed some wild oats and was involved in the Countess' attempt to poison Sir Thomas Oberbury, Knt., who apparently knew too much.

Hawley proved to be the most obstreperous or misunderstood member of the inner shrine, yet he seemed to have been the most influential in London circles and lost heavily in the commercial end of the settlement. After a few years he was given the treasureship of the Colony of the Virginia, but a sudden death prevented any great service to that colony. His brother, Gabriel, also played an important part in the pre-sailing negotiations as well as Sir Richard Letchford, of Shellwood, Surrey, Knt.

Besides the establishment of a Province for the worship of Roman Catholics and, as it was also stated, an outlet for the supposedly unemployment from the rapidly growing population of an agricultural state, the Province of Maryland offered many visible and invisible returns. Economic conditions were bad at that time in England, and while it was said that the country was overpopulated, it was more the lack of employment and opportunities during the twilight of the feudal period, and before the introduction of the industrial age, than over population. Enthusiasm for Lord Baltimore's colony was confined to the respectable and the well-to-do, for there is no evidence whatever that as a class the "surplus population" had any great yearnings for a new and perilous existence beyond the seas. Lord Baltimore and his stockholders made all manner of inducements and promises to secure the first contingent of colonists, but ultimately it was proved that the appeal was to the gentlemen and younger sons who were unsettled and had a desire to better their economic positions. In the manner of land speculations by the exportation or transportation of prospective settlers to Maryland and also by trade with the Indians, ships' captains and certain English agencies at home ultimately reaped some profit, but it took several years before dividends became visible.

A holding company had been formed in London for the exploitation of Maryland trade before the sailing of the Adventurers, with William Peasley, Esq., brother-in-law to Cecilius, Lord Baltimore, as the treasurer.[9] Shares or stock were sold at £15 each, with Lord Baltimore holding about half.

Among the Adventurers who held stock were Leonard Calvert, Captain

---

[9] Chancery case 1637, Public Record Office, London.

Cornwalys, Edward Wintour, Frederick Wintour, Richard Gerard, John Saunders, Mr. Wiseman, Mr. Greene, Mr. Fairfax, and Jerome Hawley.

Another investor was Edward Robinson who paid William Peasley £20 to be put into stock for trade with the natives of Maryland, but later Robinson became dissatisfied with the returns so instituted a suit in chancery which threw much light on the financial undertaking and operation of the stock company. Robinson likewise financed the transportation of five settlers in 1633, for which he received 2,000 acres.*

Sir Richard Lechford, Knt. was another investor who, on October 7, 1633, entered into an agreement with Leonard Calvert to "adventure £401/13/8 upon a voyage to be made by Leonard Calvert and others to Maryland". Calvert put up three-fourths of the amount, while Sir Richard contributed the remaining quarter. It was furthermore agreed that Calvert was to make an accountancy of the profit and benefits periodically. Sir Richard at that time delivered £50/8/6 to Leonard Calvert and "entered to be paid in the Middle Temple".[10]

On October 15, 1633, Cecilius, Lord Baltimore, conveyed to his brother, Leonard, one-eighth interest in the "Dove of Maryland of the burthen of ffortie Tunne. . . . now remayning and being in the River Thames, London" and also one-eighth of all equipments. The conveyance was witnessed by George Calvert, a brother to the contracting parties, and John Boles, secretary to Cecilius, whom he sent on the initial voyage.[11]

On September 20, 1633, Lord Baltimore, Leonard Calvert, Jerome Hawley, Thomas Cornwalys and John Sanders negotiated with Richard Orchard, Master of the pinnance "Dove".† He was to receive £4 monthly, whereas his mate, Samuel Lawson, was to receive £2/10/-, boatswain Richard Kenton £2, gunner John Games 12s, John Curke and Nicholas Perrie £1 each, and a boy-servant to the Master 10s. In addition to the boy-servant of Richard Orchard, he was to have the transportation of another boy-servant without costs.[12]

In preparation Lord Baltimore was certain to keep his Adventurers in excellent spirits during the voyage, for Leonard Calvert supervised the loading into "the Ark sailing on September 1633 divers tonnes of beer to the use of Lord Baltimore . . . Gabriel Hawley did bespeak and provide beer for the ship".

On September 28, 1633, John Bowlter, Purser of the Ark, gave his note for 105 tons of beer for the use of both ships, as follows:[13]

"Received from Leonard Leonards, Brewer, 105 tonne of Beare for the

---

* The names of these colonists have never been proved.
[10] Fund Publication no. 35, pp. 13-14, 17-18.
[11] Fund Publication no. 35, pp. 15-18.
† A pinnance was a small light vessel generally two masted and schooner rigger, often in attendance on a larger vessel as a tender or a scout.
[12] Public Record Office, London; reprinted Md. Hist. Mag., vol. 1, p. 353.
[13] Public Record Office, London.

use of the right honoble the Lord Baltimore and other gentlemen as by the particular accompts doth appeare: 9 for the p according as by the noate of directions appeareth and also ffive Ton of harbr Beare received for the Ship Ark and the pinnace Dove. I say recd by me £19/19/-."

(signed) John Bowlter

Beere* del[d] to the Ship Arke, Richard Low, M[r] for the use of the Right Honorable Lord Baltimore.[14]

	£	sh	d
28 in harbour beere...............	6	00	00
More teen ton at 3[lb] p ton..........	30	00	00
more thirtie five ton at 48[sh] per ton..	84	00	00
mor sixtie ton at 40[sh] per ton.......	120	00	00
	240	00	00

In addition to the beer which seemed to have been several grades, there were "12 pipes of Canary wine" at £14/10 per pipe or £174.† There was also "fflower Demiculleverins" costing £82/12/-.‡

To protect the ships from pirates, as it was always necessary during those perilous times, both vessels were well fortified. John Bowlter gave his receipt for "4 Sacars§ or ordinance waying 99cwt. 9qr at 14sh the cwt or £69/9/6".

Another receipt was given for Deales, sawn pieces of timber 9 inches wide, 9 inches thick, and at least 6 feet long, and other provisions amounting to a value of £28/5/-. Loaded also on either the Ark or the Dove were cut wooden planks and other essential equipment for the construction of a barge upon arrival.

The Ark and the Dove as early as September 1633, were in the Thames and the various Adventurers who were planning to sail were gradually joining the ships with their few personal belongings. When the heavily entrenched and hostile Puritan Parliament actually saw the elaborate preparations, a great rumpus was started in the Star Chamber, the meeting place of the King's Councilors in Westminster Palace, London. All kinds

---

* While beer and wine were part of the daily diet of 17th century Englishmen, somehow the spirits which the Adventurers enjoyed daily left their marks and have descended rightfully to the gentry and aristocracy of present Maryland, for no where in the United States has the enjoyment of eating and drinking reached such a zenith as in Maryland. "Eat, Drink and be Merrie in Maryland" is a popular saying. During the terrific twenties with the noble prohibition experiment, the Government planned a law enforcement agency for Southern Maryland at Leonardtown, not far from the original settlement of the Adventurers, but no one in the town would lease a single square foot of space to Uncle Sam's crusaders.

[14] Public Record Office; Md. Hist. Mag., vol. 1, p. 354.

† A pipe was a large cask more or less definite capacity used for wine being one-half ton or approximately 126 gallons.

‡ Demi-culverin, a cannon of about 4½ inches bore, used for fortifications.

§ A sacar was an old form of cannon, smaller than a demi-culverin used in the 17th century on ships and land fortifications.

of false and vicious rumors flew here and there. It was alleged that all Roman Catholics were in league with Spain and that the two ships were concerned in some foul conspiracy and intrigue against the English Colonies in America. Annoying delays occurred and several who had planned to sail became discouraged and returned to their native parishes.

It was not until late in October that the two ships were able to sail from London for the port of Cowes, Isle of Wight, their next destination. The Privy Council dispatched Edward Watkins to submit to all the Adventurers the Oaths of Supremacy which contained clauses repugnant to Roman Catholics. Before the ships were actually out of the Thames, Watkins and his accomplices stopped the ships at Tilbury Hope, on the left bank of the Thames a strongly fortified town since the days of Henry VIII, where Watkins forced all to take the oath. Reporting to the Council, he stated that he offered the oath to all on board who took it, numbering 128, and the Master stated that "some fewe others were shipped who had forsaken the shipp and given over their voyage by reason of the stay of the said ship".[15]

Secretary John Coke on October 19, 1633, advised John Pennington, Admiral of His Majesty Ship Guarding the Narrow Seas, that a ship which "caried men for the Lord Baltimore to his new planntation is or about New England. . . . the companie has taken the oath of allegiance. . . . all then present did subscribe". Coke thereupon referred to a letter which called the ship "Charles of London but since we are informed that her name is the Ark of London and that one Richard Low is Master and Captain Winter hath charge of the companie".[16]

The ships finally got out of the Thames into the English Channel and encircling Margate and Ramsgate they passed through the Straits of Dover and kept close to the southern shore of England until they reached Cowes on the northern coast of the Isle of Wight. More unavoidable delays occurred owing to the unfavorable concurrence of the wind and tide.

Gabriel Hawley, brother to Jerome the Commissioner, was interested in the Adventure and the delay of the ships caused him to billet a number of men and women who were joining the Adventurers with three inn-keepers in Cowes—James Clements, John Herricke, and Joseph Smith. The men and women were "to be entertayned" at the rate of one shilling each per day until the departure of the vessels. On the day of the final sailing Hawley was unable to discharge several pressing obligations incurred in the contemplated voyage as well as the billetting of the men and women with the inn-keepers. His creditors became impatient, and poor Mr. Hawley was unpolitely lodged in Fleet Street Prison.[17]

The three inn-keepers appealed to Lord Baltimore for payment, inasmuch

---

[15] Pub. Record Office, London; Md. Hist. Mag. vol. 1, pp. 352-353.
[16] Archives, vol. 3, p. 23.
[17] Fund Pub. no. 9, p. 106.

as Gabriel Hawley had directed them, but Lord Baltimore denied all personal responsibility. They sued both Lord Baltimore and Hawley and finally the suit went to the Privy Council.[18]

> "Most humbly shewing that whereas Gabriell Hawley his Lordshipp's deputy, did entertayne men and women for Maryland, part of Virginia, and billetted them in severall houses of your petitioners at Xlld the day; Soe it is, that the said Gabriell Hawley, just upon the poynt of the shippes setting saile, took the men soe entertayned from several petitioners, and pretended th Lo: Baltimore, his Master, would give your petitioners good satisfaction".

The total sum amounted to £60 or thereabouts besides some other pertinent charges. Lord Baltimore was cleared of all financial responsibility, but it was declared that Hawley was legally "bound for their keeps".[19]

In the court proceedings it is not quite clear whether they were the personal transportees of Hawley or others. He stated, however, that he was acting as an agent for Lord Baltimore but, from the results of the law suit, it may be concluded that Hawley had contracted to send Adventurers to the Province and, therefore, he was legally bound for their maintenance instead of Lord Baltimore. It also developed that Gabriel Hawley in or about the year 1630 had spent ten months in the Colony of Virginia, but for the past five years had lived in London.

As the two ships were lying at Cowes, Lord Baltimore, drew up elaborate instructions, dated November 15, 1633, to his brother, Leonard, and the two Commissioners which were masterpieces in forethought and wisdom.* They were to preserve unity and peace between the Protestants and the Roman Catholics and that all acts of the Catholic religion were to be performed as privately as may be and that the Catholics "be silent upon all occasions of discourse concerning matters of Religion" on sea as well as on land.

While en route he instructed his Commissioners to learn from any of the Adventurers of any known plots and schemes which they had heard or knew of to overthrow the Province and to thwart his plans for the settlement of Maryland. All knowledge was to be sworn to under oath and sent to him by the next ship.

Knowing fully the unfriendliness of the Virginians, Lord Baltimore warned them against going first to Jamestown or Point Comfort, but as they entered the Chesapeake to anchor off the settlements at Accomacke on the Eastern Shore and to enquire of them some desirable place to settle. He advised that the site selected for settlement be "healthful and fruitfull,

---

[18] Archives, v. 3, p. 24.

[19] State Paper Office, London, "America, West Indies, and Maryland".

* The original in the handwriting of Lord Baltimore on parchment is among the Calvert papers at the Md. Hist. Soc., Balto.; copy is printed in Fund Publication no. 28, pp. 131-140.

next that it may be easily fortified. . . . that it may be convenient for traffic with the English and the savages".

After the selection of a suitable location and steps taken for a permanent settlement, they were to dispatch a messenger "conformable to the Church of England" to Jamestown and to deliver the letters from the King to Sir John Harvie, the Governor, and likewise to present Sir John letters from His Lordship. The messenger was also to acquaint the Virginians of their peaceful and neighboring intentions and to present the Governor with a "butt of sacke" with the compliments of His Lordship.† If possible to ascertain the reasons for the animosity of the Virginians against his Province, but at all times to maintain amiable relations with them, especially in trading but that it was a courtesy to trade with him and "not of right". They were not to quarrel with the Virginians and to have as little as possible contact with them during the first year.

Clayborne's attitude had already given Lord Baltimore much concern, so a polite letter was to be written and to advise him of their arrival in the country and that they had direct authority from the King and Parliament. The messenger was likewise to be a member of the Church of England, and that they were to request a conference with Clayborne. By all means they were to be courteous to Clayborne, and to advise that his plantation was within the precinct of the Maryland grant and "His Lordship is willing to give him all the ancouragement he cane to proceede". The island (Isle of Kent) on which he was seated would be granted to him, but certain London merchants who were in partnership with him were also desirous of a grant, but inasmuch as he was aware of certain differences between him [Clayborne] and the London merchants, he would postpone all treaties with them until he could learn from him "how matters stand between them, and what he would desire of His Lordship". The Commissioners were furthermore instructed that he [Lord Baltimore] did not intend "to do him any wrong, but to shew him all the love and favour that he cann". In the event that Clayborne refused to accept the entreaties of Lord Baltimore, the Commissioners were "to lett him alone for the first yeare, till upon notice given to his lordship of his answer".

After selecting the most suitable place to settle, the Adventurers were to assemble on shore and have "his ma^ties patents to be publikely read by his L^opp Secretary John Bolles". The Governor and Commissioners at that time were to announce that "his L^opps affection and zeale is so greate to the advancement of his Plantacon and consequently of their good, that he will imploy all his endeavors in it, and that he would not have failed to have come himself in person along with them this first yeare, to have beene partakers with them in the honour of the first voyage thither, but that by reasons of some unexpected accidents, he found it more necessary for their good, to stay in England some time longer, for the better establishment of

---

† A butt was a large cask holding 126 gallons of wine, a sacke usually referring to Spanish wine.

his and their rights, then it was fitt that the shipp should stay for him, but that by the grace of god he intends without faile to be with them next year". Then the Oath of Allegiance to His Majesty should be taken by all.

They were to erect a fort immediately for protection and safety patterned after medieval castles of old which protected the lord and his vassals from neighboring enemies. Then they were to build a house for the seat of the government, and a church or chapel. Nearby they were to plan a town and to send Lord Baltimore a plot or diagram of it. The planters were to construct houses with sufficient grounds in back for gardens. Robert Simpson, the surveyor, was to lay out the sections for each Adventurer, and that they "assigne ever adventurer his proportion of Land both in and bout the intended towne". The surrounding area was to be surveyed into an estate for His Lordship's own use, for he fully expected to join the settlement within a year as stated in his letter. The surveyor was furthermore to draw a map for His Lordship of the surrounding rivers and bays.

Each Adventurer was to see that his servants immediately planted corn and produced other "victuall" for the settlement. All men were to be trained in military discipline and regular musters were ordered. They were also to prospect for any deposits of salt, iron ore or other minerals. Above all they were to "bee very carefull to do justice to every man without partiality".

The final instructions were to make a duplicate of all letters to him "least they should have failed and not be come to his lopps hands". All details and plans therefore were well thought out by Lord Baltimore and his advisers.

The ships were now lying snugly in the picturesque harbour of Cowes awaiting final orders to draw anchor. The Adventurers were becoming impatient with the undue interruptions and delays, consequently they were anxious to get on their way. A day or two before sailing, however, Leonard Calvert and the two Commissioners, Jerome Hawley and Thomas Cornwalys, went aboard the Dove and in the presence of William Fitters, Gent., equerry to Cornwalys, gave final instructions to Richard Orchard of the Dove, to follow always in the course of the Ark.

THE VOYAGE

The two ships which had sailed somewhat inauspiciously from Cowes on that bleak November morn by the afternoon made only moderate progress between the headlands—not more than eight nautical miles. From the beginning the wind which had not been altogether too favourable ceased entirely and in its lone stillness the ships, unabled to proceed, sought anchor off Yarmouth Castle on the Isle of Wight at an hour shortly after midday. In the midst of anchoring, the warden of the castle saluted them with the "festal thunders of the cannon", as Father White expressed it, which vibrated every nook and corner of the great oaken hulls of the vessels.

Although they had sailed from Cowes with but minor difficulty, Commander Robert Wintour and the Commissioners were still not without some apprehensions of last minute interference from the King's Councilors of State. Whispers were even buzzing among the sailors that messengers from London would intercept with orders to turn back. The Protestant crew, apparently not too much in sympathy with the unfavourable publicity given Lord Baltimore's plans of colonization, stalled and did everything possible to effect a delay. Commander Robert Wintour and Richard Orchard, Master of the Dove, were careful to exercise utmost caution and tact, for seamen of that day were principally a handful of dirty-mouthed, hard-fisted brutes who had no conception of the obligations of even the middle class, but lived up to the tradition of the seaman race. Their sulkiness on this occasion was audacious even in that day of strict discipline and obedience between master and servant. Those on the Dove were destined to give more trouble upon the arrival in Virginia waters.

The wind remained unfavourable all that afternoon and as night fell they were still in Yarmouth harbour, but after sunset a slight sea mist slowly crept up engulfing both land and water. In the darkness of the night the lanterns here and there on the ships and the scattered lights on shore, seen faintly through the fog, left forever a melancholic picture upon the minds of all. Many were leaving their native England forever—some leaving their families behind not knowing whether they would ever return.

The gentlemen and gentlewomen had already been assigned to their miniature cabins with bunks, small and compact, and by necessity shared by several. Under each bunk was a drawer for the personal belongings. The ceiling was low, not more than five foot-one, so even the medium height of them had to stoop. Their mattresses for the most part were stuffed with straw, though a few were of flock.

The artisans and menial servants found places on the crowded "twendeck" below, where on the hard wooden planks of the ship's floor they slept on straw pallets covered only with a coarse sheet and hopharlot with a round log under their heads for pillows. They slept as close to one another as possible, not only for warmth, but the scarcity of space.

The few maid-servants shared one corner of the twendeck, but there were few if any partitions. Comforts, privacy and conveniences were almost totally lacking. At night the atmosphere reeked of ale and bodies.

Many were constantly and abominably seasick, and by the stench of vomit and other odors resultant upon the days and night confinement in so small a space was not pleasant to behold.

The crowded slave ships of that epoch and thereafter had no less comforts and while much sympathy is being aroused over the unsanitary and crowded conditions of the slave ships which brought the Negroes to the Colonies, our ancestors other than the very wealthy shared the same discomforts and hardships—only our English settlers were civilized, whereas the Africans were savages—and many were cannibals, so necessary precautions were taken for the safety of the crew and the fellow passengers.

There were small lamps and candles in the gentlemen's quarters, but the ship's few lanterns furnished the only illumination for the servants. Night's lights, however, were not primarily necessary, for they reverted to the days of the past generations awaking at dawn and retiring at nightfall.

Only the gentlemen and gentlewomen changed at night, for many had only the clothing which they wore, and besides it was needed for protection against the winter's cold, until they reached the tropics, as no portions of the ships were heated. So cold, heat and body dirt were shared by the highest and the lowest on the ships.

Cooking was done by charcoal on deck over a bed of sand in a wooden or iron fire box protected from the wind by a hood. The diet was a monotonous one of salt meat, dried fish, cheese, hard tack, and dried peas or beans. For drink they had ample wine and beer, and water in cask which was not always too pure.

Their actual first night out passed without the usual mishaps. Most of them slept well and the deep silence of the night was broken only by the rhythmic lapping of the water against the side of the vessel. All were up at day-break and appeared on deck before their breakfast of barley, salt herring, and hard bread—washed down with copious draughts of beer. The fog had lifted during the night leaving a pale, misty dawn. The sea gulls with their grey wings were wheeling silently around the mast, but they were still within sight of their homeland.

Father White assisted by Father Altham celebrated early Mass before the improvised altar which had been constructed in the small and narrow passageway leading from the cabins to the forward deck—but many had to kneel outside in the open—not being able to crowd into the small covered passage.

No breeze! They were forced to remain in Yarmouth harbour all that day—hoping at each hour of the clock that a favourable wind would come up. Governor Calvert and his Commissioners were anxious to proceed without further delay, as was the crew now that the ships were underway.

As evening neared and the final rays of the northern sun were streaming over the western horizon, they realized another day was passing, for turning to the East one was conscious of the hand of night rapidly approaching. Governor Calvert and his boyhood friend, Thomas Greene, whom he had persuaded to join him and who had invested some stock in the adventure, were on deck, when a wind first favourable and mild ascended upon them, for at that moment they had no indication of a storm brewing. Commander Wintour ever alert began to issue orders to his seamen to prepare for sailing, when suddenly without much warning a heavier wind approaching the velocity of a gale descended upon the town.

Within a short time a French baroque anchored in the harbour was forced from her moorings and was running afoul. The clouds overhead were now black and heavy, for a storm was unmistakably apparent. The seamen on both vessels were preparing to meet the occasion, when the baroque with a terrific force was being blown towards the Dove. Master Richard Orchard of the Dove in order to prevent a serious collision with resultant damage, gave orders to set sail at once towards the sea. Commander Wintour of the Ark seeing the dilemma of its pinnace issued immediate orders to sail without further delay and to follow in the course of the Dove.

The storm continued unabated. The two ships were drifting rapidly out to sea. Both continued on their way uninterrupted all during the night. A number of the Adventurers were making their initial sea voyage, and on that second night with coldness becoming more intensified each hour, few actually slept. The waves as they hit the side of the boat were becoming mightier and the cricking and cracking of the great timbers were becoming more frequent and louder as the wind drove them farther out to sea. Some were becoming bitterly homesick, while others were feeling the effects of claustrophobia in the tweendeck.

Seventeenth century Englishmen were traditionally early risers, especially at sea, and as expressed previously all were up at dawn on that third morning. During the night the wind shifted and the storm was believed to have passed. After Mass a typical 17th century breakfast was served.

The wind being now favourable, the two ships were nearing Hurstand Castle. At ten by the ship's clock they passed the fortress-like castle and were honoured by a salute from the castle's warden. Within a short space they had reached the Needles of the Isle—a terror to sailors even in favourable weather as the double tide rushes in from the sea. If the storm of the previous night had passed, another one which proved of greater tensity than the day before was in the making. The Ark narrowly escaped from being dashed to pieces against the rocky coast at the point of the Isle, so a sigh of relief went up from those who were watching the difficulty experienced by Commander Wintour in his piloting through the Needles. Both ships, however, entered the English Channel and the commanders were proud of their navigation.

The Dove was having some difficulty in keeping up with the Ark, so in a moment of sea calmness Governor Calvert and the two Commissioners standing on the poop, or the short deck built over the after part of the spar-deck, while the Dove was at the side of the Ark called to Orchard and instructed him that in case of a storm or accident or that they should be separated at sea, the Dove was to proceed to St. Christopher's and there to remain until the arrival of the Ark.*

For some strange trick of fate the channel was rather peaceful all that day and night, and the two ships made excellent progress, as Leonard Calvert wrote to his partner and friend, Sir Richard Letchford, "we sayled 60 leagues cleare of the lande end of England". They were slowly leaving the channel and were beginning to realize that the mighty sea spread out into vast nautical distances. Instead of the sucking waves of the night before, there were mere ripples on the purple-blue water all during the day. Some of the colonists even believed that the worst had passed. Governor Calvert and his younger brother, George, were not so optimistic, for they had sailed the North Atlantic only a short time previously to their father's Province of Avalon on the bleak coast of Newfoundland. They knew the roughness of the ocean at that time of the year, and the seasoned sailors were likewise not fooled.

Already several of the Adventurers who had not been accustomed to a seaman's life were beginning to feel its characteristic effects and began to complain of a peculiar *mal de mer*. In fact several of the women had already taken to their allotted space on the twendeck and had even refused food.

Fortunately during the fifth day the wind remained favourable, which was Sunday, and by the sixth day, or Monday morning, several of the early risers by the morning light saw for the last time their beloved England as the ships passed Land's End of the Cornish Coast. About nine o'clock they left behind them the western promontory of Cornwall and the Scilly Isles. They were now well out into the ocean and were beginning to feel the sharp, bleak, biting cold of the North Atlantic and realized that crossing the ocean at the advent of winter was not the most propitious time for a sea voyage. But the English was a race accustomed to hard, long winters, reduced rationing, heatless houses, and with Spartan courage they were well prepared physically and mentally for whatever confronted them.

The commander of the Ark ordered his men to control its speed as much as possible, lest the pinnace of just one-seventh its size be left too far

---

* See testimony of William Fitters who was present when Calvert gave the order.

behind. Then there was the desire of mutual protection in case of any approaching evil, for the ever danger of the unspeakable Turks and other pirates who infested the sea of that day was a constant menace.

About three o'clock in the afternoon several of the crew who were on watch sighted a ship in the distance and immediately made a report to the Commander and Governor Calvert. Orders were given at once to the crew to be on the alert, and those who had invested shares in the adventure were particularly concerned lest it should be a pirate ship.

Within a short time Commander Wintour recognized the merchant flag of His Britannic Majesty. As the vessel came nearer, it turned out to be the "Dragon", a ship of 600-ton burden, destined for Angola which had sailed some days previously from the port of London. Almost all the Adventurers rushed on deck. To them who had become a little weary of so much water and no land, the "Dragon" brought much joy and comfort. It was their sixth day out and life on the crowded vessels was becoming a little monotonous.

Salutes and greetings were exchanged. The Ark displayed all her festive flags and bunting, including the Calvert standard with crosslets and paley of gold and black. The clangor of trumpets responded from both ships. The miniature Dove did not wish to be eclipsed on this occasion, so Master Orchard and his first mate, Samuel Lawson, gave equaled salutations and displayed their colours. To the Adventurers it was a glorious sight to see the flags of England fluttering in the breeze and sunlight and with a sense of English pride they breathed the free air of the sea.

Smooth sailing persisted until the evening of Monday, November 25th, and at night most of them slumbered peacefully. The sun shone for part of the day and some of the land lovers, beginning to feel a little improved in their equilibrium, appeared on deck. Several of the menial servants who had indulged too freely at grog-time of the "240 divers tonnes of beere" in order to drown partly their home-sickness, but not to forget a natural tendency for its taste, were out on their allotted portion of the deck and were beginning in their merriment to indulge in too coarse language. But they were having a jolly time and even the few maid-servants who claimed they were a little shocked, actually enjoyed it. In fact some flirtations were already apparent, and as the sex disproportions were most glaring, the maids and widows had assured themselves that they would not remain spinsters much longer.

Towards evening a sudden and peculiar gust of wind that usually ushers in a storm swept around the ship, coming up from the South towards the North West. It grew darker every moment and the mutter of thunder was heard in the distance. Then flashes of sharp lightning preceded each clap of thunder as they came nearer and nearer. Soon blinding rain like sheets of arrows hurled from above poured down upon the ship and sea. The waves roared and as they broke at the ship's bow with a violent force, the heavy frays washed on deck and almost covered completely the bow. The cricking and cracking of the timbers became more intensified than two nights previously and some even thought the Ark would break in two.

All the women grew hysterical and took to below like little chicks in a storm scurrying under the wings of the mother hen. Votive candles were lighted by the Roman Catholics, and prayers and supplications on knees were offered to all the Saints except the godless pilot who was loud in his complaint against the commander. As each moment came, they thought they would be engulfed ignominiously in the perilous sea.

The rain and hail sent icy draughts through the unheated cabins and the hold of the ship, and cloaks and blankets were insufficient to maintain warmth. Mistress Ann Cox whose fortitude and courage were outstanding throughout the voyage comforted them as much as possible during the entire night. But the worst was yet to come. Many were unable to partake of the salt fish, bread, and pottage which was the fare for the evening.

The captain and crew of the English merchantman became alarmed and signaled their concern to Commander Wintour. As the storm became more terrifying, the pilot of the merchantman experienced greater difficulty in directing the ship's course to Angola and, in desperation, signaled the Ark that they were turning back to seek shelter at Falmouth.

Master Orchard of the Dove likewise manifested considerable alarm and in some miraculous manner was able to come sufficiently close to the Ark in order to signal Commander Wintour that if it were in distress or danger of shipwreck, his men would display two red lights from the masthead.

Many on the Ark were likewise uneasy, though Commander Wintour who was commanding the ship for the first time, had either confidence or sheer courage in his ability of his 300-ton ship.

Several entreated Governor Calvert and his councilors to follow the lead of the merchantman into Falmouth. Pressure was so great that he and Commander Wintour summoned a conference of those who had stock in the adventure. Several of the older men who were conscious of the grave danger were particularly concerned, but Edward Wintour and his brother, Frederick, two young near-beardless youths, were enjoying it as if it were great sport. Richard Gerard, although he had invested in the project, was likewise enjoying the experience and took great delight as the ship rolled and pitched.

Governor Calvert and his two principal advisers, Jerome Hawley and Thomas Cornwalys, left it entirely in the hands of Commander Wintour, with the option of returning to the nearest port as the "Dragon" had done or continuing the course towards the next lap of the journey which was the Irish Coast. But the constant, rain-swept Irish Coast was notoriously famous for its breakers and frequent shipwrecks and they could not expect much haven except by Divine Providence. Commander Wintour, displaying that daring fearlessness which characterized him throughout the voyage, was determined to weather the storm regardless. Governor Calvert placed his confidence in him, but some of the doubting gentlemen were not so sure of their destiny.

The wind blew at a terrific rate, its roar became louder and louder as it whistled through the riggings, and the sea became rougher and waves higher. Sleep was out of the question. Those who usually had to bunk on deck were unable to do so from the ruthless waves which tossed over the side of the ship. The slightly inebriated servants of the afternoon were now cold sober. Both Roman Catholics and Anglicans were frequently on their knees, with many Hail Marys and prayers to St. Christopher and St. Botolph, the patron saints of all sea-travelers. Cries and curses went up from the heartless crew.

Many of the Adventurers who had been accustomed to the prayers and liturgy of the Anglican faith were huddled below and they realized more than ever, with the driving wind penetrating all portions of the ship, what the parish priest meant when he offered up that petition at both matins and vespers for all travelers on perilous seas.

In the meantime Master Orchard of the Dove was having his troubles. His crew which from the very beginning had never been too cooperative were now in fear of their lives. The little 50-ton pinnance was unable to withstand the terrific beating it was receiving from the wild terror of the sea. Everything seemed hopeless and lost. He gave orders, so either John Curke or Nicholas Perrie climbed the masthead and placed the two signal red-lights.

It was Midnight. The sea was likened to a roaring cavern of darkness, then a sudden glare of lightning ripping open the jet black sky above. A crash of thunder—then the descent of more rain. A sailor of the Ark on watch spied in the distance the two red lights. The first mate was immediately informed and within no time Commander Wintour and Governor Calvert and others were on deck.

Grief and fear struck all and prayers were offered by Fathers White and Altham for the safety of their compatriots on the Dove. Then the two red lights became dimmer and dimmer, and finally disappeared from sight in the night's blackness. Going to the rescue of the Dove was out of the question. All hope was therefore abandoned for the pinnance and then came the realization that everything on board were lost. The Dove carried besides its crew a few artisans and had the greater bulk of the supplies for effecting a settlement and the trade-goods to bargain with the Indians. It carried also the livestock, herbs for the gardens and seeds to start the vegetable gardens. The only conclusions was that the Dove had been swallowed up in the angry whirlpools of the North Atlantic with everything vitally needed gone.

It was another great disappointment to Governor Calvert as well as the twelve others who had stock in the settlement, for the loss of the "trucks" stored in the Dove was irreplaceable and they saw only financial difficulty confronting them. Yet they were bound to fulfill their objective and had that courage to face the situation regardless.

The Ark pitched and tossed all that night. Several of the seasoned sailors who had weathered many an ocean tempest swore that it was the worst within their memory. The dawn brought no relief, only a changing and unfavourable wind coming up from the South West, so the Ark braved it all and made but little headway on account of being compelled to tack frequently, that is, to change the course in order to bring the wind to the other side of the ship.

As dawn changed into morning, Mass was offered for the repose of the souls of those who had perished with the Dove. That day and the next two, very little progress was made, owing to the variable winds, currents, and again more tacking. It seemed as if the Ark would make two paces and then lose three by the heavy wind and strong waves.

Hoping that the next day, Friday, would bring some relief, Commander Wintour was up early consulting his first mate, but the tempest became more intensified and the sea pitched more ferociously, with driving rain, wind, sleet, hail, and a dumb-still coldness never before experienced by the Adventurers. The ship rolled around like a porpoise. Trusting that the worst had passed, they braved the night with fortitude, though like the night before very few were able to sleep.

The next morning they were unable to see the sun rise—only an opaque watery grayness proclaimed the coming of dawn. The Ark sailed or pitched on, only to encounter another tempest more ferocious and devastating than the previous ones. Great angry waves encircled the vessel and every minute the men and women thought that the end had come. Many were prepared for Fathers White and Altham had heard confessions at almost every hour of the day and absolutions had been given to the Faithful.

The next day was the Feast of St. Andrews, that apostle fisherman so well acquainted with the sea. The Roman Catholics celebrated it not only at the early Mass but at matins, benediction, and at complines. But in spite of the many prayers and thanksgiving, the sea remained its angry and dreadful self. The wind howling through the riggings which once brought terror was now accepted with resignation.

During the early services the clouds blackened all around in a frightful manner, with sharp streaks of lightning and heavy rolls of thunder which again struck consternation into every mortal on board. Several of the Protestants, conscious of the danger and seeing the spirit and faith of the Roman Catholics, turned to that religion during those believed dark, last hours.

The superstitious sailors, certainly not followers of the Roman doctrine, believing that the evil spirits which were against the settlement of Maryland were using their vicious and evil powers upon an adventure sanctioned only by the Devil.

Towards evening it cleared slightly—sufficient to be conscious of a faint sunset, but to make matters worse one or two of the mates on deck spied a sunfish endeavouring to make his way against the course of the setting sun. To all travelers of the sea it foretold another storm. Commander Wintour came out on the quarter deck in time to see it before its disappearing into the emptiness of watery space.

The sunfish fulfilled its omen, for about ten o'clock most of the men and women had taken to their bunks and those destined to sleep on the opened decks had for several nights found space in the narrow passageways which at times made walking almost impossible. As Father White stated "that night a black cloud hung low and rained down a direful tempest". It was followed by a whirlwind so dreadful that orders were given to the seamen to take in the sails, but before they could do so calamity struck again and the mainsail under which they alone were sailing was spitted in twain from top to bottom. One part was blown into the sea nearly taking one of the coxswains with it, but the other portion with much difficulty was fortunately recovered by several of the sailors.

The stoutest hearts among the Adventurers became more frightened and distressed. As the storm continued with no abatement, in fact with increasing ferocity, the minds of the bravest, whether Adventurer or seaman, were struck with terror, for seasoned sailors confessed that they had seen the best ships go down in lighter storms.

The Roman Catholics and the Anglicans prayed more fervently, and Fathers White and Altham were kept busy hearing more confessions and giving absolutions before ultimate destruction. Lamentations were given to the Blessed Virgin Mother and to St. Ignatius* who had been consecrated the Patron Saint of the New Province, to St. Michael and all the tutelar Angels. Even the hardest and roughest sailor made his peace with God and as Father White wrote "strove by the sacrament of penance to purge his soul".

They waited patiently for the next calamity. Although it was not supposed to be known generally, the rudder worked itself loose from the terrific pounding of the increasing waves and was finally lost in the sea. A coxswain who had been carrying on a flirtation with one of the serving maids confided in her, but within no time the whole ship was aware of it.

The Ark was being carried directly out of its course. The navigators thus were forced to abandon the ship to the menacing restlessness of the sea with the consequence that the Ark tossed about here and there like a pea in a dried pod.

After several days of untold storms, the sea ultimately ceased its raging.

---

* Ignatius Loyola, a Spanish gentleman, born 1491, died 1556, founded the Society of Jesus, canonized in 1622.

But the northern sun which eventually shone was cold and unfriendly, yet thanks offerings were given by all and, for the first time since they sailed slowly out of Cowes harbour, a feeling of security was felt and actually enjoyed.

Within a short time as almost as if a miracle had occurred, somewhat without nautical warning the waves subsided and the ocean took upon itself a deep, silent calm. As expressed by the Commander and his mates, "the sea was never more tranquil". Yet there was that persistent humming in the riggings as the ship sailed on and which was to become a sort of music to the Adventurers.

The Ark continued on its course and was now encircling the Spanish coast, but even with a favourable sea the wind was not too propitious. After the fear of being lost at sea during a storm, the minds of the Adventurers now turned to the next great hindrance to sea travel—the apprehensions and fears of the insufferable Turks and other pirates.

The Turks at that time, however, were celebrating their annual Feast of Ramadan, so they felt a little sense of security for a while, but feasts made no difference to the Christian pirates or other non-Christian robbers of the sea.

The calmness of the sea had given the Adventurers more time to think of matters other than destruction and loss, so during the now soft, semi-tropical sun the men get out their decks of playing cards with what coins they possessed for stakes. Other seventeenth century games were indulged in and those who at first could not manage to surmount seasickness were becoming better sailors. The servants and the seamen were now enjoying their daily rations of beer at grog-time, while the gentlemen were relishing the Spanish and French wines which had been brought aboard.

Soon the Madeira Islands discovered and colonized by the Portuguese were passed, but no landing was made. The climate was becoming more and more semi-tropical, and although the dazzle of the bright sun was new to the English, it offered more relaxation to them. The Ark was now making rather good time.

One day a crewman on watch sighted three vessels, all of which appeared much larger in tonnage than the Ark, and it looked as if their commander were steering directly towards them. The only thought was the unspeakable Turks. The alarm was sounded and each seaman hurried to his position with all mortars and guns set for action. The few women on board took to the lower deck or their cabins. Some wished the Commander to attack, but Wintour knew his strength and doubted that he was able to take the initiative in a sea battle against three. But the fright was soon over, much to the relief of all, for the ships turned out to be friendly merchantmen en route to the Fortunate Islands, now known as the Canaries. Salutes were exchanged and they all went their way.

The sun, as the Ark nosed toward the southwest, became more golden, and each evening as it set, it washed both sky and sea with its brilliant rays of yellow gold, crimson red, and sometimes deep purple. They had now been out a number of days. Some were becoming a little restless of the cramped quarters, but for the most part with a capacity for simple delight they were beginning to enjoy life on ship board, strangers to one another a few days ago were now becoming friends, and cliques were being formed.

The sea was now perfectly calm and the warmer climate encouraged recreation on deck to a great degree. And the once restlessness found its outlet in more games and pastimes. There was that ever struggle among the servants to get the few decks of cards in the mornings after their routine chores had been accomplished. And the daily ration of beer at grog-time always brought on merriment, and was the highlight of the day.

The gentry had their movements of fun, likewise, but Governor Leonard Calvert and the other gentlemen who had invested their resources in the Adventure and felt a certain responsibility were ever making decisions and drafting plans for the success of the new Province. With Governor Calvert was his ever-present private secretary, young Peter Draper, Gent.

Gradually, the Adventurers were being introduced to the semi-tropical heat as they approached the South Atlantic and it was not too long before they found the sun in full force and effect. Many who had not traveled beyond the area of their English countryside was beginning to find it slightly unbearable after the freezing and abnormal stormy weather experienced immediately after leaving Cowes. They were not prepared for it, with their heavy winter clothing—then again the endurance of the English and the Scot for cold was known even in that day, but they found the change too sudden and drastic. The seasoned sailors were used to it, and the gentlemen and gentlewomen whose wardrobe was more extensive than the provincial servants and artisans were able to adjust themselves better than their servants. Some had already complained of illness aided by the lack of sufficient salt to preserve their provisions.

As the Feast of Christmas approached, preparations were made for a grand celebration. After the usual masses to commemorate the Nativity, Governor Calvert ordered extra rations of beer and wine and the Adventurers deemed it was the occasion to celebrate as they never celebrated before. In fact youthful high spirits caused certain excesses. Wine flowed freely among the gentlemen as well as the servants until it almost reached the stage of a seventeenth century brawl.

One of the servants got a little too fresh with his words and a little too free with his hands with a maid-servant of Father White and his face was unceremoniously slapped. Shouts went up from the servant's quarters and much fun was directed towards the offender. Although the maid-servant showed her temper and displeasure, inwardly she was rather flattered that so much attention came her way. As Father White who certainly did not see the conflict between the two, expressed the whole Christmas celebration as "some drank immoderately".

The next day about thirty were seized with a burning fever and stomach disorder. As Father Andrew later reported to the Society of Jesus, "If you expect sea-sickness, usual to those who are making a voyage, no one was attacked with any disease till the festival of the Nativity of our Lord".

Mistress Ann Cox administered to the sick and slightly inebriated ship-mates, and her calm and silent devotion to the afflicted and her intuitive knowledge of nursing won her the admiration of all. In spite of the remedies used and several bleedings by the chirurgeon, Mr. Richard Edwards, twelve died and were buried at sea.

Among those who imbibed too freely and without discretion were two Catholic gentlemen, Nicholas Fairfax and James Barefoot, whose death caused great grief and regret among the Adventurers. It saddened the hopes of all, especially Governor Calvert, for manpower was greatly needed in the settlement, and Lord Baltimore had visualized attracting more than those who actually embarked on the expedition. It was the first tragedy from death, but others were soon to follow.*

The ship ultimately arrived safely at the Fortunate Islands, better known as the Canaries, and set anchor. There were other ships in the harbor and the soaring beauty of the raking masts and the swell of the great sails of the seventeenth century vessels made a vivid picture against the lush vegetation of the Canary's coast line.

They were well received by the Spaniards and the few Portuguese who had remained after Spain gained sovereignty. Governor Calvert consulted with his commissioners about the type of food and trade-goods they could obtain from the islanders. After several days spent at the Canaries, they headed for St. Christopher in the West Indies, or St. Kitts, as it is now popularly called, but fearing at that season of the year other ships might have been there and acquired the surpluses from the settlers and natives, they decided to make Bonavista opposite Angola on the east coast of Africa. They had made but a few nautical miles when the commissioners reconsidered lest provisions might fail them at Bonavista. Considerably out of the course, they turned their sails directly towards the Barbadoes. It was a wise decision, for at their arrival at the Barbadoes, they were advised that a hostile Spanish fleet was lying at the Isle of Bonavista for the purpose of prohibiting foreigners from trading in the much needed commodity of salt.

Leonard Calvert writing to his partner, Sir Richard Lechford, stated that they went out of their course to the Barbadoes "to furnish ourselves with seede corne for our plantinge that yeare in Maryland which wee had little hopes Virginia would afford us, and therefore were unwillinge to put

---

* Although over-excess of food and alcohol was attributed as the cause, it was no doubt a combination of poisoned food, lack of sanitation on ship board and the sudden change from freezing weather to a sub-tropical climate—and also aggravated by other degenerative ailments of the individual.

ourselves to their mercy for a commodity which did so necessarily concerne our whole substance".

They arrived at the Barbadoes making very good progress on January 3, and entered Carlisle Bay, but ever cautious of the great coral reef which completely surrounded the island even beyond the three-mile limit. Again good luck or Divine Providence was in their favour, for the Ark barely escaped another fate equally as disastrous as being ship-wrecked at sea. The Negro slaves and some notorious and desperate white servants had organized an armed conspiracy to slaughter all their English masters and their families, then to capture the first boat which sailed into Bridgetown and effect an immediate evacuation of the Island. The Ark was that first ship, but the conspiracy was nipped in the bud, however, because plans of the contemplated atrocities leaked out. The leader was executed and security and peace again were restored on the island. The very day that Leonard Calvert presented his compliments to the Governor of the island, eight men were under arms in order to prevent any possible uprising.

They were in hopes of receiving many articles of trade from the English inhabitants and Governor of the same blood, but apparently some Virginia agent or enemy of the Roman Catholic colony had already prejudiced the Barbadians against Lord Baltimore and his adventure, for a well organized and planned conspiracy raised the prices of commodities to near prohibitive levels. They refused to sell a single bushel of wheat which grew luxuriously in the central Dutch portion of the island for less than 10½ florins. For a turkey they demanded 5 florins, for a guinea hen from 2 to 5 florins. Beef and mutton which the colonists craved after subsisting on salt meat and fish for weeks were unobtainable. Potatoes which grew abundantly and wild on the island were had for the hoeing and hauling, and as their food reserve was virtually exhausted, all they lived on for days thereafter were bread and potatoes.

While anchored at the Barbadoes to their surprise the pinnace Dove, which they had given up for lost, sailed into the harbour with but few scars of a rough sea voyage. After her disappearance in the blackness of that night, she made for the Scilly Isles off the southwest coast of England where many a ship had been wrecked on their rocky coasts. Rejoicing was great, for it seemed like divine providence that the Dove had been preserved. Richard Orchard, its master, had brought her safely through, but he had disobeyed orders, as in case of separation they were to join one another at St. Christopher.

They remained in Carlisle Bay for 20 days, unreasonably long to be among their hostile compatriots. The Ark was already to sail from the Barbadoes for St. Kitts, and as a precaution Governor Calvert, Jerome Hawley and Thomas Cornwalys went aboard the Dove to give some last-minute instructions, but Richard Orchard, the Master, had absented himself. It developed that he was somewhere on shore, and did not return until three or four days later. He made his apologies to the Commissioners, but he had gone into the interior of the island, as he stated, to collect some debts. His absence delayed sailing fully a week.

The two ships set sail from Bridgetown at the same time on January 24th and headed northward. Within a day or two, the Ark lost sight of the Dove around Montseratt or Nevis, and when the Dove again joined the Ark on January 29th at St. Kitts, Orchard stated that he had been chased by some small Spanish vessels or frigates and almost sustained capture.

St. Christopher or St. Kitts had been settled by Sir Thomas Warner in 1623, but five years later it was divided between the British and the French. The Adventurers remained there fourteen days taking on a fresh supply of water and to "shift our ship for the second part of the voyage".

Saying farewell to their few compatriots whom they found at St. Kitts, the Ark sailed first westwardly and then northwardly to the Colony of Virginia with many forebodings and actual fear of trouble. Leonard Calvert was well aware of the schemes and intrigues of the Virginia agents in London and even the work of William Clayborne himself who made a personal trip to England to forestall the settlement. Although George Calvert, the First Baron, had been a member of the Virginia Company which financed the Virginia experiment which was primarily in the beginning a trading company to enrich the investors, Lord Baltimore's colonists were bringing England to a new continent with English traditions, customs, and a way of life of Old England—a permanent settlement for all who believed in God and the Trinity.

The leaders of the Virginia settlement regarded the Maryland Province with envy and jealousy, and actually exerted every conceivable effort possible at Court and in Parliament to prevent the consummation of Lord Baltimore's plans. Governor Calvert and his younger brother, George, had not forgotten how their father and step-mother with the rest of the family had been grossly insulted by the Virginia populace, when they paid a friendly visit to the Virginia Colony en route for England after the abandonment of the Province of Avalon on the coast of New Foundland.

Disregarding instructions from Lord Baltimore to avoid Jamestown or Point Comfort, they landed at the latter on February 27,* just 34 days after leaving the Barbadoes, but in the meantime they had experienced for the first time the terrific coastwide currents of the American Continent and squalls of the now Carolina coast, not to mention the difficulty they had with the treacherous currents around the cape later to be known as Cape Hatteras. But the mighty Ark fought the tricks of the seas as well as her pinnace and came bravely through.

Instead of looking sympathetically towards a sister colony which would strengthen the British claims in America and give mutual protection against unfriendly Indians and the Spaniards, the Virginians, who apparently considered themselves paramount in that area, did everything possible to

---

* Letter of Leonard Calvert to Sir Richard Lechford.

embarrass and prevent the settlement. But Lord Baltimore had his friends at court as well as enemies.

As the Ark and the Dove nosed towards Old Point Comfort after entering the Chesapeake, Leonard Calvert was prepared so far as possible to cope with the evil intrigue of the Virginians, and his valued commissioners, Thomas Cornwalys and Jerome Hawley, had in their possession letters from King Charles I and the Chancellor of the Exchequer to Governor Harvey of Virginia. Leonard Calvert also had the letter of instruction from his brother, Cecilius, who had already experienced the discourtesy of the Virginians only a few weeks previously.

They also had some passengers to land in Virginia, so presumably en route the Ark had taken on a few travelers at the Barbadoes or St. Kitts whose destination was Virginia. As Leonard Calvert stated "staying there some 8 or 9 dayes to land some passengers and to deliver the kinges letters to S[r] John Harvey".[1]

They found all the inhabitants of Virginia under arms and on the alert. It was rumored vaguely, as it was said, that six Spanish ships were approaching the Colony to reduce it into submission and to place all under Spanish rule. Father White stated in his journal that the "thing afterwards proved to be in a measure true", but there was always that feeling in the minds of the Marylanders that the Virginians mistrusted the friendly motives of them and were prepared and expected armed conflict. The Spanish story is now known to have been a subterfuge, and at that time they were prepared for any overt actions of the Adventurers. The Spanish story had the flavour of the propaganda which was circulating around London, and which had likewise reached Virginia, that the Popish Colony of Lord Baltimore was in league with Roman Catholic Spain.

Much to their surprise the Governor of Virginia, after the Marylanders assured him of their peaceful intentions, was kindness personified. They were entertained in a sort of way, "kind" as Father White put it, and the ships remained in Virginia waters for eight or nine days. But the overtures of Governor Harvey later developed to be more artful than sincere, for it was learned that he had designs on recovering from the Royal Treasury a large sum of money which was due him and desired no adverse criticisms even from the Marylanders. Yet all during Harvey's tenure of office Harvey displayed much sympathy with the Marylanders.

Much, however, was accomplished in those few days in Virginia. They found several men around the James with no particular ties with Virginia who were looking for additional adventure and who willingly joined the colonists. And it was there perhaps that Thomas Cornwalys engaged a young intellectual gentleman, Cuthbert Fenwick, to be his secretary and steward. Fenwick agreed by written indenture to serve him for a limited period in return for passage money to Maryland and maintenance. Fenwick

---

[1] Calvert Papers, Md. Hist. Soc.

ultimately proved of great service to the Province, and being a scion of an ancient family noted for centuries in Northumberland, he proved a distinct social asset to the already aristocratic flavour of the Province of Maryland.*

With scant fresh supplies from the Virginia plantations for which they paid dearly, and the purchase of a pinnace, the Adventurers left Old Point Comfort on March 3, and sailed up the Chesapeake Bay until they reached the Potomac which they rechristened St. Gregory, but soon reverted to the old Indian name. The name of St. Gregory was also given to the southern promontory of the river, and the northern cape, now Point Lookout, was dedicated to the honour and glory of St. Michael and all the Angels.

Leonard Calvert, relative to the entrance to the river and its description, stated "we made choyse of the most southerly river to set downe in, and (as I have found it) the fairest; beeings 7 or 8 leagues broad at the mouth affordinge a deepe channell from side to side, the land beinge high and free from swampes and marshes; grown over wth large timber trees, and not choaked up wth any under-shrubs, but so cleare as a coach may wth out hindrance passe all over the Countrie".[2]

At the mouth of the river, and extending along the shore for considerable distance, they beheld hundreds of natives all armed and running around in a great state of excitement. Governor Calvert in his letter to Sir Richard Lechford stated "they made a genreall alarm, as if they intended to summon all the Indians of America against us, this happened more by the ill reports our enemies of Virginia had prepossessed them with all, of our cominge to their contrey with intention to destroy them all and take from them their countrey".

The natives had seen the Virginians in their small river crafts making exploratory trips as well as for trading. Captain William Clayborne, a Puritan of the radical caste and the arch-enemy of the Maryland colonists, had already established his trading post on Kent Isle, now within the charter rights of Lord Baltimore, and another post at more remote Palmer's Island at the head of the Chesapeake. But the Indians had not seen so great a fleet as presented by the Ark and her pinnances. Messengers on foot and in canoes were dispatched everywhere to announce "that a canoe as large as an island had brought as many men as there were trees in the woods". That night bonfires were kindled throughout the northern shore of the Potomac by the Indians in order that they might watch the action of the invaders.

Governor Calvert and his Commissioners displayed no hostile gestures nor made any overt acts, but proceeded slowly along the northern bank which was to be a part, in fact the southern boundary of their royal grant,

---

* Cornwalys stated that he brought Cuthbert Fenwick from Virginia, and he most likely meant the Colony of Virginia, yet no headrights were ever claimed for him in the Colony.

[2] Calvert Papers, Md. Hist. Soc.

until about 30 miles from the mouth of the river the fleet reached three islands known as the Heron Group from the immense flocks of heron which nest there. They gave the name of St. Clement's to the first and largest, now known as Blackistone Island, and St. Catherine and St. Cecilia to the two smaller of the group.

THE LANDING

It was March 25, 1634, the initial day of Spring and the first day of the Julian calendar, as well as the Feast of the Annunciation of the Blessed Virgin, all of which were propitious for joyous and solemn celebration and a memorial day for each Adventurer who had survived that voyage of 123 days or slightly over four months from the sailing from Cowes to their destination.

Spring was well advanced that year and the new land of Maryland with its pines and cedars blended harmoniously with the virgin foliage of the hardwoods and the many indigenous wild flowers which grow plentifully in early spring.

The Adventurers viewed the landscape with mixed and solemn apprehensions, for they were bringing to a new land a virgin ambition mingled with nostalgia for the scenes of their childhood and the family ties which they had left behind. From their English homes they had conceived a fresh pattern of life in an unknown wilderness and there it was. For them it was then necessary to perfect and bring forth on a new continent another part of England—though separated from it by a great ocean.

After deciding on the possibility of what they considered a safe and convenient place to disembark, the Commissioners selected the larger of three islands lying near the shore of the Potomac not too far distant from the mainland. Before any great exploratory parties had been sent into the interior of the island, Governor Leonard Calvert ordered all on shore for a general Te Deum. The three vessels anchored as close as possible to the shore line, but the ship's small tender had to be used for landing. To the island they gave the name of St. Clement after the fourth Bishop of Rome.* According to Father White's Relation, "We landed first at St. Clements to which access is difficult except by fording because of the shelving nature of the shore".

Father White directed several of his retainers to construct a huge cross from one of the native trees. It was hastily hewn together and, on that virgin day of Spring in 1634, led by Father White who was assisted by Father Altham, all the Roman Catholics, and not a few of the Anglicans, gathered for the first sacrifice of the Roman Mass ever to have been celebrated in one of the Originial Thirteen English Colonies.† As Father

---

* First of the recognized successors of St. Peter of whom anything is definitely known. It is claimed that he was ordained by St. Peter. His feast is celebrated on November 23rd.

† Catholic Mass had been celebrated on some of the Carolina sea islands, but then under Spanish sovereignty.

White wrote to the Jesuit headquarters in Rome, "In this region of the world it had never been celebrated before". In formal acclaim they took possession of the country "for our Saviour and for our Soveraigne Lord King of England".

After the consecration and the benediction, they took "up on our shoulders the great cross which we had hewn from a tree" and in solemn procession Governor Calvert and the other Roman Catholics participated in the litany of the Holy Cross, chanting with great humility, and on bended knees they planted the cross as the symbol of their faith, as expressed by Father White "with great emotion of the soul".

In the meantime, or after Mass, several of the maid-servants had collected the soiled linen of the gentlemen for laundrying, but as they were being rowed ashore, the uneven bed of the river and a little unexpected squall upset the boat—maids, linen and all went into the water. The frightened maids were rescued by the husky sailors who were watching attentively from the ship, but most of the precious linen was lost, especially some of the church linen of Father White which proved a great loss to the cleric.

The next day Governor Calvert, ever cautious, and with the advice of his commissioners resolved to visit the chiefs of the nearby Indian tribes and paid initial respect or homage in the ancient English tradition. Many sachems or hereditary chiefs were subject to the King of the Tribe and upon the advice of Captain Fleete it was necessary to explain their coming and to court good will. Before sailing up the river he ordered a group to construct a barge and to begin immediately on some preliminary defenses for the protection of the colonists.

Taking the Dove and the pinnance procured in Virginia, Governor Calvert and his Commissioners, set out up the Potomac with swelling sails and ultimately landed some four leagues to the seat of the Indian chief. Upon the approach of Governor Calvert and his retinue the savages fled into the interior with great consternation and fears. They continued their journey for another nine leagues up the river until they reached the Indian village known as "Patawneck". Calvert proceeded with great caution, however, to the village not far from the shore. Upon a sort of dais supported by his principal tribesmen sat the "Werowance" or "Emperour of all those pettie indian kinges called the emperour of Pascatoway" who turned out to be a mere youth in his teens, but who was under the domination of his uncle, Archibu, his tutor and regent, whose gravity and prudence held the government of the tribe together. Archibu welcomed them and expressed pleasure of their coming.

Governor Calvert declared his "good intentions in comeinge to those parts. I settled a firme peace wth him and likewise obtained leave from him, to make use of what place I would use for myselfe and our country to sett down".[1]

---

[1] Fund Publication no. 35, pp. 20-21.

Father White had remained in the boat with the baggage, but Father Altham explained to the chieftain the errors and pitfalls of the heathen, and that they had come in peace and benevolence not for the purpose of war, and that they wished to imbue their race with the precepts of civilization in order to be saved by the word of God and to receive eventually the rewards of heaven. Father Altham stated that he wished to discuss more matters with them, but for the lack of time he would return before long.

"This is agreeable to my mind", said Archibu, "We will use one table, my attendants shall go hunt for you, and all things shall be common with us".

More nobler words were never spoken by a primitive chieftain, for in analyzing the Indian, in spite of his sometime savagery, there was great nobility of character, as can be seen in many of the later portraits and paintings of the chiefs, and certainly in the reception and good will extended to the Maryland Colonists.

It was at one of these receptions with the Indians or en route to Piscataway that Governor Calvert made the acquaintance of Captain Henry Fleete, a well-seasoned Virginian and fur trader, who was then living with or trading with the Indians. The Marylanders induced him to join them which he readily did and greatly aided the Adventurers by his knowledge of the terrain and waterways and also by his fluency in the languages of the local Indian tribes.

In "A Relation of Maryland", printed in 1635, it is stated that "At paschatoway . . . met with one Captaine Henry ffleete an English-man who had lived many years among the Indians".

After having paid sufficient respects to Archibu and his court, the two pinnaces sailed farther up the Potomac to the village of Piscataway, believed to be at the head of a creek of that name where the present village of Piscataway is now located. About 500 Indians with their chieftain all stood on shore equipped with bows and arrows ready to defend themselves in case of any contingency. Governor Calvert gave them the sign of peace, followed by like signs from others on board. Captain Fleete went ashore to greet the Werowance in his own language and to invite him to a parley. The Werowance or chief, however, with some degree of apprehension, with one or two of his bodyguards, paddled out to the pinnace which contained Governor Calvert and his official party. Coming on board with an exchange of amenities and with assurance of benevolence and peaceful pursuit, the Werowance gave the Adventurers permission to settle in whatever part of his empire they might wish.

While the Werowance was aboard the Dove, many of his tribesmen came down to the shore expressing much alarm, whereupon the Werowance ordered two of the Indians that had accompanied him on shipboard to go ashore to assure them that there was no cause for fear. The messengers returned and related that his tribesmen still feared for his life, but he immediately appeared on deck and in their sign language reassured them of his safety.

The Governor and his party returned to the settlement of St. Clements or to the Ark much encouraged and satisfied with their contact with the neighboring Indians and their desire to cooperate with no apparent hostility.

While the Commissioners were paying their respects to the native chieftains, the Indians around St. Clements had laid aside their first apprehensions and realizing that the colonists had not come to wage war and waste became less timid and mingled familiarly with the guards who were posted day and night for any overt acts.

The natives asked many questions in that sign language known to all races and it was amazing and amusing how they admired everything the Adventurers had on especially the jewels of the gentlewomen and the simple gew-gews of the maid-servants. Their simple minds ran in the manner of their canoes being hollowed from a trunk of a single tree and did not conceive the construction of a ship. The eternal question was "where in all the earth did so large a tree grow from which so immense a mass of ship could be hewn?".

Their greatest fright which struck all with consternation was the ships' cannon. They were much louder than their twangling bows and when they were fired many trembled but stood immobile and faced their ground stoically. They compared the cannon to great thunder and the displeasure of the gods.

Guards had been posted night and day on board the Ark and on St. Clements while the Governor and his party had ascended the river. In the meantime, minor preliminary land protection had been started on the island. Then men were felling trees to build a palizado or fort, and a barge had already been constructed from pieces which had been brought over from England. Leonard Calvert on his trip to and from the Indian Emperor viewed "many parts of the shoare on each side of the river . . . in all wch tract I could not finde, what I most wished for, to wit some field cleered and left by the Indians".

Upon his return from the Piscataway, Governor Calvert, his Commissioners, and Captain Henry Fleete, on a bright sunny day in April, started out in the barge to explore the surrounding countryside and to select a desirable site. "Wherefore I [Leonard Calvert] went . . . more towards the mouth of the said river, where (by directions of our Captaine Henry ffleet who was very well acquainted with all parts of the river, and of the Indians likewise) I found a most convenient harbour and pleasant countrey lyinge on each side of it".*

* Capt. Whitbourne writing in "Description of Province of New Albion", printed 1648, reprinted in Force Tracts, stated "Maryland which I found healthier and better than Virginia".

They gave the name of St. George, now the St. Mary's, to the river in commemoration of the Patron Saint of England. They observed two deep inlets near the confluence with the Potomac, one capable of sheltering 300 ships of the largest class, as expressed by Father White. To the larger of the bays, or inlets, the name of St. George was given and to the more inland one that of the Blessed Virgin Mary.

About five miles up the river on the right bank, they were impressed with the physical features for a permanent settlement "so charming in its situation that Europe can scarcely show one to surpass it", thus reported Father White. There was considerable shore line capable of the landing of ships and above was a sort of bluff suitable for the erection of the castle and other public buildings. Upon landing they discovered that it was the site of an Indian village called Yoacomac, where the king of the same name dwelt with his tribesmen. Governor Calvert and his retinue were again graciously received and entertained. That night the king gave Calvert his own bed which consisted of a mat laid on boards. The next day they explored the possibilities of a permanent settlement and soon made a definite decision.

Governor Calvert displayed his trade-goods, so with axes, hatchets, hoes, and several yards of English cloth, all of which met the coveted eye of the Werowance, or King of the tribe, as well as his vassals, they bargained and bought approximately 30 square miles of the territory which they called "Augusta Carolina". A treaty of amity and friendship was negotiated with the Werowance. The believed spot is now marked with an impressive monument. The Adventurers were to occupy one part of the town, which they christened St. Mary's, but reserved the other portion for the temporary use of the tribe. On March 27, 1634, Governor Calvert took full possession of the settlement.

King or Werowance Yoacomac, prior to the visit from the colonists, was planning to abandon his village and to move farther up the Potomac to elude the blood-thirsty Susquehannocks of the North who frequently swept down and devastated his land. The Susquehannocks being traditionally more warlike and better fighters were constantly raiding the village of the Yoacomacans who were ever in fear of their lives.

It was agreed that at the end of the harvest the Indians would desert their village and leave it entirely to the Marylanders. Governor Calvert and his party soon returned to his barge and the temporary settlement on St. Clements, and in three days the Ark and the two pinnances sailed up the St. George's River. The Indians who formerly dwelt in the section of the town allotted to the colonists cheerfully gave up their houses and even left them some corn.

The land had already been cleared and been subject to cultivation by the Indians, so the Adventurers were spared the labour of felling trees and the digging up of stumps. The colonists actually lived in the Indian huts until they could build their homes after the English pattern. Some of the tribesmen offered to remain with the Adventurers until the next spring and assist in their peculiar farming methods and to instruct them how to cultivate tobacco and maize—two commodities to which the Adventurers had not been accustomed in their native England.

Father White writing in his journal stated, "Truly, this is like a miracle that savage men, a few days before arrayed in arms against us, so readily trust themselves like lambs to us, and surrender themselves and their property to us".

The first few nights the Adventurers slept on the ships, but during the day they were busy constructing first a "Court of Guard" or guard house and then a store house. In the meantime the Werowance of the Patuxent tribes paid them a ceremonial visit and many other Indians from several parts of the country came to welcome them as well as to satisfy their curiosity. After they completed the store house and unloaded the supplies and produce from the ships, Governor Calvert ordered a grand and formal entry on shore with the Colours which consisted of the flag of England and the armorial standard of the Barony of Baltimore. With the traditional English love of pageantry it was attended in semi-military formation by all the gentlemen and the servants in arms which impressed the natives as they stood in the background with silent emotion of awe, veneration and approbation. In the presence of the Werowances of the Patuxent and Yoacomaco and many tribesmen, Governor Calvert issued orders for a volley to the Colours which was answered by the guns from the ships in the harbour. Again the Indians trembled with stoic fearlessness "at the thundering of the Ordnance".

The Colonists had not been at the newly christened settlement of St. Mary's many days before Sir John Harvey, the Governor of Virginia, with his staff, who was always friendly to the Marylanders, arrived to pay his formal respects. Governor Calvert was entertaining him and the Werowance of the Patuxent in the great cabin of the Ark, when one of the Werowance's retainers came into the cabin and seeing his chief sitting between the two English governors became alarmed and was about to leap overboard. It had not been forgotten that his chief had once been taken prisoner by the Virginians and seeing him in such a position believed him again a captive of the English.

The Werowance of the Patuxent tribes remained with the colonists several days and departed with great respect and esteem for the Adventurers. Before leaving he cautioned the Yoacomacos to be careful and to keep their covenant with the Marylanders, and as his canoe was about to take off for the Patuxent area to the north, he said to Governor Calvert, "I love the English so well that if they should goe about to kill me, if I had but so much breath as to speake, I would command the people not to revenge my death, for I know they would not doe such a thing except it were through mine owne default".

From the Indians at the Barbadoes they had been able to secure some corn which they began to use in preference to the remainder of the supply of meal and oats which had been brought from England and which they decided best to preserve for future contingencies. But the women-servants were unacquainted with the preparation of corn, especially in its use as breadstuffs, so the squaws taught them how to mix it for baking to which the Marylanders gave the name of corn-pone—a name still retained today in the Southern States.

The store houses of the Indians were well stocked with corn from the previous harvest which the Indians freely exchanged or bartered for truck or trade goods. The Adventurers were able to acquire at least 1,000 bushels which the hierarchy planned to send to the Puritans in New England in exchange for salt fish and other essential commodities. Within a short time Master Richard Orchard was on his way to Boston in the Dove.

Activity had also been brisk in the planting of seed corn and preparing house gardens which they sowed "with English seeds of all sorts" and they "prospered exceeding well". The artisans after completion of the guard and store houses began on the construction of their cottages as the Indian huts were proving unsatisfactory for English standards.

The Adventurers were making excellent progress, but losing no time was William Clayborne whom Captain Thomas Young, in his letter to Sir Toby Matthews written at Jamestown in July 1634, described as one "might read much malice in his heart". He and his emissaries circulated false reports among the Indian tribes that the Marylanders were Spaniards whose treachery was now well known to all the American tribes and that they had come to harm them. The Indians immediately became less friendly with definite signs of hostility and became reluctant to trade in the stock of beaver that remained from the past winter trappings.

These unexpected events forced Governor Calvert to lay aside much other essential work and to finish in due haste the fort which was accomplished within a month. Leonard Calvert writing to Sir Richard Lechford, Knt., of London, and his business partner, stated that it was "settled one-healfe mile of the river . . . within a pallizado (palisade) of 120 square yards with four sides. . . . we have mounted one peece of ordnance and placed six murderers in parts most convenient; a fortication (we thinke) sufficient to defend against any such weake enemies as we have reason to expect here".[2]

Before the completion of the fort and the palisade, which they sometimes called the castle, Cyprian Thorowgood was sent on an exploratory expedition up the Chesapeake Bay and also to report on the possibilities of the beaver trade for that year. According to his own report, "he set sail on April 24th with seven men and went as far north as Palmer's Island". Leonard Calvert no doubt referred to him when he wrote "Whilest we

---

[2] Fund Pub. no. 35, p. 21.

were a doinge these thinges a shoare, our pinnance by our directions followed the trade of beaver, thorow all parts of the precincts of pvince".

During the time that the Yoacomacos remained with the Marylanders, and in spite of false rumors circulated by Clayborne, they and the settlers hunted together for deer and turkeys which some of them freely gave as presents, while others would sell them for knives, beads and the like. The natives furthermore brought them from time to time great stores of fresh fish. The Indian women and children began to come frequently to the houses of the Marylanders which was an excellent sign of their confidence and friendship, for it was discovered by experience that the Indians never attempted any overt acts where their women and children would be subject to danger. The Adventurers did not cease, however, to eradicate the suspicions out of the natives' mind by treating and using them in the most courteous manner possible.

On the initial visit to Virginia, they had secured, though somewhat reluctantly, some hogs, poultry and cattle, both male and female, which would furnish them with future stock. Then they built a water-mill for the grinding of corn adjoining to the settlement which lay on mill creek at the north end of St. Mary's.

Before the return of the Ark to London, the colony was well established, houses had been constructed, a fort and palisade had been erected and some trade had been accomplished with the natives, but the Virginians had gotten a start on them and obtained the best of the crop and trappings. All of these facts were carried back to Lord Baltimore by Commander Wintour of the Ark.

RETURNED VOYAGE OF THE ARK

The Ark remained in Maryland waters but a few months after the initial landing and settlement, as it was the intentions of the Commissioners to return her to London as soon as possible with skins bargained from the Indians. It may have carried some of the home-sick Adventurers who financed their own passage, but the servants or redemptioners were under contract so, whether home-sick or not, they were compelled to remain.

She sailed from St. Mary's the latter part of May with a much smaller supply of beaver than anticipated. When she sailed, she carried Governor Leonard Calvert as far as Point Comfort in Virginia, where on May 30, 1634, he addressed a lengthy letter to Sir Richard Lechford, of Shellwood, County Surry, Knt., a Roman Catholic gentleman and his business partner, by which he described the voyage of the two ships to Maryland and mentioned a number of business matters. "I have in beaver (wch came in lately since my comeinge wch my brothers ship from St. Maries from Maryland to James River in Virginia) as much as will satisfie for the courtesy I desire of you, but I cannot send it now by reason the ship cannot stay till I send for it".[1]

The Ark was back in London by August 30, 1634, when certain cargo was loaded thereon for the use of Lord Baltimore and others, as well as some goods consigned to planters or merchants in Virginia.

The Ark was preparing to sail on September 15, 1634, when Cecilius, Lord Baltimore, wrote from Wardour Castle to Secretary Windebank, and referred to the "returne of my shipp from my Maryland plantation". He spoke of "Clayborne's unlawfull proceedings" and requested a letter from the King "may not bee gotten so suddainly, before the departure of this shipp . . . and will sett sayle from thence within a few dayes . . . for my plantation will be in greate danger of being overthrown now in the infancy of it, if it be not strengthened sometime by such favourable and lawfull protection as I now desire".[2]

Those who returned on the Ark therefore brought first-hand information about Clayborne's shenanigans, and the intelligence arrived just at the time of "my Wive's lying in Child bedd detayning me heere [Wardour Castle] for sometime".[3]

There is therefore evidence that the Ark was preparing to return to Maryland on September 15, and there is also evidence of a ship sailing

---

[1] Fund Pub. no. 35, p. 23.
[2] Archives, vol. 3, p. 25.
[3] Archives, vol. 3, p. 25.

for the Province about Michaelmas, or the feast of St. Michael, celebrated on September 29, and arriving in Maryland during the early part of December. So it can be assumed that this ship was the Ark of London which brought the second contingent of colonists to Maryland.*

The following loadings were made on "le Arke of London" with Richard Lowe Master, destined for "Virginia" in the interest of Lord Baltimore: 30 August 1634.

> 111 bales
> 2 boxes
> 6 casks
> 3 yds course freez
> 15 smale groce glass beads
> 35 doz box combs
> 3 " Ivory combs cost 8s per doz.
> 17 " horne combs cost 2s per doz.
> 13 wt brass kettles
> iiijc Axes

2 Sept. 1634.   In ark for Virginia. Phillip Pinchen, 1 bale cont. 1 yrds freeze.

4 Sept. 1634.   In Ark for Lord Baltimore.

> 5 packs cont. viijc yrds course freeze
> xij Cask
> j box cont. 45 smale groce sheffeeld knives
> 30 doz hoes
> 40 " hawkes bells
> jjc Axes

4 Sept. 1634.   for Thomas Cornwallis j case cont vijc ells hinderlands.

---

* Those who are known to have come in 1634 were: Thomas Pasmore; Richard Williams; Thomas Price; Thomas Wills (Wells) in "his own rights" that is financed his passage; Henry Baker; Henry Tailor.

THE DOVE AND RICHARD ORCHARD

Richard Orchard, the Master of the Dove, was cantankerous from the very beginning. It was as late as September 20, 1633, when the Dove was already in the Thames that Lord Baltimore contracted with him to command the 50-ton pinnace which was to serve as a tender to the Ark. One-fourth of the ship was owned by Thomas Cornwalys and his partner, James Saunders, and the remaining portion by Lord Baltimore, Jerome Hawley, Richard Gerard, and Frederick Wintour.

When the Dove sailed from Cowes in attendance with the Ark, it had in addition to the supplies for equipping the settlement and trade goods for the Indians, a few passengers.[1] As the storm-tossed sea became too perilous for the Dove to follow the Ark, it turned back and found safety with the Dragon in the Scilly Islands, some distance off the coast of Cornwall. When the sea became more propitious for sailing, Orchard did not follow instructions by going direct to St. Christopher, and to await the Ark in the event of any unforeseen contingencies, but in convoy with the Dragon made for the Barbadoes. He went there, as he testified on the pretensions of collecting some debts due him.

Mention has already been made of his delaying the departure from Barbadoes for St. Christopher and the chasing of his ship by the Spanish around several of the West Indian Islands. After arrival in Maryland and progress was being made with the settlement, Governor Calvert ordered Orchard to sail the Dove for New England with a cargo of corn and other commodities in exchange for essential provisions needed by the Adventurers, and to return direct to Maryland as soon as possible. Orchard arrived in Boston on August 29th and contrary to orders he remained around the village settlement until October.

On his way south to Maryland, against specific instructions, he headed for Point Comfort in Virginia, where he arrived sometime in November 1634. Ironically, Calvert, Jerome Hawley and Captain Cornwalys with several of their retainers were in Jamestown at that time including the very able servant, William Fitter, of Captain Cornwalys. Upon their hearing that the Dove had anchored at Point Comfort, Governor Calvert and his party went immediately to the settlement at that place. The surprise of Orchard has not been recorded, but certainly embarrassment, conflict and dissension were apparent. In what manner the Marylanders arrived in Virginia is not known, but they then made plans to return in the Dove. Orchard refused to leave Virginia, demanding wages as the cause. He

---

[1] Testimony of William Fitter, Public Record Office, London.

48

assumed from all indications an antagonistic mood and replied, "in a mutinous manner that neither he or the said Pinnace the Dove would or should budge or goe from thence before he was satisfied with his wages".

The Commissioners did not have the required amount of currency with them as demanded by Orchard, but upon their arrival at St. Mary's they agreed to pay him where "their means lay", and to satisfy the crew of their wages. From later testimony it was revealed that Orchard was paid part of his wages. Orchard remained adamant. The Commissioners beseeched him not to forsake the Dove, for if he "shoulde leave her they knew not how to gitt Mariners to carry her to Maryland". At that time St. Mary's was about a two or three days' sail.

Orchard apparently exercised great influence over his crew. He, John James, and Nicholas Perry appropriated a bateau belonging to the Dove and went ashore at Point Comfort. Later Richard Kenton left the ship. Only one member of the crew remained, being "one little boy". After the crew deserted the pinnace, a violent storm arose around Point Comfort which greatly endangered the ship.

While the Dove was lying in the harbour crewless, Orchard, James, Perry, Kenton and another member of the crew named Robins came aboard, but when asked by Calvert and Hawley, then aboard the ship, what they wanted, Orchard replied "in a mutinous and braveing manner towards the said Captain Calvert and Mr. Hawley in soemuch that fearing an outrage", William Fitter sent "for the Cap^n of the Castle at Pointe Comfort to come to assist them and at their first cominge aboard her the said Orchard layd hands on the said Mr. Hawley and jostled him".

The entire crew deserted the pinnance, except Mate Warreloe, and two servants of Calvert and Cornwalys who had been sent on the voyage to New England. With much difficulty and with considerable delay, the Marylanders obtained mariners in Virginia to sail the Dove back to St. Mary's, but they refused to carry her to England.

While the ship was lying idle at St. Mary's awaiting trained mariners to sail her for England with trade goods from the Indians, a parasitic sea-worm indigenous to Maryland's waters did much damage to the hull.* In the meantime the Maryland traders had acquired during the autumn and early winter a substantial stock of beaver which from lack of scientific knowledge of preservation during the long, hot summer deteriorated.

It was not until August 1635, or nearly a year thereafter, that the Councilors or Commissioners could engage mariners to sail the Dove for England. When the Dove drew anchor at St. Mary's, she had 1000 wt of beaver and other skins, and a great quantity of wainscott timber consigned to Lord Baltimore, but the ship was lost at sea and nothing further

---

* "Teredo Navalis" which in June usually feasted on the coat of pitch, tar or lime off the timber and by degrees eat the planks into cells like those of honeycomb. See, "The Tobacco Coast", by A. P. Middleton, pp. 35-36.

was heard of it, by which Baltimore and the Commissioners sustained heavy financial losses. Secretary Lewger writing to Lord Baltimore in 1638 stated that he had acquittances from Wintour, Gerard, and others for their shares of beaver and peake which were delivered to them, and sent the other stock by the Dove "where they miscarried".

Orchard, after he and his crew deserted the Dove in Virginia, apparently had no difficulty in getting passage on a ship returning to England. On April 1, 1636, he instituted in London action against Leonard Calvert, Jerome Hawley, Thomas Cornwalys, and James Saunders, the owners of the Dove and demanded indemnity. Fortunately, Hawley and William Fitter both of whom were in Virginia at the desertion were in London at the time of the lawsuit.

Lord Baltimore stated that the agreement with Orchard was to sail the Dove to Maryland and to return her to England. Wages were to be paid at the end of twelve months or at the completed voyage, but if the voyage lasted more than twelve months, then payment was to be made for the portion thereof. Baltimore furthermore declared that Orchard entered into service on November 22, 1633, the day on which the two ships sailed from Cowes, and that certain payment had been made to Orchard in Virginia. Orchard contended that his duties began on October 16, 1633, with Leonard Calvert. Testimony was made that Orchard disobeyed orders, went to the Barbadoes "to accommodate and follow his occasion to seek or look after the recovery of a debt or debts which were due unto him there" and that he tarried a few days at Montserrat and Nevis and thus delayed arrival of the Adventurers in Maryland.

In June 1634, while in Maryland, Orchard was ordered to go in the Dove to Massachusetts for fish and other commodities. Baltimore stated that if Orchard had shown diligence he could have gone and come in seven or eight weeks, but he "neglected and followed his own pleasures and occasions that he took three or four months and returned to Virginia and thus prevented his finishing matters in a Year".

Orchard in court testified that on November 19, 1634, in Virginia, he came aboard the Dove but left it, and returned on Saturday the 22d. He maintained that he paid the mariners under him part or all of which was due them and that, after he demanded pay from Leonard Calvert and was refused by him, he went to the Governor and Council of Virginia with his complaint and that they heard the matter and ordered the Maryland Commissioners to pay Orchard and his crew.*

At court it was stated that all during the voyage Orchard was "very insolently, quarrelsomely and rudely, and did wastefully consume the said pinnace's victuals and commit divers outrages and misdemeanors".

In order to get the Dove back to Maryland, the Maryland Commissioners "were enforced with much ado and great expense, did get other mariners to

---

* What business did the Virginia Council have to make such demands?

carry them in the said pinance to Maryland and the said other mariners would not carry the said pinance further than Maryland but the said Commissioners were enforced to leave her there . . . with divers merchandise and goods of great value for want of mariners to carry the Dove to England". Lord Baltimore declared that he sustained losses to the value of £1000.

Jerome Hawley after returning to Maryland from Point Comfort departed on a ship as it touched Maryland enroute to England and as mentioned previously was in London at the time of the lawsuit. William Fitter, Gent., an equerry of Captain Cornwalys, had also returned to England and was at that time in attendance on Madam Cornwalys at her home in Holborn.† Both Hawley and Fitter agreed that when they departed from "Mariland there were beavers and divers other goods in the common storehouse wch was to been brought for England when they could gett mariners to bringe her from thence".

William Fitter gave a very interesting and enlightening testimony in defense of Lord Baltimore. He was styled of "Mariland in the West Indies, gentleman, aged 55". He stated that he had known Lord Baltimore for about four years, and Leonard Calvert, Jerome Hawley, Thomas Cornwalys, and John Saunders for the same time, and that he had known Richard Orchard for about three years.

That Thomas Cornwalys for himself and his partner, John Saunders, bought one-fourth of the "Dove" and that on two several occasions he had paid Gabriel Hawley, Merchant, for the use of Lord Baltimore £100 on behalf of Thomas Cornwalys and John Saunders. That ever since Thomas Cornwalys and John Saunders (while he lived and since his death, Valentine Saunders, his brother) have been the reputed owners of one-fourth of the "Dove". To his knowledge Lord Baltimore, Jerome Hawley, Richard Gerard, and Frederick Wintour were the owners of the remainder.

Orchard set to sea in the "Dove" which carried some passengers.‡ At Cowes Leonard Calvert, Jerome Hawley, and Thomas Cornwalys went aboard the "Dove" and in the presence of him, that is, Fitter, gave Orchard instructions to follow the Ark. "And about three dayes after at sea findinge the said Pinnace Dove sluggishly to follow the Ark and they the said Calvert, Hawley, and Cornwalys standeinge upon the poope of the Arcke did in this deponat heareing call to the said Orchard the Dove beeing then close to her and willed him that yf by storme or accident hee shoulde seperate at sea from the Arcke to ply for St. Christopher and there to stay untill the Arcke came hither or hee should receive further order from them what course to follow".

---

† This fact leads one to believe that Madam Cornwalys did not accompany her husband in the Ark, but joined him later.

‡ Fitter referred to Passengers. Are passengers synonymous with Adventurers, or were they paying passengers going to one or more ports which the Ark and the Dove had planned to touch en route?

Orchard disobeyed instructions and went to the Barbadoes instead. "That when the shippe Arcke was ready to sail from the Barbadoes the said Leonard Calvert and Thomas Cornwalys went aboard the Dove to have her sett saile . . . they discovered that Orchard was ashore & then they remained 3 or 4 days while Orchard was ashore. When Orchard came ashore, he made his apologies and that they remained fully a week while they would have done otherwise. The Arcke arrived about a fortnight before the Dove. The Arck and the Dove sailed together but the Arcke lost sight of the Dove about a day or two about Monserratt or Nevis and when she came up again to the Arcke he heard the said Orchard say shee the Dove had been chased by some vessells or friggots".

Fitter furthermore swore that after Orchard and his crew forsook the Dove in Virginia, and Calvert was able to get mariners to bring the pinnace to Maryland, it was not until August 1635, that they could persuade mariners to bring her to England. The "said Mr. Hawley came from thence before they coulde gett Mariners to bring the Pinance and when Mr. Hawley came from Mariland there was beavers & divers other goods in the comon storehouse wch was to bee brought for England when they could gett Mariners to bringe her from thence". That he went from Virginia to Maryland in the Dove and remained in Maryland the entire time the Dove lay idle at St. Mary's. He was in Maryland when the "dove last bound for England . . . and there is no news of her arrivall here".[2]

Lord Baltimore and the owners of the Dove lost their suit.[*]

---

[2] High Court of Admiralty, 13, vol. 52, p. 373, Public Record Office, London; transcript at Library of Congress, Washington.

[*] Studying all facts and testimonies objectively, Orchard had no suit against Baltimore, but justice was distorted in that day as it is today. It must be remembered that London was then politically in the hands of liberal forces who were violently anti-Roman Catholic.

SOME EARLY PROBLEMS

With the loss of the entire official records for the first three years of the Province which included proceedings of the 1635 General Assembly of all freeholders, probate records, and undoubtedly land grants and conveyances, the historian is thwarted in his pursuit of truths and facts, but a few records have escaped destruction and through personal letters to Lord Baltimore, still extant in the Calvert papers, from the Jesuits, Governor Leonard Calvert, Captain Cornwalys and others a very fair picture can be painted of the life and times of the early Adventurers and the many difficult and perplexing problems which confronted them.

Those first two or three years were certainly trying and exasperating ones for Leonard Calvert and the Commissioners. Calvert, only in his 23rd or 24th year, has been depicted as a weak personality, but his letters to his brother are certainly, when analyzed subjectively, not the exponents of an unstable and vacillating character. Cornwalys has been credited, deservedly no doubt, with being the guiding spirit of the colony, and Jerome Hawley, the other Commissioner, may have been grossly misunderstood. Cornwalys stated that the differences between Hawley and Lord Baltimore originated primarily through jealousy.[1] From extant records Father White with his vast experience in combating forces both spiritually and lay must have been a great power and substantial pillar upon whom young Leonard Calvert leaned on many a trying occasion. The vast services of Captain Henry Fleete should not be overlooked, for he knew the country and the natives well, but being an Anglican he was not able to reach sympathetically the ruling triumvirs as Father White.

Before houses could be built the surveyor had to lay out the various town plots allotted to each gentleman in the proposed city of St. Mary's, but no task was more important than the plantings for the essential foodstuffs and trade crops.

The Indian huts which were offered to the colonists were not conducive to the English way of life and served only as make-shifts until cottages could be erected. The Indian houses consisted of curved arbours, or half oval in form about 20 feet long and ten feet high, covered with animal skins. During the winter they built their fires on the ground or on deep sand laid upon their flooring and permitted the smoke and fumes to escape from an opening in the roof which could be closed during inclement weather.

At first the carpenters and sawyers with certain skilled and unskilled

---

[1] Fund Pub. no. 35, p. 179.

labourers were kept busy constructing the fort and palisade for protection from the enemy as castles had served their forefathers only a few hundred years previously. There were no trained architects among the Adventurers so far as it is known, but the several house carpenters who knew their trade found the Maryland trees well suited to their requirements.

Many of the labourers were lazy and shiftless, while others pretended before sailing to have been trained particularly in certain essential crafts when they were not. Furthermore, death often took away an excellent artisan and left only an inferior one in his place. The settlers who arrived late in 1634 and early 1635 were less than Lord Baltimore anticipated, and through death at the end of 1635 the settlement at St. Mary's and Mattapanient had less than the original Adventurers who arrived on the Ark and the Dove. Furthermore, a limited number of Adventurers had returned to England.

The land which had been cleared and cultivated by the Indians for some years was ready for the spring crops and the gentlemen planters lost no time in seeing that the farm-servants prepared the soil for seeding. The Indians introduced them to their corn or maize culture and soon the Adventurers were enjoying their bread of corn meal as they formerly enjoyed wheat and barley bread at home. It was this crop of corn on which the Adventurers had built much hope at the beginning for export, but production for the first year was in such insufficient quantities, owing to the cornbore, that they were required to barter with the Indians for their own use. Samuel Mathew writing to Sir John Wolstenholme in 1635 stated that the cornbore was "an unusual kind of wevell that last yeare eate our Corne". For meat they sustained on the wild game of the forest, and the rivers and bays were abundant in sea food such as fish, crabs, oysters and terrapin which were found without much effort.

It was not until February 1634/5, nearly a year after the actual settlement that Governor Calvert called the first General Assembly at St. Mary's City of all freeholders to meet and discuss the affairs of the Province, as outlined by Lord Baltimore in his instructions to the Colonists. The list of the freeholders who attended is regrettably lost, but Governor Calvert presided and all freemen sat on equal footing with the exception perhaps of Jerome Hawley and Captain Thomas Cornwalys, the Commissioners or Councilors, who from their position and prerogatives exercised undoubtedly certain privileges not accorded others. It can be assumed that it was a successful and harmonious occasion as no unfavourable references have been made to it in extant letters.

The many promising signs for a successful settlement were more often discounted by discouragement from the individual Adventurers. Within a year or so Thomas Greene who had invested in the adventure contemplated deserting the Province and returning to his home in Kent. William Fitter, Gent. had returned by April 1636, and we do not know why Richard Gerrard and perhaps other gentlemen of fashion departed for England.

Lack of liquid wealth was a condition prevalent among the majority of the colonists for twenty or more years, except those gentlemen who possessed private resources in England or gained the upper hand in the lucrative fur trade with the Indians.

Economic conditions and public morale improved during 1639 and much of the early discouragement vanished. Father White wrote to Lord Baltimore that every day matters were taking a favourable turn by the increase of planters from Britain and that the last harvest had been most successful of "large cropps this Yeare of Corne and Tobacco".

The conflict of distinct personalities also played its part in early dissention. Leonard Calvert and Cornwalys had their differences, for Calvert writing to his brother in April 1638, referring to Cornwalys stated ". . . though it hath been his fortune and myne to have had some differences formerly, yet in many things I have had his faithful assistance for your service".[2]

On April 25, 1638, Leonard Calvert wrote his brother that Jerome Hawley intended to move his wife and family to Virginia. And in the same year Cornwalys in writing to His Lordship referred to the financial difficulties of Hawley in England as well as in Maryland: ". . . he is not too bee blamed for laying hould of some probably way to repaye his misfortunes".[3] Cornwalys also commended Madam Hawley and the part she played during the trying years. ". . . by her comportment in these difficult affeyrs of her husbands hath manifested as much virtue and discretion as can be expected from the Sex she owes, whose Industrious houswifery hath Adorned this Desert that should his discouragements fors him toe withdraw himself and her, it would not a little Exlips the Glory of Maryland".[4]

Other problems facing Governor Calvert, besides the economic and the personal element, were certain political aspects of a young State such as legislature, appointments and the defense of the Province. The ever annoyance and jealousies of the Virginians, especially those who had settled on Kent Isle and at the head of the Bay who found themselves under Maryland sovereignty and their persistent refusal to pay homage to the Lord Proprietary or his agents were paramount problems for the young Governor to encounter. It began with bloodshed on the Eastern Shore and ultimately led to armed conquest.

The major appointments such as councilors, justices and the secretary were made directly by Lord Baltimore, but the Governor under the name of the Lord Proprietary had express power to create a number of minor offices and not a few major ones. The official title of Leonard Calvert was bestowed or reiterated on April 15, 1637, when he was commissioned

---

[2] Fund Pub. no. 28, p. 190.

[3] Fund Pub. no. 28, pp. 188-189.

[4] Fund Pub. no. 28, pp. 180-181.

"Lieutenant General Admiral Chief Captain and Commander as by Sea as Land". With the commission came the authority to appoint a deputy if he "should happen to dye or be absent out of our said Province".*

The two Commissioners whom Cecilius, Lord Baltimore, had appointed before sailing soon evolved into those of Councilors, for Jerome Hawley during his testimony in London during the summer of 1637 referred to the "Councillors" of Maryland. It has generally been accepted that the Council as such did not exist prior to Lord Baltimore's order of April 1637, which was not promulgated until the arrival of the first secretary, John Lewger, in Maryland seven months later.

For the first couple of years no important appointments were made, for the Province was small and Governor Calvert with the aid of the Commissioners or Councilors were able to cope with all matters great or small. Under date of April 15, 1637, as mentioned in the foregoing, John Lewger, Gent., in London acting under instructions of Cecilius, Lord Baltimore, authorized the appointment of a council and other officers as Receivers, Bailiffs, Marshals, and Magistrates.[5]

Sergeant Thomas Baldridge was or had been made High Constable of St. George's Hundred, an office at that time not below the dignity of a gentleman, and Robert Perry had the office of Marshal. John Langford was appointed High Constable of Kent.

When Lewger arrived in Maryland, he brought many plans and instructions from Lord Baltimore. The Council was enlarged and at the second General Assembly of January 1637/8, it was composed of Captain Thomas Cornwalys, Captain Robert Wintour, Esq., and Mr. John Lewger, Gent., with the Governor presiding.

Cornwalys writing to Lord Baltimore in April 1638, relative to the displacement of Jerome Hawley with Lewger, stated "I should bee Sorry toe change Mr. Hawley for him [Lewger] whoe I preceave stands not soe perfect in your Lops favour as I could wish him". Cornwalys was also somewhat apprehensive of Lewger, for in the same letter he wrote that he did not doubt "but yr Secretary was a very fit subject for his duties, if he did prove toe Stiff a maintayner of his own opinions and Somewhat toe forward in Sugiesting new businesses for his owne imployment".[6]

Other important appointments were Commanders for the Isle of Kent, as that portion of Maryland in the beginning was not given the status of a county or even a hundred but, owing to double-dealings of the early appointees to that tinder-box and the calibre of the men, those appointments certainly proved a source of much concern to Baltimore. At the Assembly of January 1637/8, Captain George Evelin held that post.

---

* Thus on his death bed in 1644 when he appointed Thomas Greene, Esq. his successor, he was acting under proprietary authority.

[5] Archives, vol. 3, pp. 49-55.

[6] Fund Pub. no. 28, p. 179.

In 1639 Cornwalys was preparing for a visit to his native England, but postponed it, though writing to His Lordship he recommended that a "Commander for Martiall Cause" be appointed for the Province.

The martial cause had by no means been neglected, for early precautions were taken to protect the Adventurers from possible attacks by enemies. The fortress or castle was completed within a very brief period after the selection of the permanent site where a guard was kept posted twenty-four hours of the day. If military officers had not been appointed before departure of the two ships from England, commissions were certainly granted shortly after landing.

During the first few years the colonists were not molested by the Indians. The Piscataway tribe along the Potomac and the Patuxent tribe immediately north were from the beginning on very friendly terms. But by 1638 through malicious propaganda as a result of competition in the fur trade and Clayborne's fight over title to the Isle of Kent, the Virginians intrigued with several of the warlike tribes, especially the Susquehannans, the Nanticokes and the Maquantequats with the result that the planters could no longer live and travel without fear of savage attacks. Even the once friendly tribes became apprehensive and began to display hostility. By a bulletin signed September 13, 1642, Governor Calvert declared the Wicomicos, the Mautacoques and the Susquehannas "enemies of the Province".

By an act passed by the Legislature in 1638 "every person within his her or their house able to bear" must have "one Serviceable fixed gunne of bastard muskett boare one paire of baldeleers or shott bagg one pound of good powder fowre pound of pistol or muckett shott and Sufficient quantity of match for locks and of flints for firelocks and before Christmas next shall also find a sword and Belt for every such person".

Each Captain of a hundred or in his absence the Sergeant or the Marshal was to conduct a monthly inspection at each dwelling house and those in default were fined 30 lbs. tob.

No inhabitant was to give an Indian "gunne poder nor shot", and no person was permitted to discharge three shots within a space of one-quarter of an hour except to give or answer an alarm. Upon hearing the alarm every householder was compelled to answer. Furthermore, every person able to bear arms was not permitted to go to church or chapel or any considerable distance from his plantation or manor without fixed gun and a charge of powder and shot.

Orders were given to the settlers in the event of an attack to proceed in haste to designated houses for safety. The householders in case of an alarm in St. Mary's Hundred were to send their men "to the Chappell yard neere the fort except any place may be appointed by the Lieutenant Generall or the Captain". The householders of St. Michael's Hundred from Trinity Creek southward were instructed to conduct their women and children safely to the house of Thomas Steerman. Lieutenant Thomas Baldridge was to command that portion of St. Michael's and to keep guard.

The householders of St. George's Hundred were commanded to carry their women and children to the house of Mr. [Thomas] Weston "such house as shall be thought most defensible by George Pye, late Burgess of that hundred". George Pye was placed in charge and given control of all men able to bear arms within that hundred.

By May 1639, the militia of St. Mary's County was without a commanding officer as Governor Calvert wrote "whereas the military band of our Colony of St. Mary's is now destitute of a Captain to lead and command them and to exercise them in discipline military", he appointed Giles Brent, Esq. "Captain to train and instruct all of said colony to bear arms in the art and discipline of war".

Captain Giles Brent ultimately issued orders for the safety and protection of the planters on the Patuxent River, stating that "they are so far from other plantations and so weakly peopled and continually exposed thereby to danger and outrage from the Indians . . . that upon the approach of any Indians whatsoever unto them in the woods, their plantations or house, they may after having bide the said Indians to depart they will shoot them". On June 8, 1644, Captain Brent issued a bulletin, however, whereby the Patuxent Indians were declared to be friends of the colonists and "were to be protected until theyr proved enemies".

On June 23, 1642, Robert Evelyn, formerly the commander of the Isle of Kent, was commissioned to "command all the English in or near Piscataway and to train them in discipline of war and to punish and correct all delinquencies".* On the same day William Blount, Esq., was commissioned Captain of the Militia for St. Mary's County.

In October 1640, an act was passed regulating marriages. No man was permitted to marry unless public notice had been published in some chapel or other public place within the Province at least three days before the ceremony. No marriage was permitted to be performed without the consent of the parents, tutor or master and within the forbidden degree of consanguinity.

The first two Assemblies were composed of all freemen of the Province, but the third Assembly summoned for February 1638/9, was however not a general one for all freemen, but was a representative body of delegates chosen by the freeholders of the Province. Summons were issued to all the hundreds including the Isle of Kent. The council and delegates assembled at the Fort in St. Mary's City on February 25, 1638/9, and by this time the Council had been enlarged to include six gentlemen, that is,

---

* A letter written by him circa 1642 stated that he and his Uncle Young had resided several years in New Albion, the Province of Lord Plowden, in Jersey, and that "Maryland a good friend and neighboure in 4 & 20 hours, ready to comfort and supply". Ref: Force Tracts, vol. 2, p. 23.

the Governor, Secretary Lewger, Captain Cornwalys, Mr. Thomas Greene, and the two Brent brothers, Fulk and Giles, who had arrived in 1638 and were immediately made members of the Council. Captain Robert Wintour had had an untimely death.

As capital was necessary to carry on the economy of the Province and to compensate the investors, the Adventurers lost no time in an attempt to secure the beaver skins from the Indians in order to send back a fair amount on the returned voyage of the Ark. Beaver fur was then in great demand, for it was beginning to become popular for the manufacture of felt hats then in vogue in England and the producers were always quite short of the raw material at that period.

Before the arrival of the Ark and the Dove, the Virginians had virtually bought all the trappings of the previous winter from the natives, and what few skins that remained in the hands of the several tribes were denied the Marylanders, inasmuch as the Virginians had circulated among the tribes that the Marylanders had come to destroy them.

Leonard Calvert writing to Sir Richard Lechford, Knt., shortly before the Ark sailed from Maryland for its return voyage to London, said, ". . . by reason of our so late arrival here we came too late for the first part of the trade of this yeare: which is the reason I have sent home so few furrs (they beinge all dealt for by those of Virginia before our comeinge) the second part of our trade is now in hand, and is like to prove very beneficial. The nation we trade with all at this time a yeare is called the Massawomeckes. this nation cometh seven, eight and tenne days journey from the Iland to us; these are those, from whom Kircke had formerly all his trade of beaver; But since they have found a trade with us".

Trade therefore with the Indians and England the first few years had not reaped the returns anticipated, and the first couple of years were rather hard pickings for even the gentlemen of fashion who had stock in the adventure as well as the indentures whose service was expiring and who then were on their own.

The first dividend to the stock holders in the Province consisted of 28 lbs. of beaver skins worth 10 shilling a pound, and an unspecified amount of corn for each share held. Some were quite satisfied with the returns while others were not. The first money or dividends received by William Peasley, the treasurer of the adventure, in the summer of 1634 was employed in the purchase of various commodities which were then needed for the Province and were entrusted to Captain Humber. The latter sailed from England for Maryland with these goods and presumably some fresh settlers about Michaelmas 1634, and arrived at St. Mary's City at the beginning of December 1634.[7]

In the summer of 1637, Edward Robinson, who had invested in the

[7] Deposition of William Peasley and Jerome Hawley, Pub. Rec. Office, London, Chancery 24/621/79; Robinson vs Lord Baltimore.

settlement and financed the passage of five settlers in 1633, became dissatisfied with the arrangement or perhaps the lack of dividends from his investment and initiated a suit in the English High Court of Chancery against Lord Baltimore.

In his bill of complaint Robinson stated that in August 1633, he paid Lord Baltimore an unspecified sum of money to finance the passage of indentured servants from England to Maryland. Lord Baltimore accepted the money, although according to Robinson he had no intentions of sending men for Robinson into Maryland. Robinson likewise stated that in August 1634, he had paid William Peasley £20 to be "putt into stock for trade with the natives in Maryland".* Robinson accused Baltimore of "dressing up" the list of Adventurers† in the Plantation with names of men who had never actually invested in the undertaking in order to "the better to drawe on others".

Most of the testimony or rebuttal at the trial were made by William Peasley and Jerome Hawley who was in London during that summer. Hawley in his testimony stated that the division of the proceeds of the first year's stock was made "by order of the Governour and Councell there resident".‡ Hawley furthermore testified that the total amount received by him did not amount to the value of his three shares, so that he "did loose and not get anything by this said adventure in the first yeares stock".

Besides the disappointments in trade during the first few years, the clash of personalities, the heavy death toll and the failure to interest more settlers to Maryland, the greatest problem and source of worry were the jealousy and envy of the Colony of Virginia encouraged by William Clayborne from deep-rooted hostility to the Calverts and the planting of a province north of Virginia. The latter is a story within itself which is reviewed elsewhere.

---

* This was the so-called second stock raised fur the Maryland settlement, the value of each share was therefore £20, but the total number of shares sold is not known.

† Apparently he meant investors and not the Adventurers who actually went to the Province.

‡ Evidence of an existing council the first year before the commissions of 1637.

GRANTING OF LAND AND THE ACTS THEREOF

Land in Maryland was plentiful, so plentiful that many did not exercise their legal land-rights, for in the very early days with limited farm labour the individual Adventurer was unable to cultivate such vast acreage. Besides quit-rents, which was the mode of revenue which Lord Baltimore expected in return for his heavy expenditures in financing the adventure, were unusually high and proved a tremendous hardship to the early planters. And realty at that time had little or no sales value. After the early formative years, however, land speculation became one of the minor economies of the Province, but in the beginning it brought but little profit to the vendor.

The Lord Proprietary, his heirs, and successors held absolute title to all domain, as granted under the Royal Charter by Charles I, so only Lord Baltimore through his resident agent had the vested power to confer land on the Maryland settlers. No land in Maryland, therefore, was ever granted by the King of England to a single subject, and under strict construction Lord Baltimore was the sole and absolute landlord, while the settlers or planters were his lawful tenants. They, however, enjoyed all the rights, privileges, and benefits of land in fee simple and entail and no restrain was placed upon them in exercising their rights of assignment, except by an alienation fee, and inheritance. Warrants were issued through His Lordship's agent in Maryland, and the grantee had the right of assignment even before the actual survey and letters patent were issued.

The issuance of land warrants was regulated by a systematic series of decrees promulgated by Lord Baltimore from time to time known as "Acts of Conditions" which stated or regulated the amount of land to be allotted to each settler or transporter of prospective settlers.

No direct taxes in a true sense were assessed the landed proprietors, but under all conditions, whether the grant was a private manor or an ordinary freehold, quit-rents were charged and paid to the agents of the Lord Proprietary at certain religious feasts of the Christian year. ". . . paying therefore yearly unto us and our heirs at our Receipt at St. Mary's at the two most usuall ffeasts in the year Viz at the ffeast of Annunciation of the blessed Virgin Mary and at the ffeast of St. Michael the Archangel by even and equall portions the Rent of fourteen shillings sterling in Silver or Gold or the full value thereof in such Commoditys . . ."* Quit-rents in kind were accepted in corn, wheat, tobacco, and even capons.

Lord Baltimore made recommendations from his English offices at frequent intervals for the granting of land by rights of service (a personal

---

* Excerpt from the manorial grant to Col. Baker Brooke, of Brooke Court, Esq., at Asquashyhe.

gift)† or for financing the transportation of prospective settlers. At first all land matters were under the jurisdiction of the governor and surveyor, but later a land office was created which had complete control of all land warrants, surveys, and the like. From all indications squatters were never tolerated, but in numerous instances a planter would settle on public domain and, as the opportunity presented itself, he would go down to St. Mary's City and file claim with proof of his land-rights which was followed by a legal survey of the Deputy Surveyor for the respective county and letters patent on parchment. In common with the English system the original parchment was the legal possession of the grantee and was to be transferred with notations thereon whenever the land was conveyed. As the plantations were often sold in moieties, the delivery of the original patent to the new owner became impractical and soon fell into disuse.

The First Conditions of 1633 were drawn up in London before the sailing of the Ark and the Dove, after conferring with several men who had been in Virginia and who had knowledge of the country and conditions. While Virginia always referred to "headrights", that is, rights to certain acreage of land according to each head or person transported, the term was never used in Maryland. "Rights to land" or "Land rights" was the usual nomenclature. Later when redemptioners became entitled to 50 acres, their claim was called "Freedom Rights".

Unfortunately, the terms of the First Conditions have not survived the years, but certain deductions can be drawn. They were based on the system of land-rights by one's personal emigration, that is, the payment of one's passage and the transportation of one's family, servants, or mere prospective planters. From the grants given under the First Conditions, it can be concluded that the Gentlemen of Fashion were entitled to about 400 acres for each person transported, though some contradictions occurred.* It is possible, however, that those who had investments in the settlement were granted a greater acreage than the mere settler.

Governor Thomas Greene perhaps stated the correct acreage in his letter to Thomas Hatton, Secretary of the Province, printed in the Council Proceedings under date of August 25, 1650.

"Luke Gardiner hath desired me to deliver my knowledge concerning what Condicons of Land his Lordp proposed to the Adventurers into this Province between the years 1633 and 1637. In Compliance wherewith I doe hereby declare that to the best of my knowledge any one transporting five men into this Province were to have 1500 acres of land to be erected into a Mannor. And I doe believe in my

---

† On July 20, 1652, Lord Baltimore authorized a warrant of 2,000 acres to "Mr. Samuell Whitlock one of the Lord Whitlock's youngᵣ sonns". Ref: Calvert Papers, Md. Hist. Soc.

* Capt. Cornwalys demanded 4,000 acres for transporting 10 men in 1633, and 2,200 acres by assignment of 5 land rights from Mr. Saunders. Ref: Patents, Liber ABH, folio 94; Liber 4, folio 623. Leonard Calvert, however, received only 3,000 acres for bringing 10 men in 1633.

Conscience the Rent was the Same and not greater then was required by the first Conditions of all".

Yrs.

Tho: Green.

The conditions of land grants to prospective settlers as expressed in "A Relation in Maryland", released in London under the imprint of September 8, 1635, apparently summarized some, but perhaps not all, of the provisions of the first act.† Ownership of land, as expressed in the conditions, was reserved only for a person or "subject to our soveraigne Lord the King of England".

A resumé of the conditions follows:

1. Any person who transported at his own cost five able-bodied free men between the ages of 16 and 50 was entitled to a manor of 1,000 acres.
2. Any person who transported himself or any less number of servants than five between the ages of 16 and 50 was entitled to 100 acres for himself and 100 acres for each servant.
3. Any married man who transported himself, wife, and children was entitled to 100 acres for himself and the like amount for his wife and 50 acres for each child under the age of 16 years.
4. Any woman who transported herself was entitled to 100 acres and 50 acres for any children brought in under the age of 6 years.
5. Any woman who transported women-servants under the age of 40 years was to have 50 acres for each servant.

Any person with no intention of going to Maryland who paid £100 English currency to convey five men to the Province, which was the amount sufficient for arms, implements, clothing and other necessary articles, was to have a tract of 2,000 acres or 400 acres for each person. Sending of men to the Province was therefore used as a speculation through the receipt of land, with the possibility of later assignment for a profitable consideration. Provisions were likewise made for investment of smaller sums than £100.*

On August 29, 1636, Cecilius, Lord Baltimore, ordered surveys for the following who had financed the passage of certain unnamed persons in 1633.[1]

Grantee	*Acreage*	*No. of transportees*	*Time for their transportation*
Mr. Richard Foster	2,000	5	1633
Mr. Edwin Robinson†	2,000	5	do
Mr. Anthony Metcalfe	1,000	2	do
Mr. William Knipe	1,000	2	do
Elinor Hildesby	100	1	do

---

† Reprinted 1910 in Hall's "Narratives of Early Maryland 1633-1684".

* Both Giles Brent and Thomas Gerard financed the passage of settlers to the Province before their actual arrival.

[1] Calvert Papers no. 192, Md. Hist. Soc., Balto.

† Mr. Edwin Robinson had stock in the commercial end of the Province and in 1637 sued Lord Baltimore before the English Court of Chancery.

At the same time he ordered the survey of a tract of 3,000 acres for Mr. John Lewger and of 1,000 acres for Mr. John Boles for personal services. Also "a warrant to Capt Henry Fleete for the 4000 Acres of land Due to him by the first Conditions of plantation" for transporting five men in 1633.[2]

No provisions for land-rights were made in the 1633 Conditions of Plantation for the redemptioners at the fulfillment of their service. Apparently, as they completed their contracts, they were expected to lease a tenancy upon one of the private or proprietary manors which many undoubtedly did. The First Conditions remained in full force and effect until 1636, when they were superseded by the Second Conditions.

Second Conditions of Plantation 1636.

The Second Conditions of Plantation issued at Portsmouth on August 8, 1636, presumably reiterated or augmented in the first clause a provision of the First Conditions as applied to the first Adventurers, and then made provisions for those who had entered the Province since the arrival of the Ark and the Dove.[3]

The provisions were as follows:

1. Every Adventurer who transported in 1633 five men between the ages of 16 and 50 was to receive a grant of 2,000 acres, also, if they claimed it, 10 acres of townland in St. Mary's City for each transportee.
2. Every one who brought in less than five persons in 1633 was to have 100 acres of land for himself and 100 acres additional for his wife, if he brought any, for each servant 100 acres, and for each child under 16 years 50 acres.
3. Those who transported in 1634 or 1635 ten men were entitled to 2,000 acres, but those who transported less than ten men, then 100 acres for himself and wife, if he brought any, and 100 acres for each servant and 50 acres for any one under 16 years of age. If they so wished, for every transportee five acres of townland in St. Mary's City.
4. Those who came in after 1635 were to have 1,000 acres for every five men transported, but those who brought in less than five men were to have 100 acres for each transportee, for each child under 16 years, 50 acres, and for each maid-servant less than 40 years of age 50 acres.
5. Every grant of 1,000, 2,000 and 3,000 acres was to be erected into a manor with "a court baron and court leet, to be from time to time held within every Such Manor".

With the dispatch and instructions, Lord Baltimore sent a draught of a manor patent with a court baron and court leet and also a draught of a grant or an ordinary freehold. Each manor lord had the privilege of selecting a name for his lordship and, in a number of instances, they

---

[2] Calvert Papers no. 192, Md. Hist. Soc., Balto.

[3] Archives, vol. 3, pp. 47-49.

selected place-names of their native English parishes. As in the first conditions, no land provisions were made for the redemptioners whose time was expiring, but the Assembly of 1640 passed an act by which each servant who had completed his or her indentureship was entitled to 50 acres.

At the same Assembly a bill which required the transportation of 20 men or women before the bestowal of a lordship was passed, but it was contrary to the provisions under the Second Conditions and was thereof deemed to be invalid. All laws, therefore, were subject to the approval of Lord Baltimore, so the requirements met with his approbation, as they were incorporated under the Third Conditions of 1641.

Father White writing to Lord Baltimore about this time or on February 20, 1638/9, cautioned him against the size of baronial estates "not under 5000 acres and reaching to 9000 is thought by every body too much", but he advised between 2000 and 4000 acres.

The Third Conditions of Plantation were promulgated at London on November 10, 1641, but they were not to become effective until the "ffeast of the Annunciation of the Virgin Mary" in 1642. Again no mention was made for redemptioners whose time was expiring.[4]

Third Conditions of Plantation, London 1641.

1. Any person of British or Irish descent who at his own charge within a given year transported 20 persons, able-bodied men, between the ages of 16 and 50, provided with arms and munition, or women between the ages of 14 and 40 was entitled to a manorial grant of 2,000 acres, or 100 acres for each person transported.

2. Any person of British or Irish descent who transported less than 20 persons was entitled to 50 acres for each man or woman to be erected into a plantation and held under some manor of the Lord Proprietary.

3. Any person of British or Irish descent who transported children received 25 acres for each boy under the age of 16 years and the like acreage for each girl under the age of 14.

Fourth Conditions of Plantation 1648.

The Third Conditions were superseded by the Fourth Conditions issued from London on June 20, 1648. All former Conditions of Plantation were revoked, and provisions for the first time were made for persons of French, Dutch and Italian descent to hold land. Each prospective land owner, however, was required to take the Oath of Fidelity to His Lordship.

Manorial grants still occupied the principal thought of Lord Baltimore in the matter of colonization and the issuance of land warrants. Any one importing 20 persons in any one year was entitled to a tract of 2,000 acres which was to be erected into a manor and held of some Honour of His

---

[4] Archives, vol. 3, pp. 99-100.

Lordship.* One-sixth of each manor was to be known as the demesne and was never to be alienated, separated or leased from the lord of the manor. Any person transporting less than 20 persons was entitled to 50 acres for each transportee and their plantation was to be held of some proprietary manor of His Lordship.

For the first time Lord Baltimore in his Conditions injected provisions for the redemptioners, but was confined to only servants of British or Irish descent. Consequently, any servant of British or Irish lineage transported at the cost of another person at the expiration of his or her term "so as be not under three years after arrival" as "if such servant transported himself" was privileged to apply for 50 acres as his freedom rights.[5]

Heretofore no mention in the Conditions referred to land grants of an organized body, but it is known that from the inception the Society of Jesus held manors and plantations without legal restraint. According to the Fourth Conditions, "Corporations Societies Fraternities Guilds and Bodies Politick as well as Spiritual as Temporal . . . in their own name or Right or in the name or names or right of any other Person or Persons" without special permission from the Lord Proprietary were prohibited from the future execution of land grants.

Fifth Conditions of Plantation 1649.

Within a year, or on July 2, 1649, Lord Baltimore executed a set of conditions with more liberal land-rights, but Governor William Stone in a letter to His Lordship on August 20, 1651, cautioned against units of 100 acres for a transportee but suggested 50 acres "the People will be too remotely scituated from one another and the whole Province perhaps in a short time taken up by a few people".

Any person of British or Irish descent who at his own charge transported 30 persons in any given one year was entitled to 3,000 acres which "shall be erected into a manor" to be held of some honour of His Lordship. One-sixth part of the manor, as in the Fourth Conditions, was to be known as the demesne and could never be alienated, separated or leased from the Royalties of the Lord of the Manor for a term exceeding seven years. The lord was empowered to convey portions of his domain to persons of British or Irish descent in fee-simple or fee-tail for the life or lives of certain members of the tenant's family.

Any person transporting less than 30 persons of British or Irish descent was to have 100 acres for each transportee "to be holden of some Manor there of his said Lordships".

Every one above the age of 16 to whom land was granted was required to take "the Oath of Fidelity to his said Lordship and his heirs Lords and Proprietarys of the said Province".

---

* An honour is a seigniory of several manors held under one baron or lord paramount. The term appears in the Rolls of Parliament as early as 1400.

[5] Archives, vol. 3, pp. 221-228.

Lord Baltimore, as expressed in his Conditions, continued to prohibit corporations from holding land without special license from him "doth except out of these Conditions of Plantation all Corporations Societies Fraternities Guilds and Bodys Politick as well Spirutual and Temporal . . . that he doth not intend that they or any of them shall be Capable of or have any Benefit by Virtue of these Conditions to inherit Possess or Enjoy any Land within the said Province either in their own name or right or in the name or names or right of any other Person or Persons whatsoever . . . without further particular and especial license first had and Obtain's therefore under his Lordships hand and Seal at Arms".

Furthermore, no person entitled to land was permitted to assign their rights to any "Corporation Society Fraternity Guild or Body Politick either Spirutal or Temporal or to any other Person or Persons in trust for them . . . mentioned or forbidden in any of the Statutes of Mortmayne heretofore named in the Kingdom of England at the time before the Reign of Henry the Eighth . . . without special license under the hand and seal of his Lordship or his heirs".

Every planter or heir entitled to rights under the Fifth Conditions had to apply for land-rights within one year after the said land shall be due or "for ever after loose their Respective Rights".[6]

The recommendation of Governor Stone had its effects, for on August 26, 1651, Lord Baltimore writing to the Governor revoked the 100 acres as the unit for each transportee "after the twentieth day of June One thousand Six hundred Fifty and two . . . shall be only 50 acres of land" except for several sections which the Lord Proprietary was anxious to encourage settlement.[7]

Governor Stone was therefore authorized to grant 100 acres as land-rights on any part of the Eastern Shore and that territory where Giles Brent was then living called "the Doages* . . . which lyeth between the Creek or River than runneth by Patowneck Town called in the mapp Patowneck River on the South and the River which runneth by Piscattoway River on the North in which last tract is included as we are informed that place where Mr. Giles Brent now resides called by him peace and also the country called there the Doages".[8]

The Conditions of 1649-1651 continued in effect until April 5, 1684, when Charles, 3d Lord Baltimore, at St. Mary's City then resident in his Province, abolished the land-right system and substituted the granting of land by "cautioned money" or fees in accordance with the acreage of the land-grant so applied for.

---

[6] Archives, vol. 3, pp. 233-237.

[7] Archives, vol. 1, p. 331.

* This territory which is now the lower part of Prince Georges Co. was once the home of the Piscataway Indians. Giles Brent had married Mary Kittamaquna, the daughter and heiress of the King of the Piscataways, and therefore in 1651 was living on the tribal lands or with the tribe.

[8] Archives, vol. 1, p. 332.

THE HUNDREDS AND THE COUNTIES

Within a short time after St. Mary's City was established and the various Gentlemen Adventurers were allotted townland with outlying manors and plantations, Governor Calvert, following the English pattern of judicial subdivision, instituted the hundred system or that ancient territorial division intermediate between the Roman villa and the Roman county, the origin of which can be traced directly to the pre-Christian era. They provided the framework for the military and civil, religious and secular expression of community life and were in no manner opposed to the feudal policies as laid down by the first Lord Baltimore.

The hundredum, using the old English spelling, was an institution devised by Julius Caesar by which a hundred families were grouped together under certain civil and military officers for mutual protection and common defense. It was also a term used to designate a Germanic tribal unit. After the withdrawal of the Romans about A.D. 410 the islanders, always disliking foreign innovations, discarded the Latin terminology of hundredum and substituted their native word "wapentake" which continued in use into modern times in certain English shires, especially York, Lincoln, Nottingham, Derby, Rutland, and Leicester. County Kent which was always individualistic had "lathes" as its subdivisions.

By the time of the Middle Ages, the hundred or wapentake had more or less lost its military features. It had developed into a subordinate unit for judicial purposes with a court of justice presided over by a magistrate, a constable and other minor civil officers. Consequently, hundredum became as often applied to the court as the district.

In the very early days the name given to the initial settlement in Maryland was Augusta Carolina and under that local name the first will recorded in the Province was probated. The name soon came into disuse and St. Mary's was adopted.

In the beginning the infant city of St. Mary's on the right bank of the St. Georges River was not given the status of an English municipality, but was incorporated into St. Mary's Hundred which included the immediate outlying plantations, but always maintained the prerogatives usually felt and exercised by a senior entity. If there was an official decree or proclamation at the formal inception of St. Mary's Hundred, it was recorded in the lost early libers. The first extant reference is found in 1637.

The Isle of Kent, at first regarded by the Council as rebellious territory, was denied for a time the sovereignty of a hundred but, as conditions improved and the inhabitants became more ameliorated and realized that their destiny lay with Maryland rather than Virginia, Kent was granted its official status. It was represented at the Second Assembly of January 1637/8. On that occasion Captain Robert Evelin, Gent., Commander of the Isle, and Robert Philpott, Gent., Councilor, who held all the proxies for the freemen of Kent, were present and were recognized by the Governor.

It was made officially a hundred at the Assembly of March 1638/9. "Isle of Kent shall be erected into a hundred & shall be within the County of St. Maries (untill another County shall be erected of the Eastern shoare and no longer) and shall be called by the name of Kent hundred".[1]

At the Assembly of February-March 1638/9, it was enacted that each hundred was to be presided over by a Commander who, at the court held after Michaelmass, was empowered to appoint a High Constable. Each hundred was to have a trained band under a sergeant who was to receive 4 lbs. tob. for every man able to bear arms "for his art & paines in training them".[2]

The first outpost from St. Mary's City was some ten miles to the North on the Patuxent River with apparently no seated plantations along the old Indian trail which connected the two settlements. The Patuxent plantations clustered around an old Indian village of the Mattapanients where Father White established his first mission for the conversion of the heathen Indians. The crude mission house and plantation later became the Manor of Mattapany-Sewall with Nicholas Sewell, Esq., as the first lord, all now within the Patuxent Naval Base.

Other settlers struck by the beauty and fertility of the Patuxent shores soon followed Father White and Mattapanient Hundred was officially represented at the Assembly of 1637/8. For a time a movement was current to discard the pagan name of Mattapanient and to endow it with the more sacred name of Conception, but the old and familiar name of Mattapanient persisted until it was absorbed into Old Calvert County. In 1640 Ferdinand Pulton, Esq., or Father Brock, a Jesuit, was authorized to hold an election for "Conception alias Mattapanient Hundred" and to vote on burgesses for the ensuing Assembly. The hundred along the south bank of the river soon became the center of large manorial estates of the major gentry and ultimately developed into an aristocratic center for the Roman Catholic overlords.

On March 31, 1638, Leonard Calvert announced that the west side of the St. Georges River was planted by several inhabitants and "is though fitt to be erected into a hundred by the name of St. Georges". He appointed Captain Robert Wintour, the first Justice of the Peace, who was authorized to have full power in the granting of warrants "to take recognisances to our case, keep a record, administer an oath", thus creating a hundred court after the medieval English system.[3] Although the official sanction was dated

---

[1] Archives, vol. 1, p. 55.
[2] Archives, vol. 1, pp. 54, 193.
[3] Archives, vol. 3, p. 70.

March 1638, some resemblance of a hundred was recognized, for St. Georges Hundred was represented in the Assembly of February 1637/8.

By 1637 four hundreds had consequently been organized, and by 1640 settlements had spread to outlying districts from all directions of the capital city, so that St. Michael's, St. Margaret's, and St. Clement's Hundreds had become integral jurisdictions. The freemen of St. Margaret's were authorized on September 12, 1640, to elect burgesses, but this hundred apparently merged with another or was dissolved as no further mention of it can be found.[4]

St. Michael's Hundred was organized out of those plantations and manors which had been seated eastward of St. Mary's Hundred and extended to Chesapeake Bay embracing Point Look Out which was part of St. Michael's Manor. On September 12, 1640, it was announced that the freemen of that hundred were to vote at the plantation seats of John Hallows and John Medley for one or two burgesses for the next Assembly.

St. Clement's, or New Towne Hundred, was likewise authorized to elect burgesses at the same time and had been organized a short time previously around the plantations and manors that had been seated on St. Clement's Bay and both banks of the Wicomico River. John Robinson, the High Constable, was commissioned to conduct the elections, but Thomas Gerard, Lord of St. Clement's Manor and Councilor, was the lord paramount in that area.

By 1640 sufficient settlements had likewise been made on the north shore of the Patuxent around St. Leonard's Creek to cause the planters to become conscious of their community and referred to themselves as of St. Leonard's Hundred. Leonard Leonardston so styled himself of St. Leonard's Hundred in the writing of his last will and testament on March 24, 1640, and Henry Bishop at the Assembly of July 1642, declared himself a burgess from that hundred. But it was wishful thinking on the part of the planters or their ambitions were thwarted by the Court of Mattapanient which had jurisdiction over that territory. Henry Bishop by presenting his credentials before the seated Assembly stated that it had been recognized by the probate of a will, but the Assembly declared that "it was not yet created a hundred and last election of Burgesses they were joyned to Mattapanient hundred".[5] It later was organized into a hundred and became the nucleus for present Calvert County.

By 1649 St. Clement's and New Towne Hundred became two separate and distinct units, with both sending delegates to the Assembly.[6] In the same year St. Inigoe Hundred had come into being and included the plantations around St. Inigoe's Creek and those of the southern-most tip of the Province. On January 24, 1649/50, Governor William Stone ordered elections in that hundred.

---

[4] Archives, vol. 1, p. 87.
[5] Archives, vol. 1, p. 130.
[6] Archives, vol. 1, p. 259.

At this Assembly, which was outstanding if not commendable, two stern and unyielding Puritan Gentlemen, Mr. James Coxe and Mr. George Puddington, who were vouched for by Governor Stone, arrived at St. Mary's City to represent the newly established plantations on the north shore of the Severn known as Providence, now in Anne Arundel County—and then trouble began.

Although the English parish had officially been a part of the territorial divisions of the shires for several hundreds of years, it was not actively developed in Maryland, perhaps inexpedient for the times, until the latter part of the 17th century, though both Anglican and Roman churches with their ecclesiastical bounds existed almost from the beginning.

Mention has already been made of the plan of Captain George Evelin, Gent., approved by Cecilius, Lord Baltimore, in 1638 for the division of the Province into Counties, Baronies, and Lordships, but it seems that the creation of Baronies never materialized beyond the paper stage.

The date for the erection of the county governments is not known, but under date of January 29, 1637/8, James Baldridge was commissioned "Sheriff and coroner of the County of St. Maries". Since the primary functions of a shrievalty constituted the administrative officers of a county since the days of the 16th century, it is evident that St. Mary's County existed.*

Within a few days on February 9, 1637/8, Cecilius, Lord Proprietary, likewise commissioned John Langford to be Sheriff and Coroner of the Isle of Kent and by implication therefore the existence of the County of Kent was recognized, but when the Assembly organized Kent Hundred in 1638/9, it was deemed to be a part of St. Mary's County.

On July 20, 1650, Anne Arundel County or the settlements around the Severn were organized, but not with a shrievalty but with a Commander in the person of Mr. Edward Lloyd who had come up from Virginia with the non-conformists. Under him was named a commission of seven magistrates.[7]

Old Charles County was authorized by Lord Baltimore on November 21, 1650, for Robert Brooke, Esq., who arrived with his family of thirteen and a retinue of 28 servants—21 men and 7 maids. It embraced both shores of the Patuxent River and thus incorporated the settlements in Mattapanient Hundred of former St. Mary's County to the Three Notch Road.[8] Charles County known today was created some eight years later or in 1658, and old Charles County virtually became Calvert County.

The Chief Justice of each county had the power to appoint an inhabitant of the county sheriff and also a coroner, whereas the sheriff had the power

---

* Before the Norman Conquest the "scirman" or man of the Shire constituted the office of sheriff, but after the Conquest the term "viscounte" was used, having been applied to similar functionaries in Normandy.

[7] Archives, vol. 3, p. 257.

[8] Archives, vol. 3, p. 308.

to choose one of his servants, if no servants, then the Governor and Council should appoint a person for the execution of all corporal correction or punishment to be inflicted on the body.

By the time of the first extant Rent Roll (undated) but after 1658 which includes the manors and plantations in the four Counties of St. Mary's, Kent, Charles and Calvert, the Province had outgrown its swaddling clothes and constituted a well organized sovereignty.

In St. Mary's Hundred was the City and surrounding townlands. St. Inigoes Hundred which began at only a short distance from the townlands contained a number of plantations and several manors, notably St. Inigoe, Cornwallys' Cross, St. Elizabeth, and St. Jerome. St. Michael's Hundred on the Bay side contained various plantations and the three comparatively small manors of Trinity, St. Gabriel's and St. Michael's belonging to the son and heir of the late Governor Leonard Calvert. St. George's Hundred was well seated with plantations and contained the Manor of West St. Mary's, once the private manor of Captain Henry Fleet, Gent., but at that time had evolved into one of the public proprietary manors of the Lord Paramount.

New Towne Hundred, which was once identical with St. Clement's Hundred, had been recognized as an integral hundred, including the plantations around Bretton Bay, and extended westward to Wicomico River, containing the three manors of St. Clement's, Basford, and Westwood of which Thomas Gerard, Esq., was the seigneur.

Calvert County which comprised both banks of the Patuxent River in that day was well organized into hundreds in spite of its being only thinly settled. On the south shore was St. Valentine Hundred which included Eltonhead Manor as well as St. Richard's and St. Joseph's. Resurrection Hundred which included the plantations and manors farther up the river, some of which are now in Charles and Prince Georges Counties, had within its jurisdictions Resurrection, Fenwick, De le Brooke, and Brooke Court Manors. St. Leonard's Hundred on the north shore, the oldest settlement in Calvert County, finally came into its own and boasted of Abington and Brooke Place Manors, with Colonel Baker Brooke, Esq., a baronial lord who had married one of Lord Baltimore's nieces. The Cliffs or those palisades on the Bay side in Calvert County were divided into North and South Cliff Hundreds. Mt. Calvert Hundred contained Mt. Calvert and Cold Spring Manors. Then there was Eltonhead Hundred to commemorate the loyal friend of Lord Baltimore who was shot by the Puritans after the battle of the Severn, and Lyon Hundred, or the plantations around Plum Point.

Kent County, the second oldest of the counties, was still thinly populated and comprised only two hundreds. Fort Hundred with the Manors of Kent Fort and Bobbing (then known as Thompson) comprised the plantations in the southern portion of the Island. The northern plantations around Love Point were in North East Hundred and contained no manors at that time.

The plantations in Charles County were mostly along the river fronts. Wicomico Hundred had been created out of the western portion of St. Clement's Hundred, or the settlements on the western shore of the Wicomico River. It included Wolleston Manor where Captain James Neale, Esq., held forth in baronial style. Then running northwestwardly along the Potomac was Cedar Point Hundred with its plantations and Causeen Manor, of which Ignatius Causeen, a French Catholic gentleman, exercised manorial rights. Portobacco Hundred comprised all the plantations and manors around Portobacco Creek and extended westward to an undetermined boundary and was rightfully the frontier of the Province. It was well seated with manors, however, and included at that time the following—St. Thomas, Rice, Mattawoman Neck, Poynton, and Christian Temple.

Not too far distant from the plantations on Mattawoman Creek was the fort at Piscataway where rangers were stationed to protect the frontier from Indian attacks. From then on was the wilderness until the Puritan settlements on the north shore of the Severn were reached—then completely isolated from the older settlements except the Isle of Kent which could be seen from Town Point, now known as Greenbury Point.

JESUITS IN EARLY MARYLAND

The influence which the Jesuits played in the early settlement of Maryland can not be too greatly emphasized, and Father Andrew White, the senior member of the Order in the Province, was responsible for more settlers coming into Maryland than other gentlemen on the Ark and the Dove. On the voyage with him were Father John Altham and two lay brothers, so the cloth was well represented. No Anglican priest was on the Ark nor did any officiate in the Province until 1650 when the Rev. William Wilkinson arrived from Virginia, a gentleman of York. A third Jesuit arrived in 1634 or 1635, for the 1635 report from Father White to the Senior House in Rome stated that there were five members of the Order— three priests and two coadjutors.

The men whom Father White personally encouraged to make the trip and whom he brought in as servants were for the most part members of the Roman faith. Any one of Anglican heritage would perhaps not have sufficient confidence or would be prejudiced in a Roman Catholic to indenture himself to a consecrated member of that faith. The Anglicans who were recruited for the Adventure engaged themselves in service to the Roman or Anglican lay gentlemen indiscriminately though no hard nor fast rule can be drawn.

In 1636 Father White reported to the Order that they had in Maryland four priests and one temporal coadjutor, so another priest had recently arrived, but in 1638 he referred to the death of a priest who had "laboured for five years" [Father Altham] and his death was soon followed by a second young priest.

In August 1637 arrived a kinsmen of Father White, Thomas Copley, who used the name of Father Fisher in the performance of his church duties and who was responsible for financing the passage of 10 Adventurers in 1633. He thus strengthened the Order and his influence was soon greatly felt through his keen interest in the development of the Order and the political and social welfare of Maryland in general. Furthermore, he brought much social distinction to the young Province, for he was the grandson of Sir Thomas Copley, of Gatton, Surrey, heir to an English barony, who espoused the Anglican tradition at the beginning of his kinswoman's reign, for Sir Thomas was closely related to Queen Elizabeth through the Boleyns.* He held an important position at court and in

---

* Sir Thomas was one of the coheirs of the last Lord Hoo and Hastings, a title he sometime used—being the gr-grandson of Jane Hoo, daughter of the last Lord Hoo who married his great-grandfather Sir Roger Copley.

1560 the Queen was godmother to his son and heir, William. Later Sir Thomas deserted the English Church and affiliated with Rome, thereupon he was banished from England. The King of France conferred seigniory upon him and the King of Spain created him a baron of the Spanish realm.

Thomas Copley [Father Fisher] was born in 1594, presumably in Spain where he was raised, the eldest son of William who was the son and heir to Sir Thomas Copley and was therefore the inheritor of the Spanish titles and in direct line to the English barony claimed by his grandfather. Thomas entered the Jesuit Order at Louvain between 1611 and 1615 and thus forsook all noble trappings in both England and Spain. He was, however, not a beloved character like Father White. His life and early training in Spain developed a strong and arbitrary discipline, quite characteristic of the Spanish Church, so his arrogance and uncompromising nature were not appreciated in Maryland among the freedom-loving Englishmen. In fact he was more Spanish than English. His unjustifiable and unreasonable demands upon the Lord Proprietary caused a breach between the Government and the Jesuits which continued until 1649, when the militant Puritans took over by force with the result that both Anglicans and Romans alike were disenfranchised.

Cecilius himself a jealous Roman Catholic was no doubt in sympathy with Copley's commands and recommendation to link Church and State and to exempt the Jesuits and their retainers from taxation, but his Province was becoming a heavy financial burden and he needed the revenue from his plantations. Furthermore, although he apparently wished secretly to unite his Province with the Church of Rome, he realized the inexpediency of it, especially when the Puritans were gaining such a strong foothold at home. Any union of Church and State would have been the death warrant for his Province.

Within a short time after the settlement at St. Mary's City, Father White, his servants, and followers established a mission at Mattapani on the Patuxent which had once been the site of an Indian village. William Lewis, who most likely came on the Ark, was made overseer and ultimately the steward of their manorial holdings.[1]

Besides establishing the Province of Maryland as a haven for English Roman Catholics, one of the primary objectives of the Jesuits in coming to Maryland was to convert the so-called savages to Christianity, but inasmuch as proselyting has always been one of the underlying motives of the Church of Rome, it was not spared in those early days. Father White writing to Rome in 1638 stated that "For the protestants who came from England this year [1638] almost all have been converted to the faith, besides many others with four servants that we brought for necessary use in Virginia".

In 1638 a prevalent sickness gripped the Province and two members of

---

[1] Fund Pub. no. 28, p. 158.

the Jesuit Order succumbed besides many planters and servants.* Father White in his letter to Lord Baltimore, "This yeare indeed hath proven sick and epidemically and hath taken away 16 of our Colony rather by disorder of eating flesh and drinking hott waters [rum or whiskey] & wine by advice of our Chirurgian rather by any great malice of their fevers for they who kept our diett and absteinence generally recorded".[2] Father White also reported the death of one of the gentlewomen who came on the Ark, though neglected to state her name saying "A noble matron also has died who coming with the first settlers in the Colony with more than woman's courage bore all difficulties and inconvenience. She was given much to prayer and most anxious for the salvations of her neighbours—a perfect example as well in herself as in her domestic concerns—she was fond of our society while living and a benefactor to it when dying".†

It was in 1638 that the impact of the proceedings of the 1637/8 Assembly had its repercussions on the Order and was the occasion of a lengthy epistle written to Cecilius, Lord Baltimore, by Father Copley on April 3, only 15 days after the close of the sessions, recommending exemption from taxation for the tenants on the Church land as well as the servants. Lord Baltimore read it most carefully and even made notes in his own hand-writing in the margin.‡

At the opening day of the Assembly on January 25, 1637/8, it was noted that Mr. Thomas Copley, Esq., Mr. Andrew White, Gent., and Mr. John Altham, Gent., of St. Mary's Hundred, had not responded to the writs of summons. Thereupon, Robert Clarke, Gent., of the same hundred, and the business agent for the Jesuits rose and explained that their absence was "by reason of sickness".[3] Accordingly, they were excused on the second day "from giving voices in the Assembly". William Lewis, their overseer, attended and reported along with Robert Clarke all proceedings, and William Lewis likewise had a number of proxies of the Catholic free-holders who for one reason or another did not attend.

---

* Estates of those administered in that year from St. Mary's of which there are records were John Smithson, Richard Lee, Richard Bradley, Jerome Hawley, Thomas Cullamore, Andrew Baker, Susan Saye, Zachary Mottershead, Gent., and Captain Robert Wintour, Gent.

[2] Fund Pub. no. 28, p. 202.

† The puzzling question has been who was this noble matron who came in the Ark? She could have been Mistress Anne Cox who married Thomas Greene, Esq., yet the statement that she left a legacy to the Order somewhat refutes the assumption. As Madam Greene, she had no estate under the law, her husband having acquired all rights at marriage. It is possible that she could have made a bequest with the permission of her husband. Could the noble lady have been Madam Ann Smith, the widow of William Smith, who died in 1635? The last record of his widow was about October 1638.

‡ All their tennants as well as servants he intimates heere ought to be exempted from the temporall gouerment. See original letter among "Calvert Papers", Md. Hist. Soc., Balto.

[3] Archives, vol. 1, p. 2.

Although the three priests then resident in the Province were excused from attending the Assembly of 1637/8, it seemed rather conclusive that the lords spirituals were to sit at the Assemblies as it was customary in England. If not, why were the names called and excuses made for their absence? It seemed as if a precedent was established by their refusals, for seats in all future assemblies were denied the gentlemen of the cloth. Protests were ultimately made by the Order, and while Lord Baltimore did not yield, the authority of the lords spiritual became all powerful and the extant letters from Father White and Father Copley are worthy manifestations of the influence of the Jesuits in that early period.

The excuse of sickness delivered by Robert Clarke proved to be mere subterfuge for Father Copley writing to Cecilius at the conclusion of the Assembly stated "it was not fitt that we should be there in person".[4]

Copley, however, followed the sessions of the Assembly most religiously and in his letter of April 3, 1638, not only gave his frank opinion and advice on lay and spiritual matters to the Lord Proprietary, but made a number of recommendations. He cautioned wisely against the necessity of transporting 20 men by an Adventurer before the conferment of manorial rights. He spoke of the contingency of death of the transportees as well as "runne away or miscarry servants" which caused a hardship upon the manor lord. He also warned against the heavy fee of one barrel of corn to be furnished by each manor lord for each of his 100 acres. "It would not be difficult for a freeholder who was labouring faithfully himself but to a gentleman who hath a companye of headstrong servants wch in the beginning especially shall scarecely maintaine themselve, this burden will cumme heavy".[5] In addition to his corn levy, each manor lord was made subject to a tax of 20 shillings for each 1,000 acres. The manor lord was furthermore forbidden to engage in trade, but "be compelled to plante", but as Father Copley explained "there is noe commoditye to be gott by planting". He also cautioned Lord Baltimore against the desire to extract too much revenue out of the planters, but by peopling the plantations "Yet against this I would desyre your lor^{pe} to reflecte that in a flourishing plantation, Your lor^{pe} shall ever be sure of a growing profit and honour. . . . But endeed the old saings are true that Roome was not bulte in a day".[6]

Father Copley complained that nothing was done at the Assembly to "promote the conversion of the Indians to provide or to shew any favor to Ecclesiasticall persons or to preserve for the Church the Immunitye and priviledge wch she enjoyeth every where else".

His principal objections were, however, the taxation placed upon the Order and their assessment for the defense of the Province and referred several times to the *Bulla Coenae.* He opposed strenuously the 15,000 lbs.

---

[4] Fund Pub. no. 28, p. 158.
[5] Fund Pub. no. 28, p. 159.
[6] Fund Pub. no. 28, p. 161.

tob. levied upon the Order towards the construction of the fort "they might free us from such kinde of taxation easpecially seing, we put noe taxes upon them".[7] Opposition was also made to furnishing 15 men from each manor to defend the Province in case of an attack and considered it "would be very unfite for us". Inasmuch as at that time the Jesuits controlled several manorial holdings, they would be subject to the same requirements of a lay manor lord. The planting of two acres of corn met with his disapproval "we find by experience that we canne not possibly employ halfe our number in planting", for they would lose their trade in beaver.

Disapproval was voiced of each manor having 100 acres laid out in Glebe land which would necessitate a pastor for each manor "wch to us would be very inconvenient". Opposition was also made to the case of a woman who fell heir to a manorial holding being forced to forfeit it to the next of kin if she did not marry within seven years, and also against the law that the Jesuits in common with other fur traders be compelled to have a license for trading. "I beseech your lordship to send me a private order that we may while the government is catholique enjoy the priviledges follow".

Among his requests were that the Church and the houses of the Order be declared sanctuaries, that the Order and their domestic servants and at least half of their "planting servants" be free from taxation and also the "rest of our servants and tenants".[8] Furthermore that in the absence of an ecclesiastical jurisdiction their causes may be heard and tried by the public magistrates but to be understood in their procedure as "arbitrator and defenders of the Church". He also recommended that they go and live freely among the Indians without licenses and that they enjoy according to their discretion certain ecclesiastical privileges.

Father Copley furthermore requested that the Order take up and keep such land as was essential to their needs, according to the First Conditions of Plantation, and if not expedient to take up their land-rights immediately to do so at some future time. Furthermore that part of the land then held by them would "prove convenient to be laide out for a towne at St. Maries". He also requested that the Order maintain a boat to be employed in their trading, but when not in use to be permitted to hire it out for profit, and to buy corn from the Indians without permission from the provincial authorities.

In closing he criticized the "Cheife of this Colony" for neglecting planting and for engaging too much "on a pedling trade" and that in "peopling and planting this place I am sure that none doone neere soe much as we nor endeed are lykly to doe soe much".

In a postscript Father Copley referred to Mr. Lewger, the Secretary of

---

[7] Fund Pub. no. 28, p. 163.
[8] Fund Pub. no. 28, p. 166.

the Province, with whom he apparently was not *sympatico*, for he stated that Lewger was one of the principal factors in maintaining that the laws of the Assembly be applicable to all members of the Province both spiritual and temporal. Another leading man of the Province at that time had also met with his displeasure, for Copley spoke of a shrive "who have formerly been a pursevante . . . is now one of the chief protestants".*

In 1639, a more detailed report of the Order was sent to Rome by the Maryland Jesuits and it referred to a great drought during the summer. In that year four priests and one coadjutor were officiating. Father John Brock, the Superior of the Order, with a coadjutor brother remained on "the plantation". Father Philip Fisher [Copley] lived in St. Mary's City "the principal town of the Colony" and Father John Gravener laboured at the mission on Kent Isle. The report furthermore stated that "Father Andrew White is still with us at Kittamaguanda Pascatoe".† There was no change in the members of the Order in 1640. Father Altham died on June 5, 1641. In 1642 Father Roger Rigby arrived and in 1654 Father Francis Fitzherbert.

In October 1639, Mr. Ferdinando Poulton alias Father Brock filed claims for a number of land-rights to which he was entitled personally, while others had been assigned him by Father White. The latter included not only those to which Father White was entitled in his own rights, but assignments to him from John Sanders, Richard Gerard, and the two Wintours.

On July 27, 1641, Father Copley filed claims for 400 acres of town land, 260 acres for transporting 26 able men into the Province in the year 1633 and 140 acres more for transporting 28 others since that year. At the same time he filed claims for a manor of 3,000 acres due under Conditions of Plantation for bringing in ten of the above named men in the year 1633.‡

No record has been found prior to 1641 for any land grants made by the Lord Proprietary to Father White nor to the Order of the Jesuits— though the Order was in possession of several manors before April 3, 1638. When Father Copley complained about the hardships of the Jesuits paying one barrel of corn for every 100 acres and implied that they would be forced to abandon one or more of their manorial holdings, he apparently referred to their purchase from Mr. Gerard "Though we should have the best lott; yet if we should choose Metapanian first, then we are sure to loose Mʳ Gerards Mannor, not with standing that we have bought it at a deer raite".⁹

Although Thomas Gerard, later Lord of St. Clement's Manor, and a

---

* A shrive was a member of the Church who heard confessions and granted absolution, whereas a pursuvant was an attendant upon a herald or a military attendant upon the King. This colonist had not been identified.

† An Indian village at Piscataway where he was much beloved by the tribes.

‡ Actually brought in by Father White.

⁹ Fund Pub. no. 28, p. 164.

kinsman of Richard Gerard, Esq. one of the Adventurers, was in the Province before the closing days of 1638, his first manorial grant was not made until November 3, 1639, and there is no record of his assigning land warrants prior to that time. Mr. Gerard's Manor was undoubtedly the unrecorded or lost grant made to Richard Gerard, the Adventurer, upon arrival or promised before sailing on the Ark. Richard Gerard returned to England before the opening day of the Assembly of 1637/8; one undocumented source stated that he returned in the year 1635.

Richard Gerard, a Roman Catholic gentleman, therefore conveyed his lordship to the Jesuits before his desertion of the Province and, from the remarks of Father Copley, Gerard got a good price for it. Seigniory was practised in Great Britain by the Church, known as tenure in frankalmoigne, and inasmuch as it was legal to convey manorial rights, unless restricted in the letters patent, the Jesuits therefore had privileges of court baron, if not court leet.

Cecilius, Lord Baltimore, honoured the Jesuits' request for a manor and granted them the Manor of St. Innago (sic) in St. Inigoe's Hundred with seigniory on 3,000 acres including the Island of St. Georges as due to Thomas Copley, Esq., according to the first Conditions of plantation as demanded on July 27, 1641, by the said Copley. It was to be held under the Honour of St. Mary's, but Father Copley immediately assigned the lordship to Cuthbert Fenwick, Gent., a Roman Catholic layman, and his heirs to be held in trust for the Order.[10]

Later Father Copley assigned to Thomas Mathews, Gent., an outstanding Catholic layman, a warrant for 4,000 acres which was surveyed into St. Thomas' Manor on October 25, 1649, with court leet and court baron. Thomas Mathews held the manor in trust until October 6, 1662, when he deeded it to Father Henry Warren, of St. Inigoe's. It was resurveyed with 400 additional acres for Father Warren of the Jesuit Order with court leet and court baron, so the Jesuits were granted seigniory indirectly by the Lord Proprietary, though statements have been made to the contrary.* There is no extant records of manorial courts held by the Order, but the Jesuits ultimately became one of the largest land owners in Maryland and large owners of Negro slaves.†

On August 15, 1650, when Thomas Copley demanded 20,000 acres due to the Order from various land-rights and assignments, Thomas Greene, Esq. stated before the Council that Father White was entitled to 8,000 acres due to him and his successors upon the First Adventure and that

---

[10] Calvert Papers no. 880A, Md. Hist. Soc., Balto.

* The manor near Chapel Point is still maintained by the Jesuits and is one of the most historic Roman Catholic Churches in Southern Maryland. The parish church is St. Ignatius and the present manor house which continues to serve as the quarters and refectory for the priests was built about 1741.

† According to the 1790 census, the Roman Catholic Church held 92 Negro slaves— 64 with Father Molyneaux at St. Thomas and 28 with Father Pyles at Newport.

altogether Father White had transported at least 60 persons to the Province.[11]

In spite of their protest, Lord Baltimore continued to tax the Jesuits' land holdings, but was liberal in granting them licenses to trade. Robert Clarke‡ their agent shipped presumably from St. Mary's City in February 10 [1637] cloth, axes, hatchets, knives, hoes to some nearby Indian village in exchange for beaver and corn.[12]

> "Shipped upon the Saint margett by Robt Clerke on the behalfe of his master, Thomas Copley Esq; one hundred and fifteene yards of truck-cloth . . . . & the said Robt Clerke doth acknowledge himselfe in the behalfe of his said master to stand indebted unto the Lord Propriet^r in three hundred and fifteene pound w^t of tobacco due for the tenths of the said truck; if it shalbe exchanged for beaver or corne without license".

Father White left religious-secular affairs to the other priests of the Church and had a sincere calling to convert the Indians to Christianity. For several years he lived and laboured with the Piscataway tribe at Kittamaquand where he eventually succeeded in the baptism of the Chief, his family, and some members of his tribe. It was at the conversion or baptism of the Chief that Father Altham succumbed to an illness from which he never recovered. At the same time, Mary Kittamaquna, an Indian princess and daughter of the Chief, was baptized and who later succeeded to the scepter of the tribe. She married Giles Brent, Esq., who held many offices under the Lord Proprietary and who was granted Kent Fort, the settlement of William Clayborne, with full rights of seigniory.*

Before the death of King Kittamaquand, he gave a large area of land around Piscataway Creek to Father White to which the Jesuits claimed title and which they refused to surrender. Conflict thus occurred with Lord Baltimore who claimed the sole right to the land, and writing to his

---

[11] Archives of Maryland, vol. 3, pp. 258-9.

‡ Robert Clarke was therefore one of the several transportees of Thomas Copley. If he were an indenture, his contract was of short duration, for he attended the 1637/8 Assembly as a freeholder. The terminology as expressed in the archives is perhaps employer-employee relationship. Robert Clarke became the Surveyor-General of the Province with a seat on the Council and married as his first wife the widow of Governor Thomas Greene.

[12] Archives, vol. 3, p. 63.

* It was not a happy marriage for the Indian Princess, as she sustained ill-treatment at the hands of Brent. Giles Brent, as her husband, claimed the kingship of the Piscataways as well as his son and heir, Giles Brent 2d. The Brents went to Virginia and in 1676 it was rumored that Governor Bacon was using his subject's claims as a pretense to involve the two colonies in war. "Wee have just cause to Suspect [Bacon] intends to embroyle yr province in a warr and that he will make the pursuit of the Piscattaway Indians his pretence to enter it and use young Giles Brent and his vaine title to his Mother's Crowne and Scepter of Pascattaway (as his ffather use to phrase it) to sett on ffoot that Brutes Courage to head all the needy and desperate persons in these parts to Our disquett". Ref: Archives, vol. 15, p. 124.

brother, Leonard, on November 21, 1642, he stated "I pray hasten the designe you wrote unto me of this yeare, of bringing all the Indians of that province to surrender their interest and right to me, for I understood lately from a member of that Body politique, whom you call those of the Hill there that Mr. White had a great deale of land given him at Pascattoway not long since by Kittamaquund, before his death wch he told me by accident, not conceiving that that place was wthin my Province, or that I had any thing to doe wth it, for so he sayd that he had been informed and I had some difficulty to satisfy him that it was wthin my Province".[13]

A new chapel was being built in 1642 and the Lord Proprietary suggested in the same letter to his brother that the Indians who "if their conversion be reall", might assist by their labour in the construction and contribute beaver and peake for the expense.[14]

When Ingle and his Puritan Purifiers raided Maryland in 1645, they burned and destroyed all Jesuit property at St. Inigoe's and Portobacco.[15] Fathers White and Copley were sent to England as prisoners of the State— some say in chains. Father White never returned to Maryland, but Copley did and died there.

[13] Fund Pub. no. 28, p. 213.
[14] Fund Pub. no. 28, p. 213.
[15] Archives, vol. 10, p. 12; vol. 14, p. 415.

POSITION OF THE ANGLICANS

For a number of years after the Reformation, when the Crown of England and Parliament threw off the cloak of Rome, the Englishmen who accepted the Reformation were known as Protestant-Catholics, and the name was even used in Maryland within the first years of the Province. The oft-repeated statement that all the Gentlemen on the Ark and the Dove were Roman Catholics and all the servants were Protestants is certainly unsustainable and is in error, but it has been repeated so often that it is difficult to eradicate the sting. It must be remembered that a servant at that time, as it is at present in the jurisdiction of the English and American courts, was any person employed by another. While there were a number of Protestant servants who were transported by the Roman Catholic Gentlemen on the Ark as domestic servants in its baser terminology, there were also a number of Anglican gentlemen who came in as servants in dignified and approved capacities.

There was no Anglican priest on the Ark to administer to the religious needs of the faithful Anglicans who held fervently to their heritage of the Established Church of England. By 1635 five members of the Catholic clericus were administering to their population, while the Anglo-Protestants had no benefit of clergy until 1650, yet the non-Catholics were always a considerable majority, even of those who sailed from Cowes, and maintained that balance throughout Provincial Maryland and even today.

In spite of heavy proselyting by the Jesuits and a number of the Anglicans in the Province going over to Rome, a substantial group of Anglicans remained true to their Episcopal birthrights and beliefs and without the benefit of the sacraments of their Church attended services regularly during the afternoon under a layman in the chapel which in the morning was used by the Roman Catholics. The names of those faithful laymen who read matins, vespers, and the litany of the English Church are unknown today, but Father Copley referred to a former priest [shrive] was was "Chief among the Protestants".

Several Anglican servants on St. Inigoe's Manor of the Jesuits protested against certain statements and accusations made by William Lewis, the overseer or steward, so Robert Sedgrave and Francis Gray drew up a petition to Sir John Hervey, Knt., then Governor of Virginia, believing that the Virginians were in a position to come to their defense. "This is to give you notice of the abuses and scandalous reproaches wch God and his ministers doe daily suffer by william Lewis, of St. Ingego's, who saith that our Ministers are the Ministers of the divell; and that our books are made by the instruments of the divell, and further saith that those servants wch are under his charge shall keepe nor read any booke wch doth apperteine to our religion within the house of the said william Lewis, to the great discomfort of those poore bondsmen wch are under his subjection".

It was planned that the petition would be circulated on a Sunday afternoon at the chapel for additional signatures, but through some maneuvering William Lewis got possession of the petition and turned it over to Captain Cornwalys of the Council. It came up for action at a court held in St. Mary's County on June 19, 1638.

On July 3, 1638, the Governor issued warrants to the High Sheriff to bring William Lewis, Robert Sedgrave, Francis Gray, Christopher Carroll [Carnell] and Ellis Beach before the Bar. Robert Sedgrave admitted being the author of the petition, and that he and Francis Gray were much disturbed by the speeches of William Lewis. Before circulating the petition Gray wanted to speak with Father Copley. On Sunday morning at the fort, Sedgrave asked Gray whether he had spoken with Copley, and Gray replied that he had and that "Mr. Copley had given him good satisfaction in it & Blamed much william Lewis for his contumelious speeches and ill-governd zeale and said it was fitt he should be punished".

Ellis Beach swore in court that William Lewis came into the room where Francis Gray and Robert Sedgrave were reading "Mr. Smiths sermons" and Lewis stated that the "booke was made by the instrument of the divell".* Richard Duke, a witness produced by Francis Gray who declared himself to be a Protestant, swore that Lewis stated that Gray could not read such books in his house.

William Lewis defended himself in that the book stated that the "Pope was Antichrist and the Jesuits Antixpian ministers". He told the servants that it was a "falsehood & came from the Devill as all lies did".

The court found Lewis guilty of an offensive and indiscreet speech against Protestant ministers, but acquitted him against the accusation that he forbade the servants from reading or using Protestant books in his house. He was committed to the Sheriff and fined 3,000 lbs. tob. John Medcalfe and Richard Browne gave bond.[1]

Thomas Gerard, Esq., a gentleman of the Council and Lord of several manors, for some reasons unknown removed the keys from the chapel and carried away the "Books", presumably the Bible and the Book of Common Prayer, which prevented the afternoon Sunday worship of the Anglicans. At a session of the Assembly on March 23, 1641/2, they issued complaints against him. Gerard was fined by the Assembly 500 lbs. tob. to be applied to the maintenance of the first clergyman of the Established Church of

---

* Mr. Smith's sermons were most likely not of the orthodox Episcopal order, for both Sedgrave and Gray were radical Dissenters and became accomplices of Ingle during the 1645 Puritan rebellion.

[1] Archives, vol. 4, pp. 35-39.

England to arrive in the Province.[2] One, however, did not arrive until some eight years thereafter.†

It was not until 1650, some sixteen years after the founding of the Province, that the Anglicans upon the arrival of the Rev. William Wilkinson from Virginia had the benefit of clergy.‡ He officiated alternately at Trinity Chapel at Popular-Hill and at the church in St. Mary's City. He continued his incumbency until death in 1663.

On April 21, 1649, the General Assembly of Maryland passed the now famous Edict of Toleration which granted freedom of religion to all who believed in the Christian faith. At that time the Assembly was composed of sixteen Protestants and eight Roman Catholics. It was accordingly confirmed by Cecilius, Lord Baltimore, on August 26, 1650.

The edict was a great and honourable advance in the direction of religious toleration which other American Colonies did not possess, but it merely confirmed or expressed in a single edict the provisions of the Royal Charter, a measure which was calculated to attract settlers so necessary to the existence of the Province. The Charter provided that the religion of the Church of England should be recognized in the Province of Maryland or the ecclesiastical laws of the Kingdom of England, yet at the same time it was expressed in such a character that the worship of the Roman Catholic Church could and would be tolerated. Knowing even in the seventeenth century the cunning intrigue of non-Christians, the framers of the edict, however, discriminated against Jews and other non-believers in Christ.

Since the founding of the Province, Lord Baltimore magnanimously had been tolerant of all Christian faiths and opened his Province in accordance with the Royal Charter to all Christians whether conformist or nonconformist. In 1643 he addressed Governor Winthrop, of Massachusetts, and offered "land in Maryland with free liberty of religion to any of the Massachusetts colonists who would transport themselves there".[3]

---

[2] Archives, vol. 1, p. 119.

† This case has been given rather fanciful and imaginative interpretations. All that is known is that Gerard removed the key and books from the Chapel. Gerard himself was a Roman Catholic, but both of his wives were members of the Anglican Church and he permitted all of his children to be raised in the Established Church of England —a condition not generally tolerated by a parent adhering to the Roman Church. Paradoxically as it may seem, several of his daughters intermarried with Protestants of the most radical type and were instigators in overthrowing Lord Baltimore's Province in 1689.

‡ He was born 1612, the son of Gabriel Wilkinson, of an ancient armorial family of Yorkshire. His father held the vicarage of Woodburn, Buckinghamshire, for over 50 years. At 14 he entered Magdalen College, Oxford, and was graduated in Feb. 1629/30. He was in Virginia as early as 1635 and officiated at parishes in Norfolk County. Upon his settlement in Maryland he brought his family of several daughters and some servants for which he was granted 900 acres—100 acres less than the requirements for a manor. No Anglican clergyman, except Robert Brooke who did not officiate as a priest in the Province, was granted seigniory in Maryland.

[3] Winthrop's Diary.

Studying the British background of events, the edict-year 1649 was a desperate and uncertain one for not only the Roman Catholics but the staunch orthodox members of the Anglican Church. The Puritans were in absolute power in England and were gaining control of the political scene in Maryland. The Edict of Toleration was therefore a policy of political expediency and was primarily a measure of prudence and self-defense for the protection of the Province against the rising tide of the Puritan enemies of the Anglican and Roman Church. It followed by two years the Act of the House of Commons of 1647 that the inhabitants of all the American plantations should "have and enjoy the liberty of conscience in the matter of God's worship". Furthermore, Charles I had been executed only three months before and the blood-thirsty and power-ridden Cromwell was then supreme in England and his followers were riding high in oversea plantations.

As always, Cecilius, Lord Baltimore, was a man of great tact, shrewdness and expediency, for being a Roman Catholic and a friend of Charles I, he could well conceive the dispossession of his Maryland Province. The most diplomatic move was to secure the favour of old Cromwell without delay. By so doing he was not double-crossing his staunch supporters in the Province nor expressing a liking for Puritanism, but cautiously acting to protect his rights as any clever, public figure or sovereign prince would do under similar circumstances.

But the Maryland Assembly under the leadership of the Puritan-sympathizer, Captain William Stone, had already partially capitulated to the maniacal Puritan element on the Severn until word was brought by Captain Samuel Tilghman, of His Majesty's Ship "Golden Fortune" from Lord Baltimore that he had not been deprived of his sovereign rights and to protect the Province in his name. Governor Stone acted, but it was too late, and the disastrous battle of the Severn in which the Puritans were victorious is one of the blots on the history of Maryland for which neither the Roman Catholics nor the conservative Anglican members of the Proprietary Party were responsible.

Until the arrival of the Dissenters in 1649 followed by the Quakers, the Anglicans were in the majority from the very inception of the Province. Father White writing to the Jesuit Order in Rome stated "For in leading the colony to Maryland by far the greater part were heretics". In 1641 he wrote, "Three parts of the people at least are heretics".[4]

Contrary to popular belief, the Roman Catholics never attained a majority in Maryland, and after the expansion of the Province westward, northward and to the Eastern Shore, the Roman Catholics remained concentrated principally in the three southern-most counties of the Province.

---

[4] The Records of the English Province of the Society of Jesus, 7th ser., pp. 362, 364.

DOMESTIC ARCHITECTURE AND CONSTRUCTION

The Adventurers soon discarded the Indian huts without flooring which the Yoacamicans unselfishly offered them and began to build houses more in keeping with their English heritage. At first they constructed, perhaps crudely, the characteristic half-timber cottages of the Tudor period favoured for shops and homes in England to which they had become accustomed. They were developed in England and remained for many years a child-of-necessity in a land where wood had become so scarce that houses had to be built with timber framework, filled in with wattle and plaster. Trees of many species both hard and soft were abundant in Maryland, so there was no scarcity, and the servants attempting to clear the land for agricultural purposes often considered them a nuisance.

When it was realized that houses could be economically and quickly built entirely of wood, new and original architectural concepts came into being. Structural strength no longer depended upon great beams or crotches alone, as used in the beginning with less labour,* but was shifted to the outer walls. The colonial clapboard within a few years came into being, along with the simpler framework and dormer windows.† In Maryland stone or brick were consistently used in the construction of chimneys and always on the outside of the house and on the sides, never in the middle as it developed in New England.

The interior of the homes of the gentlemen was paneled, and Jerome Hawley wrote in 1635 that red oak which was plentiful was used for that purpose.

No evidence exists of the importation of bricks from England. Chemists have analyzed the composition of the 16th century brick in Maryland and elsewhere and found that its chemical elements correspond to clays in the vicinity. "A Relation of Maryland 1635" states "wee have made as good bricks as any in England".[1]

When the second generation of Marylanders arrived, they had no knowledge of the architectural influence at home, thus they followed a path of their own in which they retained the best of the Jacobean tradition of England and adopted a style typical and distinctive Maryland to conform to the climatic conditions of a summer, sub-tropical climate quite

---

* Such structures were recreated for the Jamestown Exposition of 1957, and were amply demonstrated in the church or first assembly hall of the Virginia colonists.

† The log cabin did not develop until a much later period. The State of Delaware claims the first house built entirely of logs—but some claim that it developed with the Kentucky backwoodsmen.

[1] Hall's Narratives of Early Maryland, p. 81.

different from temperate England. Eventually the characteristic "marine type" developed along the rivers and bay and then spread to the backlands along the smaller streams and creeks. The shingle roof was carried down to form a porch held up by wooden pillars which not only became a favourite place for the family to sit leisurely during the summer but protected the great room, hall and master's bedroom from the intense noon-day sun. Even though it was singularly Maryland, it carried out in an unmistakable manner a combination of simplicity and function. The high-pitched roofs of interesting angles afforded windows at the end on both sides of the huge chimneys and was usually the only window for the bed room. While some houses of greater pretension had dormer windows adding a purely romantic feature to the exterior, many of the typical smaller Maryland plantation houses lacked that feature.

The Maryland marine type for its functional purposes was either copied by the younger colonies to the South or brought there by early Maryland emigrants, as it can be seen today in the Carolinas and other more Southern States.

While the English noblemen and gentry were constructing large mansions of fifty or more rooms, the Maryland squires and even the smaller planters in the 17th century built a small functional house, compact for their individual requirements with outlying dependencies for their servants or slaves, livestock, and other plantation needs. It was the 18th century which ushered in the large pretentious dwelling in Colonial America.

No trained architect was among the Adventurers so far as it is known nor is there record of any in the early ensuing years. Carpenter was the 17th century equivalent to the present day architect and should not be confused with the twentieth century definition of the word. Sons of the planters' gentry class soon displayed their interest and artistic ability in the designing and construction of plantation houses and public buildings and ordered books of both English and French printing as aids in their plans for design. The term house-carpenter was not used until a number of years after the early settlement. The "carpenter" of that day planned and supervised, while the skilled joiners did the actual work assisted by unskilled labourers.

The millwrights brought with them the Continental wooden windmill whose sail-covered arms would use the power of the wind to grind grain, saw lumber or pump water, but Maryland had so many streams that water mills soon became the fashion.

The first reference to a water-mill in Maryland is one built by Cornwalys which took two years to construct and which, in writing to Lord Baltimore in April 1638, he complained bitterly against the stupidity of the mill-wright.[2]

"The building of the mill was I Assure yr. lop: A vast Charge untoe

---

[2] Fund Publication no. 28, p. 174.

mee, for besides the Labor of all my owne seravts for two yeers, I was
at the Charge of divers Hirelings at 100: weight of Tob: in the
monthe with dyet when Corne was at 2: and 300 weight the Barrell,
all wch besides divers materialls for it at Excessive rates is all utterly
lost by the Ignorance of a fooleish milwright whoe set it upon A
Streame that will not fill soe much in six weeks as will grinde six
bushells of Corne, soe that myself nor the Colony is any whit the
better for all the payns and Cost I have beene at about it. . . . I
intend toe bestow on 100^b or 2: more in removeing of it toe a better
Streame. . . .".

On April 16, 1638, Captain Cornwalys wrote to Lord Baltimore about
the construction of his house: *

". . . in the meantime I am building a house toe put my Head in of
sawn Timber framed A Story and half hygh with a seller and
Chimnies of brick toe Encourage others toe follow my Example, for
hithertoe we live in Cottages, and for my part I have not yet had
Leysure toe Attend my pryvate Conveniency nor Profitt wch is not a
little necessary for me, having run myself & fortune allmost out of
breathe in Pursute of the Publick good. . . .".

Although Captain Cornwalys in 1638 referred to his building a "sawn
Timber framed house", by June 5, 1640, when Mrs. Mary Throughton
was granted 50 acres of townland, he had constructed a dwelling of brick.[3]
According to the patent, her land bordered "St. Barbara" and "partly west
to the swamp below the brick house lately set up by Capt. Thomas
Cornwallys Esq.".†

There are references in 1638 to Captain Henry Fleete's dwelling on
West St. Mary's Manor, and the fact that Captain Cornwalys wanted to
exchange his manor for "St. Peter's", the dwelling of the late Jerome
Hawley, Esq., would indicate that at the time of Hawley's death, he had
one of the most commodious dwellings in the town. It was then that
Secretary Lewger, who had lately come into the Province, advised Lord
Baltimore that he was building on Captain Fleete's side or on the west
side of St. Mary's River.

Secretary Lewger also in his letter of 1638/9, to Lord Baltimore expressed
the desire of Cornwalys for Hawley's residence and actually suggested a
grant. "If you can hinder the Captaine [Cornwalys] from obtaining that
house [Mrs. Hawley] by any other meanes than yr lops grant, he will
exchange Captain ffeets mannor and all the mannors in the country rather
than let St. Peter's goe (so they call Mr. Hawlie's house) to wch he is so
much affected for the Saint's sake that once inhabited it".[4]

---

* This house of sawn timber, and a story and a half high can not be the manor
house now standing on Cross Manor in St. Mary's County attributable to Captain
Cornwalys.

[3] Patents, Liber 1, folio 67, Land Office.

† The location of this brick house does not seem to fit the present brick house on
Cross Manor.

[4] Fund Pub. no. 28, p. 200.

Very few references can be found for the description of the gubernatorial residence of Leonard Calvert, but as the seat of the chief executive, it was certainly one of the ostentatious dwellings of the young settlement. It stood near the fort or castle and was claimed by his son and heir, William, upon his arrival in the Province after the royal restoration in England and proprietary restoration in Maryland.

The Governor's Palace, Mr. Hawley's St. Peter's, and the manorial dwelling of Captain Fleete have all passed into obliteration, but Mrs. Throughton's house and her barn were only demolished a few years ago. Overlooking St. Inigoes Creek stands the last brick manorial dwelling of Captain Cornwalys on the "Manor of Cornwalys' Crosse" undoubtedly the oldest house today in Maryland and a show place of the country.

Although Lord Baltimore visualized a town in St. Mary's County, a town or city as it was known in the 17th century England was not conducive to the virgin Province of Maryland. At no time was St. Mary's City a closely compact town, but rather a scattered village with houses set upon town plots of 20, 30, and 50 acres, though there is evidence that at least one row of houses was built. The failure of this urban life led the members of the squirarchy and gentry to establish themselves in the country and thus the plantation and manorial system became the dominant feature of early Maryland life. The county planters of less modest station built their homes in the most delightful spots of a virgin countryside amid primeval forests, so a very large number of comfortable dwellings and their dependencies each with their land around them rose and thrived.

SOCIAL STATUS OF THE ADVENTURERS

The degree of social structure of the Adventurers who sailed on the Ark and the Dove, according to the standards of the 17th century, has been the subject of much discussion and some erroneous statements have been made without any constructive approach to truth or even scientific analysis. The oft-repeated untruth that *all the gentlemen were members of the Roman Catholic Church and all the servants of the Protestant faith* is definitely subject to modification.

It is true that most, if not all, of the so-named seventeen Gentlemen of Fashion were members of the Roman Catholic Church, but a number of the Anglicans were certainly members of the county gentry either minorum or majorum. It was also quite apparent, and subsequent evidence substantiates it, that the county gentry far exceeded the immortal seventeen and that there were a few gentlewomen among the Adventurers. It should also be borne in mind that the definition of servant in the 17th century had a broader and more elastic meaning than the word servant of today. Several members of the county gentry actually came in under the nomenclature of servant—Anglicans as well as Roman Catholics.

In the 17th century, and even today in a legal technicality, one who was employed to render service and assistance in some manner whether trade or profession was termed a servant. Apprentices and indentured servants for a specified period of time became a well recognized institution in England for, in order to be employed or to serve another, a specific form of indentureship was essential and executed in expressed legal phraseology. This was necessary for the secretary, assistant or clerk in business, an apprentice in learning a trade or profession, and an ordinary unskilled worker.

Governor Leonard Calvert besides his body-servants had his stewards for his three manorial holdings, his lawyer, secretary, and even an equerry or chamberlain—all classed as servants.

Cecilius, 2d Lord Baltimore, who followed out his father's conception understood fully that in any organized state of society, especially a pioneering plantation whether aristocratic or plebian, well trained artisans, farmers, craftsmen, smiths, millwrights and unskilled labourers were essential for the structure and maintenance of a permanent community. The original settlers could not therefore be composed entirely of the *gentium majorum* or even *gentium minorum,* but on the Ark and the Dove were esquires, gentlemen, yeomen, and servants—the four principal social groups comprising English society of that day below the rank of royalty, peerage, and knighthood.*

The social strata were therefore composed of many cross sections of life's stations, with the servant group perhaps the most elastic class. For this group Lord Baltimore drew heavily from the younger sons of the yeomanry who were willing to indenture themselves to pay for their transportation in return for service. They were to perform work as farmers and the younger boys as field hands, for agriculture was acknowledged as the basic economy of the new province, though the fur trade with the Indians was to be fostered and recognized as offering the most profitable return. The sons and daughters of the urbanites and small village yeomanry furnished such necessary occupations as sawyer, joiner, cooper, brickmason, tailor, seaman, mid-wife, maid-servants, and many other trades peculiar to that epoch. The ship was not without its chirurgeon who was acquainted or equipped with the art of healing, did the bleeding when the patient's temperature was too high, was the apothecary, and the extractor of teeth—besides combined with his duties as a doctor was the job of cutting the hair of the gentlemen.

Records failed to name the highly important and essential artisan who was the Cooper, but there was certainly one or more on the Ark or the Dove. In that day no commercial ship sailed from a home port without several who were usually engaged for the voyage of both ways. On board ships everything was stored in casks, and as they expected to load the returning vessel with colonial goods, Lord Baltimore certainly took care of this necessary function.

It was customary to load ships in British ports with a large number of roughly shaped staves, for on the outward journey the cooper or coopers would be busily engaged in making barrels in which colonial produce would be stored for the return trip. Coopers of that day were among the most highly skilled of all craftsmen, for they worked to no written measurements or patterns. To make a barrel of a specified girth and capacity they depended on long experience and craft instinct alone. The craft was not confined to barrels for many utensils of a housewife were made by the cooper such as wash-tubs, water-pails, and small tubs for the storage of butter and other foodstuffs. Sycamore was the favourite wood as it did not leave a "woody" taste on food.†

In a study of the social structure it is necessary to repeat "the near twenty gentlemen of very good fashion who had gone to his plantation", for the

---

* Merchants have been omitted, for at the turn of the century, merchants and tradesmen in England were drawn from both the county gentry and the yeomanry. Small shop keepers in the larger cities had, for several centuries, existed having been supplied by the younger son of the yeomanry leaving the parental small farms for the urban centers. Peasantry as known and defined on the Continent in a true sense was non-existent in England in the 17th century.

† Apparently few sycamores grew in early Maryland, for Jerome Hawley said they used white oak for "pipe staves" and the red oak for paneling.

names of exactly seventeen appeared in the now noted pamphlet entitled "A Relation of Maryland". They and other members of the gentry who came to Maryland were all men who were proud of their inheritance and conscious of the responsibilities it carried.

Among the immortal seventeen were two sons of an Irish Peer, son of a baronet, two sons of a knight or a peer,‡ one definitely the son of a knight, and one is reputed to be the nephew of the Earl of Middlesex, formerly Baron Cranfield.

Furthermore, the Maryland Plantation and its visualized peculiar social structure attracted a number of the younger sons of the gentry who indentured themselves in various degrees of professional capacities in order to have their passage financed and then sheer youthful adventure played its part. This class of indentures included besides the private household staffs and secretaries of the esquires and gentlemen, those who were to assist the gentleman in his trade with the natives and the surrounding colonies. His Lordship's Surveyor was listed as a servant of Father White.

The gentlemen of fashion and estate were naturally the first to engage in the fur trade with the Indians which was followed by shipments of wood, salt, corn, and tobacco to the old country. The Jesuits were also quite active in all manner of trade and commerce of that epoch.

The Adventurers were therefore a composite group, with members of the squirarchy and gentry and many servants who, upon their freedom, assumed their place in the social class of his or her respective position as Gentleman, Planter, Craftsman or House-wife.

In the preparation for the settlement of Maryland, the prospective Adventurers probably recruited their servants from their own countryside, but for such positions as secretary and higher grades of occupations they recruited that supply from the homes of the county gentry who most likely maintained town houses in London.

The servants on the Ark and the Dove therefore can be said to have come from all walks of life. Some made excellent planters and assumed their social position at the termination of their indentureship. Others found their level in the planters group and became substantial subjects. The sons of the yeomanry had knowledge of agricultural practice in England and could easily adapt themselves to the peculiar conditions of farming during the sub-tropical summers of Maryland, but the indentures recruited from the towns, unless they were familiar to the crafts, had difficulty or an unwillingness to adapt themselves to field work on the manors and

---

‡ Edward and Frederick Wintour are styled sons of Lady Anne Wintour. If she were the wife or widow of a knight, she would be correctly styled Lady Wintour, but by being addressed as Lady Anne Wintour it would indicate, if the proper form be used, that she was the wife or widow or a peer, or a lady of high nobility who had married a commoner and who thus retained her rank. They were also referred to as the sons of Sir John Wintour.

plantations. Some, as found in all social groups, had no sense of morality or of responsibilities.

Although there were no instances of kidnapping of servants for the Ark and the Dove, kidnapping of children and indigent and friendless men and women became such an evil by ships' captains or their agents that an ordinance was passed on May 9, 1645, against the practice. Bristol which was an active port for the American trade by a law of 1654 required all servants going to the American plantations to be articled, enrolled, and questioned.*

During the first couple of years social life as known in England of that day was negligible. The planters had other compelling contingencies to face in the establishment of England in a raw and primitive land. But social amenities gradually forced their way into the fashionable life of the country. Jerome Hawley, Esq., constructed "St. Peter's House", the first pretentious dwelling in the Province, though Leonard Calvert as a bachelor presided over the Governor's Palace. So it was at St. Peter's House graced by Madam Hawley, once the Widow Courtney of that great Devonshire family, that Governor Calvert, Thomas Greene and his consort, Captain Thomas Cornwalys and a few other gentlemen with their ladies comprised a diminutive court circle in the Maryland "desert" as Cornwalys referred to the countryside in less than two years after the settlement.

They were the scions of the squirarchy who then clung and praised the splendours of fading feudalism and martial aristocracy that chivalry, honour and the Christian faith were enshrined in a glorious circle.

---

* The old enrollment books were discovered in 1924 in the vaults of the Bristol Council House, and have since been made available to researchers.

FACTORS CONTRIBUTING TO THE ARISTOCRATIC STRUCTURE OF MARYLAND

At the time Lord Baltimore was formulating plans for his Province beyond the seas and encouraging prospective settlers, the feudal age was still lingering and had not altogether given way to the materialism of commerce which was then dawning in 17th century England. Many of the conservative younger sons at that period who still regarded the cultivation of the soil as the rightful pursuit of a gentleman looked upon the Colonies as a medium for the life befitting their birthrights. Some had gone to the Colony of Virginia and the West Indian plantations, but Maryland had far greater attractions. There were more liberal land grants for the prospective planter and the aristocratic tradition which found its outlet in the institution of lordships or manorial lords, so dear to the heart of the squirarchy, with the pomp and ceremonies of a Lord of the Manor and a feudal entourage, appealed to the best of the emigrating Englishmen. The Puritanism in New England, the small-town provincialism of the neurotic Quakers with their restrictions on pleasure and fine dress, and the alleged outlawry of the Carolinas did not appeal to the younger sons of peers or the scions of the great county families. Consequently, during the early part of the 17th century, the conservative younger sons of the Roman Catholic and Anglican squirarchy sought Maryland in ever increasing number.

George, Baron of Baltimore, had accepted the teachings and beliefs of the Roman Catholic Church and that faith had likewise been accepted by all members of his immediate family. According to George Macauley Trevelyan, late of Trinity College, Cambridge, in his "England Under the Stuarts", the Roman Catholics of England in the 17th century consisted principally of the country gentlemen and their servants in the outlying counties and even more than the Anglicans were the non-industrial part of the population. London like all cities was strongly liberal in politics "for sixty years London had been the home of anti-Spanish and of anti-Catholic feeling".

By the sixteen-thirties the adherents of the Roman Church were not popular with the rising Puritanical influence which was gradually permeating into the Anglican or Episcopal Church. At this time the Puritans and other non-conformists were rapidly leaving the Anglican Church and becoming not only a strong religious block but a formidable political party as well. In fact Puritanism bespoke more of politics, destruction, and persecutions than the way of God and Christ.

Being fully aware of the persecutions to which the followers of the Roman faith were subjected by the puritanical element, and with a desire to offer freedom of conscience in the matter of religious worship without fear of intimidation, Lord Baltimore naturally favoured his friends and the members of his Church who were interested in his colonization project.

Besides establishing the Province as a haven for Roman Catholics, it was the vision of George, Baron of Baltimore, to create in the New World an integral part of England patterned after Anglo-Saxon institutions of the ancient regime. Everything before the departure of the Ark and the Dove was visualized with that objectivity and for a number of years thereafter the actual settlement of the Province conformed to that social and economic pattern. It should not be overlooked that the Englishman of an island race was different from other Europeans. To him England was and has been the whole world. If the conservative Englishman did decide to leave the land of his ancestry, he wanted to emigrate to that place where the traditions of Old England prevailed.

From the beginning the Province of Maryland therefore offered to free Britishers an opportunity to begin life anew, and the adventure appealed particularly not only to the members of the upper yeomanry who were conscious of the social restrictions in their native shires and considered Maryland an opportunity for social advancement, but to impoverished and adventurous scions of the county gentry and squirarchy. But the aristocratic propensities of the Calverts, as mentioned previously, attracted from the inception younger sons of peers and members of the *gentium majorum* and their retainers.*

---

* Besides the noble Calvert family and the Gentlemen of Fashion on the Ark and the Dove, other noble families and members of the various orders of knighthood were associated with the ultimate settlement of Maryland. On July 20, 1652, Lord Baltimore issued a warrant of 2000 acres for "Mr. Samuell Whitlock, one of the Lord Whitlock's younger sonns". Ref: Calvert Papers, Md. Hist. Soc., Balto.

George Plowden, Esq., who settled in Maryland, was the son of Francis, Baron Mount Royal, and grandson of Sir Edmund, Lord Plowden, who was granted New Albion, a platatine, in Jersey about the time that George, Lord Baltimore, received his charter for Maryland.

The senior member of the DeCourcy family of Queen Annes County which was in Maryland as early as 1650 was the rightful heir to the oldest barony in Great Britain at the death of the 21st Lord Baron of Kinsale about 1760. Ref: Letters of the daughters and the son-in-law of the late Lord Kinsale to William de Courcy, of Queen Annes County, deposited in the Manuscript Division of the Library of Congress.

Jerome Whyte, Esq., Surveyor General of Maryland under Cecilius, Lord Baltimore, was the grandson of Richard Weston, Earl of Portland, KG. Scions of the Howards of Norfolkshire whose ancestor Thomas Arundel-Howard was created a Count of the Holy Roman Empire with the title to descend to all male and female heirs settled in Maryland. Col. William Digges, Esq., in his will of 1697, mentioned a plantation in Maryland which formerly belonged to Sir Thomas Oldcastle. The senior member of the Wyvill family became heir to the baronetcy which he waived categorically. The consort of Henry Darnall, Esq., of His Lordship's Kindness, was the niece of the 13th Earl of Shrewsbury. A number of other scions could be cited.

They brought England with them, for Maryland was the only English colony of the 17th century which featured strictly the ancient life of Old England. The English counties, hundreds, parishes, towns, honours, proprietary and private manors, plantations, and leaseholds of 17th century England were all planned and became a vital reality of old English life in Maryland. In other words Maryland's way of life was a continuation of the pattern of the English county gentry. And it has virtually remained such even to this age of material-industrialization, especially on the Eastern Shore and in Southern Maryland.

Maryland was unlike the Virginia settlements to the South or the Pennsylvania settlements to the North. Virginia at its inception was based primarily on trade and commerce as the objectives of the commercial Virginia Company so amply set forth in its charter, and Pennsylvania was a community of an astute religious sect which drew its adherents mostly from the small tradesmen and urbanites of the cities. They were morbidly afraid of gaiety and fine clothes, would not fight in combat to protect their homeland, but developed a bargaining power equaled to the Semitic tribes which came out of ancient Asia. Nor was the Maryland Province founded on the principles of the New England Colonies whose settlers had rebelled against the way-of-life of Merrie England and aimed to live a cold, materialistic, puritanical and abstemious existence far away from their native country. In fact the Puritans and Pilgrims of New England aimed to form a State separate and distinct from England, with absolutely no allegiance to the mother country. From the very beginning therefore a marked contrast existed and continued between Maryland and New England, where in the latter a concentration of social life occurred in towns and villages with complete democracy, while in Maryland the isolated life upon the great manors and plantations with indentured servants and Negro slaves were conducive to an aristocratic structure of society.*

Life of the average early Maryland Adventurers other than the Gentlemen of Fashion was circumscribed within a small radius. The Adventurers remembered their native villages and parishes and saw perhaps for the first time the great town of London from which the Ark and the Dove sailed to Cowes and thence to Maryland—but beyond that the great hinterland of Maryland was a vast and unknown wilderness. They knew and all heard of the rebels on Kent and the few Puritan adherents within St. Mary's possessed a sympathetic understanding of their aims. Later the rebellious Puritans of Providence or Ann Arundell Towne held an identical compassion, but to the aristocrat and orthodox Anglicans and Roman Catholics those communities and their inhabitants were not a part

---

* Bruce states in his Economic History of Virginia, 1896, vol. 2, pp. 572-3, that the Puritans in New England were more numerous and bred faster, and on account of geographical and climatic conditions were engaged in the more ordinary occupations of a white man's land.

of their social life, but they were compelled to recognize their economic and political aspects. But in spite of the vast differences, a few marriages between Puritans and Roman Catholics occurred which always prove the rule.

A brief review of the social classes of England from which Maryland drew for her plantations and manors will present a better understanding of the Province's social structure during those formative years.

Squirarchy and Gentry

The squirarchy and gentry were those classes of English society who descended from freemen, bore coats-of-arms duly registered at the College of Arms, and ranked immediately below knighthood. Many of the squirarchy were descended from younger sons of the peers or had peerage connections but without titles and were often referred to as the untitled aristocracy. Between the two groups no social feuds existed, for they were forever mingling and inter-marrying. Gentry both *majorum* and *minorum*, however, ranked below squirarchy, perhaps having less land. Both groups were composed principally of large landed proprietors and lords of manorial estates of the various shires, the wealthy ones sometimes maintaining town houses in London. It was these substantial classes that gave English society intellect, culture, and achievement.

Under English common law of primogeniture and entail only the eldest sons of landed proprietors could inherit the parental land, where their forbears had held manorial courts from the early Norman period, and it was the scions of this class who sometimes for feats in battle as well as in civil achievement were elevated to knights and at other times to the realm of the peerage. Any acquired land through purchase could only be willed to younger sons, but so often in that day the land of England was so entailed that very little was available through commercial transactions. While the English custom of primogeniture and entailed estates forbade the younger sons to dwell on the family estates, they were not forbidden, like the children of noble houses and the *haute monde* of the Continent, to seek their fortune in commerce and trade. The younger sons sometimes sought commissions in the army and navy and there was always the tradition for the youngest to take Holy Orders. Then the discoveries of the New World with its colonization offered new opportunities in navigation and shipping, in addition to the lure of becoming a rich colonial planter. Before emigrating it was the custom to sell their property but, as it was usually the younger son, he was given his share before departure or, as in many instances, he inherited after his residence in Maryland.

During the seventeenth century when cities were becoming potential factors in the economic life of England with its essential business, trades, and other occupations, many of the younger sons of the squirarchy and gentry accepted positions in trade with no embarrassment or stigma to their social position, and it did not prevent their names from appearing in the Herald's Visitations of the epoch of those who were entitled to bear arms. The extant Visitations of London frequently list drapers, haberdashers and the like.

The ceremonious title for the squirarchy was Esquire, abbreviated as Esqr which always followed the name, and the consort of the squire was addressed as Madam and when used always indicated an untitled lady of high rank. To this class belonged the unmarried or grown-up woman or maiden who was addressed as Mistress with her Christian name as a title of courtesy and respect. It persisted throughout the seventeenth century and for a considerable part of the eighteenth but was superseded by the more informal and plebian title of Miss. The sons of knights were also privileged to use the title of "Esqr".

The appellation "Gent." was given to members of the county gentry and "Gentlewoman" was applied to their wives and was frequently employed besides their names whenever they appeared in official records.

The squirarchy and gentry of town and country of the 17th century were not accustomed to manual labour or even the many personal performances in the matter of dressing and other intimate acts of every-day life, so servants of various degrees comprised their retinue privately as well as publicly.

In many of the early inventories of the Maryland gentry at their death, a sword is listed when there is no visible proof of the deceased serving in the provincial militia. In the seventeenth century the sword was the symbol of the gentleman of honour and was worn by him on all state and social occasions. It also became the exponent of the cavalier or royalist during those hectic days through which Maryland passed shortly after its founding, when traditional government and royal prerogatives were matched against Parliamentary revolt and the torch of destruction. The sword in the inventory was thus an indication of the social status of the deceased and a cherished possession brought with him from his English home.

YEOMANRY AND SERVANTS

The yeomanry, always freemen, composed the small landed proprietors of the shires, and like the gentry there were the *majorum* and *minorum*. It was from this class of English society that the artisans of the cities were drawn. The women of the yeomanry were usually addressed as "Goody", particularly a married woman, and when a woman rose from the lower ranks to a higher station, she was addressed as "Goody-madam". The word wench was commonly used in that day to imply a girl of the rustic or working class.

In Maryland, as in all other colonies, an opportunity existed for the ambitious to advance through intelligence, industry, and personal charm, and concurrently the indolent and shiftless regardless of birth relegated to a lower stratum. Sometimes through marriage, and sometimes through his own sheer ability, the man rose in social position and acquired the right to bear "Gent." beside his name. A number of families who were perhaps members of the yeomanry in Britain within the next generation were eventually accorded the title of "Gent." behind their names, so at the beginning of the eighteenth century, the significance of "Gent." had somewhat lost its English meaning. On the other hand descendants of some of the best families of England, regrettably through unfortunate circumstances, soon lost their social prestige and became plain small planters or farmers of the yeomanry, with a definite so-called middle-class status. A new class of provincial gentry therefore developed whose only claim to the use of "Gent." was wealth or a fortunate marriage with a daughter of the squirarchy—though it has always been an unwritten law of society that a woman assumed the social rank of her husband.

In Britain as well as in the Colonies opportunities were always greater and more rewarding for the woman to advance her social position through her personal charm and other subtle functions.* In Maryland particularly the great disproportion between the sexes undoubtedly encouraged easy and early marriages. George Alsop writing on life in the Province stated that the women that came over to the Province had the best luck as in any place of the world, for they no sooner were on shore but they were courted into copulative matrimony.†

Although Maryland was patterned after Old England, peculiar social conditions arose to meet the exclusive needs of the new world. The place of the original indentured servant was soon filled by other willing settlers who were desirous of emigrating to Maryland, and as a rule the newly freed servants did not apply for reindenture. There was usually a fresh supply. Many ultimately became large landed proprietors within a few years, while others became small planters. Then in Maryland, as elsewhere in the colonial world, a new social order developed—that of the planter which ranked below the gentleman and was drawn mostly from the ranks of the gentry and upper yeomanry.

From the very beginning titles or distinction in social status in Maryland

---

* Anne Clarges, a needle-woman and daughter of a blacksmith in the Savoy, exercised her functional charm and married the celebrated General George Monck and eventually became the Duchess of Albemarle. In the present day many Peers wishing to enhance their estates and political power now marry women who are descendants of once nomadic, Mongolian tribes of Asiatic Jews whose parents have gained power through trade and banking, so the Jewish, non-Christian blood among present day British peers is greater than they would care to admit. The Crown has even created a number of Jewish peers and only recently made noble the blood of a nonconformist, socialist Jewess by creating her a member of the House of Lords.

† A character of the Province of Maryland, reprinted in Gowan's Bibliotheca Americana, edited by John Gilmay Shea, 1869, p. 59. Alsop lived about 30 years in Maryland.

were religiously employed, as it was customary in England. Esqr was placed beside the name of the man when he could claim that title, as well as "Gent." when he deserved the title or rose to it. At the settlement of the Province the prefix "Mister", as one of courtesy, was well established as a customary ceremonious title to those below the rank of squirarchy and above an undefined level of social position. It was usually abbreviated as "Mr.". Then there was the title of "Planter", by far representing the larger class, a word or class which had been recently added to the English vocabulary as one who was the proprietor of a plantation or cultivated estate in the West Indies and the Southern Colonies.

Yeoman and the various forms of artisans were used and given as titles to the individual such as Carpenter, Taylor, Cordwainer, and the like. At the First Assembly of which there is a record, that is, 1637/8, we find a Carpenter and a Brickmason among the freeholders.

SERVANTS IN MARYLAND

Indentureship was an ancient institution on the Continent as well as in England which grew out of the training of young men for expectant knighthood. In their training the postulant had to serve the noblemen into whose house he was placed in all kinds of menial duties which were never considered a stigma upon his social prestige and then gradually advance to the services of an aide or equerry. Scions of the higher orders of nobility went through the same basic training as the sons of the gentry.

From this medieval institution developed the custom of Englishmen, rich or poor, proletariat or bourgeois, to keep their children at home until the ages of seven or eight and then place them in service into the houses of other families, binding them for another seven or eight years. As the custom became more elastic, the sons of all social classes were placed as apprentices under an indentureship, during which time they performed the most servile offices. Then there was the various wardships which the guardian had at his disposal, for orphans of rich and poor, high and low were bought and sold like any other commodity.

In Maryland the agreements between the gentlemen who transported servants in 1633 were apparently private covenants and the length of service varied according to the age of the servants and the respective covenants. In the beginning the time of service, however, was usually four years,* and the master was responsible for the passage of each and every one of his servants, the clothing during the indentureship, and keeps. For youths the time was longer. No servant was permitted to marry without the permission of the master, and the master always had the right for a valuable consideration to assign his servants without permission of the individual. A servant could redeem his indentureship for a valuable

---

* In 1638 Father White wrote to Lord Baltimore and mentioned "the servants time now expiring". Fund Pub. 28, p. 202.

consideration before his period of servitude terminated.† At the expiration of the indentureship the one-time servant became a freeholder, was entitled to buy and sell land and have the privilege of the franchise.

It can be roughly estimated that fully 80 percent of the Adventurers on the two ships sailed under a contract of indentureship. A servant during his period of service received no pay, but all necessary subsistence was furnished him or her by the master.

After the Ark and the Dove a new class of younger sons of gentry background found their way to Maryland. The younger sons in England, as expressed elsewhere, were victims of primogeniture and entail and often indentured themselves which set an example and brought culture, education and gentle living to the new-world settlements. They came as tutors, secretaries, stewards, clerks to merchants, gentleman planters and in various other capacities in agreement with their masters for their transportation and "keeps", until they had fulfilled their contract and as in Maryland received 50 acres of land and other stipulated provisions furnished by law. They were then able to start a new life beyond the seas or the "western planting" which it was sometimes called in England.

It was the policy of those days to work long and hard, and the servants in Maryland were subjected to the routine of the English household and work shop. At the Second Assembly a question was put before the House whether the servants should be permitted to rest "on Satturdaies in the afternoone", but it was declared that "no such custome was to be allowed".[1]

Many of the bond servants must have often longed for their own fields and the comfort of their own cottage, and often at the close of a long arduous day spent at toil, must have hoped for the end of their indentureship, yet the average bondsman reverenced his contractual agreement with his master and realized it was law and custom of the land which was of over-whelming importance.

The Assembly of February-March 1638/9 passed an act to limit the time of "Christian" servants which would indicate that already some black savages from Africa, besides the few on the Ark, had arrived. By that act all persons of 18 years and above brought into the Province were to serve four years from the time of their arrival. All persons under the age of 18 years were to serve until the age 24 years unless "except likewise any other time were Contracted for by Covenant". Maid servants at the age of 12 years or under were bound to serve seven years, but if they were above the age of 12 years, they were to give only four years of service.[2]

The Second Conditions of Plantation in 1636, and undoubtedly the first, as well, made no provisions for land-rights of the bondsmen at the

---

† John Court, Gent. and John Pope "bought their time of service" from Capt. Fulk Brent who transported them in 1639. Ref: Liber ABH, folio 23, Land Office, Annapolis.

[1] Archives, vol. 1, p. 21.

[2] Archives, vol. 1, p. 80.

expiration of their service. It was not until the Assembly of October 1640, that a law was passed which entitled the one-time servant to receive land which became known as freedom rights. The act as passed by the Assembly stated that "A Servant at the end of his Service shall have by the custome of the Country one good cloth suite of Keirsy or broad cloth a Shift of white linen one new pair of stockings and Shoes two hoes one axe 3 barrells of Corne and fifty acres of land, five whereof at least to be plantable, women Servants a Years Provision of Corne and a like proportion of Cloth & land".[3]

The introduction of Negro slavery into the colonies and especially into Maryland presented an entirely new social order. Negroes and Spanish mulattoes were among the lower servant-class on the Ark and the Dove, but it was some 20 or 30 years before the wholesale traffic in the Negroes from the jungles of Africa became an economic force. Secretary Lewger writing to Lord Baltimore in 1638 stated "for negros I heare of none come in this yeare". Its introduction precluded to a large extent the system of indentured servants from becoming an important social institution in provincial Maryland after the seventeenth century, but indentureship was firmly established in the formative days of the Province's growth.

At first land and redemptioners became synonymous with personal wealth, for land was the hallmark of quality and prestige, as Negro slaves plus land were in the succeeding generations. A landless man, that is, without even a tenancy, was beneath notice in Provincial Maryland.

But the magnanimity of the Calverts was their undoing. By the complete tolerance to all Christian doctrine, they invited the Puritan, the Quaker, and the non-Conformist which is another story in the annals of Maryland. And in most instances the Dissenters of the first generation could not and would not conform to the pattern of the Maryland squirarchy and county gentry.

---

[3] Archives, vol. 1, p. 97.

MARYLAND FEUDAL SEIGNIORY

The feudal laws form a very beautiful prospect. A venerable old oak raises its lofty head to the skies, the eye sees from afar its spreading leaves; upon drawing nearer, it perceives the trunk but does not discover the root; the ground must be dug up to discover it.

MONTESQUIEU.

As English customs from the beginning were definitely very strong in Maryland, they were exemplified in no small degree by the institution of seigniory by the Calverts. The lord with his freeholders, tenants and bond servants was all bound by a multiplicity of variations governing the principle of English manorial law and economy which were so much a part of Britain at the time of Maryland's settlement. The plantation system on the other hand was a new order in world economy and was common at that time to all settlements in America. The early English colonies of New Found Land and those on the rock-bound New England Coast were all styled the "American Plantations", but the manorial system was not typical colonial but was a part of English life and land tenure long before the Conquest.

When George, Lord Baltimore, was visualizing his Province across the sea, perhaps somewhat with an Utopian rather than a realist view, the feudal age with its manorial society was still strong in the hearts and minds of Jacobean Englishmen and the dawn of material industrialism had not made its advent upon the minds of the urban and agricultural working classes. In fact today in England the rights of the lords of the manors and the conveyances of those rights are still exercised and respected.

Lord Baltimore had spent his childhood in conservative and rural Yorkshire and had associated with the society of the English royal court in his capacity as statesman, and later as a continental traveler he came in contact with a more rigid and astute court society, all of which were to his liking. So it was with understanding that he planned his Palatinate with a manorial economy and all the features of English conservative social life for the gentry which would be attracted to his Province.

The manor therefore became a distinctive Maryland colonial institution and in no other English colony did the order reach its full flowering as it did in early Maryland. The Dutch in New Netherlands had its patroon system, but it was not then under English sovereignty. South Carolina was supposed to have had one, but its grandiose plan existed on paper only and died by its own weight, for it was not conducive to the polygonaceous classes of French Huguenots, Spanish renegades, sanctimonious Quakers,

Barbadians, pirates and calculating Puritan traders from New England which arrived and settled around the Cooper and Ashley Rivers, but who ultimately established a respectable and near-homogeneous society.

The system definitely set Maryland off from the other English colonies up and down the Atlantic Coast* and contributed further in creating Lord Baltimore's Province the most essentially English of the Thirteen Original Colonies. It was the closing days of the old feudal period of the English Tudors with the Stuarts inheriting the mantle of their distant kin through Margaret Tudor who married James IV of Scotland and who became the great-grandmother of Charles I of England.

The system contrary to modern writers whose chief aim is to debunk America's colonial grandeur took firm roots in Maryland with all the trappings and rigid formality of an English baronial court. Before the arrival of the Virginia non-conformists and the subsequent revolution of 1654, the Calverts had created at least forty-one lordships which embraced no small area of the young Province. It acquired a very firm hold on both sides of the Chesapeake, but more especially in Southern Maryland which early became the seat and social center of the Province's aristocracy.

The rôle which was therefore played by the feudal order of seigniory with baronies and honours in the Province of Maryland was far greater socially, politically and economically than most modern historians and antiquarians have given.† The whole political structure for the first seventy-five or more years was adjusted virtually to the existing and contemplated manorial system both private and proprietary. While the detailed proceedings of that first General Assembly of 1635 are not available, practically the entire morning of the Assembly of March 16, 1637/8, was consumed with matters pertaining to the manors, the manorial lords, officers of the manors and the taxation of the lordships. Every Act of Conditions of Plantation decreed by Cecilius from the first in 1633 to the one of 1652, the last issued by him, contained vital and pertinent measures concerned primarily with the manorial system to be established in the Province and the methods by which individual manors were to be erected and maintained.

Prior to the Norman Conquest of 1066 the term manor indicated a land unit of varied size belonging either to the Crown, the Church, a nobleman

---

* The 1619 Virginia Assembly decreed that such powers as Court Leet and Court Baron were incompatible with the democratic establishment of the Colony of Virginia with its uniform system of local government which was contemplated by the fundamental laws and constitution enacted by the Virginia Company in 1618. *See,* Va. Hist. Mag., vol. 32, p. 188.

† Professor Charles McLean Andrews, of Yale University, a prominent historian of the past decade has brought out the significance of private lordships in Maryland before the student. In his "The Colonial Period of American History", vol. 1, pub. 1934, he states "On the social and tenurial sides, Maryland stands in a class by itself among the colonies of the English world. No such form of aristocratic and seigniorial life characterized either the Barbadoes or Leeward Islands".

or a commoner.* The Domesday Book published shortly after the Conquest outlined their functional duties all with the lord, seneschal, beadle, reeve, villein, cotter, socman and free man.

The historian rejoices over the wealth of early manorial accounts and court-rolls which have survived in old England, but it is lamentable that only one such record, for a brief period only, has been preserved in Maryland.† Then it is a court-roll and not the accounts. The early Maryland records of both the provincial court and land conveyances and leases are full of multifarious references, so that existence and operations of manorial courts are well substantiated by documentary evidence. The American antiquarian then need not permit the loss of the early private manorial rolls to reduce him to a pessimistic belief that no general account of the Maryland manor and its occupants is possible. From the extant references, life thereon can be pieced together by the preceptive student with substantial accuracy and well-defined conclusions.

The Maryland manor was in itself a small sovereign state subject to its own individual rights and privileges but conformed to the over-all structure of the institution and the laws of England. Each manor was to operate according "to the Law or Custome of England", as expressed in each and every letter-patent of the hundred or more manors created by the Lord Proprietary. In Maryland the prerogatives of a lordship descended to the son and heir under the ancient law of primogeniture, but ultimogeniture was not unusual in England and conformed especially in County Kent. No such condition has been noted among the Maryland manorial patents.

The early structure of the manorial order was laid down by the Battle Abbey Customals during the early period of the Conquest, though, as expressed previously, the system existed in Britain during the Anglo-Saxon period.

It was naturally modified by subsequent statutes. As new centuries brought fresh ideas and enlightenment, customs were altered and deflections were made in the straight forward operation of the old law. But one must be on his guard against imagining too great an uniformity. Each maintained interesting variations and individual details, for there was no

---

* The numerous proprietary manors which operated in Maryland to the American Revolution of 1775 correspond to those of the Crown; the Church acquired manors in Maryland under a private trusteeship but the laws of the Province prohibited the Church from out-right grants by letters-patent from the Lord Proprietary.

† Extant references infer that baronial courts were held regularly in Maryland during the 17th century, but as the manor-court roll or proceedings were the private property of the lord, only one known and partial roll of a baronial court is extant, that is, St. Clement's Manor, held under the lordship of Thomas Gerard, Esq. The complete extant court-roll is printed in vol. 53, of the Maryland Archives and gives an informative picture of the functions of a Maryland manor.

steady or clear cut pattern.* The pattern was set by the stipulations expressed in the granting of the lordship. Most creations had the privileges of court leet and court baron, but many jurisdictions or prerogatives did not extend beyond the limitations of court baron.

One of the characteristic features of the manorial system was its insistence on manual labour as one important element in the return a man made to his lord for the privilege of holding land on the domain. The tenants might and generally did make money payments, in Maryland principally in kind, but his obligation to render a specified amount of work from time to time was all important.†

In return for the creation of a lordship, the manor lord owed not only fealty to the Lord Proprietary but a monetary consideration called quit rents which varied according to the size and fertility of the manor. Such fees were to be paid at certain feasts on the Christian calendar and consisted of English currency or in kind.‡

The Statutes of Merton enacted in 1233, though modified by other statutes, laid down specific regulations that the lord was to leave "sufficient pastures" on the manorial commons for his free tenants. Most manors had their own water or wind mills and all tenants were obligated to have their corn and other grain ground at the manorial mill. Fines were imposed upon those who attempted to save themselves the millers' toll by grinding at home with a quern. Thomas Cornwalys, Esq., was the first on record who constructed

---

* When Jane, Lady Baltimore, consort of Charles, 3d Baron of Baltimore, was granted the Manor of Charles' Gift, formerly Little Eltonhead Manor, she was to enjoy ". . . such Courts Perquisitts and Profits of Courts rights royalities Liberties Privileges Jurisdictions and Immunities Royal Mines Excepts . . .". Liber 19, folio 484, Land Office.

Walter Notley, of County of Fermanayh in the Realm of England, Gent., was granted Court Leet and Court Baron on 20,000 acres and was to enjoy "all prequesities and Profitts . . . [courts were to be held] from time to time for and held by the Steward or Stewardes to bee appointed by the said Walter Notley and his heirs". Ref: Original patent in Calvert Papers, Md. Hist. Soc., Balto.

† When Robert Slye, Esq., leased a 1000-acre plantation on St. Clement's Manor from his father-in-law, Thomas Gerard, called "Bushwood or the White poynt" the consideration was "two barrells of Indian Corne or twenty Shillings in mony Every yeare Which is to be paid at the Nativity of oᵣ Lord". Ref: Archives, vol. 53, pp. 631-632.

John Langford who held a tenancy of 100 acres on St. Gabriel's Manor, one of the lordships of Governor Calvert, paid an annual rent of "6 barrells of corne & 12 Capons". Ref: Archives, vol. 10, p. 93.

‡ The fee on Eltonhead Manor granted to Edward Eltonhead was to be paid at the Feast of the Annunciation of the Blessed Virgin Mary and at the feast of St. Michael the Archangel and was £5 Sterling in Silver or Gold or the full value thereof "in such Commoditys as we and our heirs or such . . . to collect and review". Ref: Liber Q, folios 27-28, Land Office, Annapolis.

The yearly rent for Prior Manor on Kent Isle granted to Thomas Adams in 1640 was "two barrells of good wheat to be delivered at the Mill at Kent ffort".

a water mill on his manor. Then there is record of the Puritans wrecking the mill of Giles Brent, Esq., on Kent Fort Manor.

The baronial court was the principal prop of the manorial order, where all met, gave homage to the lord, expressed their grievances and were punished for minor offences.* It was a court, however, with varying powers and some manors dealt solely with indentured servants, while others only with matters arising from the economic administration of the manor. Others not only the indentures but the freeholders were in question and not only economic matters were transacted but criminal charges were investigated. Fines and levies were raised and the breaking of the lord's peace and other minor matters which would seem to belong to the Provincial High Court of the Lord Proprietary were discussed, yet the functions of the manor court were limited. As we come closer to the actual workings of the manor courts, we must remember that, while they all conformed to a general pattern, each had its own particularities and customals. The lord with privileges of court baron only was somewhat restricted in his jurisdiction, whereas the one with court leet took care of graver matters.

The manor court provided a speedy and comparatively inexpensive way of obtaining redress for injury or wrong. While we can not agree with some writers that "all foreign elements in the shape of advocates or professional pleaders were excluded", it is true that in general the procedure of the Maryland manorial courts were simple enough to be followed by the average tenant and he did not require an attorney to plead his cause.

The old patriarchal system prevailed sufficiently in Maryland for a man to be able to go to court in reasonable expectation of receiving protection from his lord, if wrong had been done him. There at the manor court he could plead redress for almost every kind of tart, before a jury of his peers with the verdict of his fellow tenants and the judgment of the steward.

When the court was summoned, it was necessary for every servant to attend unless he had permission to absent himself. Fines were imposed for all absentees. The attendance of the freeholders was another matter.† His compulsory appearance was generally a question of the bargain struck between him and his lord when the land was leased.

---

* Robert Cole, Gent., a freeholder on St. Clement's Manor was fined 2000 lbs. tob. for marking "one of Lord of the Mannors hoggs", presumably with his own mark. Ref: Archives, vol. 53, p. 628. Luke Gardiner, Gent., another freeholder, caught two wild hogs and was fined 1000 lbs. tob. for "not restoringe the one half to the Lord of the Mannor". *Ibid.*, p. 628. Robert Samson and Henry Awsbury, tavern keepers on St. Clement's, were accused of selling drink at an unlawful rate. *Ibid.*, p. 636.

† When Jacob Young leased a tenancy from George Talbot, Esq., Lord of Susquehanna Manor, now in Cecil County, he and his successors were required "ye all times hereafter when any court or courts shall be held for the mannor the said Jacob Young his heirs and assigns . . . shall from time to time when required does such suite and service to and att ye said Court and Courts as is customary and usuall in mannors in England". Ref: Cecil Co. Deeds, Liber 1, folio 96.

In general, however, the lord and his tenants found it mutually convenient to compromise, and as certain customs and changes took place in manorial life in England and its counterpart in Maryland, the will of the lord was softened and no longer the autocractic voice of the 15th and 16th centuries.

Life on the Maryland manor centered around the court and various officers connected with the operations thereof. At its head was the lord himself and as a number of Marylanders possessed several manors, some in various parts of the Province, he was often the lord in absentia. At the settlement of Maryland the civil officers of a manor were much less than those of the Plantagenet or Tudor eras and were usually measured by the size of the seigniorial holdings of the lord. The manor in Maryland was too compact to maintain the functionaries on the larger manors in England such as hayward, the messor in charge of sowing and gathering of the crops, the shepherd, ploughman, carter, and the like, but the steward, the bailiff, the constable, the reeve, the scribe, the muster-master were, however, essential to all manorial administrations and constituted the staff on the Maryland manors of which we have record. They were the paid agents of the lord and in this manner a whole hierarchy of officials and minor servants was created.

The steward or seneschal was the voice and executive of the lord and was always a gentleman of rank and standing. One steward on St. Clement's Manor was John Ryves, Gent., and another was Thomas Manning, Gent. The steward on St. Gabriel's Manor for Mistress Mary Brent was James Gaylord, Gent.

To the steward was committed the duty of holding periodic courts, to preside over them, to hold the View of Frankpledge*, if the particular manor had that privilege, and was the dispenser of justice. He was second in importance to the lord and had the management of the agricultural exploitation of the land. He could be strong or weak as well as harsh, but he was usually a beneficial patriarch to the tenants and servants and at times something considerably less than that, but in any case he controlled the tenants' well being on the manor to a very great extent.

He did not necessarily have to live upon the manor, but came at fixed times and sessions, although in Maryland it is believed that most of them did dwell upon their charges. He sometimes held the stewardship on more

---

* View of Frankpledge was the manorial court enquiry as to the proper observance of the law with regard to good behavior which provided that the lord was responsible for his charges and their appearance in court. Normally held by the High Sheriffs, it was a valuable privilege and entitled the lord to retain the profits of jurisdiction of the manorial Courts. If the crime of a tenant or bond servant were of sufficient severity to be carried to the Provincial Court and the accused fled rather than paid for his crime, the lord was responsible. In some parts of England frankpledge was known as tithings—both terms, however, were used in early Maryland patents.

than one manor. This seems to have been true of Thomas Gerard, Esq., who held rights on three manors within a limited radius of each other.

The bailiff or beadle was of great practical importance on the manor and was usually appointed by the lord. His duties were mostly associated with the activities of the manor court and at court sessions his prerogatives were second only to the steward. He summoned the tenants and freeholders to the court, collected all fines imposed on them, or evicted them from their holdings by order of the court. As the harvest season came round he visited the tenants and servants and warned them of the days they would have to appear to gather in their lord's corn, tobacco and other crops. He committed all offenders to the stocks, ducking pool and the whipping post—the latter was certainly not spared in the matter of justice whether the offender was gentleman or villain. The tenants at a manor court held on St. Clement's in Maryland presented the condition that "the Lord of the Manno^r hath not provided a paire of Stocks, pillory and Ducking Stoole", so it definitely established that such instruments of correction existed on the Maryland manor.[1]

The reeve was the third man in the administration and was always chosen from among the servants or tenants each year usually at Michaelmas. He kept the manorial accounts such as production, sales, purchases, the births and deaths of the varied livestock, in fact it may be stated that every item of manorial economy was his principal concern. In ancient days only a serf could serve as a reeve or one of "villein blood". The centuries, however, had brought changes in England economically as well as socially, and at the settlement of Maryland England was without a single serf in the realm, yet 200 years before that half the population was under serfdom.

The reeve was compelled to live on the manor, for it was his duty to see that the farm servants rose in good time, usually at sunrise, and got to their labours in the field quickly. He overlooked the ploughing, carting, marling, seeding and supervised the care and feeding of the livestock. He also issued the various food and clothing allowances to the indentured servants at stated intervals, and he was expected to hale before the manor court all those who failed or faltered in their service and allegiance to the lord. It was also his duty to maintain the proper upkeep of the manor house, the servants' quarters, the farm buildings and agricultural implements. In short there was no end to the variety or the extent of his labours. It was a very unpopular office and often a tenant or bond servant would refuse to serve in that capacity and the lord or his steward would have difficulty in finding the right person.

Courts were frequently held out of doors in fair weather, a custom not too unusual in England, as the manor house of the Maryland lords of the 17th century were rather compact and small to assemble all the freeholders and residents at a single session. Court days were always holidays and if

---

[1] Archives of Maryland, vol. 53, p. 634.

the Maryland lord followed the ways of England, they were likewise feast days at the lord's expense.

By and large it remained true that the manorial courts of Maryland were sources of revenue sufficiently valuable to enrich the manor lord in a virgin land where profits were limited from the original medium of gain. In the beginning, however, they were monetary liabilities, for Thomas Greene, Esq., permitted his 10,000 acres to revert to the Lord Proprietary for insufficient tenants and only three bond servants to operate them.

The granting of land in Maryland was subject to the Lord Proprietary or through his local agent and if not bestowed as gifts for friendship or service, the patents came under a series of "Acts of Conditions of Plantation", the first being promulgated in 1633, the provisions of which have not survived.* In 1634 Governor Leonard Calvert was granted lordships on three manors aggregating 3,000 acres for transporting ten able-bodied men in the voyage of the Ark. Consequently, it can be assumed with some reservations that 300 acres was the unit for each man transported under the first condition.

While each manorial granting contained more or less individual privileges as set forth in the patent, the General Assembly early passed a series of laws applicable to all lordships relative to certain over-all requirements and their obligations to the Lord Proprietary. For instance every lord of a manor was assessed 20 shillings for each 1000 acres of his manorial domain, plus one barrel of corn annually for each 100 acres to be paid at Michaelmas. A lord was required to hold muster under a Muster Master who had the power to assess fines and to punish all delinquencies, if these duties had not already been assigned to the bailiff. Specific quantities of munitions were required to be kept by the manor lord and to defend the Province in the uprising of the inhabitants or an attack by an enemy. In such contingency each manor lord was under obligation to furnish fifteen men for the militia. Furthermore, he was to maintain them while in service with food at his own expense and to furnish them with powder, shot and arms. One severe restriction placed on the manor lords was the prohibition of trade, as their domains were to be strictly agricultural entities.[2] This was a serious handicap at that trying period, as it developed then and later that the wealth in the Province was not acquired in corn and tobacco but in the fur trade with the Indians and the ultimate importing of manufactured goods from British merchants for resale to the planters. For a tenant on a manor to strike a bailiff or any other officer his land and goods were forfeited to the lord.

Many considered these laws too strict and in time worked as a serious handicap to the manor lords. As mentioned previously, a howl went up from Father Fisher [Copley] when he learned that the manorial holdings

---

* See section on "Granting of Land and the Acts Thereof".

[2] Fund Pub. no. 28, p. 160.

of the Jesuits were subject to the same fees and requirements as any other manor. The laws were later relaxed to the great relief of the early lordships, nonetheless, after a few years manorial holdings were extremely popular and bestowed certain coveted distinctions upon the individual. Some applications for seigniory were rejected by his Lordship's agents, although they qualified under the law of conditions for the granting of a manor.†

As only a few manors contained less than 1,000 acres, 100 acres of each in the beginning of the system were to be laid out as a glebe with an officiating pastor. This provision likewise was justly contested by the Jesuits believing that there would not be sufficient priests for each manor.³ Again this followed the English mode of the great squires of Britain having their own chaplains. Furthermore, the presence of a man of God on the premises always gave them a sense of power and spiritual security.

Whenever a *feme sole* fell heir to a lordship and she failed to acquire a husband within seven years, the manor was automatically forfeited to the next of kin.

Alongside of the private manors were the already mentioned proprietary or public manors which were large domains under the direct tenure of the Lord Proprietary who administered the units, issued leases, collected rents, and maintained justice through his land agent in St. Mary's City or in a number of instances actual stewards assigned to one or more manors. The proprietary manors, which should not be confused with the private manors, were surveyed and established from the early days and until the Revolution were an integral part of the intricate land structure of Maryland.

Perhaps the most interesting proprietary manor was the authorization by Cecilius, Lord Baltimore, by letter of 1651 to survey 8,000 to 10,000 acres of land at the head of the Wicomico River in what is now Charles County to be called "Calverton Manor" for six Maryland tribes of Indians—the Mattapanians, Wicomocons, Patuxents, Lamasconsons, Kighahnixons and Chapticos. Courts leet and courts baron were to be held with Robert Clark, Esq., one-time the business agent for the Jesuits and later Surveyor General, as the steward. One thousand acres were to be the desmene land of the manor and leases of not more than 50 acres were permitted for each Indian except the "Werrowance or Chief Head" whose acreage or lease-hold was not to exceed 200.⁴

Calverton Manor was surveyed and laid-out, but the nomadic Indian of the free and open country would not or could not be regimented into the

---

† On Sept. 7, 1640, Giles Basha, one of the malefactors on the Isle of Kent applied for a manor of 1100 acres for transporting at his own charge five able-bodied men-servants. On Sept. 26, following, a warrant was given to lay out for him 1100 acres on any part of the Western Shore or against the Isle of Kent not afore disposed of, but no mention was made of a court baron in the grant.

³ Fund Pub. no. 28, p. 165.

⁴ Archives, vol. 1, p. 330.

English way-of-life, and as a domain for the various tribes, it was wholly unsuccessful from the very beginning. Later leases were let to Britishers and it existed as a public manor of the Lord Proprietary until the Revolution.

The importance of manorial economy in the formulative days can also be gauged by the sessions of the early assemblies. At a sitting of the General Assembly of March 13, 1637/8, a bill for the exact services to be performed by the various manors were read in open session. During the morning of March 16, following, the freemen of the Province or their proxies passed the following five bills relative to manors by "general consent not one vote dissenting".[5]

1. For the bounding of the manors.
2. For the peopling of the manors.
3. For supporting the manors.
4. For settling of glebes upon the manors.
5. Against the alienation of manors.

Furthermore, a bill was passed for the creation of baronies, the latter being a higher and greater form of seigniory with a squire or a gentleman holding a hereditary title with certain privileges over a number of manors and freeholds.[6]

At the same Assembly it was enacted that at the first manorial court held after Michaelmas each lord or his steward was to appoint a tithingman with power to execute all precepts and warrants.[7]

The bills passed and the impact of the manorial system and taxation of the lordships were so great that it was the subject of a ululation in a form of a letter to the Lord Proprietary from Father Fisher [Copley], because the several manors controlled by the Jesuits were not exempt from taxation.[8]

Documents substantiate the fact that the "Gentlemen of Fashion" in the Adventure were promised or actually given by Lord Baltimore extensive manorial estates upon or before departure from England subject to immediate lay-out by the surveyor after settlement. These large manors were maintained for a few years, but within a short period the Gentlemen, realizing the difficulty of cultivation and maintenance with so few farm labourers or servants, undoubtedly permitted several to escheat to the Lord Proprietary. Furthermore, the excessive quit-rents originally assessed by Cecilius worked as a hindrance to the Adventurers in possession or taking-up large unimproved manorial holdings aggravated by a limited number of freeholders to lease tenements.

---

[5] *Archives of Maryland*, vol. 1, p. 13.
[6] *Archives of Maryland*, vol. 1, pp. 19-20.
[7] *Archives of Maryland*, vol. 1, p. 54.
[8] *Fund Pub.* no. 28, pp. 157-169.

There is definite proof of existing manors in the first year or so held and maintained by Thomas Greene, Jerome Hawley, Richard Gerard, Capt. George Evelyn, and the Jesuits, yet the letters-patent to the individual proprietors are not extant today. Richard Gerard was sufficiently calculating to obtain a good price from the Jesuits for his lordship before departing permanently for England. Thomas Greene had 10,000 acres but permitted them to escheat to the Lord Proprietary. Jerome Hawley retained his lordships which became the factors in some litigation after his death. Another early manor was granted to Captain Henry Fleete which was later assigned to Captain Thomas Cornwalys, when Fleete deserted the Province and returned to Virginia.

The Maryland squirarchy, gentry, yeomanry and even the servantry were substantially English to the core in every instinct, having been born and bred into the ancient traditions, social customs, and mannerisms of Great Britain with an intense love for freedom as their inalienable birthrights. The glorious age of Elizabeth was still fresh in the minds of the older Maryland squires who wished to emulate it in their new homes overseas, consequently the squirarchy and gentry, particularly, as it is the case of all members of a higher social order, cherished a love for things British with the result that Maryland has always been known to be more English than her sister colonies. In fact Marylanders brought old England with them.

One of the most significant characteristics of their love for their native hearth was the official naming of the manors and plantations after their estates or parishes in England. The Roman Catholics were prone to name their manors or plantations in memory of their patron saints, and a wide variety of English and foreign saints were commemorated in this manner, but the Roman Catholic Neales named their manor "Wolleston" after their ancestral holdings in Northamptonshire, whereas the Anglican Stones named their manor "Poynton" after an ancestral seat in Cheshire. The Anglican Tilghmans gave the name of "Canterbury" to their manor from the town in Kent where the family originated, while Jerome Whyte, Esq., a Roman Catholic, named his lordship "Portland" after the earldom of his distinguished grandfather, Thomas Weston, KG, the first Earl of Portland and Lord Treasurer under Charles I.

The Maryland Adventurers, therefore, like their kinsmen in Britain clung to the ancient feudal orders fostered in no small degree by the Calverts, in spite of the then current rise of ruthless realism by the Puritans at home as well as in the Colonies, until the early part of the eighteenth century when Negro slavery forced the manorial system to become uneconomical and the further desire of the yeomanry and minor planters to maintain small freeholds in fee rather than a lease-tenancy upon a large baronial estate. It was the genesis of that independence of mind and body of the second generation which sprung up among free people in a primitive land with opportunities for those who were denied certain privileges at home to throw off the adornments of feudalism, yet the proprietary manors of the Calverts functioned with more or less profit, certainly with success, until the opening days of the Revolution when Maryland was lost to the sovereignty of the Calvert family.

Before the advent of the eighteenth century with the progress and materialistic wealth which it brought to the Maryland planters, baronial manors, according to source records, had been created by the Lords Baltimore on at least eighty-seven of their subjects, with the acreage of approximately 255,000.* A greater number, however, were actually granted that can not be proved by the extant letters-patent on file at the Land Office in Annapolis. Now and then references are made to certain manors which certainly existed and functioned as such, but the historian is thwarted as to their creation and the gentlemen or squires who were so honoured.

In spite of the fading days of the manorial system in Maryland and the emergence from the old age rigidities of feudalism to a strictly plantation economy with Negro slave labour, the seigniorial glory of the Lord Barons of Baltimore with all their arrays of rank and might was still fervent in the eighteenth century, for Benedict Leonard Calvert, 4th Baron of Baltimore, in 1722 issued writs of court leet to his brother uterine, Major Nicholas Sewall, to him and his heirs forever on the ancestral seat at Mattapany-Sewall on the Patuxent.

Bohemian Manor in Cecil County functioned economically as a manor in strict primogeniture unitl the opening days of colonial unrest against Great Britain. Thus, from the beginning Maryland possessed a character, a way of life, a setting and an outlook which set her apart from her sister Colonies.

NOTE: An excellent study of the private manors in Maryland was done by Donnell MacClure Owings, Ph.D., in 1938 and published in the Maryland Historical Magazine, vol. 33, pp. 307-334. In preparation he read all extant land grants issued by the Calverts of 1000 acres or more to check whether court leet or court baron was mentioned or implied in the patent. He excluded in his brochure for known reasons those warrants and letters patent issued by Lord Baltimore of expressed baronial privileges to prospective colonists who failed to take them up. Whether or not they were never taken up, these warrants and letters patent are of incredible historic interest and are included in "Seigniory in Early Maryland", by this author and published under the auspices of the society of "The Descendants of Lords of the Maryland Manors". The list in the mentioned publication also contains proved manorial holdings found in various sources perhaps not available or unknown to the earlier writers of Maryland's unique land structure. Original parchment patents were found among the once buried Calvert Papers in the Maryland Historical Society, especially one to Walter Notley, of "Fermanaghshire, Realme of England, Gent.".

The study of private manors by Dr. Owings did not contain a number of lordships

---

* When the compactness of Maryland and her limited population of that day are considered, 255,000 acres, more than a quarter of a million, were definitely not an infinitesimal portion of her seated plantations. If the great proprietary manors were considered with their lease holds, the aggregate acreage before 1700 under manorial economy would perhaps have reached nearly half a million acres.

on which manorial courts or peculiar manorial rights were exercised or those whose letters patent presumably were lost or destroyed in the various uprisings in Maryland. The functional exercise of certain gestures characteristic of seigniory was obvious proof of manorial practices, as proved by several subsequent documents. One may be cited, as when James Gaylord, Steward to Mistress Mary Brent held court on St. Gabriel's Manor in 1656, thereby implying that Mistress Brent had the prerogatives of seigniory.

The brochure of "Seigniory in Early Maryland" contains therefore a list which were rightfully proved by source documents at the Land Office, Annapolis, at the time of its printing in 1949. It does not contain unfortunately several additional ones which the author has proved since publication.

The "Order of Colonial Lords of Manors in America" published in 1944 "Material for the Study of the Maryland Manors" compiled by the Hon. Montgomery Schuyler, of New York. It is a most constructive and worthwhile publication and contains articles or excerpts of the Maryland system printed in other publications. It includes also the list of private manors edited by Dr. Owings, but it does not include the comprehensive list compiled by the genealogist for the "Descendants of Lords of the Maryland Manors".

CLAYBORNE AND INGLE

From the inception of the Province of Maryland when George, Lord Baltimore, visualized his Palatinate until the defeat of anarchy and Puritan rule in Maryland and the recovery of the Province by the Calverts in 1658, Captain William Clayborne, of Virginia, was the principal trouble-shooter, the arch enemy of the Marylanders and the personification of Satan himself in the minds of the Roman Catholics. These trying years from 1633 to 1658 presented for Maryland a shifting picture of alternating inter-colonial warfare—first on the Isle of Kent and then at St. Mary's City accentuated with several naval skirmishes in the Bay.

When the background of the two men, Calvert and Clayborne, in this early drama is analyzed with their social, political and religious concepts, a more perfect understanding of the conflict is manifestedly apparent. William Clayborne was born in Crayford Parish, County Kent, England, where he was baptized in the Established Church on August 10, 1600, and was descended from an old county gentry family which had lost much in social prestige during the past few years—though his father and his grandfather had held the office of Mayor of King's Lynn, Norfolkshire. In 1617 young Clayborne was sent up in Pembroke College, Cambridge, a hot-bed of liberalism, for his formal education, and soon embraced the ultra-liberalism of certain fire-brand groups which were beginning their intrigue in undermining both Church and State. McMahan in his "History of Maryland", stated "Clayborne espoused the parliament cause for which he was well fitted both by his natural temper and his deep sense of un-redressed wrongs".[1]

It was an age, however, when liberalism was looked upon with disfavour by the better classes and not of today when it is deemed a fashionable asset.

His unredressed wrongs at Cambridge can only be a matter of conjecture in retrospect, for during his college days his long drawn-out and losing battle with the Marylanders was part of a future destiny, then unknown. Perhaps, the limited success of his father as a merchant and his mother, Sara, the Widow James, having once been the wife of a brewer as well as the daughter of the Brewer Smith did not elevate the social position of his family but caused a sense of insecurity within him as he encountered at Cambridge the scions of greater gentry houses than his own and also the sons of the peerage. It was a time when the ranks of society were kept more separate than they are today and Clayborne perhaps found an outlet for his restlessness in the political concepts of the Puritans. Furthermore,

---

[1] Vol. 1, p. 201.

he was the second son and what landed estate his father would leave at his death would revert by law to his older brother who became without much lucrative success a hosier—a craft not too approved in the days of inherited wealth and the leisure pursuits of the major county gentry on their great manorial domains.

The Claybornes of that branch and generation had therefore relegated to the position of respectable tradesmen and in a political sense, especially William Clayborne, could not be classified as Royalists or Cavaliers, whereas the Calverts through their personal charm and mental discernment had acquired great wealth and an unimpeachable social position.

In 1621 Clayborne, just turned twenty-one, was chosen by the Virginia Company, as the Surveyor General of its commercial and exploiting project in America. The primary objectives of the Virginia Company, sometimes known as the London, were exploitation and the mining of gold and copper. Another visual project was to discover a more direct passage to the Pacific Ocean. Colonization and the establishment of a permanent part of England in the New World were only incidental to the success of trade and mining, whereas the settlements with their plantations were not an end in itself through the development of the company's more obvious resources. Dissensions broke out almost immediately among the leaders who were bent only on a quest for riches and high adventure. On the other hand the Marylanders came to create another England in the wilderness of America under English institutions with the Barons of Baltimore as the hereditary ruling overlords subject only to the Crown.

Upon Clayborne's arrival in Virginia he pointedly met and secretly intrigued with many of his co-thinkers, for it was known that from the arrival of the liberal-minded Sir Thomas Dale, Knt., in 1611 the Puritans and other non-conformists had been emigrating to the Colony of Virginia in great number. While they may not have attained a majority of the population, their influence was decidedly formidable. Furthermore, their militant organization and strict party discipline against less organized orthodox conservatives were not only far-reaching, but most effective as it is always in a radical organized minority. Within a short time Clayborne was appointed to the Virginia Council, then Secretary of State, and within a few years he was well recognized as one of the most aggressive personalities of the Colony. His official duties to the State, however, did not interfere with his desire for economic gain and wealth through trade, with the result that he soon developed into the principal trader of the Colony and into an energetic and clamorous agitator.

On the other hand while the family of George Calvert may not have been as old in social recognition and prestige as the Claybornes, George, Lord Baltimore, had improved his station by contracting a marriage with the ancient Crosland family, had been elevated to the peerage, granted considerable land in Ireland, and attained an envious position as a court favorite, whereas the Claybornes had remained a provincial family in rural

Kent and Norfolk. Furthermore, the son and heir of George, Lord Baltimore, had contracted a brilliant marriage with one of the oldest and most powerful peers of the realm. Subjectively, one can recognize a deep-rooted animosity of a liberal dissenter from the orthodox teachings of the Established Church of England for a conservative and Royalist who became an adherent to the Roman Catholic Faith.

As the power and influence of Clayborne successively increased in Virginia, he became fully cognizant of the vast economic resources of the Chesapeake Bay and its basin in the then lucrative fur trade with the Indians. As early as 1611 the Virginia Company had established a settlement at Accomacke on the Eastern Shore and had traded unhindered in the Bay from the very beginning of that outpost.

In 1627 William Clayborne approached Sir George Yardley, Knt., then Governor of Virginia, with the intentions "this Springe to emply himself with a sufficient Companie of men in a shallope for discoerie of the Bottome of the Bay of Chesepeck". Accordingly, permission was granted him by Sir George to "go and make his voyadge . . . and saile into any the rivers, Creekes, portes and havens within the said Bay . . . to trade and truck with the Indians for furr skinns, corne, and any other comodities". The commission, however, was limited only "during the tyme of his said voiadge and retourne from the same".[2]

Lord Baltimore and his family arrived in Virginia from his Province of Avalon in October 1629. He, an investor of the commercial enterprise which gave life to the Colony of Virginia, guilelessly let it be known around Jamestown of his interests in establishing a province similar to his adventure at Avalon in a more temperate climate.

In January 1629/30, according to the minutes of the Virginia Council, Clayborne requested permission to trade in the Chesapeake to the mouth of the Susquehanna River which times perfectly with the announcement of Lord Baltimore's plans for an English settlement. It has already been mentioned of Clayborne taking the first ship for England to thwart Lord Baltimore's plans. At that time Clayborne had not been granted royal permission to trade nor had any settlement been effected in the upper Bay.

While in England Clayborne contracted with Clobery & Co., Merchants of London, by which Clobery was to finance trading posts in the Colony of Virginia and in return Clayborne, as the colonial agent, agreed to supply the company with beaver and other such commodities as might be obtained from the native Indians in America.* On May 16, 1631, with the partnership clearly formed, he was granted a Royal license by the Kingdom of

---

[2] Archives of Maryland, vol. 5, pp. 158-159.

* The partners were William Clobery, John Delabare, Maurice Thompson, Simon Lurgis (Surgis), and William Clayborne. Each was to receive one-sixth of the profits except Clobery who had one-third interest.

Scotland† to trade in any and all parts of North America not already preempted by monopolies and to establish trading posts. The license by no means granted him sovereignty over his contemplated trading posts nor did it imply that the Virginia Colony could exercise rights of sovereignty. According to the 1609 charter, the Virginia Colony extended 200 miles northward from Point Comfort or about as far north as the present site of Chester in Pennsylvania. On June 26, 1624, the charter or patent of the company of English merchants trading in Virginia "and pretending to exercise a power and authority over his Majesty's good subjects there should be thenceforth null and void".

James I and his successor Charles I both declared that the annulment of the charter simply abolished the sovereignty of the Virginia Company. Later Charles I implied that the annulment of the charter made the limits of the Royal Colony transitory.

William Clayborne returned to Virginia well pleased with his contract with Clobery & Co. On August 17, 1631, he established a trading post on the lower tip of Kent Isle in the Bay with a number of redemptioners and some traders sent out by Clobery & Co., and also with some Virginians from around the James River and Accomac. From the beginning the Virginia Colony assumed supreme jurisdiction over the trading post which ultimately developed into a series of plantations and in 1631, 1632 and 1633 the Isle of Kent and Kiskyacke were represented at Jamestown in the House of Burgesses by Nicholas Martiau, a Huguenot, who had settled in Virginia.[3] Clayborne furthermore assumed the prerogative to issue warrants and surveys for land patents, a privilege or right not embodied in his Scot trading license.

Lord Baltimore received his Royal grant on June 30, 1632, within a year after the establishment of the trading post on Kent. When the news reached Virginia, a number of planters and especially merchants vigorously protested and immediately forwarded a petition to the Star Chamber against the granting of land to an English subject which they considered a portion of their Colony in direct violation of Virginia's prior rights of domain.

Among the many objectives which Virginia and Clayborne built up their case was the statement that the Maryland Charter granted Lord Baltimore the right to establish a Province only "in a country hitherto uncultivated". A trading post of the early seventeenth century did not signify by any means a settled territorial unit, or a series of plantations organized into a hundred,* but merely a small designated area whereby two or more parties

---

† Why a Scot license? Scotland as a sovereign State had no claims to the English Colonies and had taken no part in exploring and claiming over-sea territory—the two kingdoms remained separate and distinct until the union in 1707.

[3] Journal of the House of Burgesses 1619-1699, pp. unnumbered, front of volume.

* Trading post, a station for buying, selling and exchange of commodities or barter as carried on in the savage parts of North America. Ref: Oxford English Dictionary.

meet from time to time to barter or sell trade goods. A license was only permission, and by no means legally defined a patent or a grant of land. Clayborne therefore had only Royal trading authority from a Kingdom which had no claims to sovereignty in America in spite of the fact that that Kingdom and England at the time were under one crowned head. Consequently, when Charles I granted the Province to Lord Baltimore technically no lawful cultivated area existed within the proprietary grant and certainly none known then by the Royal personage. After the State decree abolished the Virginia Company, Virginia became a Royal Colony with its boundaries more or less undefined but subject to the will of the Crown.

On July 3, 1633, the Star Chamber issued its reply and virtually confirmed the rights and claims of Lord Baltimore to the territory as defined in the Royal Charter, but further advised that the Virginians, if they so wished, had the "course of the law", but both colonies were to have free and unhindered traffic with the Indians.[4]

The controversy within a short time reached the King and on July 1, 1633, Charles I addressed a letter to the Governor and Planters of Virginia advising them of the plans of Lord Baltimore "to transport to that part called Maryland a good number of our Subjects who may require friendly help and assistance on their first arrival . . . requested them to allow his [Lord Baltimore] servants and planters to buy and transport to their Colony such Cattle . . . at reasonably rate".[5] Sir John Harvey, Governor, a man of understanding and never unfriendly to the Marylanders, stated in a dispatch now filed in the Public Record Office that "many [Virginians] say they would rather knock their Cattle on the head than sell them for Maryland".

A number of petitions were accordingly forwarded on each ship which departed from Virginia waters for the home country, but one significant one was sent forth in November 1633, with the signatures of Sir John Wolstenholme, Knt., and many Virginia planters and merchants urging that "the said Lord Baltimore may settle in some other place".[6] Consequently, it is quite evident from the initial settlement of Maryland that the Virginians assumed a hostile attitude and became unreconcilable to any colonization, though miles apart, from their settlements on the James River and isolated outposts.

As authorities in England had but little knowledge of the geography of the overseas possessions and could not apprehend seriously the over-lapping or encroachment upon another in such a vast, unhabited area, implications through royal decrees and the charter of the Maryland Palatinate therefore lowered the former northern boundary of the Virginia Colony

---

[4] Public Record Office, London.

[5] *Ibid.*

[6] Archives, vol. 3, pp. 24-25.

to the southern boundary as expressed in the newly created Province of Maryland, that is, the Potomac River.

In the meantime George, the first Baron, had died and Cecilius had succeeded to his father's estates and title, had been recognized by the House of Lords and with the traditional pomp and ceremony had taken his seat as the Second Lord Baron of Baltimore. Clayborne had married into a respectable gentry family, the Boteler [Butler], of his native parish, whereas Cecilius, now the Lord Proprietary of Maryland, was son-in-law to the great and mighty Earl of Arundel.

The trading post or settlements of Clobery & Co., on the Isle of Kent with Clayborne as the overseas agent, now fell *ipso facto* under the jurisdiction of the newly created Province of Maryland. Cecilius recognized this legal factor and all he requested was the expression of fealty from Clayborne and the colonists of Clobery now settled within the legal domain of his province. Cecilius' instructions to his brother and the commissioners on the Ark manifested a worthy and magnanimous approach to the delicate situation which had arisen and certainly indicated the desire for a peaceful and amicable solution to the conflict.

The following is an excerpt from Lord Baltimore's instructions to his brother, Leonard, relative to the treatment of Clayborne:[7]

"That they [Commissioners] write a letter to Cap: Clayborne as soone as conveniently other more necessary occasions will give them leave after their arrivall in the Countrey, to give him notice of their arrivall and of the Authority & charge comitted to them by his Lopp and to send the said letter together wᵗʰ his Lopps to him by some trusty messenger that is likewise conformable unto the Church of England wᵗʰ a message also from them to him if it be not inserted in their letter wᶜʰ is better, to give him kindly to come unto them, and to signify that they have some business of importance to speake wᵗʰ him about from his Lopp wᶜʰ concernes his good very much; And if he come unto them then that they use him courteously and well, and tell him, that his Lopp understanding that he hath settled a plantacon there wᵗʰ in the precincts of his Lopps Pattent, wished them to lett him know that his Lopp is willing to give him all the encouragement he cann to proceede; And that his Lopp hath had some propositions made unto him by certaine mʳchants in London who pretend to be partners wᵗʰ him in that plantation . . . and that they desired to have a grant from his Lopp of that Iland where he is: But his Lopp understanding from some others that there was some difference in partnership between him and them, and his Lopp finding them in their discourse to him, that they made somewhat slight of Cap: Clayborne's interest, doubted least he might prejudice him by asking them any grant this Lopp being ignorant of the true state of their business and of the thing they desired, as likewise being well assured that by Cap: Clayborne his care and industry besides his charges, that plantation was

---

[7] Fund Pub. no. 28, pp. 134-135.

first begunn and so far advanced was for these reasons unwilling to condescend unto their desires, and therefore deferred all wth them till his L^opp could truly understand from him, how matters stand between them, and what he would desire of his L^opp in it. wch his L^opp expects from him; that thereupon his L^opp may take it into farther consideration how to do justice to every one of them and to give them all reasonable satisfaction; And that they assure him in fine that his L^opp intends not to do to him any wrong, but to shew him all the love and favor that he cann, and that his L^opp gave them directions to do so to him in his absence. . . . If he do refuse to come unto them upon their invitation that they lett him alone for the first yeare, till upon notice given to his L^opp of his answere and behaviour they receive farther directions from his L^opp, and that they informe themselves as well as they cann of his plantation and what his designes are, of what strength & what Correspondency he keepes wth Virginea, and to give an Account of every particular to his L^opp".

Petitions and letters between England and Virginia went back and forth with each sailing vessel. Extracts from the Minutes of the Virginia Council on March 14, 1633/4, stated "that they knew no reason why Capt. Clayborne should give up the right of the Isle of Kent to Lord Baltimore".[8] Sir Francis Windebanke, Secretary of State, in a letter to Governor Harvey of Virginia requested him "to protect them [the Marylanders] against Clayborne's malitious practises".[9] It consequently appeared that at least one English statesman was well aware of Clayborne's disposition.

From subsequent developments Clayborne from the beginning of his ambitious plans had some misgivings about his authority to establish plantations at the trading post, but undauntedly assumed the power believing that he could get away with it, to use a modern expression. From the court minutes of the Admiralty suit some years later, "William Claiborne did saye & affirme unto the sd Wm Cloberrye and Companie or some one of them that unless hee had a speciall commission from the king's most excellent Majestie of Great Britain he could not proceed upon the said discoverye or plantation".[9a]

On September 29, 1634, Charles I addressed Governor Harvey of Virginia in part thanking him for the courtesies he had personally extended to the Marylanders, but principally to justify his grant to Lord Baltimore and that the dissolution of the Virginia Company's charter had forfeited their specific domain "a part of that Territory upon the devolving of the old companies' rights". There was consequently no doubt in the mind of Charles I, and apparently upon advisement of the best legal talent of the day, that, the dissolution of the commercial Virginia Company abrogated the territorial claims and that he had absolute legality in granting the Maryland Province with boundaries as defined in the Royal Charter.

---

[8] Public Record Office, London.

[9] *Ibid.*

[9a] Md. Hist. Mag. vol. 26, p. 387.

Furthermore, Charles I stated that "in respect of the vastances of that country, there being land and profit enough for the entertainment of many thousands".[9b] At that time and for considerable time thereafter it is evident that Virginia wanted to claim, if not control, the entire Atlantic sea coast in defiance to the prerogatives of the Crown.

In spite of the legality of the Maryland grant as expressed by Royal authority and of Lord Baltimore's overtures to Clayborne, the indomitable Virginia trader remained defiant and adamant. Still waiting to hear Clayborne's case through his brother, the Governor of Maryland, whose attempted conference with him in Virginia had failed, Cecilius in London delayed any approach to a compact with Clobery relative to the suzerainty of his Province.

After the Maryland Adventurers had established amiable relations with the Indians and progress was being made in the construction of their settlement, the unpleasant reaction of Clayborne's treachery and the spreading of false rumors among the natives with accelerated force caused much unrest within the young colony. In order to improve relations Leonard Calvert with his Commissioners and their staffs sailed for Virginia to confer with the Governor and Council and also with Clayborne to make overtures for his recognition of Lord Baltimore's sovereignty over Kent.

Upon their arrival at Point Comfort in July 1634, they also found Captain Thomas Young, a friend of Lord Baltimore, whose ship was in the harbour. Point Comfort at the mouth of the James, like St. Mary's City became to the Marylanders, was a sort of receiving station for the Virginia Company. There the emigrants were first quartered before their settlement or in the case of indentured servants they were claimed by their respective masters and often resold to other enterprising merchants. So Point Comfort was the logical point for the Maryland commission to land and be received by Clayborne in a diplomatic and peaceful conference.

From Captain Young's letter to Sir Toby Mathews, Knt., we obtained much human interest and the series of events at the apparent first official visit of the Marylanders to Virginia after the initial settlement at St. Mary's.[10]

Sir Toby was the son of the Archbishop of York and a schoolmate and life-long friend, of George, 1st Baron of Baltimore, and a witness to his last will and testament. In Captain Young's letter to Sir Toby, he stated that the Marylanders were there to hear and compose "the differents which were growne between those of my Lords Collony and this Cleyburnes". Captain Young entertained Clayborne aboard his ship, and did not report too complimentary remarks back to his friend, Sir Toby. He spoke of him as "subtle and fayre spoken but extreamely averse from the prosperity of that [Maryland] plantation".

[9b] Public Record Office, London; Archives, vol. 3, pp. 26-27.

[10] Reprinted at Hall's Narratives of Early Maryland; original stated to be at the Virginia State Library, Richmond.

According to Captain Young, Governor Calvert "fell sicke by the way and returned to Maryland", but it was while he was at Point Comfort on May 30, 1634, that he wrote to Sir Richard Lechford, Knt., and among other matters spoke of the arrival of the Ark in Virginia on its return voyage to England.

Clayborne refused to receive the Marylanders under the pretext, according to Captain Young, that he had to go to his plantation, as some Indians had murdered a boy-servant belonging to him, but "I playnly perceaved that the principall and mayne reason of his retreat was to absent himself from that meeting".

Captain Cornwalys in his discourse with Captain Young stated that Claybourne "had dealt very unworthyly and falsely with them. That he had also laboured to procure the Indians to supplant them by informing them that they were Spaniards and that they had a purpose to destroy them and take their Country from them. That the Indians had a purpose to have attempted it, had they not bene dissuaded by one Captayne Fleet . . . Cleyborne had bene offered all faire correspondence, with as free liberty to trade as themselves, but he refused it, wherefore the Governor gave order to forbid him to trade . . . Conspiracy and practices of Clayborne were proved by Confessions from the Indians and likewise by confession of Christians upon oath".

The only friends of Lord Baltimore in Virginia among the Councilors besides Governor Harvey were "Captaine Purfree a souldier and a man of an open heart, honest and free, hating for ought I can all kinds of dissimulation and baseness, the other an honest playne man but of small capacity and lese power". Captain Samuel Mathews, the leader of the Virginia Council, and a liberal gave his firm support to Clayborne, as Captain Young described the condition "incendiary of all this wicked plot of Cleborne". Mathews had married a daughter of Sir Thomas Hinton whose son, Young Hinton· was a member of the King's Privy Chamber, and as Captain Young expressed it, Mathews "grows, as is conceaved, much bolder by his alliance, as hoping by his power to find great strength in England". Furthermore, Captain Young reported that it was treason in Virginia to speak well of Maryland.

With further stupid resistance on the part of Clayborne to acknowledge the sovereignty of Lord Baltimore, the Royal grant, and his tenancy on Kent under the Lord Proprietary, it therefore became necessary for the Marylanders to exercise their legal rights and to persuade the planters and traders on Kent to recognize the overlordship of the Calverts. To have done otherwise would have shown weakness and fear on the part of Lord Baltimore and his trusted subjects in Maryland.

Cecilius therefore sent word to his brother, Leonard, in September 1634, to seize Kent Island and to arrest Clayborne and hold him a prisoner. News of His Lordship's intentions reached Clobery & Co. In October 1634, William Clobery, John de la Barre, and David Moorhead petitioned the King against the "attempt of Lord Baltimore to dispossess them of the Isle of Kent discovered by William Clayborne, and which they have peopled and settled and that Clayborne and the traders be permitted to the said Island and Trade without interruption".[11]

Winter passed and the Marylanders took no initiative, and in the meantime Clayborne enjoyed diplomatic leniency. The Virginia Council in March 1634/5, however, writing to the Board of Trade in London stated "for that they [Marylanders] signified unto Captain Claiborne that he was now a member of their plantation and therefore should relinquished all relation and dependence of this Colony [Virginia] . . . we are bound in duty and by our Oaths to maintain the Rights and Privileges of this Colony". It is therefore evident that the Virginia Council backed Clayborne and actually gave him its moral support and encouragement.

On March 26, 1635, just a year after the settlement of Maryland, one of Clayborne's ships the "Long Taile" under the command of Thomas Smith, Gent., left Virginia to trade with the Indians for corn and furs in the Chesapeake. According to Smith's own account, they arrived at Mattapany in the Patuxent some miles from the Bay on April 4th, and the next day Captain Henry Fleete and Captain Humber, who had recently brought a group of colonists to Maryland, with a company of men from St. Mary's came over land and demanded what authority Smith had to trade in Maryland waters. Fleete, it must be recalled, cherished no fraternal love for Clayborne, for as a former rival in the fur trade in the Bay, Fleete was arrested in 1632 by Governor Harvey on Clayborne's demands for trading without a license.

Smith showed Fleete and Humber his commission from Clayborne, but Captain Fleete stated that the commission did not permit Clayborne to trade any farther than the Isle of Kent and that he and his men must leave Maryland at once. Captain Humber who had already had some unpleasant dealings with Clayborne in Virginia declared that the commission was fraudulent and persuaded Captain Fleete to seize the ship and cargo. Thereupon, Fleete and his men boarded the vessel and ordered all the seamen on shore without arms to the consternation of Smith and his crew. They capitulated, however, with no great struggle.

The next day Captain Fleete placed the Virginians, who had lay all night on the ground in the woods, on a barge and commanded Smith to sail the "Long Taile" to St. Mary's City. Upon arrival Smith was brought before Governor Calvert who questioned him about Clayborne and his persistent refusal to cooperate with the Marylanders and to acknowledge his sovereignty. Smith stated that Calvert gave Fleete "a little latine booke and made him kiss it".*

---

[11] Public Record Office, London.

* Presumably a Roman Catholic prayer book or missal as Governor Calvert apparently wanted the solemn truth from Fleete.

Smith recited the instances leading up to his capture and the forcing of his men to leave the ship.† The Governor turned the matter over to Captain Cornwalys, whom Smith described as his Deputy, for the Governor was "away from home" for two days. Cornwalys stated that "they [Fleete and Humber] did noe more then what they had order for to doe", for all vessels found trading in the territorial limits of the Province of Maryland were subject to search and examination of trading licenses. Captain Cornwalys questioned further the letters of commission held by Smith and stated that Clayborne had permission to trade only on Kent. It was therefore quite evident that Maryland acknowledged the right of Clayborne to trade on the Isle of Kent, but questioned his aggressiveness in assuming that he could barter and trade within the several tributaries of the Bay where the Marylanders had settled.

When Governor Calvert returned to St. Marie's, Smith stated in his report that "one Mr. Greene sent his Marshall for me".‡ They met at the house of Captain Cornwalys, where the Governor questioned Smith whether he traded for himself or Clayborne. Calvert likewise examined the commission to trade and declared that Clayborne and his men had no rights to trade within his Province except on the Isle of Kent. The "Long Taile" was therefore confiscated with all goods and equipment aboard in accordance with the law of admiralty.

Smith thereupon stated, "I demand of you, how we shall get home". But "hee told wee should not returne to Kent, but hee would send us for England or for Kecotan". Governor Calvert, however, expressed regrets over the fact that he had no boats to transport them to Virginia, but as Smith reported "hee at that time had 3 Boates riding at his dore".

Smith pleaded for himself and his men and that they were in great need of corn, but transportation as well as their entreaties was categorically refused. They were sent away "without peece [arms] or victualls". Through the assistance of certain Indians, Smith and his men found their way back to Virginia, apparently in a very unhappy frame of mind.[12]

Upon their return to Virginia and the various versions related of the seizure, Clayborne saw blood. He immediately dispatched an armed sloop the "Cockatrice" to make reprisals upon Maryland shipping. Captain Cornwalys at that time was trading with two armed pinnaces in the Pocomoke River on the Eastern Shore within the territorial grant of Maryland, when the "Cockatrice" overtook him on April 23, 1635. From the statement of some of Clayborne's men, it is apparent that the Virginians fired the first shot.§ The Marylanders were prepared and after a brisk

---

† For Smith's account of his capture, see, Fund Publication no. 28, pp. 141-145.

‡ Mr. Greene was Thomas Greene, Esq., one of the councilors, and it is thus shown that the dignitaries of Maryland lived in state with "marshalls" or retainers in their retinue.

[12] Smith's own account printed in Fund Pub. no. 28, pub. by Md. Hist. Soc.

§ Statement of Governor Sir John Harvey, of Virginia, at Plymouth, Eng.

skirmish several men were killed and some wounded. The three Virginians who were mortally wounded were Lieutenant Radcliffe Warren, of a gentry family, John Belson, and William Dawson. It was decidedly a victory for the Marylanders.

On May 10, another armed naval engagement in the harbour of the Great Wighcocomoco at the mouth of the Pocomoke occurred in which Thomas Smith, of "Long Taile" fame, with blood in his eyes for his grievance against the Marylanders over his treatment in the Patuxent, commanded for Clayborne and defeated the Marylanders with more bloodshed. On the "St. Margaret" commanded by Captain Cornwalys was young William Ashmore one of the Adventurers on the Ark who fell a victim of the Virginians' wrath.

About this time conservative Sir John Harvey, Knt., Governor of Virginia, was having a difficult time with the powerful leftish Dissenters in that colony, so much so that he knew that the diplomatic gesture was to retire to his English estates. Before returning, however, he appointed Richard Kemp, Esq., Secretary of State, Governor ad interim.

At Plymouth on July 14, 1635, writing to Secretary Windebank, Sir John was not very complimentary of the Virginia law makers ". . . concerning the affayres of Virginia, I signifed that the Assemblies being composed of a rude ignorant and an ill conditioned people". Furthermore, he wrote, ". . . for whilest I was aborde the ship and readie to depart the Collonie, theare arrived Capt: Claiborne from the Ile of Kent with the newes of an hostile encounter twixt sum of his Pople and those of Marylands and Captaine Francis Hock tould me that the relation of sum of Captin Claiborne's owne compayne, it was they [Clayborne's men] that sought out the Maryland Boates, which were trading among the Indians and twice assaulted them".[13]

In the same year Robert Vaughan and John Tompkins were trading at the head of the bay near Palmer's Island, when they were captured by Thomas Smith and John Boteler and taken as prisoners to Kent, with their truckings commodities confiscated. How they were able to return to St. Mary's is a story not at present known.[14]

After Clayborne's victory over the Marylanders in May 1635, he retained undisturbed possession of Kent for at least two years, but in the meantime a quarrel was brewing between him and Clobery, his financial backer. Clobery & Co. was dissatisfied with the quantity of beaver which was being sent over by Clayborne and which Clobery declared was insufficient to repay the financial advances already made to Clayborne. Clayborne had reported the year previously that "we were much hindered and molested by the Indians falling out with us and killing our men and by the Marylanders hindering our trade".

---

[13] Colonial Papers, vol. 8, no. 69; Archives of Maryland, vol. 3, p. 38.
[14] Halls' Early Narratives of Maryland, p. 154.

Clobery demanded an audit of the accounts, for according to their agreement with Clayborne he was expected "to give just and true accounts of all tradeings truckeinge buyeinge sellinge barteringe planteinge soweinge increase in Cattle" which Clayborne apparently had failed to do.[15] As a result a bitter feud developed between Clayborne and Clobery and ultimately went before the Court of Admiralty in London. In April 1638, Clayborne was examined upon a charge of "piracy and murder".

At this point in his career Clayborne had not only the Marylanders to fight but Clobery as well. Clobery claimed that five ships were sent with indentured servants—first the "Affrica" with 20 redemptioners, the "James" with 30, the "Revenge" with seven, and the "John and Barbara" and the "Sara and Elizabeth" with 18 each also loaded with supplies which Clayborne had made no account. Clayborne claimed that only 17 arrived on the "Affrica" and not more than 22 on the "James" and "Revenge" combined. He furthermore declared that a fire on Kent in April 1631 consumed most of the supplies.

Clobery being dissatisfied with Clayborne's results accordingly sent over Captain George Evelyn, Esq., who arrived early in 1637. He was armed with power of attorney and to request Clayborne to turn over the Isle and all property thereon to him in the name of Clobery & Co. Furthermore, Evelyn carried instructions for Clayborne to take an early ship for the port of London and to settle his accounts. Clayborne sailed about May of 1637.

Captain Evelyn, the oldest son of Robert Evelyn, of Godstone, Esq., was from an old gentry family of Surrey which was proud of its heritage and armorial bearings, but which had maintained town houses in London for several generations where George was born in 1592. He and his younger brother, Robert, had been in Virginia off and on at an early period as well as their uncle, Captain Thomas Young, who had explored the Chesapeake and parts of the North Atlantic Coast. It was his uncle, Captain Young, a friend of Lord Baltimore, who reported the refusal of Clayborne to confer with Marylanders at Point Comfort. At first Evelyn was antagonistic to the Marylanders and Governor Calvert whom he considered an up-start,* but soon became convinced of the righteousness and legality of Lord Baltimore's claims.

Before sailing for London, Clayborne attempted to force a bond from Evelyn not to surrender the island to Governor Calvert under any condition, but Evelyn refused to give any assurance at that time except to express in very strong language that Lord Baltimore had no just claim to

---

[15] Claiborne vs. Clobery & Co. in the High Court of Admiralty, Md. Hist. Mag., vol. 26, p. 386.

* In referring to Leonard Calvert, Evelyn said, "What was his grandfather but a grazier—what was Leonard Calvert himself at school but a dunce and a block-head, and now has it come to this that such a fellow should be Governor of a province and assume such lordly airs".

the Isle of Kent. Clayborne sailed for England on the first available ship, and in the meantime George Evelyn made a trip to Jamestown and attached all of Clayborne's property there in the name of Clobery & Co.

As mentioned previously, the arrogant house of Evelyn considered the Calverts as parvenus, but after some consideration and fore-thought and not without some political and dexterous maneuverings Captain George Evelyn invited Leonard Calvert to occupy Kent and to declare his complete and absolute sovereign authority.

Captain Evelyn has often been accused of treason and artful double-crossing, but it must be remembered that Clobery & Co., was partially sympathetic to Lord Baltimore's claims and from evidence of the times would apparently have been contented to maintain their trading-post under Maryland's overlordship, if it had not been for their powerful and arbitrary agent in Virginia. Clobery was definitely displeased with Clayborne's shenanigans, yet they were not completely ready for Maryland occupancy of their settlement and trading-post. Captain Evelyn, it must be remembered, was not an agent for Virginia nor Clayborne, but for an English merchandise house. Evelyn came to realize, as later expressed by him, that Clayborne, as an agent for Clobery, had only commercial rights and the authority to establish a trading-post and thus had no sovereignty over the island and no power to issue warrants and grant land in the name of Virginia. In April 1638, Lord Baltimore granted Evelyn seigniory on a manor in St. Mary's County of 1,200 acres for financing the transportation of 22 men into Maryland, mostly from Kent Isle.†

Feeling the sincerity and understanding of Captain Evelyn, Governor Calvert appointed him Supreme Commander of Kent. In November 1637, he returned to the Isle and summoned all the inhabitants and freemen to assemble at the fort, as the ruling authority he urged them to acknowledge Lord Baltimore as their overlord. He furthermore delivered the message of Governor Calvert, whereby all who swore homage would be absolved from any previous contempts against his government, "but the said Freemen

---

† Evelyn named his manor "Evelynton" which occupied present Piney Point in St. Mary's County. Out of Kent he transported John Ascu, Edward Deering, Andrew Baker, William Williamson and his wife, John Hatch, Philipp West, John Dandy, Thomas Baker, and John Hobson, all of whom were alleged to be servants of Clobery & Co. All were employed in the seating of his manor, according to the Bailiff of the baronial court held on the manor, and per testimony the labour of Clobery's servants compensated Evelyn to the value of 15,000 lbs. tob. Depositions were also given that three of the servants, that is, John Hatch, Andrew Baker and Thomas Baker, had been sold in London by Clobery for £30 to one Owen Philipps, but Evelyn consigned the three to John Lewger, Secretary of Maryland. Ref: Archives, vol. 5, pp. 183-184.

Other men transported by Evelyn to seat his manor, some of whom played important rôles in the later affairs of the Province were Thomas Hebden, David Wickcliff, Randall Revell, James Coughton, Hugh Howard, John Walker, Henry Lee, John Worthley, John Richardson, John Hill, William Medcalfe, Edmond Parrie, Matthew Rodham, Roger Baxter, Thomas Orley, Thomas Keene, and Samuel Scovell.

did not consent thereunto". With Captain Evelyn was Zachary Mottershead, Gent., of St. Mary's‡ who carried the Charter of Maryland as evidence that Kent was within the bounds of Baltimore's Province.

Evelyn furthermore stated that while he had formerly spoken against the Maryland patent and the Clayborne's claim was firm and good, he was then "better informed and was formerly mistaken".[16]

John Boteler, Gent., brother-in-law of Clayborne,§ who exercised great influence on the Isle, asked Evelyn, "Are you an agent for Clobery & Co. or for Maryland?". To which Evelyn replied, "Both".[17]

At that time also exercising great influence on the Isle was the implacable Thomas Smith, Gent., of Long Taile fame, who "was of such power amongst them that they [Boteler and Smith] perswaded them [Clayborne's men] still to continue in their former contumance".[18]

Evelyn returned to St. Mary's and was the principal factor in urging Governor Calvert to invade the Isle of Kent and assert his authority after three years of a cold war. According to the deposition made in 1640 by John Boteler, brother-in-law to Clayborne, Evelyn invited and persuaded Calvert to come to Kent and take possession. Perhaps Governor Calvert needed very little persuasion, however, towards the end of November 1637, he embarked in his pinnace from St. Mary's City for Kent to capture Thomas Smith and John Boteler and to bring the islanders under submission. About this time the Maryland court issued a warrant for the arrest of John Boteler, Thomas Smith, and Edward Beckler, of Kent "To answere the severall crimes of sedition, pyracie and murther".

With Calvert were Captain Thomas Cornwalys who was appointed commander of the expedition and Sergeant Robert Vaughan who was in charge of the twenty picked musketeers from the provincial militia. After a week's sailing with unfavourable wind and "the weather so fowle in the bay", the punitive expedition was compelled to return to St. Mary's and await more propitiable weather conditions. In the meantime Clobery & Co. issued warrants to arrest a number of their men on Kent for an alleged insurrection.

At the beginning of February 1637/8, Governor Calvert received news that the warlike Susquehanna Indians at the head of the Bay planned to declare open war on the Marylanders that spring in retaliation for their

---

‡ He died intestate and apparently without issue. Letters of administration were issued on Apr. 6, 1638, to James and Thomas Baldridge. He was alive on Mar. 14, 1637/8, when he attended a session of the Assembly.

[16] *Ibid.,* vol. 5, p. 209.

§ He was born about 1601, being aged 39 in 1640, and was a native of Roxwell Parish, Essex. His sister, Elizabeth, was the first wife of William Clayborne and the mother of Clayborne's children.

[17] Archives, vol. 5, p. 203.

[18] Fund Pub. no. 28, p. 182.

assisting certain neighbouring tribes against them. The Susquehannians, ever an ally of Clayborne, were consistently raiding the tribal lands of the Indians in Southern Maryland, plundering their villages and crops, ravaging and carrying away their squaws. War with the Marylanders furthermore had been encouraged by Thomas Smith who with men from Kent had in the summer of 1637 re-established or strengthened a fortified trading post on Palmer's Island at the head of the bay about four miles below the falls of the Susquehanna River. At that time Smith and Boteler were preparing to send an additional contingent of men and supplies to strengthen the settlement which they declared was outside of the jurisdiction of the Province of Maryland.* Palmer Island was definitely within the Maryland grant, but Clayborne had used the island as a trading rendezvous with the Indians as early as 1629.

John Fullwood alias Sande, a native of Hope Parish, Herefordshire, had lived for a number of years among the Susquehanna Indians and had become familiar with their language. Captain Clayborne and his agents trading in the upper waters of the bay had frequently met him in connection with their bargaining for beaver with the Susquehannians and the tribes which came down from what is now the western part of New York State to trade with the Virginians. Through Fullwood, Clayborne was successful in persuading the King of the tribe "to come with people and settle Palmer's Island" of about 200 acres which was conveniently located as a trading-station.†

In April or May 1637, the King of the Susquehannas ceded to Clayborne the entire island with a great deal of land on both sides of the river and bay. Again there was a conflict of ownership and the right to grant land. Did the Susquehanna King have the power to grant land or did the King of England? Clayborne, however, did not question the legality of his grant, but brought several servants up from Kent and the Indians assisted them in felling trees and planting corn. Houses and a fort were constructed on the northern portion of the now uninhabitable island.

Being somewhat apprehensive by the continued aggressiveness of Clayborne and his covenant with the Susquehannians, and after consultation with the Council, Governor Calvert set sail from St. Mary's for Kent in company with Captain Thomas Cornwalys and Captain Evelyn and "with thirtie choice musketeers", including the reliable Sergeant Robert Vaughan. The primary objective was to capture Smith, Boteler, and Blecker and then grant complete amnesty to the islanders, if they would swear allegiance to Lord Baltimore.

---

* Governor Calvert in his letter to his brother stated that the northern boundary of the Province was the south boundary of New England "your [Lord Baltimore] pattent limits the Province to the northward where New England ends". Ref: Fund Pub. no. 26, p. 188.

† Known also as Watson and Garrett Island. It was granted in 1622 to Edward Palmer, a share-holder of the Virginia Co., who died in 1624 before taking up his claim.

The expedition encountered better weather this time and ultimately landed a little before sunrise‡ at the southern-most tip of the Isle, known as Kent Fort, which contained barracks and one of Clayborne's dwellings— "a small ffort of Pallysadores". The gate towards the bay was firmly barred, but one of the musketeers who was familiar with the fort soon directed them to another entrance which was unbarred and apparently unguarded. They entered without detection of the guard or without any notice of the men housed in the fort who were undoubtedly all asleep. Neither Smith nor Boteler were at the fort, but at their respective plantations some distance away.

Apparently without a gun being fired, Calvert and his men were able to subdue the entire contingent of islanders lodged at the fort and prevented any of them to escape and give the alarm to the rest of the inhabitants. With the captured islanders from the fort well under guard, the Marylanders marched them in direction of Boteler's plantation called the "Great Thickett" some five miles from the fort, and at the same time Calvert issued orders to the mariners of the pinnace to sail about one-half mile from Crayford* and to await him there. Ordering Ensign [Robert] Clarke who "came once with Mr. Copley from England"[19] to take ten musketeers and capture John Boteler, and then meet him at Crayford about two miles from Boteler's plantation.

Boteler, Clayborne's brother-in-law and confederate, was taken utterly by surprise, and was marched no doubt with a little argument by Ensign Clarke to Calvert's planned position near Crayford before Calvert had arrived at the designated point of rendezvous. Then Sergeant Vaughan with six musketeers was sent after Thomas Smith who "lived at a place called Beaver Neck right against Boteler on the other side of a creek". By the time Calvert reached the anchored pinnace, Sergeant Vaughan already had rebellious Smith completely under his control and brought him before the Governor of Maryland. Indignation must have been ripe, as the turbulent Smith again faced Governor Calvert as a prisoner.

Reading the riot act to both Smith and Boteler, Calvert placed them under guard aboard the pinnace and commanded the crew to return to St. Mary's City with orders to deliver the two "chiefe delinquents" to the High Sheriff of St. Mary's. The pinnace was then directed to return to

---

‡ Evidence varies. Boteler deposed that there were about 40 men and that they arrived at night, see his deposition, printed in Archives of Maryland, vol. 5, pp. 212-220. Leonard Calvert writing to his brother stated 30 men and that they arrived before sunrise.

* Crayford was Clayborne's dwelling-plantation, named after his native parish. When John Boteler made his peace with the Marylanders, there are implications that it or another tract which was given the name of Crayford was granted to him with manorial privileges. After the death of Boteler without issue, it escheated to the Lord Proprietary, and there is evidence that it became for a time one of the proprietary manors. Later Crayford became the name of a hundred on the isle.

[19] Fund Pub. no. 26, p. 184.

Kent for Governor Calvert and his staff who had remained with him in order to establish law and order.†

Governor Calvert then announced a court or general assembly to be held on the Isle and summoned all freemen to appear in person. By proclamation he absolved all the inhabitants, except Boteler and Smith, if within 24 hours they paid him due homage as overlord and submitted to the rule and authority of Maryland. Mr. Robert Philpot whose father was the keeper of "Hygh parcke" [Hyde Park] in London was the first to swear fealty to Governor Calvert.[20]

Within the time limit, the entire freeholders of the island surprisingly acknowledged the complete sovereignty of the Calverts. The Governor instructed them to chose their delegates for the forthcoming General Assembly soon to be held at St. Mary's. In addition Governor Calvert promised to send John Lewger, Esq., the Secretary and Surveyor General of the Province, to the Isle and reaffirm their land grants from Clayborne under the Great Seal of Maryland.‡

According to Calvert's letter to his brother, dated April 28, 1638, there were about 120 men able to bear arms "as neer as I could gather", but no estimate was made of the women and children. Before returning to St. Mary's, Calvert made Robert Philpot, Gent., the Commander of Kent, with William Coxe, Gent., a native of the Parish of Scarcliffe, Derbyshire, and Thomas Allen as joint or deputy commanders.

Some unlucky star had placed Thomas Smith, Gent., at that time on Kent. He had retaliated with the Marylanders for his humiliating treatment while he was trading with the Indians in the Patuxent by defeating the Marylanders at the naval battle in the Great Wighcocomoco, but Maryland had not forgotten his intrigue and already a price was on his head. Upon Calvert's return to St. Mary's, Smith was tried for piracy, condemned by the court and hanged without the benefit of clergy.§ With

---

† Some historians state that Calvert returned to St. Mary's with the prisoners, but in his letter to his brother, "I gave order for the carrieing of Boteler and Smith to St. Maries in the Pinnass I came in, and with them sent most of the Soldiers as a gard upon them commaunding them to be delivered into the custody of the sheriffe at St. Maries until my returne and my Pinnassee returne to the Ileand to me". Ref: Fund Pub. no. 26, p. 185.

[20] Fund Pub. no. 28, p. 193.

‡ In granting the land to the freeholders as given them by Clayborne, the Maryland patents always stated "according to the pretense of a grant from William Clayborne" or words to that effect.

§ He left two daughters and a widow Jane. She had the great misfortune to marry gentlemen who became involved, or not always being on the winning side. She was born about 1617, being aged 40 in 1657. See, Archives, vol. 3, p. 351. She married secondly Captain Philip Taylor, of Accomac and Kent, being on Kent at the time Calvert subdued the island. He was aged 30 in 1640, was a native of Marden Parish, Herefordshire, and was with Clayborne when he first settled Kent. After the death of Taylor, by whom there was issue, she married thirdly William Eltonhead, Esq., of Eltonhead Manor, St. Mary's County, who was shot by the Puritans at the battle of the Severn when he was fighting under the banner of the Lord Proprietary.

him was hanged Edward Beckler, but what part he played in the affairs of Kent and the Calverts, it is not known.

Mr. Boteler, the brother-in-law of Clayborne, was more fortunate than Smith. He played his cards better than his compatriot. Within a short time Governor Calvert released him from the custody of the High Sheriff and had him as a guest in the Governor's Palace—though well watched and perhaps still under guard. Boteler finally came to terms and his life was spared. He was made one of the early magistrates of Kent, and on March 27, 1638, Calvert commissioned him Captain of Kent Island Militia but it later developed that his allegiance and loyalty to his brother-in-law, Clayborne, were too great and he soon broke with Governor Calvert.

Governor Calvert, according to the statement of Boteler, returned to the island with about fifty armed men and completely reduced the island "under the Government of Maryland" and confiscated the estate of Clobery & Co. as well as that of Clayborne.

After Kent had been subdued without bloodshed and was passively peaceful for a time, Governor Calvert sent Sergeant Robert Vaughan, William Brainthwaite, Gent., who succeeded Evelyn as Commander of Kent, and Reynold Fleete, a brother of Captain Henry Fleete, to take possession of Palmer's Island. At the same time he dispatched a letter to William Fullwood with the Susquehanna tribe advising him that the land, servants, cattle, and goods were confiscated to the "Lord of Maryland", and that Sergeant Vaughan had been commissioned to take charge of Clayborne's servants on the island. With the expedition went two pieces of ordnance which had been taken from Kent Fort. In June Governor Calvert arrived personally on the island with his staff and "coming to Fort and houses there erected did displant the same and killed divers hoggs there and carried away from thence all the men and Neate Cattle".

Vaughan was again successful on his mission, and on June 30, 1638, he made his report to the Council, filing a complete inventory and the disposition thereof of all property taken by him and his assistants belonging to Clayborne, Smith, and one Sergeant Howard, of Kent.[21] A pair of tables were turned over to Reynold Fleete. Among the livestock were one cock and one hen with seven chicks. They killed the cock and the chicks, but delivered the hen to Mr. Lewger.

From the report it seems as if there were only four men at the post, namely, Edward Griffin, William Jones, William Freeman, and Richard Reymond, all listed as servants, who were transported to St. Mary's as political prisoners.

Repercussions on the conquest and capture of Palmer's Island were felt with mixed sentiments at St. Mary's City. Jerome Hawley defended Baltimore's title to it, but John Boteler "grew more confident of proceeding in planting it for his Brother Cleyborne". Hawley, however, considered it unlawful to hinder the settlement of the island, but Calvert writing to his

---

[21] Archives, vol. 3, pp. 76-77.

brother, Cecilius, stated "Hawley let the title fall for some design for his own for trade with the Sasquahannoughs".[22] Whatever Hawley's designs were, he died soon afterwards, and this colorful character passed forever from the Maryland scene.

Apparently, Palmer's Island remained deserted until about 1643, when Governor Calvert established a garrison there which was called Fort Conquest, and detailed ten men to protect it. In an account filed or sent by John Lewger to His Lordship about that time, he accounted for an expenditure of 1000 lbs. tob. for planting the garrison at Fort Conquest.[23]

In the meantime the English Parliament had created a Board of Commissioners to handle the affairs of the growing American plantations and one of the first cases to be placed on the agenda was the conflict of Maryland and Virginia over the sovereignty of Kent. With trained legal acumen, the board rendered its decision in April 1638. The claims of the Colony of Virginia and any sovereign rights over Kent were completely ignored, as the matter was treated merely as a personal dispute between Clayborne and Lord Baltimore. According to the board, the Lords Baltimore had a hereditary grant of suzerainty under the Great Seal of England to the Province of Maryland as expressed in the Royal Charter, whereas Clayborne had simply a trading license under the Seal of Scotland, therefore, this contingency could not be placed in bar of superior claims. Kent Island thus was adjudged to be the rightful domain of Lord Baltimore.

As a consequence of the board's decision, the Maryland General Assembly passed a bill of attainder against Clayborne. On January 2, 1638/9, Governor Calvert ordered the High Sheriff of the Isle of Kent to attach the property of William Clayborne and his partners. He and his accomplices were accused "to have Trespassed and Committed Waste upon the same to the disturbance of the peace of our said Province and to our damage of a 1000[1] sterling". He was summoned to appear at court to be held at St. Mary's on February 1, 1639/40.[24] It is needless to state that Clayborne made no appearance and the Maryland Court for a time took no further action.

Somewhat chagrined Clayborne retired to his seat in Virginia defeated, but undaunted to await a more opportune time to strike. On August 2, 1640, "Capt. William Clayborne of Kecoughton* in Virginia, Esq." gave power of attorney to George Scovell, of Nancimun, Va., to recover all debts and property due him "by any person or persons inhabiting in the province of Maryland". Scovell thereupon petitioned the Governor and Council of

---

[22] Fund Pub. no. 28, p. 188.

[23] *Ibid.*, vol. 4, p. 275; vol. 3, p. 134.

[24] Archives, vol. 3, pp. 82-83.

* Clayborne's home at the mouth of the James near present Hampton, named after an old Indian village. His plantation served as a base for his operations and intrigue against the Maryland plantations.

Maryland that Captain Cleyborn (sic) upon his departure from the Isle of Kent had left an estate "within your province at his departure undisposed of on 24 March 1637/8". It was therefore evident or guileness on the part of Clayborne that he technically acknowledged the sovereignty when he referred to "within your province". The terse reply by the Marylanders was that it was possessed by right of forfeiture to the Lord Proprietary for "certain Crimes of Pyracy and murther".[25]

A few more or less peaceful years passsed, but it was more like the proverbial calm before the storm. In the summer of 1643 Governor Calvert sailed for his native England, perhaps for business, but it is quite possible that he was anxious to revisit his old haunts and to see his kinsmen and friends whom he had not seen for over ten years. Then it was said that he foresaw trouble and resolved to make a voyage to England to consult his brother in person.

Before sailing he appointed Captain Giles Brent, Esq., then his Commander on Kent, the Deputy Governor with full authority during his absence, dating his commission as of April 11, 1643, which was ratified by the Lord Proprietary on July 14, following. Why Giles Brent was selected, we know not, but Captain Cornwalys who had shouldered many a past responsibility was overlooked and also the influential Lewger who soon quarreled with Brent. On August 26, 1644, Brent suspended Lewger from all offices and revoked all commissions granted to him.

Brent was a jealous Roman Catholic and like all men of action, he had staunch friends as well as bitter enemies. By marrying an Indian maiden, though a tribal princess, he had somehow lost face with some of the Maryland gentry.† And being a Roman Catholic and a Marylander, he was certainly not popular with the Virginia Puritans.

In 1640 the Lord Proprietary had granted Giles Brent the entire southern tip of Kent Isle which virtually embodied the former trading settlement of Clayborne, with the most ample prerogatives of seigniory perhaps ever conferred on any Maryland subject. He was made Commander of Kent in February 1639/40, and one of his first acts was to seize all debts, goods and chattels which he found on Kent belonging to Clayborne and his men who had followed him to Virginia.

He established his seat on the manor and apparently constructed a manor house of some proportions and a mill along with other dependencies. With

---

[25] *Ibid.*, vol. 3, p. 92-94.

† The comment on the marriage of Giles Brent's daughter made by Charles Calvert to his father, Cecilius, in 1672 throws some light on the feeling against the children of the English-Indian alliance. "Major ffitzherberts Brother who Maryed the Indian Brent has Civilly parted with her And (as I suppose) will never Care to bed with her more, soe that yor Loᴘᴘ needs not to fear any ill Consequence from that Match, butt what has already happened to the poore Man who unadvisedly threw himselfe away upon her in hopes of a great portion which now is come to Little". Ref: Fund Publication no. 28, p. 264.

a number of Clayborne's men remaining on the Isle and taking the Oath of Fealty with their tongues in their cheeks, Brent, however, was not popular among certain liberal elements of the inhabitants.

When Governor Calvert arrived in England in the summer of 1643 matters were far from merry in Merrie England, even safe. Public affairs were becoming more and more disturbed by the dissension between King and the powerful Puritan element which had successively been elected to Parliament. Armed conflict between Puritans and Royalists were inevitable and soon many of the aristocrats were to lose their heads, with the result that the rising middle-class attained wealth and titles—and with wealth came ultimate power.

In 1642 the King and his court left London and perhaps at that time Charles failed to realize that he would never return to his Royal Palace of Whitehall, The Parliamentarians had London firmly in their hands. The Royal Court was sometime at York, but often at other county towns, for Charles I, like kings of old, took the field in combat. Civil War between Royalists and Puritans actually broke out on September 20, 1643, at the battle of Newbury in Berkshire. As the primary objectives of the Puritans were to purify the Church, they thus traveled through the shires sacking and burning the castles of the ancient nobility and the manor houses of the conservative county gentry which was apparently their method of purification.

Trading in Virginia and Maryland waters for several years had been one Richard Ingle, of Redriff, County Surrey. As to his background little is known, but he was the commander of his own ship which he called the "Reformation", aptly named, for he was one of the most rabid and unprincipled Parliamentarians of his day, in fact he possessed all the snuffling, self-righteousness of the worst example of Puritanism. There were also rumors of piracy which were no doubt justified, because even knighted gentlemen were not adverse to the lucrative profession, if it brought them gain without capture.

On his frequent sailings into the Chesapeake he had uttered traitorous statements that the King was no King, that the sole authority emanated from Parliament, and other like remarks. In February 1642/3, while his ship was at anchor in Accomac, Virginia, he was ordered arrested by the authorities there in the name of the King, having stated that "I am Captaine of Gravesend for Parliament against the King". He defied arrest, and standing on his ship with his cutlass drawn shouted, "I deny it in the Parliament's name. He that come aboard, I cut off his head".[26]

In January 1643/4, his ship was in Maryland waters and while anchored in the Potomac near St. Clement's Island and at another time in St. George's River, he had continued his remarks against the Royal authority. William Hardige, a tailor of St. Mary's City, had no hesitancy in accusing him of high treason.

---

[26] Archives of Maryland, vol. 4, pp. 223, 234, 238.

Captain Giles Brent, then Acting Governor, had previously received instructions from the King to seize any ship licensed by Parliament trading in his dominions beyond the sea. Hearing of Ingle's boasts, he therefore ordered his arrest.[27]

Brent thereupon directed Edward Parker, High Sheriff for St. Mary's County, to place Ingle under his custody, seize his ship and cargo, and to prevent his joining his ship. Parker obeyed the orders and placed Ingle under the custody of John Hampton, who turned out to be a Puritan sympathizer, and several guards namely William Durford, John Durford, Frederick Johnson, and perhaps others. According to testimony, Hampton permitted Ingle to beat and overpower the guards and thus escape to his ship in St. George's River. Later, however, developments indicated that Hampton may not have been altogether the villain.

In the meantime two of Lord Baltimore's closest adherents and Roman Catholics became involved in some unorthodox manner with Ingle, perhaps for believed personal gains. Before Ingle's arrest, Captain Cornwalys had apparently negotiated some private business with him, certainly the consignment of merchandise to the value of £200. When Ingle made his escape and reached his ship, Cornwalys went aboard and directing his discourse to Hampton, said "All is peace, and willed him to deliver up his rapier to the gunner of the ship and told him that all was quiet and peace and willed the said John Hampton to go out to the rest of the guards and will them to deliver up their arms to the gunner of the ship".[28]

Charges were preferred against the sheriff. Brent immediately issued warrants for the arrest of Cornwalys and Captain James Neale as accessories in the escape that they did "aid, encourage and bett", but Neale denied the charges and asked for a jury trial by His Majesty's Court.[29]

At court in 1643, Cornwalys stated that he fully understood the matter, that Ingle had been accused of matters of no importance by the malice of one William Hardige, a tailor. Nonetheless, Cornwalys was fined 1,000 lbs. tob. by the court, but upon appeal the fine was reprieved.

Ingle was likewise fined 1,000 lbs. tob. and the various suits which had been instituted against him were suspended on the condition that he "leave in the country for the public need one barrel of powder and 400 lbs. shot."[30]

It seemed as if the word of a Puritan in that day was no better than a communist of today, for Ingle sailed from Maryland without satisfying the condition of powder and shot and directed his course straight for London carrying Cornwalys with him as a willing and friendly passenger. London then being under the complete control of the Parliamentarians, the Proprietary Government of Maryland had no appeal to the King's customs for the satisfaction of Ingle's unkept promises.

---

[27] *Ibid.*, vol. 4, p. 231.

[28] *Ibid.*, vol. 4, p. 23.

[29] *Ibid.*, vol. 4, p. 252.

[30] *Ibid.*, vol. 4, p. 261.

Gratitude was never a part of human frailties, certainly so with Ingle, for when his ship docked in London, he had his benefactor Cornwalys cast in prison "upon 2 feigned accons of 15,000 lbs. Sterl.". It was only through the intervention of friends that Cornwalys was released. In the meantime the merchandise of Cornwalys to the value of £200 on the "Reformation" was sold by Ingle and appropriated to his own use, justifying himself by saying that it was taken "by force of warr".

Cornwalys faced further trouble. One Mary Ford, widow, accused him of kidnapping her two children which proved to be a Puritan frame-up, inasmuch as the bill of complaint filed by the woman indicated the intrigue of Cornwalys' enemies and could not have been entirely known to the complainant.

Goody Ford accused Cornwalys of "setling of a Papist faction in Mary-Land" and used other vitriolic adjectives pertaining to Lord Baltimore and his Province. She stated that Cornwalys stole her two children—a boy of 3 or 4 years of age and a girl of about 5 or 6 years, and carried them to Maryland and seduced them to Papish practises. She furthermore swore that Cornwalys "from his owne shipp commanded the men in his owne boate to shoote at them, hee having noe other ground to fix this his Accom on . . . hee the said Cornwalys by that comand slew an honest Gentleman one Mr. Warren and hurt others w[ch] murther is yett by him unanswered for". Then she accused Cornwalys and Brent of seizing the ship of Ingle "& would have forc'd the marriners to goe for Bristol to fight against the Parliament calling them Rebells".[31]

Cornwalys was in the Lion's Den, for London was in the hands of the insurgents and Parliament and various committees were issuing petitions and decrees right and left contrary to the charter held by Lord Baltimore. On November 28, 1645, the "Committee of Lords & Commons for Foreign Plantations", signed by W. Jessop, Secretary, read a petition from the "Diverse the Inhabitants of Maryland settling forth the tyranical Government . . . ever since its first setling by Resucants". On December 25, 1645, the Lords and Parliament ordered the settling of the Plantation of Maryland under the Command of Protestants.[32]

By sailing with Ingle, Cornwalys was thus in England during the two years of Plundering by the Puritans, but his house and affairs left in the hands of his steward, like other property of Royalists whether Roman Catholic or Anglican, suffered.

Ingle in defending himself in London stated that he arrived in Maryland on his ship "Reformation" and found that the Governor of Maryland had a commission from Oxford* to seize all ships and goods belonging to the Government of London.

---

[31] *Ibid.*, vol. 4, pp. 169-170.

[32] *Ibid.*, vol. 3, pp. 164-165.

* Decree issued by Charles I from his court at Oxford to seize any Parliamentary ships tarrying in Maryland waters, or perhaps elsewhere.

At London on March 2, 1645/6, Cornwalys stated that Ingle came to Maryland as a Master of a trading ship and uttered treasonable words against the differences between the King and Parliament. He was arrested and his ship and goods were seized by the Governor of Maryland, but he, however, "found means to free Ingle and to restore him to his ship and goods".[33]

With Governor Calvert out of the Province, Cornwalys in a British prison, Acting Governor Brent and Secretary of State Lewger at loggerheads, the Puritans winning battle after battle in Britain, Puritan Clayborne with his maniacal hatred of the Calverts, realized his great opportunity had arrived and it was time to strike another blow, especially when Brent in Maryland seized Ingle's ship in the name of the King. The latter incident caused great excitement and afforded the ever watchful Clayborne his chance for revenge.

Sometime between Michaelmas and Christmas of 1644, that is, in the autumn of that year, Clayborne with his own ship and the "Cock" belonging to his Cousin Thompson, with ten or eleven accomplices reached Kent Isle without detection of the Proprietary Militia. He contacted his two friends and sympathizers, Thomas Bradnox and Edward Comins, and then traveled among the islanders stirring up trouble claiming that he had a royal commission from the King to recover Kent Isle.

With his force from Virginia and what insurgents he could muster on Kent, they proceeded to march on Kent Fort Manor, the seat of Captain Giles Brent, which was about a three-mile distance from their place of rendezvous. They stopped at the house of John Abbott en route, and there some of his recruits became suspicious and questioned the validity of the royal commission. Clayborne displayed a piece of parchment, but the majority of them doubted its validity and refused to continue the march. According to Thomas Bradnox's statement, "Whereupon he [Clayborne] betooke himself to his vessels and departed".[34]

The indomitable Clayborne was again subdued but not defeated. The accelerated success of the Parliamentary Party in England gave him greater confidence and audacity, for he aimed at nothing less than the complete control of Kent and ultimately of all Maryland.

In September 1644, Governor Calvert returned from England and rumors were already current that Clayborne and Ingle were preparing to invade the Province. If Clayborne had not already arrived on Kent Isle flashing a piece of parchment as a purported commission from the King, he was making plans to do so. His attempt failed at that time, and apparently the Marylanders for the next two years remained apathetic or failed to realize fully the intrigue and the revengeful force behind Clayborne. The apathy was certainly demonstrated for the Marylanders were

---

[33] Archives of Maryland, vol. 3, p. 167. By this statement Cornwalys may have been the factor which permitted the guards around Ingle to be overpowered.

[34] Archives, vol. 3, p. 458.

wholly unprepared for the Claybornian invasion two years thence. It could have been likened to an unheralded volcanic eruption.

The opportune time arrived when Ingle again sailed into Virginia waters with several armed vessels and immediately communicated with his compatriot Clayborne. Shortly after Christmas 1646, Clayborne and his Cousin Thompson with a force from Virginia of about 20 insurgents invaded Kent Isle and found several of their confederates on shore to welcome them with open arms, especially Edward Comins and Thomas Bradnox.

Clayborne let it be known that he had a commission from Sir William Berkeley, Governor of Virginia, to take over the island and all the land and personal property which were formerly possessed or claimed by him. That he had been offered the Governorship of Virginia and could thus have it, if he so wished. He and his insurgents successfully captured Kent Fort Manor and Captain Giles Brent, its lord, was arrested and carried to England, as a political prisoner "unjustly", as he later stated.[35] His manorial holdings on Kent were left in the custody of his sister, Mistress Margaret Brent, but the rebels established their garrison there with Clayborne's Cousin Thompson as the commander-in-chief. Within a short time Captain Peter Knight, Merchant, another Puritan fire-eater, arrived from Virginia. At Kent field he and Lieutenant South mustered the men and proposed that they go down in warlike manner and capture St. Mary's City. Nothing short of entire conquest and submission of Maryland under Puritan despotism were the ultimate goal of the Virginia radicals. Provisions were being loaded on the ships, but some of the men became apprehensive and requested that Clayborne show them the authority by which he was acting under Sir William Berkeley. He refused, so "The inhabitants and men withdrew from the design". Then Clayborne again urged the men to accompany him and stated that he would take them down in his vessels, three in number, disembark them at Point Lookout in Maryland and then go to Chicacacon, his place in Virginia, for reenforcements. Again his confederates were suspicious and refused.

There was just cause for the suspicion on both attempts by Clayborne to capture St. Mary's and his purported commission from Sir William Berkeley. It is difficult to conceive that Sir William was at one time in league with Clayborne, for in 1646 he gave assistance to Leonard Calvert to recover his Province and Virginia loyalists aided in driving out the rebels.[36]

Although his attempt to capture St. Mary's City failed, the Puritans had things pretty well in hand on Kent. Clayborne returned to Virginia, but before sailing he relinquished his authority to his Cousin Thompson who later turned it over to Peter Knight. Thomas Bradnox was made a captain of the Puritan forces.

---

[35] Archives, vol. 4, p. 148.

[36] *Ibid.*, vol. 4, pp. 458-459.

Property of the loyal subjects of Lord Baltimore on Kent fell a prey to the Puritan plunderers. Innumerable acts of incendiarism and pillage occurred in rapid succession. A tobacco barn, another house on Kent Fort and a hog sty were burned. Peter Knight made use of the mill on the manor of Captain Brent for his own profit and like Ingle's men who took St. Mary's City went around the Island pillaging the loyalists. Edward Comins, another worshipper of Cromwell, sacked the houses and would leave the proprietors and the servants destitute of provisions. Thomas Bradnox even forced the heretofore fearless Mistress Margaret Brent out of the manor house of her brother and made it his garrison. He burned one of her dependencies on the manor, killed her cattle and wasted her corn and other provisions. He kept Captain Robert Vaughan, a loyalist, a prisoner in his house for three weeks, burned four hogshead of his tobacco and was the cause of losing two of his indentured servants. Many other depredations occurred, with the Roman Catholics the greatest sufferers.

The invasion and ultimate capture of St. Mary's fell to Ingle. So rapid were his movements and so advanced his preparations for conquest that Governor Calvert and the provincial militia were unable to offer any effective resistance. He and his court hurriedly crossed over and took refuge in Northern Virginia. There he remained for nearly two years in exile surrounded by his staunch supporters who also had to flee and others who were banished from time to time by the Puritan dictators. Governor Calvert was well received in Virginia, for the heretofore Colony for exploitation of resources rather than settlement was now receiving a higher social level of English emigrants and besides the Northern Neck of Virginia where he found asylum had received many excellent families from Southern Maryland which had settled on the bays and rivers of the south bank of the Potomac.

Ingle roamed about the countryside impressing corn, tobacco, cattle and household goods. His ships were stuffed with plunder which were exported and turned into hard cash for the benefits of the rebels. It was during his occupation that many of the early Maryland records were lost or wilfully destroyed. The Catholic chapels and missions were burned; Fathers White and Copley were sent to England as prisoners. The settlers who remained never forgot the occupation and for long after those two years of Clayborne and Ingle rule were referred to as the "plundering time".

Captain Cornwalys was in England during the plunder, but his estates suffered. Later he instituted action against Ingle for trespass and for the pillage of his property during his absence in London stating in his brief "he [Ingle] landed some men near his house and rifled him to the value of £2,500 and then coming into England complained against him as an enemy of the State".

Ingle considered himself a crusader by confiscating property to his own use "from those wicked Papists and Malignants in Maryland" and that he "relieved the poore distressed Protestants there, whose otherwise must have starved and bin rooted out".

While Leonard Calvert was in exile away from the wrath of the Puritans and possible execution, after a number of months he made a diplomatic move by appointing Captain Edward Hill, a Protestant, Governor during his absence. The appointment was made on July 30, 1646, but within a short time Calvert had regained the governorship and the late appointment of Hill became of no force and effect.

In 1645 Sir William Berkeley, the Royalist Governor of Virginia, returned from England. Ultimately with his personal assistance and a force of anti-Puritan Virginians, Governor Calvert and other Marylanders in exile were able to return to Maryland and restore order. As the combined forces landed at St. Mary's and other points, Clayborne and Ingle made tactful and timely departures. By the autumn of 1646 Governor Calvert was fully restored to power.

Before their escape, however, they and their confederates committed all sort of damage. When Peter Knight left Kent, he crippled the mill of Kent Fort which by testimony was in good repair when he took it over, removed the doors of the houses from their hinges and carried off all hardware, and slaughtered most of the cattle.

Peace and order were finally restored, with Governor Calvert offering amnesty to the rebels. Thomas Sturman, Francis Gray, John Hampton, Richard Sedgrave, and John Sturman were apprehended and gave bond to the Lord Proprietary for 2,000 lbs. tob. Robert Smith, Thomas Yewell and Thomas Lewis escaped to Virginia, but would often raid the coast at night. Edward Comins was arrested and fined 20,000 lbs. tob. to be paid to Mistress Margaret Brent for the damages done to Kent Fort Manor.[37]

At Kent on April 16, 1647, Governor Calvert pardoned the following men—Thomas Bradnox, Edward Comins, John Watham, Thomas Pott, Robert Short, Francis Lumbard, John Ayres, Zacharias Wade, Richard Cottsford, Edmund Lennin, and Walter Joanes. They all took the Oath of Fealty, but the indefatigable Bradnox continued to keep in communication with the rebels in Virginia. Fealty and pardon meant little to him, for shortly afterwards he stole a neighbor's two year-old steer. It seemed as if Mrs. Bradnox was in on the steal, for she cautioned two men who cut up the animal not to reveal the theft.[38]

In a letter addressed to His Lordship by the Assembly, it was stated: "Since the beginning of the Heinous Rebellion first in Practice by that Pirate Ingle and afterwards almost for 2 years continued by his Complices & Confederates in which time most of your Lordship Loyal friends here were spoiled of their whole Estate and sent away as banished persons out

---

[37] *Ibid.*, vol. 4, pp. 435-437.
[38] *Ibid.*, vol. 3, p. 182.

of the Province those few that remained were plundered and deprived in a manner of all livelyhood and subsistence only Breathing under that intollerable Yoke which they were forced to bear under those Rebells which then assumed that Gov^t of your Lordships Province unto themselves . . .".

At the restoration of Proprietary Government Robert Vaughan, a loyalist on Kent, was made the Commander of the Isle and was ordered to attach all property of the late rebels.[39]

Lord Baltimore thereupon issued a decree that any contract made by his subjects with any of the insurgents during the occupation should be considered invalid and of no cause and effect, declaring the years of the rebellion from February 15, 1644 to August 5, 1646.

Certain malcontents in Virginia, however, were ever defiant. The Virginia Assembly granted a commission to Edmond Scarborough, of Accomac, a controversial figure, to seat Palmer's Island and to trade with the Indians in the Bay and the headwaters. Lord Baltimore hearing of the act immediately advised his then Governor, Captain William Stone, Esq., of Poynton Manor, to prevent such action and "to seize upon his or their Persons Boats and Goods".[40] Scarborough remained, however, securely at The Stages, his plantation in Accomac.

At the death of Governor Calvert on June 11, 1647, Captain Edward Hill from Checakone, Virginia, on June 20, 1647, addressed the Council in a lengthy epistle and announced his claim to the governorship by right of his appointment by Calvert in exile. Thomas Greene who had been appointed Governor by Leonard Calvert on his death bed replied to Hill and advised that under such emergencies if the Governor "shall happen to dye or be absent out of the Province" the Council had full power to elect a person from the Council, but not being a member of the Council his appointment was "grounded uppon false pretence". Furthermore, Hill was advised "to desist from such unlawfull wayes".[41]

Affairs remained rather quiet for a time in the Province, but the old conspirators were active some few years thence when the King lost his head, the House of Lords was abolished, and Cromwell with his ruffians came into complete and absolute power. Maryland again fell under Puritan domination, with Anglicans and Catholics both disenfranchised indiscriminately. Governor Leonard Calvert had passed on, but Governor Thomas Greene, Esq., an Adventurer and Royalist to the core held the reign of power. His loyalty to the Lord Proprietary and his courageous defiance of the uncompromising Puritans have made him the scapegoat of liberal historians who have accused him of being a highly bigoted Roman Catholic, but his fearlessness in the face of over-powering opposition, loyalty to the Crown, and firm convictions made him a greater

[39] *Ibid.*, vol. 3, p. 183.
[40] Archives, vol. 1, pp. 328-329.
[41] Archives of Maryland, vol. 3, pp. 188-189.

character than any writer or Maryland historian has given him credit. His gubernatorial regime was brief, for Lord Baltimore was forced through expediency and the unpopularity of the Roman Catholics while the Puritans controlled Parliament to appoint the liberal or pseudo-Puritan, William Stone, then of Hangar's Creek in Accomac as the governor of his Province.*

Stone settled first in St. Mary's City bringing a number of planters from Accomac with him and it was also under his tenure of office that the non-conformists around Norfolk in Virginia started their journey to the Severn, then the uplands of Province. And with them came more trouble for the Loyalists of St. Mary's.

On May 2, 1649, contemplating being absent from the Province Governor Stone appointed Thomas Greene the "Leievetenent Generall Chancellor Keep of the great Seale Admirall chiefe Justice Magistrate and Comander as well as by Sea by land of this his Loppr Province of Maryland and the Islands".[42]

The absence of Governor Stone was apparently of a short duration for on September 20, same year, again having an occasion to be absent he appointed Thomas Greene Acting Governor but in the event that he was unable to serve then Thomas Hatton, His Lordship's Secretary.[43]

Greene accepted the office for a second time and it was during his Acting Governorship that the news of the execution of Charles I by the Puritans reached Maryland. Thomas Greene ever loyal to the Crown and the House of Stuart published by proclamation on November 15, 1649, that "his eldest sonne Charles the most renouned Prince of Wales the undoubted rightfull heire to all his ffathers dominions is hereby prlaymed Kinge Charles the second of England Scotland ffrance & Ireland defender of ffaith & c . . . Long Live King Charles the second".[44] There was much rejoicing by the Royalists and the King's health was drunk in many a home by the provincial aristocracy.

On the same day Acting Governor Greene pronounced pardon or gave amnesty to all inhabitants for such offences against the Crown and the Lord Proprietary since the last general pardon and also from "all ffine forfeiture or penalty".[45]

The Puritans, especially in Calvert County and the liberals in other parts of the Province, rose in angry protest and denounced the Proclamation and almost hung Governor Greene in effigy. The Puritan townsmen at Providence on the north shore of the Severn gathered at the local tavern

---

* For the genealogy of the Stone family, see, "The Stones of Poynton Manor", by Newman.

[42] Archives, vol. 3, p. 231.
[43] Archives, vol. 3, pp. 241-242.
[44] Archives, vol. 3, pp. 243-244.
[45] Archives, vol. 3, p. 244.

and with body temperatures rising to fever heat castigated the "Papist Greene" in no uncertain terms. Political affairs were again terse and open rebellion was averted by only a few months.

Upon the return of William Stone and the resumption of his gubernatorial duties he repudiated the action of Thomas Greene in proclaiming Charles II as King of the Realm and openly gave his support to the Puritans and the Commonwealth.

An excerpt from "The Lord Baltamore's Case", published at Westminster Hall in 1655 and reprinted in the Force Tracts, vol. 2, p. 27, throws some contemporary light on the matter, but inasmuch as Greene had been appointed Acting Governor by Captain Stone during his absence, it would seem that it was Stone who relieved Greene of his duties and not the Lord Proprietary.

> "It hath been confessed by the Lord Baltimore, That one Captain Green his Lieutenant-Governor of Maryland, did soon after the death of the late King proclaim his Son Charles Stewart King of England & c . . . for which his Lordship saith he did by a Writing under his hand and seal (which is one of the parchments remaining with this Committee) revoke the Commission granted to the said Captain Green and appointed one Stone in his room but there is no such cause mentioned in the said Writing".

The hospitality and sanctuary granted the Puritans and malcontents from Virginia by Lord Baltimore had repercussions in many directions. The Virginians ever alert for an opportunity to embarrass Maryland reported to Charles in exile that Cecilius, Lord Baltimore, was disloyal by harbouring increasing numbers of enemies to the Crown in his Province. Charles from his court on the Isle of Jersey on February 15, 1649/50, issued a Royal Commission to Sir William Davenant, Knt.* to supersede Lord Baltimore's gubernatorial authority, though not to deprive him of his sovereign rights as lord of the soil. "Whereas the Lord Proprietary of the Province and Plantations of Maryland in America doth visibly adhere to the Rebells of England and admits all kinds of Schismaticks. . . . That Wee reposing speciall trust and confidence in the courage, conduct, loyalty, and good affection to Us, of you Sir William Davenant . . . doe by these presents, nominate, constitute and appoint you Our Lieutenant Governor of the said Province or Plantations in Maryland with all Forts, Castles, Plantations, Ports. . . ."[46]

With several retainers Sir William sailed to assume his new duties, but

---

* Davenant, poet laureate, dramatist, and staunch Royalist, was born 1606 at the Crown Inn, Oxford, of which his father was proprietor. Shakespeare always stopped at the Crown while passing through Oxford and it was rumoured that he maintained great admiration for the proprietor's wife. Stories developed that Davenant's paternity was Shakespeare, a legend which Davenant himself did not discourage. He died in 1668 and was buried in Westminster Abbey.

[46] Public Record Office, London, reprinted in Hall's Narratives, pp. 179-180.

his ship was intercepted by a cruiser belonging to Parliament before it had cleared the English Channel. He was interned at Cowes until the next year and then sent to the Tower to await trial for high treason. He was ultimately released, it is said, on the personal intercession of Milton. The latter is subject to questioning inasmuch as both Milton and his father were rabid Puritans but during the Commonwealth Milton held the secretaryship to the Committee on Foreign Affairs.

Sir William would have brought much literary refinement and culture to the provincial court at St. Mary's which then became dimmed by stoic Puritanism following the prohibition of the drama and all forms of amusement in England as ungodly and which was carried out in so far as possible in Maryland by Richard Preston and his ilk.

Stone held the reign of Government only until March 29, 1652, however, when the Commissioners from Parliament namely Richard Bennett, Edmund Curtis and the relentless William Clayborne from Virginia again came into power and took over the Government. By June 28, 1652, the Commissioners had restored the governorship to the ever vacillating Stone upon his promise to issue all writs in the name of the Keeper of the Liberties of England or the Commonwealth. Within a few months Cecilius, Lord Baltimore, advised Stone that his Province had not been lost to him and that Parliament still recognized him as the overlord. Stone thereupon announced that writs would again be issued in the name of His Lordship. It was his undoing and within a short time the Commissioners deposed him a second time and put an end to the rule of William Stone. And almost the end of Stone for at battle of the Severn which turned out to be a Puritan victory he nearly lost his head. Only the Puritans believed in the firing squad rather than beheadment. For the next five years the Puritan Commissioners acting under the name of the Commonwealth of England held complete sway and only non-Conformists were permitted the right of franchise.

During the supremacy of the Puritans or non-Conformists, the Maryland renegades recognized the sovereignty or ownership of Kent and Palmer Islands by Captain Clayborne. In 1652 the Maryland Puritan Commissioners, the then ruling power of the Province, negotiated a treaty with the Susquehanna Indians, traditional enemies of Maryland, by which they granted them all land on the west side of the Bay from the Patuxent River north and from the Choptank to the North East Branch of the Elk "Excepting the Ile of Kent and Palmers Ilands which belongs to Captain Clayborne. But nevertheless it shalbe lawfull for the aforesaid English or Indians to build a Howse or ffort for trade or any such use or Occasion at any tyme upon Palmers Iland".[47] The Puritans thus alienated more than half of the Province of Maryland which by Royal Grant had been given to the Calverts and which they had no legal right to convey.

---

[47] Archives, vol. 3, p. 277.

From the strict construction of the accord, it looked as if the Puritans were alienating their own settlement at Providence on the north shore of the Severn peopled by malcontents from Virginia and who were virtually chased out of that Colony for their non-conformity.

Although the Puritans of the Severn and the Patuxent in now Calvert County had succeeded in their revolution to defeat the gubernatorial rule of the Calverts and were living with satisfaction under the rule of the Parliamentary Commissioners, they still were not content to recognize Lord Baltimore as their sovereign lord or land-owner. On January 3, 1653/4, written at the Severn River by Edward Lloyd and signed by 77 "house-keepers & Freemen & Inhabitants", they addressed a petition to Richard Bennett and William Clayborne "Commissioners for Virginia and Maryland" against subscribing to the oath of fealty to Lord Baltimore and complained of great "grievances and oppressions". Likewise on March 12, 1653/4, 60 house-keepers and freemen of the Patuxent subscribed to a similar petition written by Richard Preston.[48]

Richard Bennett and Will Clairbourne (sic) replied from Virginia on March 12, 1653/4, "We advise and require you, that in no Case you depart from the same (taking Oath of Fidelity), but you continue in your due Obedience to the Commonwealth of England".

The second Puritan reign in Maryland lasted from 1649 to 1658, when Lord Baltimore was able to regain sovereignty, though the Puritans or Parliamentarians in England had always respected his ownership as a landlord, but not as a ruler of a Palatinate.

Clayborne lived long and hard, but on March 13, 1676/7, he petitioned Charles II as "a Poor Old servant of your Majesty's father & Grandfather" for redress and reparation. At that time he was approaching seventy and perhaps time had dimmed his memory of loyalty but not his malice for Maryland. How could a one-time Puritan and Dissenter be a poor servant to Charles I whose head was cut off by the party, and how could he have been a loyal servant during the time when the Puritans drove his son, Charles II, to his exile in France? His statement perhaps contained more truth as to his service to the grandfather, James I, for during his reign Puritanism had not reached its mercurial force, yet the seed was planted in the latter years of Elizabeth. Charles II was then in undisputed power and had been recalled from the palace of St. Germain in France at the down-fall of Puritanism by the death of Cromwell when freedom-loving Englishmen were only too happy to welcome the restoration of the royal regime and be relieved from a reign which promised reforms but brought only tyranny.

Clayborne stated that at his own charge he discovered and planted the Isle of Kent, though he made no mention of the greater assistance made

---

[48] Force Tracts, vol. 2, p. 28. The list of subscribers was not given; it would have been an excellent census for those living in the Puritan camps in that year.

by Clobery & Co., and accused Lord Baltimore by force of arms in a hostile manner of confiscating his estate to the value of £10,000 in goods, cattle, servants, and many plantations. Furthermore that the plantations on Kent were under the jurisdiction of the Government of Virginia and that warrants were issued to arrest men, and one man was brought and tried in Virginia for felony and many were arrested for debts and sent to Jamestown, that Lord Baltimore wounded and hanged a man without trial and in like manner they displanted "us at Palmer's Island".

Clayborne did perhaps sustain personal losses of an unknown value—and from the depositions made by a number of free-holders on Kent, Clobery did neglect his servants and Clayborne personally supplied them with food from his own estate.* It would seem from all source records that if Captain Clayborne had recognized the claims of Baltimore, there would have been no confiscation of his property within the territorial limits of Maryland as expressed in the Royal Charter. His obstinacy and undeviating approach to the Maryland cause were definitely his economic loss, but jealousy and deep-rooted hatred of the Puritans for the Royalists and Roman Catholics were undoubtedly the basis for his relentlessness.

Clayborne died a short time after his final petition, and thus passed from the scene the conflict of jealousy of fifty or more years between the two "fruitfull sisters" whom John Hammond in 1656 compared to Leah and Rachel.

---

* See the depositions in Archives, vol. 5, pp. 181-239.

EPILOGUE

It was the spring of 1958 that I had planned to spend some time on the Isle of Wight and one of my first objectives was to pay homage to the memorial which the State of Maryland placed at the harbour of Cowes during the 1934 tercentenary to commemorate the sailing of the two ships from that port.

I had spent the greater part of the morning at Osborne House, the favourite retreat of the late Queen Victoria, and was sitting on a public bench awaiting the bus to return me to the town of Cowes proper. An English lady was likewise waiting for the bus and seeing that I was an outlander to those parts engaged in conversation. During our causeries I enquired of the location of the monument or memorial which commemorated the sailing of the Ark and the Dove. She frankly admitted that she had no knowledge of it and also expressed some chagrin in not knowing more about her native isle, as she considered herself well informed on its history.

En route on the bus down to town I asked the driver of the location and where would be the most convenient stop to reach the harbour and the memorial. He likewise had never heard of it and an accommodating fellow-passenger who offered his assistance knew nothing of such a memorial. My next thought was to seek a Bobby—a member of that wonderful institution of British policemen who are noted throughout the world for their kindness, knowledge and well-breeding, but I had not gone but a few paces after alighting from the bus when I came to a police station.

I entered and was courteously received by the sergeant and three officers. I made my enquiry and again to my surprise no member of the police force present had ever heard of the Ark and the Dove and had no knowledge of any memorial or monument erected in the town. Then came the fatal blow and most unkindest cut of all to my Maryland pride and Southern chauvinism. The sergeant in all earnestness said, "You do not mean the Mayflower, do you. That large monument in Plymouth harbour?" I may add that Plymouth is some 160 miles from Cowes as the crow flies.

The sergeant telephoned the librarian of the town who fortunately was able to advise of such a plaque. The sergeant hung up the receiver and then pointed to the youngest of the three Bobbies, "Why, it is right on the esplanade in front of your home'". At that time the wife and mother-in-law of the young Bobby had arrived as he was about to go off duty. They escorted me to the esplanade and en route the Bobby possessed a charm of manner certainly not found in the American police force. He who had only been married a few weeks was very proud of his old English name of Sutherland. His bride was a native of Australia.

The esplanade which affords a magnificent view of the harbour may be described as a good-sized rectangular, cemented open space running for a short distance along the water side with a low classical balustrade surrounding all sides. On one of the corner balusters which acts as a post for one of the entrances and which also now serves as a convenient resting place for bicycles we discovered a simple copper plaque which told the story of the Ark and the Dove. After removing a number of bicycles which enabled me to read and copy the inscription I took several shots with my inexpensive camera.

Nearby was an aged retired gentleman who had no doubt come to this spot every day for a number of years whenever the weather was propitious to relax and dream into the past sitting calmly on a bench with his pipe and cane. He became quite intrigued at my interest, so after I had copied the inscription and taken a few snapshots, he rose and with the aid of his cane came over slowly and adjusting his glasses read the inscription and then serenely returned to his bench and resumed his tranquility.

All bicycles were carefully replaced.

"On the 22nd day of November A.D. 1633 Leonard Calvert brother of Cecil Calvert, Baron of Baltimore with his co-adventurers set sail from this port in the Ark and the Dove to establish in America the Palatinate of Maryland under a charter granted by the King of England which conferred upon the people of Maryland all the Rights of Englishmen to be theirs in perpetuity Rights which the people of Maryland have ever cherished as their greatest, most valued heritage. Upon the site granted by the Cowes Urban District Council to the Society of the Ark and the Dove this tablet is erected November 22, 1933, by the State of Maryland".

PART II

NUMBER OF ADVENTURERS ON THE ARK AND THE DOVE

The number of Adventurers on the Ark and the Dove and a complete list of their names will ever remain a controversial and undetermined factor. Although it was officially stated that the Oath of Allegiance had been administered to about 128, it occurred at Tilbury on the Thames some few miles southeast of London in October and before additional Adventurers had joined the ships at Cowes prior to sailing in November.

On October 29, 1633, Edward Watkins reported the following to the Privy Council.[1] "According to yr Lops oder of the 25th daie of this instance moneth of October I have been at Tilbury hope where I found a shipp and a pinnance belonging to the right honble Cecill Lord Baltimore, where I offered the oath of Allegiance to all and every the persons aboard whether any more persons were to goe the said voyage, he answered that some fewe others were shipped who had forsaken the shipp and given over their voyage by reason of the stay of the said shipp".

The absolute, official list of those who took the oath of supremacy is presumably not extant, nor has any semi-official list been unearthed.* A fire at the Public Record Office in London early during the last century is believed to have caused its destruction.

Cecilius, Lord Baltimore, writing to Thomas Wentworth, Earl of Stratford, in January 1633/4, stated that "There are two of my brothers gone with very near twenty other gentlemen of very good fashion and three hundred labouring men".†

---

[1] Pub. Record Office, London; see also, Md. Hist. Soc., vol. 1, pp. 352-353.

* Watkins stated that "all and every the persons" subscribed to the oath which would therefore include the Roman Catholics on board. The Catholics naturally found the oath obnoxious, as it has been said, "No Roman Catholic could take it". Nathaniel Claiborne Hale in his biography of William Claiborne "Virginia Venturer", p. 173, stated "Evidently the Roman Catholic priests and some hundred or more laymen who could not conscientiously subscribe to a denial of papal authority either concealed themselves in some way or boarded the vessels farther down the channel". It would have been difficult for any one or more persons to hide in such compact quarters on the Ark and the Dove. It is possible, and this author is of the opinion, that the few Catholics who were on board subscribed to the oath with their tongues in their cheeks as a means to an end, hoping for absolution in the next confessional. Certainly Leonard Calvert, his younger brother, and the two Catholic Commissioners were on board as the ships sailed from London, but some of the other Catholic gentlemen of fashion could have joined the ships at Cowes.

† A Relation in Maryland, published 1635 in London, gives a list of only seventeen gentlemen. See reprint in Hall's Narratives of Early Maryland, p. 101.

Lord Cecil in the House of Lords shortly after the sailing of the ships stated about two hundred. The Lord Baltimore's Case, printed in London in 1653, stated that "The Lord Baltemore hereupon in 1633 sent two of his own brothers with above 200 people to begin and seat a Plantation".[2]

More than 100 years later Governor Horatio Sharpe, of Maryland, on December 15, 1757, by his message to the Lower House of the General Assembly in reviewing the history of certain provincial proceedings stated: "The first Settlement that was made in this Province after the Lord Baltimore had obtained his Patent was made by his Lordship Brother and between Two and Three Hundred other Persons in February 1632/3".

Besides the seventeen Gentlemen of Fashion as given by Lord Baltimore, the most positive proof of the Adventurers is through the established claims for landrights instituted by those who guaranteed or paid for certain colonists who sailed on the two ships with the intentions to settle permanently in Maryland.

Names mentioned in Father White's Journal gave authentic proof for a few. Furthermore, the proof of certain men being in St. Mary's a short time after the initial settlement is also *prima facie* evidence that they were on the Ark or the Dove—certainly when proof is lacking to the contrary.

Yet there were Adventurers on that voyage whose identity is still unknown. The names of the transportees of the five passenger-investors who did not sail on the ships but who financed the transportation of fifteen Adventurers have not been established. Also five men whom Captain Henry Fleete transported when he came up the Bay to join the Adventurers are unknown.

The Chancery suit of Edward Robinson vs. Cecil, Lord Baltimore, initiated in the summer of 1637 over investments threw many lights on early Maryland, and referred to servants or redemptioners on the voyage over, presumably financed by Robinson, yet no specific names were mentioned.

Jerome Hawley in his testimony stated that the two Calverts in the first year brought over "no less than forty servants". But Leonard Calvert claimed in 1641 land-rights for only fifteen men whom he brought in during 1633. No other demands were made by him and no record exists of any transportees or servants sent personally by the Lord Proprietary except his secretary, John Bolles. If the two Calverts referred to are Governor Leonard Calvert and George Calvert, Esq., (younger brother of Cecilius, Lord Baltimore) no claims nor assignments were made by young George according to extant records. Consequently, approximately twenty-five settlers whose names are lacking were brought in by the Calverts during the first year. The "first year", however, could mean those who came in the second ship, for the chancery case previously referred to proved that a ship under Captain Humber which left England at Michaelmas

---

[2] See "Narratives of Early Maryland", by C. C. Hall, 1910, p. 167.

arrived in Maryland during December 1634. The passenger list of this ship is likewise missing.

No list is extant of the servants transported by Jerome Hawley, Esq., one of the financial backers of the Adventure, and certainly a man of his position would have brought in a number equaled if not greater than his colleague Thomas Cornwalys. Furthermore, there is evidence that Gabriel Hawley, Esq., brother to Jerome, financed several Adventurers whose names are unknown.

John Saunders who died en route and a business partner of Captain Cornwalys had ten transportees in his retinue, five of whom he assigned before his death to Father White and whose names are known. When Captain Cornwalys claimed land-rights for the five whom John Saunders had assigned him, he failed to name them specifically but claimed his land-rights thereof. Consequently, there were five additional names lost to the historian.

Thomas Greene, Esq., received an assignment of redemptioners from Nicholas Fairfax who died en route, and also from William Smith, an Adventurer, the names of which have not been proved.

The number of 300 stated by Cecilius, Lord Baltimore, in the first instance can be considered a loose and inaccurate remark or perhaps an exaggeration or idle boast. It was apparently made to encourage settlement of those who had the matter under consideration. The figure of 200 quoted in 1653 was perhaps more correct. But proving the passenger list from sources other than official, the number falls well short of 200.

It should first be admitted as expressed elsewhere that mortality among the first settlers was at a high level. There is also evidence that a number of transportees or servants were brought over for whom no land-rights were claimed. Certainly each and every one of the so-named seventeen gentlemen of very near fashion had at least one body-servant, and certainly Mistress Ann Cox had a maid-servant.

Only three of the Fashionable Gentlemen proved land-rights, while there is the record of only four who assigned their claims to another party. As a consequence, land was plentiful and with the quit-rents set by Lord Baltimore being rather excessive at the beginning, many apparently failed to exercise their rights while others were not anxious to consider assignment for a valuable consideration. The liberal policy of granting land, and the difficulty of making it productive with so few farm labourers apparently acted as an obstacle to land claims and many rights were not exercised or even assigned. Furthermore, some land-rights under the 1633 Conditions of Plantation were proved as late as 1650, so it is evident that much land was available, but the Adventurers were in no hurry to acquire vast tracts with the burden of heavy quit-rents in the form of taxation.

Then it is difficult to separate those who actually sailed on the Ark and the Dove from those who came on the second ship which arrived within the calendar year of the initial settlement. Several joined the ships in Virginia. This could signify any of the English settlements in the Caribbean where the ships touched as well as the Colony of Virginia, for *Virginia* in that day was the geographic term applied to all territory claimed by the sovereigns of England in the Western Hemisphere. Furthermore, there was frequent intercourse between the two colonies during the early months, so settlers already in Virginia could have entered after the initial arrival of the Ark and the Dove, but yet came in during the year 1633/4.

Psychologically it was an age of restless adventure, as the young had boldness in their blood and the desire to see or share a new adventure after having experienced a life in one settlement or another. It was somewhat like the Spanish conquest for El Dorado, because the new Province of Maryland in their minds perhaps promised more than they had found in their present state. They knew not where they were going nor what they would actually find, but the spirit of adventure led them on. Consequently, a few or even more than a few attached themselves to the Adventurers as they were anchored here and there en route.

Consequently, these facts lean a certain authenticity to the belief that more Adventurers whose names are proved as coming to Maryland on the Ark or the Dove actually came, especially when proof of entry can not be established through the application of land-rights and the like.

Several unofficial lists have been prepared by interested parties and organizations, but all subject to varied criticisms and even corrections. It is quite apparent that the referred-to lists contain several who never saw the Ark or the Dove, and lack many who actually did.*

Through certain mediums a synthetic list, which may also be the subject of criticism, has been compiled during this study of some thirty or more years. The list is therefore flexible, but proof or evidence for each name is cited, and even then the list contains only 113 Adventurers, or—with the crew 121, when the actual number is believed to be approximately 175 rather than the casual statement of 200—yet no figure can be cited with any degree of accuracy.

---

* The Society of The Ark and The Dove published in its constitution and by laws 110 Adventurers, including members of the crew. The list in "MacKenzie's Colonial Families of America", vol. 5, contains 119 names, including several members of the crew and three unnamed wives of which no proof was cited. The list of the late Hester Dorsey Richardson published in "Side-Lights on Maryland History" contains a more conservative list of 97, including members of the crew.

WOMEN AND CHILDREN ON THE ARK

One of the most intriguing subjects regarding the initial voyage of the Ark and the Dove to Maryland is the number of women and children among the Adventurers. That there were women, there is no doubt, but so far no evidence of children has come to light—though there must have been a number of youths still in their teens.

The number of women were perhaps greater than the extant records indicate. Lord Baltimore was too much of an organizer not to realize the value of women in a settlement to insure prosperity, contentment and permanency. This was certainly true of his Colony at Ferryland in New Found Land, for we have a list of 31 colonists who in 1622 remained with Governor Edward Wynne, of which eight were women or girls. So in selecting or encouraging Adventurers for his Province of Maryland, he certainly did not overlook this aspect, but the records prove so few.

Father White stated in his report to the Jesuits when speaking of the landing on St. Clement's Island "here the youngwomen who had landed for the purpose of washing, were nearly drowned by the upsetting of the boat—a great portion also of my linen being lost—no trifing misfortune in these parts". In his narrative he stated "here by the overturning of a shallop we had allmost lost our mades [maids] which we brought along".

In both instances women and maids were in the plural, but so far only two women have been proved definitely as being among the Adventurers, although a third can be accepted by inference. As Lord Baltimore planned everything for a permanent settlement, certainly more women made that historic voyage. It is not beyond the realms of truth to believe that a mid-wife was aboard the Ark. In that day one was essential in all communities, and in the absence of doctors it was the women of the household who practised the quaint lore of the art of healing and the ancient use of herbs, mingled with charms and a little white magic.

Mistress Anne Cox is definitely proved as one of the gentlewomen, and she could have been the "noble matron . . . who coming with the first settlers into the colony with more than women's courage bore all difficulties and inconvenience".[1] If Mistress Anne Cox, later Madam Greene, were not that noble matron, then at least two gentlewomen were on the Ark.

Land-rights were proved for Mary Jennings, a maid-servant of Father White. No further record of her has been found, so she either failed to survive the hardships of the first years or married and lost her identity.

---

[1] Calvert Papers, Md. Hist. Soc.

Neither she nor any husband claimed land-rights or "freedom-rights" so far as extant records.

There are no records of wives accompanying the married gentlemen, nor servant-maids with indentured husbands. Madam Hawley, consort to Jerome Hawley, Esq., was in the Province at an early date and was in residence at the time of his death in 1638. No evidence has come to light to indicate her coming on the Ark with her husband, but it is not altogether unlikely, for we do not have a list of the transportees of Jerome Hawley. If she did not, she therefore came with him on his return voyage in 1635.

Captain Thomas Cornwalys was apparently married at the time he sailed on the voyage or married upon one of his return trips to England, yet we have no record of his wife being among the first Adventurers. We have proof, however, that he was married by 1638 and his wife was in England.[2]

Circumstantial evidence would also indicate that Anne Smith who was made a widow by the death of her husband, William Smith, before September 22, 1635, was a passenger on the Ark—either as his wife or a spinster whom he married after the ship left England.

Further proof that several women were on board is through the lawsuit of the three innkeepers at Cowes against Gabriel Hawley when it was explicitly stated that "men and women" were lodged.

Under the Second Conditions of 1636, provisions were made for land-rights to a married man and his wife who came in 1633. It would seem, however, if no wives were brought, that it would not have been necessary to include that provision.

---

[2] Fund Pub. no. 28, p. 170.

HIGH MORTALITY AMONG THE ADVENTURERS

While two hundred or less Adventurers braved the bleak Atlantic in the winter of 1633, remarkably few survived the first three years, and relatively few left descendants. It is known that some returned to England, presumably more than it is known, but it was the gentry who could afford to pay their return passage, whereas the redemptioners who comprised fully 75 percent of the passenger list was forced to remain and wait until their time of service had expired. If he were without sufficient funds, which was usually the case of a redemptioner, he had to bargain with some ship's captain in order to earn his return passage. The latter condition is believed to have been negligible, for the majority of them succumbed early to various diseases characteristic of the times.

The Ark carried with it Richard Edward, a doctor or chirurgeon, as one was called in those days, who likewise acted as the barber to the gentry— for in that day the profession of a doctor was combined with that of a tonsorial practitioner as well as the extractor of teeth.

The lack of sanitary knowledge and the fact that the redemptioners were all crowded in the hold of the ship or "tween deck", with very little bedding and with less change of clothing were propitious to the breeding of bacteria. Sanitation to a minor degree was known for they swabbed all quarters daily with vinegar and aired the bedding in fair weather.

In those days it is known that many of the ablest servants sent over died on the ship and those who did survive were so weak from exposure and lack of proper nourishment that it was months before they were serviceable for a full day's work. This may not be so true of the servants of the Ark, but it was certainly true of other ships. Then, rules of health even among the civilized nations of the seventeenth century were little understood and practiced. Functional habits were free and filthy, according to our present standards, among the rich as well as the poor, and while facilities for bathing on the two vessels were inadequate, our ancestors washed less frequent than standards of public decency demand today.*

There was the usual indisposure owing to *mal de mer* but according to Father White virtually no sickness occurred until the Christmas celebration which was due solely to over indulgence.

The Adventurers left England in the midst of winter presumably with only heavy clothing, for clothing of the Englishman was necessarily heavier

---

* At the dedication of the monument at Runnemede by the American Bar Association in 1957 Sir Hartley Shawcross stated that "King John was not one of our cleaner kings; it is recorded that he bathed eight times in six months".

than what was required in the milder climate of Maryland and Virginia. As the Adventurers neared the Caribbean with its tense tropical heat and the peculiarities of sudden climatic changes, the average Adventurer manifestedly was not accustomed to it, so it required sometime to adjust himself to the sudden transition, particularly when it is believed that one had but the heavy outer garments with perhaps a shirt or two for a change.

Many were stricken during the Christmas celebration which then lasted the traditional twelve days to the Feast of the Epiphany, when Father White reported that twelve died—two being members of the Roman Catholic faith whom he named, but he failed to name the non-Catholics.

After landing and as summer approached, mortality must have been extremely high among all classes, especially the servants. The heavy death rate could not be attributed altogether to a state of lowered physical resistance which courted disease, owing to the hardship of the voyage, for they all had ample rest and exercise at the Barbadoes, St. Christopher, and the Colony of Virginia. Yet some failed to survive the rigours of that transatlantic passage, for at times there certainly must have been bad drinking water and although the food was well salted, it often spoiled during the latter part of the voyage and which they courageously washed down with copious draughts of beer.

Reading contemporary narratives of that period reveal conditions almost unbelievable. One seaman writing of his trip to America stated that the bread was so full of midgets that if you left it on the board [table] it would walk. Conditions on some of the ships carrying colonists to Virginia were likewise deplorable. Lady Wyatt, consort of Sir Francis Wyatt, Knt., who crossed the ocean in 1622 wrote to her sister in England that the vessel was so infected that she "saw little but throwing folke overboard . . . few els are left alive that came in that shipp".

The high standards, however, set and maintained by the Marylanders prevented the almost unbelievable depraved and cannibalistic conditions which existed during the first few years in the Virginia Colony.† And no time did the death toll take such a large number as it did in Virginia. When Newport, Gates and Somers arrived from the Bermudas in 1610, just three years after the initial settlement, they found only approximately sixty inhabitants.

---

† The inhabitants remaining upon the arrival of Captain Christopher Newport in 1610 told of the "starving time, when it were too vile to say, and scarce to be believed, what we endured; but the occasion was our owne, for want of providence, industrie and government . . . so great was our famine that a Salvage we slew . . . the poorer sort tooke him againe and eat him, and so did divers one another boyled and stewed with roots and herbs; And one amongst the rest did kell his wife, powdered her, and had eaten part of her before it was knowne, for which hee was executed, as hee well deserved". Author's note: With the rivers full of fish and the forest full of game, it seems no justification for a famine or the barbarous acts of cannibalism. But it must be remembered that the colonists sent over in the beginning by the Virginia Co. were of the lowest social stratum.

But it was the first summer in Maryland which played its havoc. The malaria mosquito to which they had not been accustomed in England inflicted fever which they called "ague" after an ailment characteristic of that day in England. Again some doubts exist whether the chirurgeon knew how to treat the malarian infection. A Dutchman in Virginia during 1630 remarked that unseasoned people in Virginia died like cats and dogs between June and August.

The winter of 1638 proved a particularly bad one. Father White writing to Lord Baltimore of the epidemic stated that "sixteen died . . . weather by disorder of eating flesh and drinking hott waters [rum, whiskey] and wine by advice of our Chirurgian rather by any great malice of their fevers, for they who kept our diett and absteinence generally recovered".

We thus have the knowledge of a doctor being in the Province during 1638, whose advice some sufferers failed to heed, for those who abstained from hot waters apparently recovered. Father White did not name the sixteen who died, but, while some may have been the 1633 Adventurers, yet others could have been those who arrived later.

Scurvy was one of the greatest enemies of seamen in that day, but perhaps the greatest disease or pestilence other than ague or malaria sustained by the colonists was dysentery. Bleeding was resorted to in all cases of high fever, but instead of aiding the patient, as we now know, it only aggravated his condition. Then contaminated drinking water was another cause of certain diseases, and the excessive consumption of beer and wine during illnesses certainly did not help the patient.

It can therefore be said that the principal causes of such high mortality were the peculiar changes in climate, the hardships endured, the lack or knowledge of sanitation, improper diet, decomposed food, and contaminated drinking water, accompanied by unintelligent methods of healing.

More Than Ten Percent Left Descendants

Of the approximately 200 Adventurers, more than ten percent left descendants. When studying the conditions of the times and the high mortality rate, it is perhaps a good average, and definitely higher than those on the three small boats which brought the first supply of settlers to Jamestown—if it were possible to discover their names.

One question which piques the curiosity of the antiquarian is what happened to the Seventeen Gentlemen of Fashion. Not too many of the Gentlemen could have died early in the settlement. We do know that John Saunders and Nicholas Fairfax died en route and that the Hon. George Calvert died within a few months as well as Thomas Dorrell. Richard Gerard returned to England, but if others did, there is no record. Of the seventeen only five—Leonard Calvert, Thomas Greene, Thomas Cornwalys, Jerome Hawley, and Robert Wiseman—remained after the first year or so to figure in the affairs of the Province.

Those who did survive and lived for five or more years in the Province seemed to have died unmarried or without issue, and thus failed to leave a posterity. In the beginning few women ventured to cross the ocean, so as a consequence many men were forced to lead a non-connubial existence. Yet Mistress Ann Cox left many descendants through her only surviving son—Leonard Greene.

The descendants of those who left issue are now scattered perhaps in every State of the Union. Captain Thomas Cornwalys and Walter Beane left issue in England, and it is sometime wondered if some of their descendants came to America at a later date.

BIOGRAPHIES OF THE ADVENTURERS

Thomas Allen

Thomas Allen was one of the retainers of Leonard Calvert in 1633, and for whom he claimed land-rights in 1641. He has generally been accepted as the Thomas Allen who died testate in 1648, leaving three orphan boys, but circumstances indicate clearly that this Thomas Allen was one of Clayborne's men on Kent.

At the General Assembly of February-March 1638/9, a Thomas Allen was on Kent when he voted for a burgess for that isle,[1] and in all likelihood he was associated with Clayborne and his trading post. This is further substantiated in September 1640, when he "prayeth to have Confirmed to him the Neck of Land which he now holdeth by Grant of Capt. Cleyborne".[2] He was accordingly granted 66 acres on a branch of Northwest Creek in the Manor of Kent Fort. It is therefore conclusive that he was one of the malcontents on Kent and was not the redemptioner of Governor Calvert. In October 1640, he was elected to represent Kent Isle along with three other Kent Islanders.

Other substantiating evidence proves that the Thomas Allen who died in 1648 was not the retainer of Governor Calvert. First, he had an absolute distrust of Roman Catholics, for in his last will and testament which he signed he did not wish that his three sons (Thomas, William, and Robert) to live with "any Papists". He furthermore did not wish his sons to be "sold for slaves or Morter-Boyes", but left them with his "very loving ffriends John Hatch & Rich: Banks". If his old friend at Accomac called James Bruse had no son of his own, he could have his son, Robert. He placed his son, William, with Philip Conner, of Kent, inasmuch as he had once expressed a desire for him. He furthermore appointed his loving friends John Hatch or in his absence William Marshall and Richard Banks to be the overseers of his estate.[3]

John Hatch had been one of the servants of Clobery & Co. on Kent and later settled in St. Mary's County where he became a foe to the Proprietary Government. There is that tie-in of Thomas Allen with one of the men on Kent before its submission by the Marylanders, and also with William Conner, another settler on Kent under Clayborne. His early connections with Virginia was also apparent when he spoke of his old friend at Accomac.

Thomas Allen possessed indentured servants at his death, one of whom

Sources:—[1]Archives, vol. 1, p. 30; [2]Liber ABH, folio 88, Land Office; [3]Archives, vol. 4, pp. 403, 447.

was William Ashbiston who had served him seven years. His three sons, all minors at his death were later captured by the Indians and ransomed for a handsome sum. They either died during their minority or were taken to Virginia, as no further record can be found for them in Maryland.

With further reference to Thomas Allen, the redemptioner of Governor Calvert, no record therefore exists for him in the Province other than the claim for land by rights of his transportation.

JOHN ALTHAM [ALCOMB], GENT.

John Altham, a member of the Jesuit Order, was brought in by Father White, served as his assistant, whose land-rights were assigned to Ferdinando Pulton [Father Brock]. Father Altham was styled "Gent." at the Assembly of 1637, and Mr. by Father White who mentioned him in his journal, that is, "Mr. Altham hath writ sometime thereof, wch himselfe can witnesse; and likewise Mr Thorowgood who drive trade with the Indians". He died in Maryland on November 5, 1640.

WILLIAM ANDREWS

William Andrews was one of the transportees of Governor Leonard Calvert, but he failed to attend the Assembly of 1637 or the following Assemblies. He apparently returned to England or was one of the early casualties.

JOHN ASHMORE

John Ashmore was transported by Leonard Calvert, but no relationship has been proved to William Ashmore, another Adventurer, who came in as a servant of Father White. He was not among the freeholders who attended the Assembly of 1637 nor subsequent Assemblies, nor did he figure in any land or testamentary proceedings. The only conclusion that can be drawn is that he was probably among the many fatalities of the early days.

WILLIAM ASHMORE

William Ashmore was transported into Maryland as one of the servants of Father White who assigned his land-rights to Ferdinand Pulton. He was with Captain Cornwalys in the pinnace "St. Margaret" at the naval battle fought in the Chesapeake Bay, when on May 10, 1635, Cornwalys defended himself and crew against one of Clayborne's armed vessels. Ashmore fell a victim of the Virginians' shot and shell and died instantly. No issue has been proved.

JAMES BALDRIDGE, GENT.

Early in the days of the Province or before 1637 appeared two brothers, James Baldridge and Thomas Baldridge. They became extremely active at a very early period in civic endeavors, but no reference can be found to

Sources: Archives, vol. 1, p. 18; vol. 4, pp. 22-23.

prove how and when they arrived in the Province. It is quite possible that they came in under the patronage of Jerome Hawley or another Gentleman of Fashion whose redemptioners are not on record. Evidence on this point is incomplete and certainly unsatisfactory from a documentary point of view, but subsequent factors would lead to the assumption that they were with the first Adventurers—certainly no evidence has been found to disprove it.

Inasmuch as indentured servants even after completing their contracts were not entitled to land rights until the 1648 Conditions of Plantation, and no letters-patent were issued to either James or Thomas Baldridge, it leans further substance to the inference that they were among the fifty or less unaccounted-for transportees or bond servants on the initial voyage. If they became entitled to land rights under the 1648 Act, they failed to exercise their rights, perhaps because they were then subjects of the King in Virginia.

On April 6, 1637, James Baldridge was appointed the administrator of the estate of Zachary Mottershead, Gent., who had died intestate.[1] He filed at court the inventory which included seven books and closed the estate on August 29, 1638.

On January 29, 1637/8, he was commissioned High Sheriff and Coroner "untill we shall signifie our pleasure to the contrary", and gave bond to the value of 1000 lbs. tob.[2] At the Second General Assembly of 1637/8, he was in attendance as High Sheriff.[3] At the elective Assembly of 1639, he voted for Thomas Gerard and Francis Gray to represent St. Mary's Hundred at which time he signed his ballot rather than making an X.[4]

It is reasonable to assume that in order to be appointed to the functions of a shrievalty within three years of the settlement neither Governor Calvert nor his brother, the Lord Proprietary, would have selected one who had recently arrived in the Province without some recommendation. He had apparently proved his worth and ability and the fact that the early appointees were with one or two exceptions members of the Roman Catholic Church proves that he being an Anglican was a man of some parts and was not a newcomer to the settlement.

Although he early held responsible positions under the Calverts, he later was involved in treasonable activities as is evident on the part of his brother with the Rebel Ingle, and for this reason it is certain that they crossed over into Virginia when law and order were restored by the Proprietary Party.

So in 1648 when the redemptioners of 1633 became entitled to land rights for their initial entry, he and Thomas Baldridge were in disagreement with the ruling heirarchy and had established themselves in the Northern Neck of Virginia. With land then plentiful on a virtually undeveloped portion of Virginia, he had no use for a Maryland patent which was taxable and at that period had a very minor sales value, but most likely what property he left behind in Maryland or was entitled to was sequestered.

His wife was Dorothy _____, whom he certainly married in Maryland. There is a reference to Mrs. Baldridge in 1647 turning property at St. Inigo House over to William Lewis. On February 4, 1646/7, Dorothy Baldridge sued Richard Duke for 200 lbs. tob.[5] Although there is evidence of the Baldridges allied with the Puritans during the Plundering Time, she was an ardent Anglican and at her death she bequeathed a chalice and a prayer book to her parish church.

Children of James and Dorothy Baldridge

1. Jane Baldridge married several times. *q.v.*
2. _____ Baldridge married Capt. Alexander Baynham. *q.v.*
3. William Baldridge married Elizabeth _____. *q.v.*

The exact time of his settlement in the Northern Neck is not known, but it was prior to the year 1651. In that year "Mr. Baldridge"* and Mr. [Thomas] Speke received from the court of Northumberland County 3490 lbs. tob. for "their charges of Burgeship" (sic), as the county's delegates to the House of Burgesses.[6]

On April 3, 1651, William Berkeley, Governor of Virginia, granted to James Baldridge and Captain Thomas Baldridge 840 acres of land in Northumberland County, beginning at the mouth of Hollis Creek for the transporting of 17 persons into Virginia to inhabit. The seventeen transportees were most likely from Maryland and included besides the two patentees Dorida [Dorothy] Baldridge, Mary Baldridge and William Baldridge.[7]

After 1653 James Baldridge and his brother appear as planters of Westmoreland County, so it is evident that they settled in that portion of Northumberland which became Westmoreland in 1653. On April 4, 1655, he attended a court session in Westmoreland as one of the Justices of the Peace.

After the death of his brother, or on August 20, 1657, he made a deed of gift to his nephew, James Baldridge, for a moyety or 420 acres styling himself "the administrator of the estate of Major Thomas Baldridge my late brother deceased". It was his brother's portion to the 840 acres which had been granted them by Governor William Berkeley. In the event, however, that "James Baldridge should marry and have no issue male, the land was to revert to his uncle, James Baldridge, or his next male heir that shall be of the name of Baldridge and if none of that name in Virginia then the next male heir to the said James Baldridge by Common Law".[8]

His last will and testament was dated November 26, 1658, and probated in Westmoreland County on January 10, 1658/9.[9]

To Daniel Sisson the first foal of my grey mare.
To wife Dorothy the residuary estate including land and all chattels for her own use and to dispose of as she shall please.

---

* Mr. Baldridge is believed to be James, as his brother, Thomas, at this period was usually addressed with a military title, although Stanard in his Colonial Register gives the service to Thomas.

His widow lived until 1662. Her last will and testament, dated November 2, 1662, was subsequently probated in Westmoreland County.[10]

To grandchild Charles Baldridge the first mare colt that any of "my mares shall bring".

To William Baldridge "son of my nephew James Baldridge" the first mare colt that comes of the colt given to her grandson Charles Baldridge.

To nephew James Baldridge 3 hogsheads of tobacco.

To Joshua, son of Thomas Butler, the next mare colt, also 2 cows.

To John Stands one cow.

To John Stands and Stephen "one year of their turn of time which they were to serve a piece".

To nephew James Baldridge the "great long gun that was his father".

Book and chalice to be sent out of England at price of 2000 lbs. tob. to be presented to the parish church at Appomattox to celebrate communion and name to be engraved in the book and chalice.

Residuary estate to three grandchildren—Elizabeth Baynham, Ann Baynham and Mary Baynham equally.

Executor—son-in-law Thomas Butler.

Sources: 1. Archives, vol. 4, pp. 24, 46; 2. Archives, vol. 3, p. 61; 3. Archives, vol. 3, p. 61; vol. 1, p. 2; vol. 4, p. 32; 4. Archives, vol. 1, p. 29; 5. Archives, vol. 10, p. 96; 6. Record Book, Northumberland, vol. 2, p. 21; also Va. Col. Abstracts, vol. 2, p. 99; 7. Patent Book 2, p. 307; 8. West: Co. Deeds, Liber 1, folio 49; 9. Wills, Liber 1, folio 106; 10. Wills, Liber 1, folio 188.

Major Thomas Baldridge, Gent.

Thomas Baldridge appeared in Maryland records about the same time as his brother, James Baldridge, which indicates an arrival in the same ship or if they entered under an indentureship, their time was completed within the same period. In 1637 he was a surety for his brother when the latter administered on the estate of Zachary Mottershead. Evidence is strong that he was with the first Adventurers.

On January 23, 1637/8, he attended the Second General Assembly as a freeholder with the titles of Sergeant and Planter of St. Mary's Hundred.[1] On the 26th of the same month he was amerced for his non-attendance at a session, but in the afternoon James Baldridge exhibited his proxy. During the same session of the Assembly, he was fined 40 lbs. tob. for striking Isaac Edwards.

On February 12, 1637/8, he attended a grand inquest as a freeman. On March 20, 1638/9, he was commissioned the High Sheriff and Coroner for St. Mary's County to serve one year which succeeded the shrievalty of his brother James.[2]

His domicile was in St. Mary's Hundred as late as February 1638/9, when he voted for the burgesses of that hundred.[3] As Sergeant Thomas Baldridge he was granted letters of administration on the estate of Edward Bateman. By October 1640, he was of St. Michael's Hundred when the freeholders of that hundred elected him and Thomas Morris to represent them at the Assembly.[4] In 1642 he was assessed 23 lbs. tob. for the expenses of St. Michael's Hundred. He was fined 20 lbs. tob. for not attending the Assembly called for all freeholders in September 1642, but within a few days Captain Cornwalys held his proxy. On November 12, 1642, he was granted a license to kill swine in any of His Lordship's forests and gave bond to the Lord Proprietary for 1000 lbs. tob.

For the defense of the Province and in preparation of a possible Indian attack, as Lieutenant Thomas Baldridge, he was to command the southern portion of the county and keep guard.[5] For an expedition presumably military from September 21 to October 13, [1642], he received 75 lbs. tob. for the services of his servant, Alexander Banum.[6]

In 1643 he was ordered by Giles Brent to take a census of all men capable of bearing arms in St. Michael's Hundred and their fire arms including swords, quantities of shot and powder and to make a return to the Secretary without delay.[7]

When John Lewger ordered Captain Henry Fleete to travel to Piscataway and make a truce with the Sesquihanowes Indians, Captain Fleete, if expedient, was to seek the advice of several men of standing in the Province, among whom was Thomas Baldridge "if be there to advise with".[8]

After having held several offices of trust and honour under the Lord Proprietary he intrigued with Richard Ingle and as Henry Spinke stated in court on December 6, 1647 "hee [William Wheatley] came under the command of Capt. Thomas Baldridge who was Capt & Comder of those Rebells" carried away corn and burned the house of Nicholas Harvey.[9]

Upon the return of Governor Calvert after the plundering period, the Governor ordered William Lewis to search St. Inigo's House for all goods found there belonging to the inhabitants and to take possession thereof. On January 20, 1646/7, Lewis recovered from Mrs. Baldridge at St. Inigo's House a number of items belonging to Mr. Copley including six pictures.[10]

When peace and order were restored after the plundering times of Ingle, Thomas and James Baldridge found sanctuary in Virginia across the Potomac. A letter dated 9 Sept. 1649, was addressed to Thomas Baldridge by his cousin, Thomas Baldredge (sic), of the Barbadoes as "Cosen Mr. Tho Baldreade liveing in Potomack river over against Maryland". The writer sent his "love to your [Thomas] brothers and sisters* and your children". He recommended to his care a gentlewoman whose name was not disclosed to his cousins stating that she had been in the Barbadoes to settle her husband's estate but did not find the islands to her liking, so was "returning" to Virginia which indicated she had previously been in the Colony. Furthermore, he hoped to spend Christmas with his cousins in Virginia.[11]

On January 30, 1650/1, when John Cocke was granted 450 acres of land in Northumberland County, they adjoined the land of "Mr. James

---

* It is apparent that the Baldridge brothers had sisters in Maryland or Virginia, but their identity is not known.

Baldridge and Capt. Thomas Baldridge" and extended to the head of a branch "issuing out of Hollowes' Creek".[12]

As Major Thomas Baldridge, he was a Justice of the Peace for Northumberland County on November 25, 1652.[13]

He died intestate presumably in 1654, certainly before August 22, of that year.

His wife was born Grace Beman, whom he probably married in Maryland, as one of the early settlers in that Province was Anum Benum [Banum, Benam]. She may not have been his only wife, for the court was reluctant to grant letters of administration on his estate to her and her newly acquired husband.

On August 22, 1654, the following was ordered to be recorded at court:[14]

"Let no will be proved nor Ad'com granted nor anything also be done in the estate of Thomas Baldridge till John Tew who married with Grace Beman the then bethrothed wife of the said Baldridge and principal creditor of the estate be first called".

Ultimately, "John Tew and Grace Baldridge als Tew . . .; widow of Major Thomas Baldridge of the County of Westmoreland, Gent., deceased", renounced the administration. John Tew signed the instrument, while his wife, Grace, made her mark.[15]

On May 6, 1654, Isaac Allerton Jr. made his "honoured friend Mr. John Hallowes, Gent." to recover by law "what part of my estate there is belonging to me out of the estate of Major Thomas Baldridge".

Administration was granted to his brother, James Baldridge, who filed the inventory at court on April 9, 1655.[16] Prior to the filing of the inventory or on September 25, 1654, as James Baldridge Sr., he had the cattle marks of James Baldridge Jr. and Mary Baldridge registered at court.[17]

On March 10, 1655/6, Walter Broadhurst, Gent., who is sometimes believed to have married one of the daughters of Thomas Gerard, of St. Clement's Manor, aged 36, swore in court that he heard Major Hallowes say that Mrs. Grace Baldridge als Tew took a pair of stockings and other personalty from his wife.[18]

Children of Thomas Baldridge

1. James Baldridge. *q.v.*
2. Mary Baldridge married 1657 Richard Heabeard.

On June 15, 1657, Richard Heabeard conveyed his plantation of 300 acres in trust to Captain Alexander Baynham and Thomas Wilsford, Gent., inasmuch as the said "Richard Heabeard intented to marry Mary, the daughter of Major Thomas Baldridge, late of Westmoreland County, deceased". The trust was for the natural life of his intended wife and then to their future children. Also conveyed were 6 cows, 6 calves, 1 mare colt and other personalty which he had received from "Mr. James Baldridge administrator of Major Thomas Baldridge".[19]

Sources: 1. Archives, vol. 1, p. 2; 2. *Ibid.*, vol. 3, p. 85; 3. *Ibid.*, vol. 1, p. 29; 4. *Ibid.*, vol. 1, p. 104; 5. *Ibid.*, vol. 3, p. 108; 6. *Ibid.*, vol. 3, p. 119; 7. *Ibid.*, vol. 3, p. 122; 8. *Ibid.*, vol. 3, p. 150; 9. Archives, vol. 4, p. 453; 10. Archives, vol. 3, p. 178; 11. West: Co. Record Book 1653-59, folio 29; 12. Patent Book 2, folio 280; 13. North: Order Book 2, folio 5; 14. West: Order Book 2, folio 28; 15. West: Record Book 1653-59, folio 25; 16. *Ibid.*, folio 45; 17. *Ibid.*, folio 28; 18. *Ibid.*, folio 54; 19. *Ibid.*, folio 82.

JAMES BAREFOOTE, GENT.

James Barefoote, Gent., died en route with twelve others from over indulgence at Christmas. Father White referred to him as "one very faithful servant of my Lorde name Mr. Barefoote". The word servant implied faithful follower and admirer of the Lord Proprietary, as he was addressed as "Mr.", applied only to the gentry. Another part of Father White's journal referred to the twelve deaths "among whom two Catholics Nicholas Fairfax and James Barefoote caused great regret with us all".

JOHN BAXTER, ESQ.

John Baxter, Esq. was one of the Gentlemen of Fashion referred to by Lord Baltimore. He seemed to have engaged in trade as an importing merchant from the items in his inventory, consisting of clothing, at the time of his death. He died sometime before February 20, 1637/8, when Justinian Snow, who had been granted letters of administration on his estate, made an inventory and filed an account with the court.

He was married at the time of his death, for in the inventory is listed "lre to his wife wth a small silver seale". Another interesting notation was the payment of an indebtedness on May 4, 1639, to Thomas Cornwalys, the assignee of Thomas White, which had been "authorized by M[rs] Baxter".

Circumstances would lead to the conclusion that he was one of the Adventurers who had left his wife in England, or if she had made the initial voyage, she had returned home. If she had been in Maryland, letters of administration would have been issued to her, and no doubt "lre" was the abbreviation for "letter" which he had written to her during his last illness. In it he was returning the cherished family seal. There is no record of their children being in Maryland. The doctor who tended him in his last illness was "Mr. Wells surgeon". Ref: Archives, vol. 4, pp. 76, 104-105.

RALPH BEANE [BAYNE], GENT.

Ralph Beane was one of the fifteen "abled bodied men" transported by Governor Leonard Calvert in 1633, for whom he claimed land-rights in

NOTE: A Roger Baxter was on Kent as early as 1642, but no relationship can be established.

1641.[1] He was not referred to by Governor Calvert as a servant, yet a subsequent record establishes him as a redemptioner of some calibre. In spite of his service in payment perhaps for his passage money or a contract after his landing, he may be classed a scion of the English gentry, for although he made his mark at times, he also inscribed his name, was a property holder in England, and was of sufficient affluence to revisit his native land. Furthermore, his brother, Walter Bayne, was styled "Gent". as well as succeeding generations which intermarried with several prominent and distinguished Maryland families.[2] He ultimately became a Maryland landed proprietor and at his death he maintained a staff of servants. He was also the owner of a boat which imported wine and "hotwater" from Virginia.[3]

By 1637 as a planter and freeholder, he was domiciled in St. George's Hundred. In 1642 the Governor called an assembly of all freeholders which was the occasion of his attendance in person for the first time, and with him came his brother, Walter, who had recently arrived in the Province after having been in Virginia as early as 1637.[4]

On January 21, 1639/40, he assigned his rights and interest in 50 acres of land granted for service to Thomas Gerard, Esq. The land was described as lying on the north shore of Gerard's Creek and lately in the occupation of John Hilliard and William Broughe.[5]

On August 30, 1649, under the signature of Governor William Stone he was granted 1,500 acres of land on the north side of the Potomac River bordering Herring and St. George's Creeks and adjoining the land of John Pritchard. Seven hundred acres were by assignment from Leonard Calvert and the other acreage was for the transporting of himself and five abled men into the Province between 1640 and 1648, an additional 50 acres due for his service, and also 150 acres due to his brother, Walter Beane, for importing himself and wife into the Province between the aforesaid years.[*] This tract or plantation of 1,500 acres was at "Piney Point commonly called Capt Evelin's or Peter Draper's Plantation".[6]

He returned to England sometime before 1653, for in that year John Hallowes made a deposition in court stating that "before Raph Beane went to England I did pay unto the aforesaid Ralph Beane". Upon one of his trips to England, he probably married, for it is doubtful whether he was of nuptial status in 1633 upon his initial arrival in Maryland.

After a resident of 21 years in the Province he died testate, but apparently leaving no descendants in Maryland. His will, dated November 12, 1654, was probated in St. Mary's County on April 24, 1655. He bequeathed his "Daughter Sarah Bean 140 lbs. of beaver and 20 Hhds of Tobacco to be sent home this present year. . . . if freight be to be had and 20 hhds of

Tobacco more the year following. . . . if my beloved brother Walter Beane goeth for England this present year and arrive safe home than my desire is that he should dispose of the Tobb & beaver for the use of my daughter. . . . discharge my beloved brother from all further debts in England". To his wife, Elizabeth, he left all the estate in her possession in England, and his friends, George Corye Smith living at the banks side in Southwarke and Joseph Ward living in St. Thomas near the Signe of the White Harte, were to be the overseers of his estate until his daughter, Sarah, came of age.[7]

From the tone of his will he, not unlike most Maryland colonists, regarded England as his permanent home. His brother, Walter, who was apparently younger, remained in Maryland and left many descendants, some of whom adopted the spelling of Bayne. There is no record of Ralph's daughter coming to Maryland.

His widow married secondly "John Tonge, of the Parish of St. Thomas Southwarke in the County of Surry Cityzen & merchant Taylor of London" who on August 9, 1658, with his wife, Elizabeth, gave their receipt to "Walter Beane of the same pish & County afforesaid for fourscore and Tenn pounds of good & lawful mony of England being the full sume of the psonall estate of Ralph Beane late husband of the abovesaid Elizabeth Deceased which he had & was possessed of in Virginia which said Sume the said Ralph Beane did give by his last will and Testamt unto his Daughter Sarah Beane".[8]

Sources: 1. Liber 1, folio 121; 2. Test. Proc. Liber 2, folio 301; 3. Archives, vol. 3, p. 177; 4. Nugent's Cavalier & Pioneers, p. 62; 5. Liber 1, folio 49; 6. Liber ABH, folio 6; 7. Wills, Liber 1, folio 60; 8. Archives, vol. 65, p. 181.

THOMAS BECKWITH

Nothing further is known about Thomas Beckwith other than he was transported in 1633 by Captain Thomas Cornwalys as a servant.

ANAN BENHAM

Anan Benham was brought in as a servant of Thomas Greene, Esq., but had completed his indentureship by the Assembly of 1637/8, for as Annum Benum, a planter of Mattapanient, he delivered his proxy to Governor Calvert. On February 14, 1638/9, he voted in Mattapanient Hundred for a delegate to the next Assembly. He was frequently sued at the Provincial Court for debt, his creditors being Captain Thomas Cornwalys and the estates of James Hitches and Justinian Snow. The last reference for him among the archives was on May 3, 1643, when Captain Cornwalys received judgement of 1,630 lbs. tob. He probably died after that date.

Sources: Liber ABH, folio 6; Liber 1, folio 17, Land Office; Archives, vol. 1, p. 4.

HENRY BISHOP

Henry Bishop was one of the Adventurers who came in at the expense of Father White and whose land-rights were later assigned to Ferdinando

Map of Ferryland made by Fitzhugh in 1693, showing the Calvert Mansion and the Various Houses of the settlement along the Moor. Taken from original copy in British Museum

*Tower of the Roman Catholic Church at Ferryland facing the site of the
Calvert Mansion. In the vestible are the armorial bearings of the Calvert Family*

Foundation of the Calvert Mansion at Ferryland at the time some archaelogical work was being conducted. Photograph taken by the author upon his visit to Newfoundland in 1932

One of the four sacars which protected the adventurers on the Voyage. Retrieved from the St. Mary's River. Now on the grounds of the State House at Annapolis.

Ark and Dove Memorial at Cowes, Isle of Wight

Pulton and Thomas Copley. On August 16, 1650, Thomas Copley, Esq., filed his claims for a number of assignees among whom was Henry Bishop.* Through the influence of Father White, Henry Bishop perhaps joined him in the settlement on the south bank of the Patuxent, later to be erected into Mattapanient Hundred.

He was of the upper yeomanry or perhaps lower gentry, and although unschooled in letters, making H B as his mark, he seemed to have possessed a certain amount of leadership, both legislature and military, and was not only selected by Governor Calvert the commander of the fort in his hundred (presumably on the north shore of the Patuxent), but was elected by his fellow planters to represent them at several assemblies. He was undoubtedly a member of the Church of Rome. He was furthermore among those who seated first on the other side of the Patuxent and who became so conscious of their settlement that they were anxious to have it recognized as St. Leonard's Hundred.

At the second Assembly of January 1637/8, Richard Garnett [Gardiner], of St. Richard's Manor, held his proxy, but on February 14, 1638/9, the freeholders of Mattapanient Hundred chose him their burgess, and at that time he was addressed as Mr. Bishop, but on all other occasions he was styled merely as Henry Bishop.

On July 18, 1642, Richard Garnett Sr. made returns to the Lower House and reported the election of Henry Bishop to represent "Conception alias Mattapanient Hundred". At the Assembly he petitioned the body against the Patuxent Indians killing his swine. At the same Assembly in August he petitioned that as a Burgess for Mattapanient, he be allowed 690 lbs. tob.—600 lbs. for 15 days of attendance, 80 lbs. for a clerk, and 10 lbs. for a drummer.[2]

On August 25, 1642, Leonard Calvert gave him permission to allow all inhabitants of his "division" to send troops only upon alarm and that they were to "repair without any delay to your ffort" and to protect the fort with his strength.

At the Assembly of September 1642, his proxy was given to Francis Posie, the progenitor of the Posey family of Southern Maryland. He was held in esteem by Cecilius, Lord Baltimore, who on July 13, 1640, appointed his trusty friend Henry Bishop to "attach any person trading unlawfully with the Indians and to hold them in custody".

He and Joseph Edlow testified in court during 1637 that John Bryant,

---

* Owing to the poor script of the 17th century, when Liber A, B, & H were recopied many years ago, the copyist mistook "Bishop" for "Briscoe". Studying the several official records of the assignment, it is quite obvious that Henry Bishop recorded in Liber 1, folio 37 and Henry Briscoe recorded in Liber ABH, folio 65 are one and the same person. This incorrect transcription has led to the false assumption that a Henry Briscoe was among the Adventurers. The extant early records of Maryland present no circumstantial evidence, inference or proof of an Adventurer, gentleman or servant, on the Ark and the Dove bearing the name of Briscoe or Biscoe.

a fellow passenger of Bishop on the Ark, met his death by the falling of a tree on Bryant's plantation at Mattapanient.[3] In 1640 he and Simon Demibiel were made the executors of the estate of Leonard Leonardson who styled himself prematurely as of St. Leonard's Hundred. In January 1643/4, he with others was summoned to court to testify against the "treasonable and pyraticall offences" of Richard Ingle, Mariner.[4]

His life in the Province extended for 25 years, but he lived presumably the life of a bachelor throughout, as the meager inventory of his personal estate, appraised at only 975 lbs. tob. would indicate the household of a single man. On August 18, 1658, William Stiles, of New Towne Hundred, proved himself a creditor to the estate of Henry Bishop "who deceased on monday 16th of the present month of August inteste" and was accordingly granted letters of administration.[5]

Sources: 1. Liber ABH, folio 65; Liber 4, folio 258; 2. Archives, vol. 1, p. 146; 3. Archives, vol. 4, p. 10; 4. Archives, vol. 4, p. 247; 5. Testamentary Proceedings, Liber IB, folio 34.

JOHN BOLLES, GENT.

John Bolles [Bowles], Gent. was the secretary or personal agent whom Cecilius, Lord Baltimore, sent to accompany the Adventurers to Maryland in 1633. In Baltimore's instructions to his brother and the Commissioners, he was referred to as "His Lordship's Secretary John Bolles" and he was delegated to read to the Adventurers when they assembled on shore the letters patent and other rights of the individuals. On July 10, 1634, he witnessed the last will and testament of George Calvert, Esq., and no doubt wrote the instrument. On August 29, 1636, Cecilius, Lord Baltimore, authorized a warrant for 1,000 acres of land to be lay out for him, apparently as a gift inasmuch as it was not stated for the financing of any adventurers. The destruction of some of the early land records precludes further history of this warrant which was probably assigned. No further record can be found relative to him among the archives.

Source: Fund Pub. no. 28, p. 136; Calvert Papers, Md. Hist. Soc.

RICHARD BRADLEY

Richard Bradley was one of the fifteen able-bodied men brought into the Province by Governor Leonard Calvert, Esq., in 1633. He was one of the creditors of the estate of William Smith, deceased, in 1635. He died early in 1638/9, for Thomas Franklin returned an inventory of his estate on March 7, 1638/9, including working tools, fowling piece, clothing, linen, and one Bible. It can definitely be accepted that he was unmarried and left no issue.

Sources: Liber 1, folio 121; Wills, Liber 3, folio 114; Archives vol. 4, p. 32.

JOHN BRIANT

Ferdinando Pulton in 1639 claimed land-rights by assignment from Father White for importing John Briant [Bryant] in 1634.[1] He became a planter of Mattapanient Hundred, but was killed by the fall of a tree in 1637.

The administration of his estate was granted to Richard Garnett Sr., as the greatest creditor, and the personal estate was not too negligible for that day. The appraisement was 1,728 lbs. tob . Among the items were "1 cock & 1 henne", so there is evidence of poultry in the colony at that time.[2]

He left a widow whose Christian name is unknown, inasmuch as in 1639 the "widdow Briant" received 40 lbs. tob. from the estate of Mr. Egerton as a debt owing to her, and likewise in 1640 the "widdow Bryant" received 10 lbs. tob. from the estate of Michael Lums.[3] No further reference can be found for the Widow Bryant who no doubt soon acquired a second husband.

In 1647 a Matthias Briant is willed a suit of clothes by Robert Tuttley, of New Towne, and in the same year he sued James Walker for 300 lbs. tob. and one "barrell of Corne dew for wages & hyre".[4]

No claims were ever made for bringing in a Matthias Briant, so there are reasons to conclude that Matthias Briant was an orphan of John Briant, the Adventurer. In 1647 he would have been at least 10 years of age, and in that day an orphaned boy was perfectly capable of inheriting clothing from a benefactor and older man. Furthermore, a boy of that day assumed responsibilities and was capable of service, especially if he were an orphan with no estate. No land grants were ever made to John Briant according to the extant records.

In 1648 as Mattias Bryant, he reported to the court that at Wicocomoco an Indian killed a swine belonging to Mr. Thompson. Later he seemed to have dropped the final t from his name, for in 1650 he appeared at court in behalf of Thomas Thomas and grants were made in the name of Matthias Brian [Bryan]. In 1651 he made his mark to an instrument as Matthias Bryan.[5]

In 1651 by a warrant assigned to him by Robert Clark, he was granted "Scotland" of 100 acres in St. Mary's County,[6] and in the same year he patented "Bryan" of 100 acres, lying on the east side of St. Clement's Bay. In 1656 he and Francis Pope were granted jointly "Brian's Clifts" in Charles County by assignment of a warrant from John Lewger Sr.[7]

At court in 1659 he swore that for two summers Thomas Cole "dyetted att the howse of David Thomas lately deceased" and that Cole considered Thomas' house as his home.[8]

Sources: 1. Liber 1, folio 37, Land Office; 2. Archives, vol. 4, pp. 30-31; 3. Archives, vol. 4, pp. 107, 113; 4. Archives, vol. 4, pp. 317, 356; 5. Archives, vol. 10, p. 140; 6. Liber ABH, folio 171; Rent Rolls 1-2, folio 41; 7. Liber ABH, folio 437; 8. Archives, vol. 41, p. 351.

WILLIAM BROWN

While the difficulty of proving the genealogical history of a member of the Brown family is manifestedly admitted, all factors indicate that William Brown who came in the Ark as a servant of Captain Thomas Cornwalys lived until 1666, and left issue.* A very good chronological history of William Brown can be sketched almost year by year from 1641, when he was entitled to a voice in the Assembly as a freeholder.[1]

Inasmuch as he deposed to be 20 years of age and upward in 1643, making his birth year about 1623, he was around 10 years of age when his parents or guardian indentured him to Captain Cornwalys. It can therefore be explained why he was not present at the 1637 Assembly, but in 1641 he would have just about attained the age of 18—presumably the majority at that time for suffrage.

His early seat was in St. Michael's Hundred, when in 1642 he was assessed 23 lbs. tob. In that year failing to appear at the Assembly of all freeholders, he was amerced 20 lbs. tob., thereby he immediately gave his proxy to Captain Cornwalys.†

He and John Thimbelly formed a partnership, and in 1648/9, John Warren sued them for 1,000 lbs. tob. At the same court Brown was sued by John Hollis for 200 lbs. tob. At this time Brown and Thimbelly engaged George Manners as their attorney to defend them at court.[2]

On January 28, 1649/50, the tract "Honest Tom's Inheritance" was surveyed for him and John Thimbelly. On September 24, 1650, by warrant a plantation of 300 acres was granted them—100 acres in right of their service and 200 acres for transporting two man-servants—John Perfitt about 7 years since and John Tobby 2 years since. The Surveyor General was instructed to lay out a plantation of 300 acres on the Potomac River or some branch or creek not formerly taken up.[3]

In 1650 William Brown received from the estate of Peter Mackrell upon which John Thimbelly administered 185 lbs. tob., and in the same year he leased a plantation from Thomas Willis and after certain payments he was to enjoy the plantation as "his lawful assigne".[4]

During the turbulent years of the Maryland Commonwealth under the Puritans the names of Brown and his partner are missing from the archives. It is understood, however, for being Roman Catholics they, like the Anglicans, were disenfranchised. When William Brown regained the franchise, there are a number of references of his serving on the jury from 1659 to 1661.

---

* The list of early settlers shows no other William Brown transported to Maryland prior to 1665, when in that year a William Brown is declared to be the son of Gabriel Brown.

† The fact that Captain Cornwalys, his former master, was given his proxy is further contributing evidence, that this William Brown was the former servant of Cornwalys. Further proof exists that the William Brown who died in 1666 was alive in 1642 and transported a servant in that year.

On March 5, 1657/8, "Brown's Woodhouse", of 50 acres, was surveyed for him at the head of Hood's Creek near John Medley's land; this he sold the same year to John Lucas.[5]

His partner and friend, John Thimbley [Thimbelly] died testate and without issue in St. Mary's County in 1659. A legacy was left to the Roman Catholic Church, to John Brown, and to Margaret, the wife of William Brown. All land in Maryland was devised to his goddaughter, Mary Brown. William Brown and John Shirtcliffe were named as executors.[6]

Children of William and Margaret Brown

1. John Brown. *q.v.*
2. Mary Brown married Thomas Kerbley; line extinct.

Being styled a planter of Bretton Bay, in January 1663/4, he conveyed to John Reddmann, of Virginia, 550 acres of land lying at the head of the bay, a portion of which had purchased from John Medley on which stood a mill.[7]

He drew up his last will and testament on February 27, 1665, it being probated at court in St. Mary's County on July 26, 1666. He mentioned no land, but bequeathed the personal estate equally to his two children, John and Mary Brown. Apparently his daughter was still under age, for the legacies willed her by her godfather, John Thimbleby (*sic*) were in his possession. The overseers, so named, were John Warren and Edward Clark, with Peter Roberts and George Shaw as the witnesses.[8] The personal estate which consisted principally of livestock was appraised at 5,610 lbs. tob. by William Tettersall and Peter Mills.

Sources: 1. Archives, vol. 1, p. 117; 2. Archives, vol. 4, pp. 478, 490, 491; vol. 10, p. 7; 3. Calvert Co. Rent Rolls, folio 28; Patents Liber ABH, folio 48; 4. Archives, vol. 10, pp. 43, 101; 5. Rent Rolls, folio 28; Archives, vol. 49, p. 573; 6. Wills, Liber 1, folio 80; 7. Archives, vol. 49, p. 572; 8. Wills, Liber 1, folio 257.

MATTHEW BURROWES

Matthew Burrowes, sometimes Burraws, was brought in at the costs and charges of Captain Thomas Cornwalys, for whom he filed land rights in 1640/1. No further record is available, so he was probably one of the early casualties or returned to England. Ref: Liber ABH, folio 94, Land Office.

GEORGE CALVERT, ESQ.

George Calvert, the third son and namesake of George, 1st Lord Baltimore, was one of the Gentlemen of Fashion who sailed on the Ark, but died within six months after the settlement at St. Mary's, so his rôle in the founding of the Province was cut short by an untimely death. On June 20, 1634, however, he, Lieut. Frederick Wintour and others from Maryland conferred with the King of the Patuxents, Capt. William Clayborne, John

Utie, and Capt. Samuel Mathews on matters involving the two colonies of Maryland and Virginia. It occurred in Maryland waters and is believed to be the first inter-colonial conference after the Adventurers left Virginia.

He was baptized July 18, 1613, at St. Martin's in the Fields, London, so was only 22 years of age at his death.* His will, dated St. Marie's July 10, 1634, was probated at London on January 19, 1634/5, being witnessed by John Boles, John Wells, Robert Vaughan and Cuthbert Fenwick. The money from his father's estate in the hands of Sir William Ashton, Knt. and Lord Cottington was to be disposed of as follows: £100 to his brother Cecil; £100 to his brother William Peasley, Esq.; £150 to his brother Leonard; £5 to his brother and sister Peasley to purchase golden crosses that they may wear in his memory. To his friend, Richard Gerard, he bequeathed all goods, merchandise, as "shall be brought into Virginia and Maryland for me for my use". The residuary was bequeathed to his brother Henry.

Leonard Calvert, Esq.

The entire early history of Maryland centered around the life of Leonard Calvert, Esq., the sixth child but second son of George, first Baron of Baltimore. Several Maryland historians, as mentioned elsewhere, have given credit to Captain Thomas Cornwalys as the principal stabilizing influence in the formative days of the Province and have penned Leonard Calvert as more or less a weak administrator holding office only by virtue of birth. There is a French saying, "Style is Man himself". When reading and analyzing the extant letters of Governor Calvert to his brother and also to his business partner, the self-expression is forceful, direct and certainly is not indicative of a character embodied with indecision and vacillation. He was only twenty-three when he embarked on the task of consummating his father's plans in the New World, but he had already been in Avalon and at Jamestown and knew the country and economic conditions and the varied problems needed to guide the colonists. He had difficult questions to solve and naturally sought council when important matters arose.

He is undoubtedly the "...... Caulford fil Mr. George" who was baptized on November 21, 1610, at the parish church of St. Martin's in the Fields, London, according to the rites of the Established Church of England. It was in this same church that the younger children of George Calvert were baptized, so it is only natural that his baptism likewise occurred there.

The one great mystifying element was his personal life. There is no

---

* Neil in his "Terra Maraie", pub. 1867, stated that George Calvert "is thought died in Virginia". It was probably due to a communication Governor Maverick, of Mass., wrote in October 1667, "That there has been a hurricane in Virginia, and it has said that Lord Baltimore's son had died". Ref: N. Y. Colonial Documents. Furthermore, Neil in his Founders of Maryland, pub. 1876, states that "George Calvert lived and died in Virginia". His death most assuredly occurred in Maryland.

evidence of a marriage before sailing in November 1633 for Maryland, and he certainly led the life of a bachelor in Maryland for ten or more years until his return to England in April 1643, leaving his friend, Giles Brent, Esq., the Acting Governor.

He remained away from Maryland for about 17 months, and during that period in England, according to tradition, he begot two children— William and Anne. He returned to his post in Maryland and presumably left the infants in the care of a nurse. The mother or his consort did not accompany him.

It has generally been stated in print with absolutely no documentation that he married Anne, one of the many daughters of Richard Brent, of Stokes, Gloucestershire, and sister to Giles, Fulkes, Margaret, and Mary— all of whom came to Maryland. No proof of this marriage can be found. Although Mistress Anne Brent no doubt saw Governor Calvert during his visit to England, as the two families had been intimate before the settlement of Maryland, she continued to live a single life in England, and in 1651 was listed as a non-juror spinster.* A diligent search has been made in England for proof of his marriage, or the mother of his children, but with failure each time.†

Although baptized in the Established Church, Leonard Calvert had followed his father upon his affiliation with the Church of Rome. At the time of his visit in England, the Puritans were becoming ever stronger in power and had directed many harsh and unreasonable laws. The Roman Catholic Church was outlawed and priests of that church were forbidden to perform the major and minor sacraments of their faith. If a marriage ceremony was performed, it was certainly solemnized in secrecy, and thus no public record is available. The mention of a wife at no time appears in the Calvert Papers, or among the Archives of Maryland. If his children figured as heirs in the wills or estates of their maternal parent, the matter has not come to light, so their maternity remains an unsolved question.

When Leonard Calvert was ill and realized that his end was near, he made no mention whatsoever of his two children or their mother. With him were Mistress Margaret Brent, his friend Thomas Greene, Francis Ankatill the priest, and Madam Mary Beane. Thomas Greene testified in court that Leonard Calvert lying on his death bed about six hours before his passing, "directed his speech to Mistress Brent" and said "I make you my sole Executrix. Take all and pay all". He then requested every one to leave the room except Mistress Brent with whom he conferred privately for some time. Thomas Greene returned to the room, then he bequeathed

---

* See Mrs. Russell Hastings' notes in Md. Hist. Vol. 22, p. 307.

† The author twice on personal trips to England has searched English records, as well as others, but with no avail.

his cloth suit to his servant, Richard Willan,‡ his black suit to his servant, James Lindsay, and his linen between them. To his godson, Leonard Greene, he bequeathed a mare colt, and "the first mare colt that shall fall within the year or if none falleth within this yeare then the first mare colt that shall hereafter fall unto Mrs. Temperance Tippett, of Virginia".

Governor Calvert furthermore upon his death bed appointed Thomas Greene to succeed him as Proprietary Governor. It was the case of "The King is dead. Long live the King", for there was much toasting and celebrating the next day for the new Governor was the choice of the conservatives and the court party.

The interment in all likelihood occurred at St. Mary's City, though the place where his remains repose is now unknown. Being a devout Roman Catholic, he was without a doubt buried in the consecrated ground or interred in the town's parish Church—most likely the latter, for peers and prominent men of State were usually buried in Churches or Cathedrals.

His nuncupative will was proved at court on June 14, 1647. The inventory was made by Captain John Price, Nicholas Causin, and Robert Percy, and filed at court on June 30, 1647. Among the items listed were a large house located at Piney Neck, three manors, a large frame house with 100 acres of townland, and thirteen books.

Only personalty could be bequeathed by a nuncupative will, but the amazing Amazon, Mistress Margaret Brent, exercised literally her prerogatives in the Governor's last words when he said "take all", and immediately possession was taken of the Governor's mansion in St. Mary's City. She furthermore assumed feudal rights on his three baronial manors and installed in some manner her sister, Mistress Mary, on St. Gabriel's Manor who functioned as Lady of the Manor with all baronial grace and privileges. Her appearance before the first Assembly called by Governor Greene demanding a seat, something totally unheard of for a woman of that period, has been widely popularized, but her aggressiveness was soon thwarted, for the stalwarts of that day wanted no petticoat rule outside of their private dwellings.

It is sometime wondered if Mistress Margaret were aware that Governor Calvert had left a legal male heir to his landed estate and a daughter who was entitled to her filial share of the personalty. His death occurred a little more than three years after his return from England, and in his closing hours he expressed no concern or affections for his children or

‡ Willan was his personal secretary, and while he was styled servant in the will, he later bore the title of "Gent." He was granted seigniory on Snow Hill Manor, was later Burgess and High Sheriff for St. Mary's County, and fought under the Proprietary Standard at the battle of the Severn. He had accompanied Leonard Calvert to Virginia during Ingle's Rebellion, and in 1650 he claimed "One hundred Acres of Land more for Transporting himself again into this Province about 4 years Since in Company with Leonard Calvert, Esqr. the late Governor and as an Assistant to him in regainning of the Province". Ref: Liber ABH, folio 46, Land Office.

wife nor provided for them in any manner—yet Margaret did not reveal the private conference while the others were out of the room. If she did have knowledge of his children, no evidence is forthcoming from the extant archives, letters and other documents of that period.

Governor's Fields, the townland and residence of Governor Calvert, had in 1641 been assigned to Nathaniel Pope who reconveyed it to Calvert by bargain and sale on January 4, 1646/7. The mansion on Governor's Fields was later occupied by Governor William Stone, the third Proprietary Governor, who had continued to occupy it long after his tenure of office whenever he was not residing at his country manorial estate on the Avon in Charles County.

Some fourteen years after the death of Leonard Calvert or in or about 1661 appeared in Maryland a youth of not more than 18 years of age who declared himself to be William Calvert, Esq., the son and heir of Leonard Calvert. From subsequent law suits it is implied that Cecilius, Lord Baltimore, and uncle of the orphan had been his guardian—thus indicating that he was raised in England.

At that time Mistress Margaret Brent had retired from the Maryland scene and in her old age was residing at her plantation in Westmoreland County, Virginia. Former Governor Stone had passed on, but in 1660 he had willed Governor's Fields to his relict, Madam Verlinda Stone, who was in possession at the time young Calvert made his dramatic entrance into the Province. Thomas Stone, Esq., the son and heir, claimed contingency in the property, while Madam Stone* who is sometime thought to be his step-mother, claimed her dower rights.

William Calvert through Thomas Manning, the Attorney-General of the Province, instituted court action for the possession of his father's landed estate. It was stated in the bill of complaint "that in the absence of the said heire William Stone, late Governor of this Province, did unto the said land unlawfully enter". The Attorney-General furthermore stated that "Leonard Calvert died seized and so the land unto William Calvert sonne and heire unto the said Leonard Calvert did descend".

Mistress Margaret Brent, then aged 60, came forth from her retirement and stated in a deposition that "I never did make any conveyance of the house and land of St. Mary's which formerly was Leonard Calvert, Esq. to Captain William Stone and that neighter he nor the heirs of said William Stone hath any right or title".[1] The jury recognized the paternity

---

* It is generally stated that Verlinda (born Verlinda Graves and not Verlinda Cotton) was the mother of all his children, but among the family papers of Thomas Stone, the Signer, in possession of Miss Mary Vivian Daniel, of Paris, Texas, a descendant of the Signer (gr-gr-grandson of the Governor) it is recorded that William Stone was twice married, his first wife being a Miss Fowke. It is of interest that when Madam Verlinda Stone died in 1675, she named only two children in her will—the youngest son, John, then a minor, and a daughter, Madam Thomas-Doyne. Ref: Wills, Liber 2, folio 364.

of William Calvert and the land was restored to him after dispossession by the Stones.

About two years after the arrival of William Calvert, the guardians of his sister, Anne, sent her to Maryland in company with two personal maids. On September 6, 1663, the Hon. Charles Calvert writing to his father, Cecilius, Lord Baltimore, said, "My Cozen Wm sister arrived her and is now att my house and has the care of my household affaires, as yett noe good match does prsent, but I hope in a short time she may find one to her own content & y^{rs} Lopps desire, I shall further what I can towards it, I have acquainted her Brother what y^r Lopp expect—he should doe for her, but in case he does not, or be not in a Condicon to doe much I shall take care she shall not want as long as she remains wth me. There came wth her two maids one to wait upon her & the other to my selfe".[2]

She did not go to the home of her brother who by this time perhaps was courting Elizabeth, the eldest daughter of the late Governor Stone whose family he ejected from Governor's Fields. From letters of Charles Calvert to his father one can sense an indifference between the brother and sister, and also some report was made to Lord Baltimore about the treatment Anne received at the home of her cousin Charles. Writing to his father, Charles Calvert stated "I received y^r Lopps letter of the 8th of Sept: & wonder very much that some should inform my Cousen Wm Calverts sister that I had noe kindness for her when I can safely say I never had any such thoughts & can say as much of Her Brother. I hope my Carriage to her & the Care I shall take to see her want for nothing will give her reason to think better on me. The Maid that came wth her waits upon her & shall remaine wth her according to y^{rs} Lopps comands". In the same letter he stated "I have Thirty to provide victualls for, wch does putt me to some care & trouble besides the expence wch is the best".[3]

It is not known how long she waited for that brilliant match to materialize or how difficult it was for her cousin to maneuver in order to get her off his hands, but it is quite obvious that she was sent to Maryland to acquire a husband. It may have taken some time to find the right suitor, Colonel Baker Brooke, Esq., but as the wealthy Widow Brooke she lost no time in acquiring a second husband, and perhaps age brought forth more charm, for she acquired in all three husbands.

Her first husband was Colonel Baker Brooke, Esq., fully 33 years of age at the time and the son and heir of Robert Brooke, Esq., of Brooke Place Manor, Calvert County, one time an ordained clergyman of the Church of England. Her second husband was Henry Brent, a kinsman of the astonishing Mistress Margaret Brent, and her third was Richard Marsham, Gent., who survived her. Issue resulted, however, only from the first marriage.

NOTE: For the issue of Anne (Calvert) Brooke, see the Maryland Historical Magazine, vol. 1, and for the issue of William Calvert, Esq., see, "Descendants of Virginia Calverts", by Ella Foy O'Gorman, pub. 1947.

Sources: 1. Judgments, Liber 28, folio 7, Hall of Records; 2. Fund Pub. no. 28, p. 244; 3. Fund Pub. no. 28, pp. 246-247.

CHRISTOPHER CARNELL

Christopher Carnell [Carnoll, Carnot] was apparently a youth in his teens at the time of his settlement in Maryland. And the fact that Thomas Copley, Esq., proved land-rights for his importation "anno 1634" may indicate that he was not actually an Adventurer on the Ark and the Dove, but may have arrived in another ship which brought colonists after the initial settlement.[1]

He can best be placed as a member of the yeomanry, unschooled in letters, and he seemed to have been always in debt and being sued at the Provincial Court. He was definitely an Anglican and was among those who in 1638 was summoned to testify against William Lewis, of St. Inigoes, who allegedly forbade the reading of non-Catholic sermons by his servants.[2] If he served Father White or Thomas Copley in any capacity, he was a freeholder by 1641, being at that time a resident of St. Mary's Hundred, and attended the General Assembly at its opening day of March 23, 1641/2. At the Assembly convened on September 5, 1642, Thomas Greene, Esq., held his proxy.[3]

On March 24, 1642/3, he demanded at court 400 lbs. tob. from Francis Posie "due by bargain for a plantation" which may indicate that he sold a plantation to Poise and was demanding payment or he may have paid 400 lbs. tob. for plantation and Posie had failed to make delivery.

Sometime after June 1644, when at the request of James Neale, Esq., he swore that John Tailor had sold a gelt to Neale which was delivered at Snowhill. He apparently left the Province and was gone perhaps about two years which coincides with the plundering. On November 14, 1649, he proved his rights to 100 acres of land for his emigration into the Province during 1646.[4] By October 8, 1646, Robert Clark, Surveyor, had already laid out a parcel of 100 acres for him on the south side of Popular Hill Creek. This tract became known as "Thomas Peteets" which he and John Nevill for 1400 lbs. tob. sold or leased to Richard Bennett "bounded on the south side of Popular Hill Creek and a swamp that lies between the plantation of the said John Nevill and the plantation of the said Richard Bennett". The earliest rent roll shows that 100 acres of "Thomas Peteets Freehould" was surveyed for Carnell on July 14, 1647, and 50 acres for John Nevill.

In 1655 he leased from James Walker, of Wicomico, land adjoining Thomas Mitchell for "yearly four shillings and 2 bbl. of good sound corne to be delivered at the dwelling house of the said Walker". By 1659 he was a tenant of Thomas Gerard, on St. Clement's Manor, when it was shown that the Wicomico Indians had stolen his "cannowe".

When he reentered the Province in 1646, he made no claims for the transportation of a wife, but he probably married after that date some maiden of the yeomanry who predeceased him. At the time of his death he was domiciled in New Towne Hundred, where his will was drawn up on November 25, 1661. He bequeathed his entire estate real and personal to his friend, John Pyper, in trust for his child, Elizabeth Carnell, and Pyper was "not to dispose of her to any, to make her a servant but to dispose of her as he the said John Pyper doth think fitt, or as his own daughter". In the event that Pyper should die during her minority, then his loving friend, John Gouldsmith, was to act. On March 17, 1661/2, John Gouldsmith requested letters of administration, and with John Norman entered into recognizance with the Lord Proprietary to the value of 8000 lbs. tob. At a court held in Charles County on October 1, 1662, Gouldsmith stated that the estate of Christopher Carnell owed him 619 lbs. tob. "by account and also for funeral charges" and demanded payment of John Piper.[5]

John Piper was a tenant of the Gerards on Basford Manor and died intestate in 1674, leaving a widow but no children named in his will. Several bequests were made to his god-children but none could be identified as Elizabeth Carnell. John Gouldsmith died testate in 1683 and made no bequests except to members of his family.

No further record can be found for the orphan Elizabeth. If she matured, she probably found a mate in the vicinity, and we know of no other descendant of this Adventurer of 1634.

Sources: 1. Archives, vol. 2, p. 258; 2. Archives, vol. 4, p. 37; 3. Archives, vol. 1, pp. 120, 176; 4. Land Office, Liber 1, folio 528; 5. Archives, vol. 53, p. 253.

Thomas Charinton

Thomas Charinton was transported into the Province by the two Wintour brothers who assigned their rights to Ferdinand Pulton. He was probably not a servant, if so, no mention was made of it at the time Pulton claimed land rights. In 1636 he cleared 50 acres of land in St. George's Hundred, for on October 4, 1640, he "prayeth to have granted him 50 acres of land which he hath in part cleared and built upon with the Privity and at the appointment of His Lorps Lt. Gen. in the year 1636". His claim was granted and he assigned his warrant to Nicholas Cossin [Causine] ffrenchman.

He settled first in St. George's Hundred, where in 1637 there is a record of his signature. In January 1637/8, at the Second Assembly he gave his proxy to Captain Robert Evelyn. He was also closely associated with the Manor of Evelynton under the lordship of Captain Evelyn and was one of the early bailiffs. In 1641 he attended the assembly in person.

He later settled in Mattapanient Hundred, where on August 3, 1642, letters of administration on his estate were granted to Captain Thomas Cornwalys. The inventory was taken on August 23, following, and indicated a small estate and definitely the estate of an unmarried man. Among the items was one "black dogge". No land grants are on record in the Land Office.

Sources: Liber ABH, folio 66; Liber 1, folio 38; Liber 2, folio 38; Archives vol. 1, p. 116; Archives, vol. 4, pp. 71, 95; Fund Publication no. 9, p. 101; Md. Hist. Mag., vol. 6, pp. 69-70.

Note: The Md. Hist. Magazine, vol. 5, p. 268, in publishing the land rights of Pulton incorrectly printed his name as Thomas Harrington instead of Thomas Charinton. A John Harrington emigrated in 1635. Ref: Liber ABH, folio 93.

RICHARD COLE

Richard Cole, one of the transportees of John Sanders, Esq., whose rights had been assigned to Father White, was of sufficient social status to attend the General Assembly of 1638/9, as a freeholder, then being a resident of St. George's Hundred.[1] He was literate. He likewise attended the Assembly of 1641, but in September 1642, he sent a proxy.[2] At the trial or suit between Henry Brookes and Nicholas Causine, he stated in court on October 12, 1650, that four or five years ago the gun exhibited in court was taken by Governor Calvert, then deceased, from Henry Brookes upon promise to re-deliver the gun to Brookes upon his return from Kent.[3] In 1649 he sued John Halfhead, one of his fellow passengers on the Ark, and on November 8, 1653, he witnessed the bill of sale of Paul Sympson, and on November 19, 1655, he witnessed the assignment of the Irish lad, John Poore, to John Lawson.[4] He was perhaps the Richard Cole who in 1660 at the Provincial Court through his attorney, John Abbington, demanded writ to arrest Richard True, a ship carpenter, for debts.[5]

No further record of Richard Cole has been found, according to this research. There were several Cole [Coale] families in St. Mary's County at an early date. It does not seem reasonable for him to be the father of William Coale, of St. Mary's County, St. Jerome's Manor, who in 1659 had a married daughter, Sara, the wife of Elias Beach, whose son was killed on an expedition to the Whorekill. The family of Ensign Robert Cole, Gent., is well established, and no connection can be established between the Adventurer of 1633 and Ensign Cole.

Sources: 1. Archives, vol. 1, p. 30; 2. Archives, vol. 1, pp. 104, 168, 172; 3. Archives, vol. 10, p. 40; 4. Archives, vol. 10, pp. 379, 568; 5. Archives, vol. 41, p. 399.

JOHN COOK

Circumstantial evidence places John Cook, a servant of Jerome Hawley, as one of his retainers of 1633/4, as no record of the transportees of Hawley is extant. John Cook had not completed his four years of service at his master's death in 1638, but he had attained his freedom by May 24, 1639, when he was a debtor of the estate of Justinian Snow. No further reference for him among the Archives can be identified.*

THOMAS COOPER

Thomas Cooper was brought in as a retainer of Thomas Greene, Esq. No record is found of his attending the early Assemblies, so probably he remained under the indentureship of Thomas Greene beyond the usual statutory four years, owing to his youth. He died intestate and undoubtedly without issue, when on August 5, 1640, Robert Clark was ordered by the court to sell his "goods" at an outcry. Numerous settlers, 57 of them, bearing the name of Cooper arrived in the Province prior to 1687 and the

---

* In 1636 Captain Cornwalys transported Daniel Clocker and a John Cook, and the latter can later be satisfactorily traced in St. Mary's County. Prior to 1687 nine John Cooks arrived in Maryland.

progenitors of the later Cooper families of Southern Maryland can be traced to one or two of these colonists.

CAPTAIN THOMAS CORNWALYS, ESQ.

Few on the Ark and the Dove could claim better background than Captain Thomas Cornwalys, Esq., of London and Burnham Thorpe, County Norfolk, where he and his family were registered in the Heralds' Visitation. On the initial voyage of the Ark, he financed the passage of twelve redemptioners, all of various degrees of service, and then en route he persuaded four other prospective settlers in Virginia to accompany him as indentures—one being Cuthbert Fenwick, Gent., who proved invaluable to him as his secretary, steward, and attorney.[1]

He and Jerome Hawley were appointed Commissioners to Governor Calvert on the voyage and immediately were made Councilors during the first few days after landing. He was one of the principal advisers to the Calverts and his extant letters to Lord Baltimore give much insight into the early workings of the Province. His intrigue with Richard Ingle lessened some of his glory, but he paid up for it later by imprisonment upon his return to England.

He was staunch in his adherence to the Roman Catholic Church and writing on April 6, 1638, to His Lordship he stated that he would "rather Sacrifice myself . . . then Consent toe anything that may not stand with the Good Consiens [conscience] of A Real Catholick".[2]

As an investor in the stock company which was formed prior to the sailing of the Ark, he held a share or two and thus was engaged in not only trade with the Indians in beaver and corn, but as a merchant he sold essentials to the early settlers by imports from England and the Continent. He is credited with the construction of the now extant Manor House outside of St. Mary's City generally accepted with being the oldest house now standing in Maryland. He was granted seigniory on a number of manors over which he held baronial courts, but regrettably the proceedings of those historic sessions have not come down to posterity.

Although he has been cannonized for his integrity and staunch Roman Catholicism, on occasions he "got mixed up" too often with the Arch Villian Richard Ingle even after he had experienced the gloom of a London prison at the instigation of Ingle. On September 8, 1647, after his release from prison and his loss during the plundering period, Cornwalys became Ingle's attorney which peculiarly was recorded at a Virginia court rather than Maryland. According to Record Book, Northumberland Co., Liber 14, folio 21, or Fleet's Virginia Colonial Abstracts, vol. 12, p. 100, "Richard Ingle of Wappting in the County of Middlesex, Maryner" granted power of attorney to "Thomas Cornwallis, Gent.", to collect all debts. The document was dated "in the three and twentieth yeare of the reigne of our Sovereign Lord King Charles" and was witnessed by William Eltonhead, of Eltonhead Manor, ffra. Manestry and John Brown.

He was one of the greatest importers of settlers for the Province, and on February 1, 1652/3, he listed all of his servants and transportees since 1633, and declared that he was entitled to 19,300 acres of land "To there is due in all for these besides divers forgotten by the loss of Books and Indentures in the time of plunder". Included were his land-rights for his re-entry into the Province in 1651 after a trip to England.

Robert Vaughan and he were the principal military officers of the Province in those formative years, though his title as captain, seemed to have been more honourary than functional, yet soon after his return from England in 1642/3, he commanded an expedition against the warlike Susquehanna Indians.[3]

It is not known whether Madam Cornwalys, who was born Penelope Wiseman, accompanied him on that historic voyage in 1633 or later joined him. There is evidence that she was in England in 1638, for Cornwalys writing to Lord Baltimore on April 6, of that year, stated "my wives [wife's] tooe probably indisposition desenable her from manageing my affaires there",[4] yet in the same letter he wrote that he was constructing a house "for the mayntayneing of myself and family". She was certainly in Maryland at one time or another and the chatelaine of his manor house on Cornwalys' Crosse. From circumstances it is apparent that some of his children were born in Maryland.

In 1658 he was granted "Planter's Paradise", of 1000 acres in Baltimore County, for the transportation in 1656 of 20 colonists—among whom were his wife, Penelope Cornwalys, and Robert Wiseman, presumably a kinsman of his wife.*

Captain Cornwalys became dissatisfied with affairs in the Province, though he seemed to have remained throughout the trying days of the Puritan domination, when he and all not pledging allegiance to the Puritans were disenfranchised. In 1659 he returned permanently to his ancestral seat in Norfolk, where he died.

His heirs retained their estates in Maryland long after their father's death, and it is possible that some of his sons actually revisited Maryland, if not, their agents kept in contact with them. In 1678, William Cornwallis, son and heir, complained that several persons had encroached upon land or boundaries of his deceased's father's plantation known as "Planter's Paradise", of 1000 acres on the west side of the north branch of Back River "to his great damage and humbly requested his Lordship to grant unto him a Warrent for the Resurvey thereof which was granted unto him". A resurvey therefore was ordered by the Land Office on February 18, 1678/9.[5]

For his descendants, see the Norfolk Visitations, Harleian Soc. Pub., vol. 85, p. 56.

---

* Robert Wiseman probably returned with Cornwalys in 1659, as he can not be further identified in the Province.

Sources: 1. Liber ABH, folio 244; 2. Fund Pub. no. 28, p. 172; 3. Archives, vol. 3, pp. 127, 131; 4. Calvert Papers, no. 1, folder 170; 5. Liber 20, folio 147.

MISTRESS ANN COX, GENTLEWOMAN

Mistress Ann Cox is the only proved lady of gentle birth who is known to have been on the Ark and the Dove. Her title of "Mistress" indicated that she was a matured-unmarried lady capable of managing her own affairs,* and it can be assumed that she traveled with at least one hand-maiden, but we have no record of that fact. She was definitely not the widowed sister of Richard Gerard, Esq., nor of Thomas Gerard, Esq., as it has frequently been printed.

She married Thomas Greene, Esq., one of her fellow adventurers, and the wedding was without doubt the first to be celebrated in the Province of Maryland. Being a woman her name did not figure in any of the business and political affairs of the early days, and the only evidence of her being on the Ark was when Thomas Greene in 1648 proved land rights or 500 acres of land to which he was entitled by her emigration in 1633.

She was undoubtedly the "noble matron" who died in 1638, according to Father White's report to the Superior General at Rome, as her death occurred about that time. Mistress Winifred Seyborn came in 1638 and later married Thomas Greene.

Although Father White mentioned no name, he probably referred to her as "coming with the first settlers into the Colony, with more than woman's courage, bore all difficulties and inconeniences. She was given to much prayer, and most anxious for the salvation of her neighbors—a perfect example as well in herself as in her domestic concerns—she was fond of our society while living, and a benefactor to it when dying—of blessed memory with all for her notable examples ample, especially of charity to the sick, as well as of other virtues".

No will nuncupative, with the consent of her spouse, has been found, but if she were the benefactor to the Society of Jesus when dying indicates some final testament, and also that she was a lady of estates in her own rights. She left many descendants.

EDWARD CRANFIELD, ESQ.

Other than listed as one of the Gentlemen of Fashion by Lord Baltimore, nothing further is known about Edward Cranfield. If he died, returned to England, or assigned his land rights to another Adventurer, no record has been found. Furthermore, he does not figure in any of the early correspondence with the Adventurers and Lord Baltimore.

---

* Mistress was a title of courtesy and respect and was the 17th century style of addressing unmarried ladies of position. Even in the 18th century it maintained its ground against the infantine term of "miss". Mistress therefore did not signify a married or widowed woman, as it is so often stated, but was considered analogous to the masculine title of Esquire. A married or widowed lady of rank and fashion was styled Madam (without an e) and was in frequent use in Maryland.

Thomas Dorrell, Esq.

Thomas Dorrell, Esq., styled by Lord Baltimore as one of the Gentlemen of Fashion who came in 1633, was a kinsman to Thomas Greene, Esq. He died before the Second General Assembly of 1637/8, and there is no record of his claiming land or making any assignments to a third party. Secretary Lewger writing to Cecilius, Lord Baltimore, in 1638/9, stated "Spoke with Mr. Copley about Mr. Dorrell's goods . . . but no will of Mr. Dorrell yet proved, no administration taken out, no inventory of the goods, some remaining in my hands". No further references to him or his estate have been found. He probably left no issue in Maryland or are his heirs known.

Source: Calvert Papers, Fund Pub. no. 28, p. 199.

Peter Draper, Gent.

Peter Draper, secretary or steward to Governor Leonard Calvert, financed his own passage in 1633, and therefore can be credited as another gentleman of fashion on the Ark. He did not attend the Second General Assembly of which there is record, at least no evidence has been found of his attendance, but in 1640 he proved his land-rights as having emigrated in 1633.[1]

"3 April 1640. Leonard Calvert Esq., demandeth 100 acres of Land due to him for transporting into the Province one able man Servant called James Hoskly in the year 1633 and assigned his interest in the said 100 acres unto Peter Draper".

"2 Aprill 1640. Peter Draper demandeth 100 acres of Land due to him by Conditions of Plantation for transporting himself into the Province in the year 1633, and 100 acres more due by assignment from Leonard Calvert Esq. and one hundred acres more due by Assignment from Owen Phillips, Gent."

"10th Aprill 1643. Peter Draper, Gent. demandeth 1300 acres of Land due by assignment of Leonard Calvert, Esq., and 100 acres more due in his own name ut Sup: and 100 acres more due by assignment of Owen Phillips ut supra:"

"Eod. I doe assigne 1300 acres of the Land demandeth by me upon Record and due by Conditions of Plantation unto Peter Draper".

(signed) Leonard Calvert.

At the General Assembly of 1642, Peter Draper was fined for his non-attendance, but within a few days Governor Calvert appeared holding his proxy, when the fine was cancelled.[2]

As secretary to Governor Leonard Calvert, he frequently sued in the interest of the Governor as his attorney, and at the time Governor Calvert left the Province in April 1643, for a trip to England, he was granted power of attorney by the Governor during his absence and was specifically requested to pay William Harrington at the termination of his four-year service his clothes and other articles under the conditions of indentureship.[3]

He died during the absence of the Governor in England or sometime before April 1644. John Lewger, Esq. was granted letters of administration, but upon the return of Governor Calvert he assumed the administration.[4] No inventory or distribution of his estate is on file, or any record of the heirs or heirs-at-law.

> "2 May 1644. John Lewger Secretary Administrator Ex officio of the Estate of Peter Draper, deceased, Sold the right of the said Peter unto 1500 acres of land upon Record in fra: pag: 81, unto Captain Henry ffleet Gent. for the price of 10th Sterling as pp bill dated".

> "13 May eod. The said Henry ffleet demandeth 1500 acres of land due by assignment of right of Peter Draper and 500 acres more in consideration of five able men undertaken by the said Henry ffleet to be transported at his Charge nto the Province to plant and Inhabit here Sometime before Christmas next at the furthest."

Peter Draper, Gent., was undoubtedly a member of the Roman Catholic Church and died without issue. Being the private secretary of the Governor, he apparently shared the same quarters with him or a dependency on his townland in St. Mary's City. In 1650 Stanhope Clarke had a land warrant which included "Draper's Neck" on the bayside near the land of Barnaby Jackson.

Sources: 1. Patents, Liber 1, folio 63; Liber ABH, folios 79, 98; Md. Hist. Mag., vol. 5, p. 368; 2. Archives, vol. 1, pp. 169, 172; 3. *Ibid.*, vol. 4, pp. 202, 208, 216, 243, 271; 4. *Ibid.*, vol. 2, p. 279; vol. 4, pp. 262, 307.

RICHARD DUKE

Richard Duke came with the first Adventurers as a redemptioner of the two Wintour brothers who assigned their land-rights to Ferdinando Poulton alias Father Brock who demanded land for his transportation in 1639.[1] He was born in or about 1613, according to his deposition in 1648, so therefore he was about 20 years of age upon his sailing on the Ark.

On July 3, 1638, as one of the servants of Father Brock, he declared himself to be a Protestant and testified that William Lewis, a Roman Catholic and steward for the manors of the Jesuits, forbade Francis Gray, a non-Catholic, from reading religious books.[2] He had not completed his service by October 6, 1639, for on that day styling himself as "Richard Duke Servt to Mr. Pulton" he made oath that John Speed, one-time servant to the late Captain Wintour, lying on his death bed stated that "Richard Browne his fellow serv^t should have all such Tob as were oweing to him the said John Speed and that Richard Browne to pay such Debts as far as he owed".[3]

He was, however, a freeholder by March 21, 1641/2, when he attended the General Assembly for the first time.[4] His early seat was in St. Michael

Hundred, where in 1642 he was assessed 23 lbs. tob. for defraying certain expenses of the Province.[5]

He was out of the Province in the autumn of 1642, for on September 5, of that year, he was excused from attending the session of the General Assembly "as being out of the Province".[6] The question is whether he was in Virginia, some other nearby Colony, or did he return to England? The latter was most likely the case, inasmuch as no further reference is found for him until November 3, 1647, some five years later, when he was sued by John Hollis [Hallowes] for 600 lbs. tob.[7]

On June 20, 1648, he declared himself to be 35 years of age and stated in court that Mr. South asked him to sell him an Indian girl, but when he replied that he had none to sell, South then requested him to accompany him up the Wiccomico in search for one. At this time Richard Duke signed his name.[8]

In October 1649, as the assignee of a warrant from Thomas Copley, Esq. he was granted 100 acres of land on the Wicomico River near Posey's Creek and bounding on the North and East with the said river, on the West with the said creek, and on the South with a line drawn east from a branch to the said creek called Duke's Branch.[9] In 1650 he was sued by Cuthbert Fenwick and Dorothy Baldridge for indebtedness.

The last reference found for him in Maryland was during 1653. In that year the following was recorded in the land records.[10]

> "Richard Duke Demandeth two hundred acres of land for Transporting himself and Wife and two children into this Province as he intends this presence Year 1653. Warrt to lay out for Richard Duke 200 acres in any part of the Province not formerly taken up ret. 25 March to stand good in case he makes good his Title by the Transport aforesaid".

All evidence points to the fact that he left issue who settled in the Province.

Sources: 1. Liber ABH, folios 65-66; 2. Archives, vol. 4, p. 37; 3. Wills, Liber 1, folio 5; 4. Archives, vol. 1, p. 116; 5. Archives, vol. 1, p. 145; 6. Archives, vol. 1, p. 169; 7. Archives, vol. 4, p. 340; 8. Archives, vol. 4, p. 392; 9. Liber ABH, folio 31; 10. Liber ABH, folio 331.

JOSEPH EDLOWE

Joseph Edlowe in 1650 at the death of Robert Wiseman, Esq., declared himself as the greatest creditor and at the same time stated that he had been a servant of the deceased.[1] There is no record of Robert Wiseman, one of the Gentlemen of Fashion, claiming land-rights for his servants or transportees, but it is certain that a gentleman of his social standing would have come into the Province with at least one body-servant. Joseph Edlowe had obtained his freedom by the General Assembly of January 1637/8, which would be about the expiration of a four-year term of service, having contracted in 1633 before sailing of the Ark.

Yet as it so often occurs in historic research, there is a contradictory of facts which are not always explainable. As mentioned above, Joseph Edlowe declared himself in 1650 to have been a servant of Robert Wiseman, but a few months previously it was stated in public print that he had been a servant of Leonard Calvert. As bond servants could lawfully be sold and frequently were, we are at loss to know who brought him originally into the Province. And the fact that he received 50 acres of land under the Conditions of 1636, also presents a question.* While no source document has been discovered that would clarify the question, the probabilities are that Joseph Edlowe accompanied Robert Wiseman as his servant in 1633.

He was one of the most colorful characters around the countryside—and could not resist in indulging in some illicit *affaires d'armour*. He settled first at Mattapanient, for in 1637 he testified to the death of John Bryant. It has already been stated that he attended the Second Assembly of all freeholders, and he also attended in person the Assembly of 1641/2.[2] His assessment in August 1642, for charges of the Province were 30 lbs. tob., and at the Assembly of September 1642, Thomas Greene, Esq. held his proxy. In 1643 he gave evidence against Richard Ingle, the arch disturber of the Peace.[3]

He was unlettered, and from the many times he sued for non-payment of obligations to him, he could very easily have been a tradesman or artisan, presumably a tailor. He administered on the estate of Christopher Martin, Tailor, who died intestate about 1640, and it would seem that they were partners, as the inventory of Martin's estate was declared to be a joint-inventory of the deceased and that of Joseph Edlowe.[4]

In or about 1641 he transported his wife, Eliner, and a man-servant. The family name of his wife has not been identified, but in some manner he was a brother-in-law of Cyprian Thorowgood who from all circumstances came with the first Adventurers.

On March 2, 1649/50, he received a grant of 300 acres known as "Susquehanough Point" on the south shore of the Patuxent between the Manors of Little Eltonhead and Mattapani-Sewell which included Half-head's Hollow. Two hundred and fifty acres were due from assignment of Cyprian Thorowgood and 50 acres upon "the advice of Governor Stone" as servant to Leonard Calvert under the Conditions of August 8, 1636, signed at Portsmouth.

On November 8, 1653, "Joseph Edlow Demandeth 200 acres of land for Transporting of Eliner his wife and Roger Webb his Servant into this province twelve years since and upwards".[4a] On June 25, 1648, he and his wife were summoned by the High Sheriff, of St. Mary's, to testify

---

* It is quite possible that Governor Stone wanted to reward several of those who had come with the first Adventurers, inasmuch as so few were alive in 1649 that the land rights of 1636 were interpreted to apply. See, Liber ABH, folios 39, 118, **Land Office.**

relative to the allegation of James Langworth that William Wheatley in 1644 removed certain corn from the plantation of Nicholas Harvey.[5] On April 12, 1650, Barnaby Jackson made a deed of gift of a cow and her increase to his godson, Barnaby Edlowe, the son of Joseph Edlowe.[6]

It seemed that as a widower he became involved in 1657 during a drinking party in at least one *affaire d'armour* with Mary Cole, a maid-servant of Henry de Coursey, Esq. Mary Cole had already been married to Thomas Bramstead but that did not prevent her having an affair with Joseph Edlowe at his house presumably when her alleged husband was around. Depositions were made that Thomas Seamor had read from the Book of Common Prayer the marriage ceremony, and according to the testimony of Samuel Gosey, Thomas Seamor "read more then the minister use to read".[7] Thomas Seamor was also "a little disturbed in Drink", according to the testimony of Arthur Ludford. Julianna Halfhead, wife of John Halfhead, stated that Mary Cole told her that Seamor followed her into a room at the house of Joseph Edlowe and wanted her to lie with him upon a chest and in the affray "the said Seamor had hurt her against the Said Chest". Henry de Coursey thereupon sued both Thomas Seamor and Joseph Edlowe for the maltreatment of his maid-servant, but later withdrew his suit.[8]

In 1657 he allegedly fled the Province, when William Sinckler sued him for a debt of 1451 lbs. tob. and demanded an attachment against his estate.[9] Presumably getting out of the affair with Mary Cole and settling the debt of William Sinckler, he became involved with Anne Barbery, another maid-servant, in 1659, and she declared him to be the father of her *enfant d'armour* which lived only a few hours after she gave birth to it rather surreptitiously, but its cries in the barn led to its discovery. The court ordered 30 lashes on the bare back.[10]

A complete list of the children of Joseph Edlowe has not been proved, but there is record of the following:

1. Barnaby Edlowe, *d.s.p.* 1665.
2. Joseph Edlowe. *q.v.*

Joseph Edlowe died intestate, when letters of administration were granted to John Walton, with Richard Collett as his surety. Walton was the greatest creditor and the orphan or orphans were placed under him. John Walton died and in 1661 Richard Collett petitioned the court for administration of Edlowe's estate which at that time was unsettled.

At the same time Joseph Edlowe, son of Joseph Sr., petitioned the court and stated that at the death of his father he was placed under the custody of Thomas Walton "with the rest of that poore Estate which was left amongst us his Children". Joseph Edlowe Jr. entered into a covenant to serve Walton for the consideration of cow and calf and sufficient clothing to be delivered yearly. At the expiration of his service of two years he petitioned therefore for his cattle and clothing from the estate of Thomas

Walton. A writ was therefore issued to arrest the administrators of Walton's estate.[11]

Sources: 1. Archives, vol. 10, pp. 10-11; 2. Archives, vol. 1, p. 116; 3. Archives, vol. 4, p. 233; 4. Archives, vol. 4, pp. 67, 92; 4a. Liber ABH, folio 349; 5. Archives, vol. 4, p. 438; 6. Archives, vol. 10, p. 87; 7. Archives, vol. 10, pp. 549-560; 8. Archives, vol. 41, p. 152; 9. Archives, vol. 10, p. 558; 10. Archives, vol. 41, pp. 329, 331; 11. Archives, vol. 41, pp. 598-599.

RICHARD EDWARDS, CHIRURGEON

There is the record of only one doctor or chirurgeon on the Ark to Maryland and he apparently was kept busy during the many days the Adventurers were on land and sea. His name was Richard Edwards and very little is known about his background and study or apprenticeship in the art of healing. The duties of a chirurgeon of that day were manifold and his profession did not place him high on the social scale. He did the bleeding when the patient's temperature was too high, was the apothecary and extractor of teeth—besides it was the duty of the chirurgeon to be trained in the tonsorial arts, so he had the task of cutting the hair of the gentlemen and perhaps that of the servants as well.

Governor Calvert writing to Sir Richard Lechford, from Poynt Comfort, Virginia, May 30, 1634, stated, "I gave signed a bill of exchange of 9 [£] for one Mr. Richard Edwards our Chyrurgeon of the Arcke".[1]

Richard Edwards was perhaps higher in learning and ability than most barber-chirurgeons of his day, for he was addressed by Governor Calvert as "Mr." and his letter, undated, found among the Lechford papers indicated a man of marked intelligence.[2]

> "Sir Richard Leatchford my service with respect remembered, you may be pleased to understand that your loving Frend Captaine Leanard Calvert having occation to make use of mee for som Commodities whome I was very willing and redy to furnish hath charged you by way of exchange to make satisfactio. my request is that your worshippe would be pleased I living soe Far of and it being soe smale a some as to take order for the paiment. so wish you health I rest."

Yours to use

(signed) Richard Edwards
Chirurgion of the Arke of Mariland

How long he remained in Maryland as the chirurgeon we do not know. He may have contracted only for the initial voyage and there are some indications of his returning with the ship in May. He is not listed as attending any of the early assemblies. Father White referred to the chirurgeon in his letter of February 20, 1638/9, relative to the sick eating flesh and drinking hot waters and wine, but he failed to name him.

Sources: 1. Fund Pub. no. 35, p. 25; 2. *Ibid.*

ROBERT EDWARDS

Robert Edwards was transported into the Province by Richard Gerard, Esq., who assigned his service and land rights to Ferdinand Pulton before returning to England about 1635. Edwards was not a freeholder at the Assembly of 1637/8. He did not exercise or have the rights of a freeman until 1640, when he voted for Thomas Gerard, Esq., to represent St. Clement's Hundred. In the same year he sued Thomas Gerard for a breeding sow due him for "wages at Christmas last", but he lost his suit. In December 1643, he was assessed 35 lbs. tob. for the defense of St. Mary's County from the assault of the Sesquihanowes during the past summer. In 1643 he sued Robert Percy for 100 lbs. tob. "due four years ago". On January 2, 1646/7, he took the oath of fealty after Ingle's Rebellion and on January 25, same year, he demanded tobacco and corn due him from the estate of John Langworth.

He received no land grants and there is no record of any administration of his estate—though he had a life span in the Province of at least 14 years. He undoubtedly was a freeholder on St. Clement's Manor, but the extant records for that manor do not begin until 1659—at which time he was probably deceased. No known descendants have been proved.

Sources: Archives, vol. 2, p. 138; vol. 10, ppp.

WILLIAM EDWIN

The land rights for William Edwin, transported by Richard Gerard, Esq., were assigned to Ferdinand Pulton, Esq., who later made claims to the Lord Proprietary.[1] At the time of importation he had about reached his 21st birthday, or born about 1612, and it is assumed, though the extant records do not reveal it, that he entered as one of the retainers of Mr. Gerard. He was literate and later was the proprietor of an inn, but while the fact remains that he was schooled in letters, an attribute of the gentry, he was addressed in one or two instances as "goodman" and his wife as "goodwife", all marks of the bourgeoise. In 1650 he signed a declaration with other Protestant subjects of Lord Baltimore that he enjoyed "all fitting and convenient freedone and liberty in the exercise of our Religion". Thus, he can be placed as a member of the Proprietary Party and not a follower of the Puritans who were then gradually usurping the government. He was a kinsman in some manner to Francis Jarvise.

His service, if any, had expired by the Second Assembly of January 1637/8, at which gathering he was styled planter, of St. Mary's Hundred, and had given his proxy to William Lewis. At the creation of St. Michael's Hundred, his plantation fell in that hundred and it is not unlikely that he held tenancy at one time on St. Michael's Manor.

On March 26, 1637, he declared his intentions to marry Mary Whitehead, spinster, and he gave bond to the Lord Proprietary for 1,000 lbs. tob.[2] The records fail to show, however, when and how his wife, Mary, entered the Province.

There is the human interest of John Nevill suing William Edwin and his wife, Mary, in 1643 for "forceable entry into his dwelling house", and of Edwin and his wife suing the Widow Whitcliff for slander in 1644.[3]

It was not until 1648 that he applied for his land rights under the Conditions of Plymouth, by which he received 50 acres of land, lying in St. George's Hundred, bounded on the West by Cooper's Creek and on the North by Packer's Creek. The name "St. William" was given to his plantation which was to be held under the Manor of West St. Mary's, the warrant being signed by Thomas Greene, Esq.[4] He settled on "St. William" and in 1658 he was sworn in as the Constable of St. George's Hundred.[5]

In August 1649, Francis Jarvise, who signed his name and declared himself to be a kinsman of Edwin, granted the latter power of attorney to recover 500 lbs. tob. from Francis Brooke, one-time wife beater. Jarvise won his case and Brooke delivered a heifer in payment. Brooke signed with a large F B.[6] In the same year William Edwin registered his cattle marks for his daughters, Elizabeth and Mary.[7]

His public inn was probably located on "St. William" in St. George's Hundred which was nearer to the important center of activities than St. Michael's Hundred, where he was earlier domiciled. It was not a small hostelry, for at one time he lodged 50 servants and their goods for Captain Richard Husbands. In January 1652/3, his wife, Mary Edwin, declared in court that Goodman Hoult had cattle at her husband's house.

On June 8, 1653, William Edwin sued at court Miles Cooke, a mate of Captain Husbands for "his trouble & Entertainment with houseroom and Dyett about fifty Servants and Storage for Goods which Came last yeare in Captain Richard's Ship". He asked for 2,000 lbs. tob. according to agreement and had refused the 600 lbs. tob. offered by Cooke.[8] In 1659 Captain Husbands before the Provincial Court, wishing to compensate the loss, stated that about seven years ago he "transported divers Scotts into Virginia and from thence into this Province in his sloope" and landed them at the house of William Edwin where they remained for some time. That Edwin arrested his Mate Miles Cooke for non-payment, while he was out of the Province.[9]

In 1656 Edwin returned to England and while there he contracted with Captain Samuel Tilghman to transport him on his return voyage to Maryland. In 1658 Captain Tilghman sued in court for payment of passage declaring that he transported Edwin "out of England on the Ship Goulden ffortune". William Edwin swore in court that he had partly paid the charge and produced a receipt signed "by John Mochar, Boteswaine, for one small Steare weighing 251 lbs."[10]

Among the guests at his inn was Benjamin Gill, Esq., father-in-law to Captain James Neale, later of Wolleston Manor. Gill while lying ill at the inn made several verbal statements as to the disposition of his estate. Later it occasioned a law suit by which Robert Cole demanded writs be issued for William Edwin and his wife to prove that Benjamin Gill declared him as a kinsman and made him the contingent heir in his will. Accordingly, in 1658, William Edwin, aged 46 and upward, swore that four years ago Mr. Benjamin Gill lay sick at his house and declared Robert Cole a kinsman and that if he died, Cole should enjoy all he had "except his sonne or Daughter or some of their children should perchance come to this country". His wife, Mary Edwin, who made her mark, swore that Mr. Gill while lying sick at her house was desirous for some one to write his will, but at that time no literate person was present. Mr. Gill stated that he had given his kinsman, Robert Cole, certain goods and referred to Mr. Neale, his wife, and their children.[11]

His wife, Mary Whitehead, died after 1658, and he married secondly Margerite .... who survived him and acquired additional husbands. His undated will was probated at court on October 13, 1663.[12]

He appointed his wife, unnamed, the executrix of his estate and devised her the dwelling-plantation during life, then to his "eldest son Michael Edwin". Personalty were left to his granddaughter, Mary Hall, and to William Guigoe. The witnesses were William Price and William Grengo.

On January 11, 1663/4, Thomas Dent made a return of the inventory approved by Robert Cager and Henry Ellery, presumably the greatest creditors. No kin signed the appraisal or did any administrator.[13]

On September 26, 1665, Margerite Edwyn, the Widdow and Relict of William Edwyn, proved her rights to 350 acres of land by assignment from "several person" and also 100 acres more for her and her husband's transport into the Province.* She assigned her warrant and ultimate patent to her son, William "orphant of the aforesaid William Edwyn". Land rights were made under the Conditions of London, dated July 2, 1649.[14]

It was therefore ordered that a tract of 350 acres be laid out for William Edwin, orphan, on the Eastern Shore in a River called Pokemock adjoining the land taken up by Captain Harwood and called the "Golden Lyon" and thence to a tree on Edwin's Marsh. It lay in Somerset County and was to be held of the Manor of Nanticoke.[15]

Issue of William Edwin

1. Michael Edwin, son and heir.
2. Elizabeth Edwin.
3. Mary Edwin married [James] Hall.†
4. William Edwin.

---

* The 100 acres were perhaps due her deceased husband for his return in the "Golden Fortune"; it is therefore apparent that she was transported into the Province and was not a native of Maryland.

† Forker Frissell, of St. M. Co., in 1661, bequeathed a legacy to Mary Halles, daughter of James Halles. Ref: Wills, Liber 1, folio 152.

Sources: 1. Liber ABH, folio 66; 2. Archives, vol. 4, pp. 24-25; 3. Archives, vol. 4, pp. 253, 258; 4. Liber ABH, folio 9; Liber 2, folio 419; 5. Archives, vol. 41, p. 119; 6. Archives, vol. 4, p. 538; 7. Archives, vol. 4, p. 514; 8. Archives, vol. 10, p. 272; 9. Archives, vol. 41, pp. 276-270; 10. Archives, vol. 41, p. 216; 11. Archives, vol. 41, p. 197; 12. Wills, Liber 1, folio 197; 13. Test. Proc. Liber I D, folios 163, 175; 14. Liber 8, folio 442; 15. Liber 7, folio 265.

JOHN ELBIN

John Elbin [Elkin] was transported in 1633 by John Saunders, Esq., who assigned his land-rights to Ferdinando Pulton. He settled in St. George's Hundred, where in 1642 as a freeholder he was amerced 20 lbs. tob. for non-attendance at the Assembly and the failure to name a proxy. In the same year he was arraigned in court for the felony and murder of the King of Yowocomoco at an Indian quarter in the woods near St. George's Creek in St. George's Hundred in the company of John Robinson, barber, and the latter's servant, Miles Ricards. The jury of twelve men rendered a verdict of not guilty "they found that he killed the Indian in his owne defence". After December 2, 1642, he was transported to the York River in Virginia by Michael Peasley.

Sources: Liber ABH, folio 65; Archives, vol. 4, pp. 177, 180, 253.

NICHOLAS FAIRFAX, ESQ.

Nicholas Fairfax, Esq., was one of the Gentlemen of Fashion who accompanied Governor Calvert on the initial sailing of the Ark. He professed the Roman Catholic faith and was one of the victims of over indulgence at Christmas, with resultant dysentery and fever. Before his death he bequeathed his friend, Thomas Greene, Esq., all his rights in the Province.

CUTHBERT FENWICK, GENT.

Cuthbert Fenwick, Gent., was either the secretary, steward or equerry to Captain Thomas Cornwalys, Esq., all of which placed him during the early years under the loose category of "servant". He possessed a keen sense of legal acumen and it is possible that he had some training in law at home, if not, he must have read jurisprudence with one of the learned gentlemen during his service.

He was not among the Adventurers who joined the ships at London or Cowes, but sufficient evidence is extant to prove that he was with the Adventurers when they sailed up the Chesapeake Bay in March 1633, and was with them when Father White and his associates celebrated the Roman Mass on St. Clement's Island on the first day of the year 1634.

Captain Cornwalys made two entries of his land-rights for Fenwick. The earlier one states that Cuthbert Fenwick was "bought" in 1633 and the other some years later states that he "brought" him from Virginia in 1634.* No record is extant of Fenwick entering the Colony of Virginia either in his own right or having been transported. Furthermore, no references have been found for him among the extant Virginia records of that period. Virginia in a broad sense embraced all English settlements in the New World and in that day was not confined to the Colony of Virginia.

* As this date was given in 1653, twenty years after the event, credence can logically be given to the earlier claim when the matter of time was clearer in the mind.

There is a remote possibility that Cornwalys acquired his services at a place other than the Virginia Colony—but it is generally believed to be the Colony.

It is also quite possible that along the way the Ark and the Dove met with some ship whose captain had several redemptioners whom he had planned to convey for a valuable consideration at an English port to some enterprising planters, and Cornwalys found the occasion propitious to increase his entourage. It is also known that one of the indentures besides Fenwick, that is, John Hallowes, was a scion of the county gentry and was later styled gentleman.

In presenting the evidence that Cuthbert Fenwick entered Maryland with the Adventurers it is well to reiterate the earlier application of Captain Cornwalys in order that a study and strict interpretation be given.

"January 17th. Memorial of rights Entred by Capt. Cornwallis 1633. Thomas Cornewallis transported himself and Eleven Servants into Maryland which is 12 for which is due to Manors 4000 acres and 400 acres of Town Land for 10 and 4000 acres for the 2 odd persons in all 4800.

"Give me by Mr. John Saunder 5 Servants and their rights 2200—Bought John Hollowes, Cuthbert ffenwicke, Christopher Martin, John Norton Senr and Junr in all 5 that year for which is due 2200 in all 9200".[1]

Cornwalys stated that he transported eleven men in 1633. His business partner, John Saunders, who died in 1634, gave him five unnamed additional servants, and then he stated that he bought five whom he named "in all 5 that year". That year could apply only to "1633", as stated in the first line of his claim. The year 1634 did not begin until March 25th, the very day on which the Adventurers landed on St. Clement's Island. It is therefore quite evident that when Cornwalys stated he bought Cuthbert Fenwick and the four others in that year it was before 1634, and consequently Cuthbert Fenwick and the four others* could not have arrived in Maryland after the initial landing date. Furthermore, the fact that his period of service expired before March 13, 1637/8, but after January 25th is another indication of his being with the Adventurers before the landing on the first day of the year 1634. He thus sustained all the vicissitudes of the early settlement along with the gentlemen and servants who sailed from Cowes.

All genealogical indicators point to the fact that he was a scion of that great North county family of Fenwick which had its seat in Northumberland and which participated in almost every border warfare known in that conflict between the Scots and the English, for ancient Scotland included Westmoreland, Northumberland and Cumberland and the Scots fought

---

[1] Land Liber 4, folio 523, Land Office, Annapolis.

* The later application for land Cornwalys omitted perhaps inadvertently the name of John Hallowes as being one of the five men he "bought" in that year 1633.

hard to regain them. He is declared to be the fourth son of George Fenwick, of Langshawes, Gent.†

It is not known whether he had accepted the Roman Catholic faith under the tutelage of his one-time master, Captain Cornwalys, during his indentureship or whether it was his birthright. He became, however, one of the leading laymen of the Roman Church in Maryland and in 1650 when it was forbidden by law for a society religious or otherwise to maintain manorial rights or own land, Cuthbert Fenwick held the Manor of St. Inigoes in trust for the Society of the Jesuits, having been assigned it by Thomas Copley, Esq., [Father Fisher]. He, however, was granted in 1651 by the Lord Proprietary absolute lordship on Fenwick Manor, sometimes called St. Cuthbert's, of 2000 acres in Resurrection Hundred with court baron and all the trappings of a feudal petty state.

Although the records of the baronial courts held on St. Cuthbert or Fenwick Manor have not come down to the present generation, there is every evidence that such courts were periodically held, according to custom, during the lordship of Cuthbert Sr. In his last will and testament he especially stipulated that his son and heir, Cuthbert, was to be recognized as the Lord of the Manor, thereby implying that the honour and dignity of a baronial court were practiced and observed. Furthermore, the younger sons of Cuthbert Fenwick Sr. were to hold certain portions of the manor as freeholders, but they were to remit the annual fees to the Manor Lord.

Cuthbert Fenwick had completed his indentureship by March 13, 1637/8,‡ when he took his seat in the General Assembly for the first time. At the Assembly of October 1640, he acted as the Attorney General *pro tempe* for the Province, and in 1641 he was a delegate from Mattapanient Hundred at the representative Assembly of that year. By 1642 he had been appointed to His Lordship's Council to serve during the pleasure of His Lordship, but he was unseated along with his colleagues by the Puritan upheaval which abolished the Council or Upper House following abolishment of the House of Lords by the radical Puritans upon Cromwell's militant assumption of power in 1649.

His fellow constituents, however, had sufficient confidence in him to elect him a delegate from St. Clement's Hundred to succeed Thomas Mathews, appearing at the session on the morning of April 18, 1650. The Assembly at that time was heavily infiltrated with Puritans and ultra-liberals, so much so that a radical Puritan was elected Speaker of the House. Upon Fenwick's entry the Speaker offered him the secret oath

---

† One genealogist at least has questioned his usually stated parentage, yet disproof to the contrary has not been cited.

‡ If his service were for four years, it would have placed his contractual agreement prior to March 13, 1633/4, before the Ark and Dove arrived in Maryland waters. He had not completed his service on the opening day of January 25th, 1633/4, for he was not summoned to the Assembly nor was he fined for non-attendance on that day and no freeman held his proxy.

which the Assembly had adopted. Up to that time no delegate had been required to take a secret oath, for the oath as prescribed by the Lord Proprietary was known and had been officially published.

Fenwick replied that he would subscribe to the oath provided that it did not prejudice his religion or conscience. A motion was made and passed that Mr. Fenwick should not be permitted to take his seat unless he took the secret oath as adopted by the liberal Assembly. Upon the motion of three members, he was admitted to the session and was given until the next morning to consider the oath. At the afternoon session, however, it was declared that the secret oath did not infringe upon the liberty of conscience and religion and thereupon Mr. Fenwick was sworn in by the other delegates.

His other offices were almost too numerous to mention, but in 1644 he was created a magistrate with Thomas Greene, Esq., to try all cases civil and criminal in the Province. He also participated in several minor punitive expeditions against the Indians.

The 1649 Assembly was the last representative one before the Puritans gained completely the upper hand. The next Assembly met at Patuxent in 1654, with the Puritans in complete and absolute power and all Anglicans and Roman Catholics disenfranchised.

When law and order were restored by 1659 and Lord Baltimore had regained sovereignty over his Province, Cuthbert Fenwick had passed on, having died testate in or about 1654. He left six sons and one daughter, and his descendants today are legion.

WILLIAM FITTER, GENT.

William Fitter was one of the retainers who came with Captain Thomas Cornwalys in 1633, and is another example of a member of the county gentry being styled servant. When he testified in London during April 1636 in behalf of Lord Baltimore in the suit with Richard Orchard, one-time master of the pinnance Dove, he was addressed as "William Fitter of Maryland in the West Indies, Gent.", aet 55". He was therefore born in or about 1571 and was in his early fifties upon his sailing for Maryland.

In his testimony he gave much human interest about the early months in Maryland and the relations of Governor Calvert with Virginia, and displayed staunch loyalty to the Lord Proprietary against the rebellious Orchard and his crew, though Lord Baltimore lost his case.

Prior to his embarkation for Maryland he stated that "he had lived two years in London with Captain Cornwallis in Holborne as his servant" and was "now [1636] Lodgeth at the house of Mrs. Cornwallis in Holborne where he had since lodged since his return from Maryland on Easter Eve last". Before his service with Captain Cornwallis he had "served the Lady Stafford and lived with her at Stafford Castle in Staffordshire".

He returned to England, therefore, in the spring of 1635 after two and one-half years in Maryland. Although he may have left descendants in England, there is no knowledge of any from Maryland records.

Sources: Patents, Liber ABH, folio 94; High Court of Admiralty 13, vol. 52, folio 373.

CAPTAIN HENRY FLEETE, GENT.

Captain Henry Fleete, a fur trader, whom Father White styled a "Virginia Protestant", was of great assistance to the Maryland Adventurers at the initial settlement and aided greatly in the amiable negotiations with the Indian tribes and continued to dwell as a feudal lord in the Province for nearly eleven years. He was the son of William Fleete, of Chatham, County Kent, Gent., a member of the Virginia Company, and his wife Deborah Scott.[1]

He was in Virginia as early as 1623, when, while trading in what is now Maryland waters, he was captured by the Indians and remained with them until about 1627 during which time he became quite affluent in several of the Indian tongues. As an interpreter to Governor Calvert and Father White and a mediator between the Marylanders and the Indians, he rendered inestimable service to the young Province and was rewarded by Lord Baltimore with extensive grants of baronial manors. His trading proclivities early aroused the jealousy and envy of the indomitable William Clayborne who recognized him as his principal competitor in the Chesapeake area and thus a rivalry which was not dimmed by age resulted. And Clayborne lost no opportunity to circumvent his activities whenever possible.*

At what time and at what place Captain Fleete attached himself to the Adventurers, secondary writers differ. Some believed that he joined the Ark and the Dove when they were anchored in the James, while others state that he joined the Calvert party when the Governor paid homage to the Emperor at Piscataway.

One Virginia writer stated that "It was Captain Henry Fleet who guided Leonard Calvert to this spot on the Potomac. He was busy about his fur trade in the River of the Patowomecke when the Ark and the Dove reached St. Clement's Isle".[2] The statement was undocumented, but from source material of the times, it was undoubtedly correct.

Father White writing in his journal stated that at their devotion on St. Clement's "Our Governour was advised not to settle himselfe, till he spoake with the emperour of Pascatoway".[3] The counsel or advice was certainly given by some one who had understanding and had had previous dealings with the Indians, and Captain Henry Fleete was the only known person among the Adventurers at that time who possessed such knowledge.

---

* Fiske in his "Old Virginia and Her Neighbours", vol. 2, p. 275, makes Fleete the aggressor rather than Clayborne. He states "There is evidence to believe that Capt. Henry Fleete wished to supplant Clayborne in the fur trade".

Father White furthermore stated that "at Patomecke towne, he found there the king. . . . Here by an Interpretour, they had some speech with Archihoe".[4] Captain Henry Fleete again seems to be the only logical one to be the interpreter on that occasion. From Patomecke Govenor Calvert went to Piscataway, the seat of the Emperor of the tribe, whereas Father White wrote in his journal "our governour tooke Captain Henrie ffleet and his 3 barkes".[5] Consequently, there is definite proof that Captain Fleete was with the Adventurers a day or two after they sailed into the Potomac. Then, Father White stated that Fleete "brought us to as noble a seat as could be wished and as good graound as I suppose is in all Europe".[6]

Governor Calvert writing to Sir Richard Lechford, Knt., on May 30, 1634, said "by directions of our Captaine Henry ffleet who was very well acquainted with all parts of the river, and of the Indians likewise, I found a most convenient harbour and pleasant countrey".[7]

It therefore appears quite obvious that Captain Fleete was cruising with his three barks in the Potomac or some of its inlets when he and his traders sighted the Ark and the Dove and the pinnace which Governor Calvert acquired while in Virginia. A bark, though generally referred to as a three-masted vessel, could also be any vessel or boat, so it looks as if Captain Fleete had a fleet of sailing vessels when he joined the Adventurers. He was certainly not alone at that time, as it would require a small crew to sail even three small barks and assist in bartering with the natives. No record has come down as who composed his party, but his three brothers Edward, John and Rainold were most likely with him at that time as well as one or two other personalities who appeared early in Maryland records and who followed him later upon his settlement in the Northern Neck of Virginia.

On August 29, 1636, Cecilius, Lord Baltimore, issued "A warrant to Capt. Henry Fleete for 4000 acres of Land Due to him by the first Conditions of Plantation" for transporting five persons in 1633.[8] It therefore can be strictly interpreted that Captain Henry Fleete had at least five men in his party at the time he joined the colonists. This warrant was apparently his patent for "West St. Mary's Manor" which conferred upon him feudal seigniory. The manor lay across the river from the townlands of St. Mary's and according to source statements, he was the first "to seat across the river". That section became the nucleus of St. George's Hundred and he was soon joined by planters other than the tenants and civil officers who were maintained on his lordship. The Lord Proprietary later granted him a warrant for 10,000 acres to be erected into a manor in any part of his Province not heretofore inhabited or taken up. He was apparently more interested in the coast-wide fur trade than the life of a feudal lord, so failed to take up the patent. At least no record exists to show the survey and patent, though it could have been among the many valuable papers destroyed ruthlessly during Ingle's supremacy.

Thomas Morris was one of his tenants and had apparently been granted "four yeare term rent free" which was later questioned by Captain Cornwalys, when the Assembly ordered that he pay 200 lbs. tob. for the next year rent for his house.[9]

On May 11, 1636, Governor John West of Virginia, ordered his arrest for his alleged participation in the seizure of the "Long Taile" in April 1635. He was then safe within the domain of Maryland. No contemporary record has been discovered, however, to indicate that he was with Captain Cornwalys at the time the "Long Taile" was seized by the Marylanders in the Pocomoke River, yet at the same time the names of all the men with Cornwalys are not known.

He and his three brothers attended in person the General Assembly of 1637/8. On February 11, 1638/9, the freemen of St. George's Hundred were summoned to meet at the house* where Captain Fleete "lately dwelt on thursday the 21st February" to vote for delegates to the first representative Assembly in Maryland.[10] There are no further records of his attending the subsequent Assemblies called by the Governor or the Council. It is known, however, that he was busy with his trading fleets and was in and out of the Province, so consequently he may have been excused. His three brothers undoubtedly returned to England or elsewhere, as no further record can be found for them in either Maryland or Virginia.

On September 25, 1640, Leonard Calvert issued the following: "I would have you to lay out two thousand acres of land on the West side of St. George River over against St. Maries unto Thomas Cornwallys, Esq., as assignee of Capt. Henry ffleet who held it by Grant from myself and the Com^r of Maryland And for Soe doeing this Shall be your warrant".[11]

The Provincial Court on March 14, 1742/3, ordered that all his lordship's tenants in Whitcliff's Creek were to pay their quit-rents at the Manor of West St. Mary's before "our Lady day next".

During Leonard Calvert's visit to England conflict either through jealousy, misplaced authority or clash of temperaments developed between Giles Brent, the Acting Governor, and John Lewger, the Secretary of State. John Lewger commissioned Henry Fleete "a Generall to make war against the Indians",[12] which met with the displeasure of Governor Brent who apparently considered the prerogatives of commissions lay within the category of the Governor rather than the Secretary of State. Brent suspended Lewger. On June 18, 1644, however, Governor Brent appointed Henry Fleete "to go up to Piscataway with your company" at the time the Susquehannas expected to conclude a treaty which would unite several

---

* A 17th century manor house is extant on "West St. Mary's Manor" and was restored by Colonel and Mrs. Miodrag Blagojevich, the Colonel being a former officer in the Royal Army of Jugoslavia. Mrs. Blagojevich was the former Elizabeth Ridgely, of Washington and Maryland. In restoration it was discovered that the present house was on the foundation of an earlier and smaller dwelling which was most likely the original manor house of Captain Fleete.

Indian tribes against the Marylanders. As Governor Brent declared "it concerned the Province to have some one there who understand the language".[13]

From Secretary Lewger, the executor of the estate of Peter Draper, Gent., Henry Fleete purchased for £10 the land rights for 1500 acres. Conse-quently, on May 13, 1644, he demanded the 1500 acres of land by assign-ment from Peter Draper's estate and 500 acres additional in consideration of five able-bodied men whom he promised to transport at his own expense into the Province "sometime before Christmas next at the furthest". It was therefore ordered to "lay out for Capt. Henry ffleet 2000 acres of land about the plantation late belonging to Peter Draper, deceased, and Certify the bounds thereof to Mr. Secretary without delay whereof fail not at peril and this Shall be your Warrant". The order was signed by Giles Brent, then Acting Governor.[14]

Records show that he maintained his domicile in Maryland as late as 1644. In that year the High Sheriff for St. Mary's County ordered two of his servants to answer "His Lordship's suit for misdemeanors".[15] On July 17, 1644, Edward Packer, a Marylander, was granted permission to trade with the Dutch and to be the commander of one of Captain Fleete's pinnace.[16]

On July 18, 1644, Captain Fleete acknowledged a debt of 3463 lbs. tob. to Governor Calvert and if not paid by December 10 next, then Fleete was willing that 6000 lbs. tob. be levied "upon any of his [Fleete] land, debts, goods or chattels within this Province".[17]

On October 5, 1644, Owen Seymour swore before the Provincial Court that he "had covenanted to serve Captain Fleete until next March in either New Netherlands or New England and had served him until this present day and was ready to serve him, but being pressed by the Governor's warrant to serve in the garrison at Pascatowat" therefore requested that attachment be made against Captain Fleete.[18]

At court throughout the year 1644 he had numerous business transactions with Mistress Margaret Brent, Cuthbert Fenwick, Barnaby Jackson, Thomas Sturman and Thomas Greene.

Although he maintained property both real and personal in Maryland during 1644, he apparently was in Virginia in 1643, for in that year the Maryland court ordered Upkin Powell to take three Maryland men to Virginia "to answere the allegaons of Capt. Henry ffleet in point of service".[19]

Several theories have been advanced as to the cause of Captain Fleete deserting the Maryland Province after he had been so graciously received and became the grantee of large manorial estates and plantations from the Lord Proprietary. One is that he quarreled with the Maryland heirarchy—another that he could no longer tolerate the strong influence of Roman Catholics. Neither of which can be found nor verified in the extant writings of the times. One has to review the political and social background in the Province at the time of his settlement in Virginia to find perhaps a cause and draw adequate inference. As late as 1644 he maintained realty and indented servants in Maryland and was active in coast-wide inner colonial trade.

He was in high favour with the Maryland overlords in 1643, when Governor Calvert returned to England in April that year. He was even offered by the Secretary of State the generalship of the provincial militia to subdue the Susquehanna Confederacy.

In February 1644/5, Captain Richard Ingle seized the Government of Maryland and a period of complete anarchy ensued for nearly two years. Governor Calvert and many of his loyal followers were forced to flee to Virginia to save their necks. It was about this time that Captain Henry Fleete settled in Virginia and while we know not why, it times perfectly with Ingle's insurgent rule. Fleete was no non-conformist and it must again be recalled, he had no love for Clayborne.

The authors of "Adventurers of Purse and Persons Virginia 1607-1625", page 172, state that Fleete opened the Northern Neck to Virginia planters and "cemented title to the region despite designs of the Maryland Calverts". The Calverts, however, had no designs on the Northern Neck or any part of Virginia which they did not possess rightfully by Royal grant.*

While it is not known definitely in what part of Virginia that Governor Calvert and his followers in exile sought haven from Ingle, it is believed to have been the Northern Neck as it enabled them to keep in close contact with the events in their Province across the Potomac. The Governor, however, made frequent trips to Jamestown, and it was through the aid of the Governor of Virginia that Leonard Calvert under the guidance of Richard Willan† could regain their Province in the fall of 1646 after an exile of perhaps twenty months.

Some of the Marylanders who fled to Virginia returned with Governor Calvert and resumed their former life in the Province, while others chose

---

* Designs of the Maryland Calverts! Another example of self-effacement by Virginians in their chauvinism and blindness for truth. The Maryland Calverts were interested only in land which they held sovereign rights as defined in the Royal Charter and clarified and interpreted by the best legal talent of that day in Great Britain. While many Marylanders of a very high calibre removed to Virginia after 1644, they were mostly the conservative element which fled from Ingle and his ruffians. Conservatism and aristocracy are hand maidens, so Virginia received a very high type of planter at the expense of Maryland. Virginia's laws against Quakers and all non-conformists sent an element to Maryland undesired in Virginia which ultimately lay the foundation for the Puritan Commonwealth of 1650 and more remotely the revolution of 1689. The establishment of the Commonwealth in Maryland in 1650 sent more conservative Marylanders to the Northern Neck, and as a result brought culture, aristocracy, and way-of-life to the Northern Neck not heretofore known in Virginia.

† Later Willan was rewarded with manorial rights on Snow Hill Manor for his bravery and support of the Proprietary government at the battle of the Severn.

to remain in Virginia. Perhaps Captain Fleete was one who for reasons undisclosed chose to remain. At that time his old rival William Clayborne was not so high in favour as he had previously been. He was no longer Secretary of State, Surveyor General, Councilor or even a burgess to the Lower House.

His first Virginia land grant on record was in 1650, according to Nugent's *Cavaliers and Pioneers*, when he received 1750 acres of land on Fleet's Bay in Lancaster County. He was styled Lieutenant-Colonel Henry Fleete and was both a Justice of the Peace and Burgess of Lancaster County. He maintained business relations with Marylanders, however, throughout his life and in 1652 he appointed John Hallowes his lawful attorney to sue William Eltonhead, Gent., for 1500 lbs. tob.[20]

Owing to the casual manner in which land and probate records were kept in colonial Virginia, no settlement of his estate is on record, and only one issue, a son Henry, has been proved. He was deceased by November 15, 1660, when "Mrs. Sarah Fleete the widow and relict of the said Henry Fleete" declared that John Manning, an apprentice, had been maintained several years by her late husband.

Sources: 1. Berry's Kentish Pedigrees; Famillae Minorum Gentium, Harleian Soc. Pub., vol. 40, p. 1297; 2. Hale's Virginia Venturer, p. 177; 3. Hall's Narratives of Early Maryland, p. 40; 4. *Ibid.*, p. 41; 5. *Ibid.;* 6. *Ibid.;* 7. Fund Pub. no. 35, p. 21; 8. Calvert Papers no. 192; 9. Archives of Maryland, vol. 1, p. 37; 10. Archives, vol. 1, p. 28; 11. Liber 1, folio 96, Land Office; 12. Archives, vol. 3, p. 151; 13. Archives, vol. 3, pp. 148-149; 15. Archives, vol. 4, p. 275; 16. Archives, vol. 4, p. 281; 17. Archives, vol. 4, p. 284; 18. Archives, vol. 4, p. 286; 19. Archives, vol. 4, p. 201; 20. Archives, vol. 10, pp. 275, 338.

FRANCISCO A MULATTO

Francisco "a molato" accompanied Father White as one of his servants—one record states in 1633, another 1635. He was apparently part Portuguese, of a nation where crossing with African slave blood was practised with great profligacy. Furthermore, Father White had spent some time in Portugal and could have brought him to England as a body servant. No further record exists for him, and if he did not succumb to an early death in Maryland, he probably returned to England with Father White in 1644.

LEWIS FREMOND

Lewis Fremond [Freeman, Froman] was transported by Father White in 1633 who assigned his land rights to Ferdinand Poulton. Later evidence indicates that he was about ten years of age at the time of the sailing and was therefore one of the few boys of tender age on the voyage. At a session of the Provincial Court of 1653/4, he deposed to be 29 years of age, therefore, it is understood why he did not attend the 1637-38 General Assembly.

He had acquired his freedom by 1639, and qualified as a freeholder of Mattapanient Hundred to vote for Henry Bishop to represent that hundred in the February-March 1638/9 Assembly.[1] About that time he was approximately 15 or 16 years of age, probably 16, which gives evidence of the majority age recognized at that time in the Province. At the 1641 and 1642 General Assemblies called for all freeholders, he gave his proxy to Cuthbert Fenwick.[2]

His residence seemed to have been consistently in Mattapanient Hundred near the Jesuit Mission and for that reason it can be assumed that his faith was that of Rome. In 1642 he was assessed 33 lbs. tob. at the levy of Mattapanient Hundred, and his name appeared frequently during the 1642-43 sessions of the Provincial Court. In 1648 he served on the jury of the Provincial Court and in 1649 he sued Elias Beach for the purchase of a pair of shoes, a pair of knit stockings, 2 lbs. of powder, and 4 lbs. of shot, "about 9 years since", thus proving that he was the same Lewis Fremond of that name in the Province in 1640.[3] Beach denied that delivery had been made, but proof was presented that delivery had been made thereupon the court ordered Beach to pay him 150 lbs. tob. at the next crop.

Although he made his mark in 1641, he later acquired the art of writing and became fluent with the language of the Indians, and acted as interpreter to Robert Brooke, Esq., when he settled on the Patuxent about 1650.

At court in 1654, he deposed to be 29 years of age, and made the following statement:[4]

> "That about a month or Six weeks after Mʳ Robert Brookes was seated in Putuxent River this Deponent being then Servant to the Said mr Brooks and Imployed as an Interpreter by him to the Indians, mr Brooke desired this Deponent to Speake to the Indians he the Imployed, that if they Saw any hogs they Should kill them, about a weeke or fortnight after, the Said Indians Came and told him of hogs which were about a quarter of a Mile from his house whereupon he bid his people goe with them and kill them at which time by mr Brooks Sons, his Servants & Indians there was killed one Boare five or Six Barrowes and Sowes, the Marks this depont doth not Remember neither did mr Brooks in this Depont hearing, give orders that the Eares Should be kept".

> (signed) Lewis ffroman

In 1650 he and Henry Adams sued Robert Brooke for 2,008 lbs. tob., and on May 19, 1651, he registered his cattle mark at court.[5] At a court held in August 1658, as Lew ffroeman through his attorney Nicholas Gwyther he sued Robert Holt for 100 lbs. tob.[6] In 1658 he was about 34 years of age, but no record of the settlement of his estate is available nor any further mention has been found for him among the extant records of Maryland.

Sources: 1. Archives, vol. 1, p. 28; 2. Archives, vol. 1, pp. 106, 168; 3. Archives, vol. 4, pp. 485, 491; 4. Archives, vol. 10, p. 353; 5. Archives, vol. 10, pp. 59, 88; 6. Archives, vol. 41, pp. 128, 137.

RICHARD GERARD, ESQ.

Richard Gerard, Esq., was truly one of the Cavaliers or Gentlemen of Rank and Fashion on the Ark, being a younger son of Sir Thomas Gerard, Bart., K.B., of Lancashire. In 1633 he was young seeking adventure, but after a year or two in Maryland he craved greater excitement, so returned to England and later sought his fortune in new fields including India and the Far East. According to Neil, Richard Gerard was about 20 years of age and remained about one year. During the Civil Wars he adhered to the King and was Governor of Denbigh Castle. At the restoration he was one of the cup bearers to Charles II.

He brought in five men—Thomas Minnus, Thomas Grogson, Robert Edwards, John Ward, and William Edwin—whose land rights he assigned to Ferdinand Pulton, Gent., a Jesuit, as proved by the latter when he made land claims on October 9, 1639.

When Captain Cornwalys settled the estate of John Sanders, Esq., "severall discharges [were shown] under the hand of Richard Gerard, Thomas White, and Roger Walton". It indicated that Gerard was either a legatee or had owed the estate. The account was not recorded at court until March 20, 1638/9, though Gerard had certainly returned to England prior to January 1637/8, as he failed to attend the 2d General Assembly.

Evidence is quite convincing that a lordship was granted him by Lord Baltimore before his embarkation from England and which he assigned to the Jesuits per letter of Father Copley to Cecilius, of April 3, 1638, "yet if we should choose Metapanian first, then we are sure to loose Mr. Gerard's Mannor, not wth standing that we have bought it at a deer raite".*

---

* Calvert Papers, p. 164. This reference to Gerard's Manor can not be a manor of Thomas Gerard, Esq., who later held lordships on St. Clement's, Westwood, and Basford. Thomas Gerard did not receive his first manor until 1641, so therefore the manor referred to in Father Copley's letter had to be that of Richard. Furthermore, it was more logical for one to convey land upon leaving the Province rather than one coming in.

THOMAS GERVASE

Thomas Gervase, probably a Frenchman, was one of two lay members of the Jesuit Order who Father White transported to Maryland. His death occurred in 1637. Ref: Calvert Papers, reprinted in Fund Publication no. 7, pp. 117, 126.

RICHARD GILBERT

Richard Gilbert was transported by Leonard Calvert, Esq. in 1633 and from a strict interpretation of the records there are no indications of his entering the Province in the capacity of a servant. It is definitely the story of an adventurer leaving his young wife and children in England on a trial voyage to a new land, with the apparent promise of returning and bringing them over if conditions proved favourable. His return voyage was undoubtedly on one of the early ships which touched at St. Mary's City, for he was back in the Province by 1637 at the latest. His seat was in St. Mary's Hundred.

He financed his second passage and those of his wife, Rose, their two children, Grace and Elizabeth, and he likewise brought two contracted servants—Walter Waterling and Thomas Thomas, with hopes of starting life anew as a gentleman planter. His ambitions and plans were thwarted, however, by an untimely death before 1638, leaving a widow and two small children in a strange land.

It is well to place him as a member of the minor gentry, for true it is that no instrument is extant to prove whether he was lettered, but his wife had definitely received early training in the art of writing, an accomplishment not always accorded the daughters of even the esquires. She signed her name in all instances and was born in or about 1609. While she was not accorded the title of Madam or Mrs. in after life, it was perhaps due to her marriage with a member of the yeomanry—at least her second husband always made his mark.

Shortly after her first husband's death, Leonard Calvert sued the Widow Gilbert for certain goods and commodities sold her husband, to which she replied in court on January 20, 1637/8, that the obligation had partially been paid, but then lacked the means to remit the balance, but she would do so whenever possible.[1]

Within a short time or on November 23, 1638, Robert Smith, Planter, announced his intentions at court of marrying the widow and that he "is not precontracted to any other woman than Rose Gilbert and that there is noe Inpediment of Consanquinty affinity nor any other lawfull Impediment".[2]

Thereafter her life became connected with that of her second husband, but she had two daughters whose father was one of those Adventurers who dared cross the ocean in 1633 to aid in the establishing a new State. And unless the two daughters of Richard Gilbert died young or were greatly deformed, they had no difficulty in finding mates at that period in Maryland history.

While documentary proof is lacking, but circumstantial evidence keen and ripe, it is believed that Elizabeth Gilbert, the elder daughter, married William Asbeston, and Grace, the younger daughter, married Walter Waterling who as a youth was brought over by her father in the same ship with her.

Robert Smith was rewarded by marrying the widow of Richard Gilbert and acquired the land rights of Gilbert as well as those of Gilbert's family and the two servants. And the land which he acquired was not devised to his step-children at his death but to his own progeny.

Sources: 1. Archives, vol. 2, pp. 10-11; 2. Archives, vol. 4, p. 51.

STEPHEN GORE

Stephen Gore came in as one of the men servants of Captain Cornwalys, for whom he established land claims in 1640. He must have succumbed before the Assembly of 1637/8, inasmuch as he did not claim a seat or can any further references be found for him in the Province.

THOMAS GREENE, ESQ.

Thomas Greene, Esq., one of the Gentlemen of Rank and Fashion and boyhood friend of Leonard Calvert, was destined to be the second Provincial Governor of Maryland. He was listed, however, inadvertently as Henry Greene in the 1635 publication of "A Relation of Maryland", as having gone to the Maryland plantations. As Thomas Greene, "of Bobbing, Kent", his father was created a Knight Bachelor of the Realm on September 5, 1622, at Windsor Castle by James I.[1] His mother, Margaret, Lady Greene, was the daughter of Thomas Webb, of Frittenden.[2]

He and his three brothers, Robert, John and Jeremiah, grew up in the Parish of Bobbing which lay in the northeastern portion of Kent and about two miles from Sittingbourne which was not too distant from Boxley where the children of George, Lord Baltimore, spent their childhood. In some manner the family or some members of it had affiliated with the Roman Catholic Church, yet his great-grandfather, Thomas Greene, had received favours from Henry VIII and at the confiscation of church lands had received the rectory of Bobbing Manor and "all manors, messuages, glebe, tithes and hereditaments in the parishes and fields of Bobbing, Iwade, Halstow, and Newington in capite by knight's service".

There was much colour and dash to the character of Thomas Greene which have not been written into the pages of Maryland history and his position as a conservative and loyal subject of the Stuarts and the Calverts has been criticized with derogation by the liberal writers of history rather than praised by the introspective student for his stand on ethical and judicial questions.

He not only professed the Catholic dogma but became one of the leading laymen of the Church during the infant and trying days of the Province. His conservativeness and social values which became a target for the liberal views of the Puritans and the rabble were his undoing later on.

He embarked on the Ark with all the prerogatives of the major gentry to which he had been accustomed for a number of generations, but so far as it has been proved, his retinue consisted of only two servants—Anan Benham and Thomas Cooper—though he transported a third servant in 1634.

He imbibed evidently with much abandonment at the Christmas celebration and no doubt felt the effects during the next few days, but the Lord spared him for some useful purpose, yet his very good friend, Nicholas Fairfax, was called to the proverbial bosom of Abraham. Feeling the end was near, Fairfax bequeathed his friend, Thomas Greene, all rights to which he was entitled in the settlement of Maryland.

Before embarkation, as it would seem from circumstances, Thomas Greene was granted by George, Lord Baron, large manorial tracts of land of which no direct records at present exist. By the spring of 1638, however, he was seized of 10,000 acres, as proved by a letter of Father Copley to Cecilius, Lord Baltimore, dated April 3, 1638. While Copley was referring to manors and the high fees and services to the Lord Proprietary required by the individual manor lords and the insufficient tenants to labour on the manors, it is evident that the 10,000 acres of Thomas Greene constituted a lordship. Father Copley stated "And accordingly Mr. Greene one of the Gentlemen that came in the Arke reffecting that besydes the losse of his halfe share of trucke, he was not to pay tenne barrels of Corne for his 10,000 acres, and that only he had three men to raise that and maintaine himselfe and his wyfe, confidently told me that he must necessarily deserte the Colyne".[3]

The 10,000 acres were certainly not under any extant Conditions of Plantation, but presumably under the 1633 conditions which has not been preserved, and inasmuch as this manor did not descend to his son and heir, it is apparent that it was either assigned or allowed to escheat to the Lord Proprietary, Thomas Greene himself being unable to remit the quit-rents and maintain such an estate at that time.

Later Thomas Greene was granted another manorial domain by Cecilius, with the same prerogatives as expressed in the ancient letters of patent perhaps to the ancestoral seat in Kent and which he gave the name of "Bobbing" in fond recollections of the family estate.

Although there is little or no word or painted description of Thomas Greene which has come down to posterity, he apparently possessed great personal charm, for, of the several cavaliers and young buxoms on the Ark and the Dove and with the ratio of about 75 men to one woman, he was the gallant who won the consent of Mistress Ann Cox, the only proved gentlewoman on board, though it is believed that there were others. And his was the only known romance which sparkled and matured on that perilous trip across the Atlantic which has come to knowledge.

In the light of present diligent research, Thomas Greene was not married at the time of his sailing from England and therefore can not be credited with the three marriages usually accorded him, with the story of leaving a young and faithful wife behind with two healthy youngsters to perpetuate the house of Greene. A document states definitely in no ambiguous wording that Mistress Ann was *his first wife*.† The full Roman Catholic rites were certainly solemnized on the verdant banks of the St. George's River one spring morning by Father White, for a crowded and congested

† "Thomas Green Esqʳ demandeth 500 acres of land on his first Wife's right vizt Mʳˢ Ann Cox for Speciall Grant of his lordship unto her coming with this province in the year 1633 . . ." Ref: Patents, Liber ABH, folio 12, Land Office, Annapolis.

ship was not propitious for an infare. His nuptials can therefore be credited with the distinction of being the first marriage to have been celebrated and consummated on Maryland soil. And as his was the first known marriage to have occurred in the Province, the birth of his son and heir, Thomas, was undoubtedly the first English child to have been born under the baronial standards of Lord Baltimore in his Palatinate on the Potomac.*

Looking at the facts and conditions objectively and with realism, the two sons, Thomas and Leonard, who were born in Maryland, were sent to England which seems only natural under the auspiciousness of the times. Their mother died leaving two helpless babes in a virgin and somewhat crude land with little or none of the 17th century comforts of old England. Women were conspicuously absent during the first few years and Thomas Greene had no known maid-servant in his household until 1638, so it was only logical that a father would feel concern for the early training of his progeny and considered that their welfare would be better in England with the opportunity of nurse-maid care at Bobbing and the ultimate chance of some basic and rudimentary factors in education, not obtainable in a pioneer settlement.

Robert Greene, Esq., the elder brother of Thomas and heir-apparent to the Kentish parental estates, came over to Maryland for a brief period soon after the voyage of the Ark and the Dove, but returned to England at a date unknown, assigning his brother, Thomas, his land-rights. It is logical to assume that the two motherless boys born in Maryland sailed under the care of their paternal uncle.

In 1638 there emigrated to Maryland Mistress Winifred Seybourne who by her title indicated gentle birth and likewise one who had arrived to the age of discretion to be recognized as a *feme sole* in matter of ethics and business. She emigrated, that is, financed her own passage thus indicating a lady of means. She no doubt arrived on the same ship with Mistress Troughan [Throughton], for on the same day, that is, July 30, 1638, Lord

---

* The condition which proves conclusively that the two eldest sons were born after 1634 is amply substantiated by the document of November 1650, when their father shortly before his death made provisions for his four sons and ultimate widow. He stated definitely that his sons, no exceptions were made, were to enjoy their estates at 18 years of age, the age of majority at that time, consequently all four sons were minors in 1650 and were necessarily born after 1632. If Thomas and Leonard had been begotten by a marriage prior to his sailing for Maryland in 1633, Thomas the acknowledged son and heir, estimating his birth in 1631, would therefore had attained the age of discretion by 1650 and Leonard almost or just about, estimating the latter's birth as of 1633.

The appointment of guardianships and the placing of their property under trustees were therefore *fait accompli* and would have been "non suit", if one or another had attained eighteen years of age as specified by their father in the instrument. Furthermore, we have the significant statement in 1648 that Mistress Ann Cox was the first wife. These facts and conditions leave no arbitrary arguments notwithstanding for the agnostic to attempt to disapprove the truth of their being born in Maryland and being the sons of Mistress Ann Cox.

Baltimore personally issued instructions for a warrant of 100 acres for Mistress Winifred Seyborne [Seaborne] for transporting herself in 1638 and at the same time a warrant of 100 acres for Mistress Troughan. It was not so long after the arrival of Mistress Winifred that she lost her independent status and married the widower Thomas Greene.

As it has been demonstrated, years would elapse before the various settlers proved land-rights and Thomas Greene was no exception. On September 1, 1648, Thomas Greene, Esq., demanded 2,000 acres of land from His Lordship's Land Office for the transportation of himself and two servants, Thomas Cooper and Anan Benham, in 1633, also the assigned rights of his friend, Nicholas Fairfax, Esq., who died en route and of William Smith who transported himself in 1633. He likewise requested land for the transportation of his servant, Thomas Willis, in 1634, the rights of Mistress Winifred Seyborne then his wife for transporting herself in 1638, and the transportation of his two children, Thomas and Leonard, in 1644. A warrant was subsequently issued for 2,000 acres on the north side of Hierom's Creek.

The correct analysis and interpretation of the above claims prove that Mistress Winifred Seyborne who later became his wife emigrated in 1638 and that six years later his two sons arrived. The instrument does not read, as it has so often been stated orally as well as in print, that Mistress Seyborne brought the two boys with her. It is quite possible that the two youngsters, both of whom were more than six years of age, came under the protection and care of the ship's captain or that of their Uncle Robert, as Thomas Greene made no claims for land for other person or persons who came in that year. If Mistress Seyborne had returned for her step-sons after she married Thomas Greene, an additional 100 acres could have been claimed for her re-entry which is certainly not on record. And the sometime caustic remark, that Winifred Seyborne had been his mistress before the sailing of the Ark and the Dove and the mother of the two sons, defeats itself by documentary facts and is not worth refutation.

On December 1, 1648, a few months after the above land-rights, Thomas Greene applied for additional land by the following rights and assignments:[4]

"Thomas Green Esqr demandeth 500 acres of land on his first Wife's right Viz^t Mrs Ann Cox by Speciall Grant of his Lordship unto her coming into this Province in the year 1633, and 50 acres more for a Maid Servt vizt Ann Pyke brought into this Province in the year 1638, and 150 acres more for a Man and maid Servt viz Henry Adams and Ann Norris brought into the province in the year 1639, and 50 acres more for a Maid Servt vizt Margarett Nutbrown brought in in the year 1640 and 50 acres more for a maid Servt Viz^t Alice Philips brought in in the year 1648, and 100 acres more by Ass^t of his brother Robert Green Esqr".

Governor Leonard Calvert had ordered previously on October 15, 1639,[5] that 55 acres of townland be surveyed for Thomas Greene, as the following will demonstrate:

> "I would have you sett forth for Mr. Thomas Gerrard* (*sic*) as assigne of Nicholas Fairfax and William Smith first Adventurers Twenty Acres and in his own right for himself and two servants brought in by the first Adventure thirty acres and for 5 acres being in all 55 acres of Townland lying nearest together about the house where the said Mr. Green now dwelleth and for so long this shall be your warrant".
>
> (signed) Leonard Calvert

> "Sett forth for Mr. Thomas Green a portion of Town Land being in figure a Romboides whereof the North side bounding upon the Town Land of Mrs Margaret and Mrs. Mary Brent is laid out for 18 perches the East side bounding upon St. Mary's Forest and beginning at a pathway leading from St. Mary's Forest and beginning at a pathway leading from St. Mary's Hill to the head of St. Peter's Creek and running by a North West and by West line to the bank of St. George River is laid out for 20 perches so that the whole area thereof is laid out to contain five and fifty Acres or thereabouts".
>
> (signed) John Lewger, Sur.

He received other land grants, one of which was for 2500 acres, but his death occurred before the patent was actually issued. Consequently in 1665, it was laid out and surveyed in Charles County for his three surviving sons who gave it the name of "Green's Inheritance". His seat, however, was at "Green's Rest", sometimes called "Green Freehould", the townland of 55 acres within the environs of St. Mary's City and bordering St. Mary's [St. George's] River.

He took a serious interest in all affairs of the Province and became one of the leading factors in the early political developments. He attended the early General Assemblies to whom all freeholders were summoned, and when the legislature became representative and the Upper House or Privy Council developed, he was one of the first to be appointed by the Lord Proprietary to that body which was a counterpart to the British House of Lords. He was also appointed one of the Justices of the Provincial Court at its inception. He retained his seat in the Council until 1647, when he succeeded to the governorship by the death of Leonard Calvert, the first Provincial Governor. His term of office lasted until April 26, 1649, when Lord Baltimore commissioned Captain William Stone, of Virginia, to succeed him in an attempt to appease the Liberals.

He was a Royalist to the core and never deviated from his convictions as a faithful servant and admirer of Lord Baltimore and a loyal subject of the King. His conservatism contrasted greatly with his contemporary and

---

* The copy in the Land Office states Thomas Gerrard inadvertently copied by a clerk, but facts definitely prove that it should be Thomas Greene.

successor, Captain William Stone, who nourished Puritan sympathies, yet never openly declared himself one.

When Governor Stone made a trip to Virginia, he deputized his predecessor as the Acting Governor and it was during that period that a ship's captain brought the news to Maryland that Charles I had been beheaded by the Puritans. Thereupon Acting Governor Greene proclaimed Charles II as the rightful successor and celebrated the occasion with wine and song and granted complete amnesty to all prisoners, much to the disfavour of the Puritans and other non-conformists. The wrath was so great that some would liked to have beheaded him. Upon the return of Stone, the action taken by Greene was repudiated.

On November 18, 1650, he executed a document whereby he assigned his entire estate in trust under certain conditions to his friends, Henry Adams and James Langworth, for the benefit of his wife, Winifred, and sons—Thomas, Leonard, Robert, and Francis. He desired his wife to have full possession of the estate during life except for a certain amount of tobacco which was bequeathed to his friend and priest, Thomas Copley. His widow was to grant his sons the designated shares in succession as they came of age, ". . . be Sufficiently maintained and Provided for . . . both for Subsistance and Education answerable to their qualify until each of them respectively come to eighteen years of age". In the event of his widow's decease and the death of his sons without issue, then three-fourths of his estate were to be distributed to charity and the residue to James Langworth and to Henry Adams, whom he had transported as a redemptioner.

He died before January 20, 1651/2, the day on which Henry Adams appeared in court as the trustee of the estate. His widow married secondly Robert Clarke, Gent., one-time Surveyor-General of the Province and steward to the Jesuit's manors. She became the mother of at least two children—Robert and Thomas Clarke. On November 16, 1654, Robert Clarke on behalf of his wife, Winifred Clarke "late wife of Thomas Greene deceased and her children by the said Greene" demanded 400 acres of land for the transportation by Thomas Greene of four servants on June 10, 165–.

In 1658 William Hewes instituted action against Robert Clarke for repairs on "Green's Rest" before Clarke married the widow of Thomas Greene. At that time Madam Greene-Clarke was deceased. Hewes claimed that Captain William Stone engaged him for the work and that the overseers of the estate of Thomas Greene should be responsible for the expenditures.

Sources: 1. Shaw's The Knights of England, vol. 2, p. 180; 2. Hasted's Kent, vol. 2, pp. 635-639; 3. Fund Pub. no. 28, pp. 159-160; 4. Land Office, Liber ABH, folio 12; 5. *Ibid.*, folios 6, 67.

Thomas Grigston

Thomas Grigston, sometimes Grogson, was transported by Richard Gerard, Esq., who assigned his land claims to Ferdinando Pulton. No further references are available. Ref: Liber ABH, folio 66; Liber 1, folio 38, Land Office, Annapolis.

John Halfhead, Brickman

John Halfhead who came over as one of Father White's indentures had an eventful and long life in the Province, acquired three wives, and after residence of 42 years was perhaps at his death one of the last surviving Adventurers, if not, the last. He was the provincial bricklayer which in that day required the molding of bricks from the local clay as well as laying them in house construction. The apprentices which he trained carried on after his passing, so the early brick plantation homes in St. Mary's County were no doubt his handiwork. He was born in or about 1608, according to a 1651 deposition, and was unschooled in letters.

At first he resided in St. Mary's Hundred and had served his period of indentureship by 1637/8, when as John Halfhead, Brickmason, he gave his proxy to Justinian Snow, Esq. In 1650 he signed as a Protestant subject of His Lordship.

Later he maintained a plantation on the Patuxent which adjoined the manorial seat of Madam Jane Eltonhead. It was there in 1651 that the death of Thomas Lisle occurred as a result of a fall from a tree. At court on October 25, 1651, Christopher Walter, aged about 12 or 13 years, one of his apprentices, swore that he was present when Lisle fell "out of tree in John Halfhead's this Depondent's Master's Plantacon at Patuxent River" and died about one-half hour afterwards.[1] Thomas Hamper likewise stated that he was at the plantation of John Halfhead when he heard "Christopher Walter John Halfhead's boy cry out Master, Master" and saw Thomas Lisle who died about one-half hour afterwards lying under a tree, being speechless for about 15 minutes before his death. At one time he had a maid servant, Jane Miccolgutt, whom he sold to Cuthbert Fenwick, Esq.

His first wife was Ann _____, a free woman, while his second wife was Juliana _____ who had been a bond servant of Mr. White. In 1657, Juliana Halfhead, aged 34, testified in the lawsuit of Henry Coursey vs Thomas Seamor.[2] By 1664, however, Juliana had died and he had married thirdly Elizabeth _____ who in 1665 swore that she was aged 49. He no doubt had several daughters who found husbands among the yeomanry or "goodman" planters in the Province, but no record has been found.

On March 2, 1649/50, in his instance styled Planter, he received "100 acres of land due to him in the said Province in respect his being Servt to us there and 100 acres more in right of Ann his first wife a Free woman and 50 acres more in right of Julian his now Wife who was Servant to

Mr. White who where all of them long Since Transported into the province". The grant was issued under the Conditions dated at Portsmouth on August 8, 1636, and the 200-acre unnamed plantation lay on the south side of the Patuxent next to the land of Joseph Edloe, according to Liber ABH, folio 118.

The inventory of his personal estate was filed at court on February 5, 1675/6, with an appraised value of 25,562 lbs. tob. Among the items were a silver cup, two thin silver spoons, 35 breast silver buttons, and an unnamed servant girl, who was appraised at 1,600 lbs. tob. A subsequent account showed 422 lbs. tob. paid to Christopher Rousby for funeral expenses and the record of a servant bought from Benjamin Massey for 948 lbs. tob.

His son and heir, John Halfhead Jr., who was born presumably of the first union, died shortly after his father or on January 6, 1678/9, by the falling of a tree.[3] His widow, Jane, married soon thereafter Henry Elliott who on July 2, 1679, filed an account with the court showing an estate valued at 25,265 lbs. tob. Disbursements had been made to Dr. Jacob Loockerman for services. A chancery case of 1678 proves that John Halfhead had leased 400 acres of land in Brushey Neck, St. Mary's County, from William Gwyther "where Henry Elliott who intermarried with Jane the Relict of the said Halfehead now dwells" on which 5 bushels of corn as rent was then due. The male line definitely died with the son and heir, as this quaint old English name is not found thereafter in Maryland.

Sources: 1. Archives, vol. 10, p. 154; 2. Archives, vol. 10, p. 551; 3. Archives, vol. 51, p. 252; 4. Archives, vol. 51, p. 222.

MAJOR JOHN HALLOWES, GENT.

John Hallowes [Hollis], Gent., born about 1613, was of Rochdale, Lancashire, England, and was in the retinue of Captain Thomas Cornwalys, having been assigned him by James Saunders, Esq. His name frequently appeared as Hollis, and there was also a John Hallowes, Carpenter, contemporary with him, but there is no evidence to assume that the Carpenter came with the first Adventurers. On March 21, 1641, Thomas Morris exhibited proxies at the Assembly for John Hallowes and John Hallowes, Carpenter, thus proving two colonists with identical names.[1]

In 1635 John Hallowes and Cuthbert Fenwick, both retainers of Captain Cornwalys at that time, were on the "St. Margaret" with a company of fourteen, when William Clayborne fired upon the pinnace and mortally wounded William Ashmore.[2]

By December 1638, he had completed his period of indentureship, when he witnessed a deed of conveyance, and on June 1, 1639, he expressed his intentions to marry Restituta Tue, declaring that no impediment existed and gave his bond for 1000 lbs. tob. to the Lord Proprietary.[3] He signed the bond. The marriage, performed by Mr. Thomas White, occurred on the day following with Cuthbert Fenwick and Robert Percy as witnesses.

She had been transported in 1636 by Captain Cornwalys. Her brother, John Tue [Tew], was in Maryland at one time, but later settled in Westmoreland County, Virginia, where he served as one of the county's magistrates. He married Grace, the widow of Major Thomas Baldridge, an early figure in St. Mary's County.

John Hallowes first established his seat in St. Michael's Hundred, and attended a session of the Assembly on March 21, 1641/2, "appeared after the house was risen". Although he attended one or two sessions, he generally gave his proxy, and in September 1642, Captain Cornwalys held the proxies of John Hollis, Planter, and John Hollis, Carpenter.[4]

At a session of the court held on May 2, 1643, John Hallowes, of St. Michael's Hundred "for consideration of 267 of good & merchantable winter Beave due from me to Captain Thomas Cornwaleys of the Crosse" placed a lien on four milch cows, two stears, and three calves, and also all swine male and female".[5]

Sometime before November 1648, John Hallowes removed to Northumberland County, Virginia, where he became one of the important planters of that section. At court in that year held in Maryland "John Tew age 21 or thereabouts swore under oath that the cow which John Hallowes carryed out from St. Maries to Appamatucks for the use of Mr. Speake of Chicasoan was marked with an hallow crop in one year".[6]

On November 23, 1648, at the Provincial Court John Hatch "complayneth against Jno Hallowes of Appamatucks for transporting out of the province Jno Walton who was indebted unto the complt in the somme of 260 lb tob and 1 hogshead and desureth of this court that the sd Jno Hallowes may be ordered to satisfy and pay the sd debt unto the Complt according to the Custome of this province in that kind providing".[7]

On September 17, 1649, Edward Hill, of Maryland, appointed John Hollis his attorney to collect all debts due him in the County of Northumberland.[8] On January 10, 1649/50, Thomas Spake, Gent. received 400 acres of land from the Governor of Virginia, adjoining the plantation of John Hallowes.[9] By 1649 John Hallowes was definitely established as a Virginia planter.

At a session of the Maryland Provincial Court in February 1649/50, Restitua, the wife of John Hallowes, appeared as his attorney to answer the suit of Marks Phelps. On June 25, 1650, at the Provincial Court of Maryland, Paul Simpson, "Marriner aged 60 years swore that about last March he being with Lt William Lewis at Appamatock in the County of Northumberland in Virginia then and there heard Mr. John Hallowes his wife say to the said Lt Lewis that she suspected hee had inveigged and intended to carry away one William Greenstead & Thomas Meredith who shee said were servants that had run away to absented themselves from their Mrs service".[10]

In 1650 he was granted 600 acres of land in Northumberland County on the south side of the Potomac River on the east side of Hallowes Creek for transporting 12 persons to Virginia, among whom were Restitute Hallowes Jr., Restitute Hallowes Sr., and John Tew. At the same time he received 1600 acres in the same county beginning at the head of Canawoman Creek for transporting 32 persons, and also an additional 200 acres on the west side of a marsh and swamp which divided the land from Thomas Speake.[11]

By September 20, 1652, he had been commissioned a Magistrate for Northumberland County, and as a Magistrate he attended sessions of the court held on January 20, 1652/3, and March 10, 1652/3.[12]

He was esteemed by Captain Cornwalys, of Maryland, for on February 22, 1653/4, he appointed his "loveing friend John Hallowes, of Nominy in the County of Westmoreland in Virginia, Gent." his attorney to collect all debts due him.

On September 20, 1655, John Hallowes, Gent., aged 40 years or thereabouts swore and examined in court stated that "he this Depont heard Mr. Dodson confess at Mr. Dedmans house that his the said Dodsons Instruments were false . . . they were tryed at Colonel Claybornes". It was signed as "Jo Hallowes" and presented at court held in Westmoreland County, Virginia, on October 21, 1653.[13]

Before the above mentioned deposition, however, John Hallowes appeared in April 1653, at the Maryland Provincial Court, "I Capt. John Hallowes doe hereby acquitt and discharge Thomas Baker of and from one Bill of 680 lb tob with Caske". It was witnessed by Richard Browne and Thomas Bennett. In June 1753, before the Provincial Court of Maryland, "John Hallowes gent. aged 40 yeares or thereabouts Sworen & Examined Sayeth That before Ralph Beane went for England I the said John Hallowes did pay unto the aforesaid Ralph Beane Sixteen hundred pounds of Tobacco & caske for the use of John Dandy".[14]

On September 11, 1653, he received a patent for 2400 acres of land bordering the Potomac River, Connawoman Creek and Nomany Bay.

At the organization of Westmoreland County from Northumberland, the plantation of John Hallowes lay in the newly created county. At a court held in that county on April 4, 1655, "Mr. John Hallowes of the Quorum" was one of the Commissioners.[15] At the same time he was commissioned a Major of the Colonial Militia, along with Colonel Thomas Speke, Lieutenant Colonel Nathaniel Pope, Captain Thomas Blagg, and Captain Alex Bainham.

By the last will and testament of Thomas Boys, dated August 1, 1656, he bequeathed "unto Major John Hallows my very loving friend my Gold ring, 2000 lbs. tob. & Cask & one of my best sture". In the event that his executors could not locate his son and sister living near Newport, Isle of Wight, then Major John Hallows, John Hilles and Thomas Wilsford were to have additional legacies.[16]

"Major John Hollis" was in Maryland during a session of the Provincial Court in 1657, when he swore that "John Nevill was indebted" to him for 446 lbs. tob. At the same time as "Major John Hollowes", he swore to be 41 years of age. It was also stated that John Dandy was apprehended for suspicion of murder, had made his escape to Virginia, and then committed unto the hands of Major John Hallowes.[17]

John Tew, brother to Madam Restitute Hallowes, died in Westmoreland County, and by his will, dated June 2, 1655, and probated on July 20, following, he divided his estate among his wife, Grace Tew, and "nephews John Hallowes Jr. and Restitute Hallowes".[18]

At court on January 10, 1655/6, Major John Hallowes declared that his servant "Sion the Turk" was then a free man. At the same time he renounced all rights to the cattle belonging to John Tew, deceased, and registered the cattle marks of his children, John and Restitute, as gifts of John Tew by his last will and testament.[19]

Children of John and Restitute (Tew) Hallowes
1. John Hallowes, probably married, but left no issue.
2. Restitute Hallowes married John Whetstone. *q.v.*

It is quite likely that Major Hallowes married a second time, in fact there is definite proof. On April 27, 1657, he assigned a patent of 650 acres of land to William Robinson and John Cammell, at which time Elizabeth his wife waived all dower interests.[20]

On June 20, 1657, Mrs. Elizabeth Hallowes, the wife of Major John Hallowes, and Sam Hallowes, the son of Major John Hallowes, filed their hogs and cattle marks with the court.[21] No further record of Samuel has been found.

He was alive on June 20, 1657, when he sold a cow to John Jenkins. No will has been found. His daughter eventually became the sole heiress to the estate and left many descendants through her second marriage.

NOTE: It looks as if his son and heir, John, married Elizabeth ...., but no issue, if any, survived. On July 20, 1655, Elizabeth Hallowes, aged 24, swore in court that her "late" husband (unnamed) and John Sturman entered into a bargain which concerned land lying between the plantations of Mr. Speke and Richard Hawkins. William Hardich, aged 38, once of Maryland, made the same deposition. Ref: Westmoreland Record Book 1753-59, folio 38.

Sources: 1. Archives, vol. 1, p. 117; 2. Archives, vol. 4, p. 23; 3. Archives, vol. 4, p. 52; 4. Archives, vol. 1, p. 172; 5. Archives, vol. 4, p. 242; 6. Archives, vol. 4, p. 415; 7. Archives, vol. 4, p. 442; 8. Archives, vol. 4, p. 513; 9. Patent Book no. 2, p. 206, Va. State Libr.; 10. Archives, vol. 10, pp. 20, 100; 11. Patent Book, no. 2, pp. 281-282, Va. State Libr.; 12. Court Order Book, no. 2, pp. 8, 15, 21, 102; 13. Court Order Book, no. 2, p. 115; 14. Archives, vol. 10, pp. 265, 279; 15. Tyler's Magazine, vol. 4, p. 350; 16. Tyler's Magazine, vol. 4, p. 351; 17. Archives, vol. 10, p. 547; 18. Fothergill's Abstracts of Westmoreland Co. Wills, p. 1; 19. West: Co. Record Book 1653-59, folio 51; 20. *Ibid.*, folio 82; 21. *Ibid.*, folio 79.

NICHOLAS HARVEY, GENT.

Nicholas Harvey first entered the Province as a transportee of Father White who assigned his land rights to Thomas Copley, Esq. When Copley, or Father Fisher, applied for his land rights on August 16, 1650, the name of Nicholas Harvey inadvertently appeared in the records as Richard Harvey.*

Nicholas Harvey can be placed as a member of the county gentry, if not, Lord Baltimore would not have conferred a lordship upon him in 1641, though he came into the Province under the status of a redemptioner. He was literate and was a trusted public servant of the Calverts, holding minor offices under them. Although his grandchildren were members of the Church of England, it is believed that he held allegiance to Rome in the matter of religion, though no definite proof of this fact can be established. He was closely associated with Father White in his mission among the Indians at Mattapanient and he gave a saint's name to his manor. Furthermore, his man-servants were Roman Catholics, all of which would indicate that he was probably a communicant of the Church of Rome.

By 1637 Nicholas Harvey had settled in Mattapanient Hundred on the Patuxent River which was the first settlement made by the colonists outside the environs of St. Mary's City under the influence of Father White. He was a member of the jury which investigated the death of John Bryant, a planter of Mattapanient, and an Adventurer on the Ark. Harvey signed the statement at the inquest.

The Maquantequats [Mattachewatt. Mancantequats] Indians were plundering the plantations of the Marylanders, consequently on January 3, 1639/40, Governor Calvert authorized Harvey to pick at least twelve men "Sufficiently provided with arms to invade the Said Mancantequats only and against them and their lands and goods to execute and inflict what may be inflicted by the Law of warr and the pillage and booty therein gotten to part and divide among the Company, that Sall performe the Service".[1]

Shortly after his expedition against the Indians, he left the Province and presumably returned to England or perhaps Virginia. On September 1, 1641, Cecilius, Lord Baltimore addressed a letter to his brother, Leonard, requesting that Nicholas Harvey be granted manorial rights. He was back in the Province by December 17, 1641, when he "prayeth a greant of a Mannor of a thousand Acres on the South side of Patuxen River by Special Warrant from his Lordship". At that time he proved that he financed his passage to Maryland and at the same time he transported his wife un-named, his daughter Frances Harvey, and the following servants—Robert Beard, Henry Spink, John Chaire, and a boy Robert Ford. He was accordingly granted a lordship on the south side of the Patuxent River

---

* See assignment of land rights by Father White to Poulton on Oct. 9, 1638. Ref: Liber ABH, folio 65-66.

which he called "St. Joseph" and thus he was one of the early landed barons to seat that section which became noted for its manorial domains.[2]

He attended in person the succeeding General Assemblies often holding proxies of the neighbouring planters. In September 1642, he controlled the proxy of Richard Garnett [Gardiner] who held a lordship on St. Richard's Manor.[3] He was held in such high esteem that occasionally he sat on committees with the Governor, Captain Cornwalys, John Lewger, and Thomas Greene.[4]

At the Provincial Court of January 6, 1642/3, the Sheriff of St. Mary's County was ordered to seize all the goods which Nicholas Harvey had taken from Chapoy Senim, an Indian, and to deliver them to Manascott of the Patuxent and to explain why he shot and killed an Indian.[5]

He was at one time sued by Robert Ellyson, the barber-chirurgeon, for 955 lbs. tob. for the treatment of Henry Spink, his man-servant. Harvey stated that Ellyson neglected his servant "endangering of the man's life" and that he had to call in Henry Hooper, another chirurgeon.[6] In spite of the lawsuit, Harvey later or in January 1644/5 called in Robert Ellyson to attend "Jane the now wife".[7]

In August 1644, he drew up his last will and testament and bequeathed his entire estate to his daughter, Frances Harvey. No mention was made of a wife at that time, so it is assumed that the mother of Frances was then deceased. By January 1644/5, he had therefore married Jane _____ "the now wife". His will was probated at court on June 28, 1647.[8]

The administration of the estate became much involved. His widow, Jane, soon married a Thomas Green and departed for "Elisabeth River in Virginia" and left her young step-daughter in the hands of her deceased husband's neighbours. She and her second husband were conscious of the dower interest in St. Joseph's Manor, so in March 1654/6, conveyed their interest or one-third to Edward Lloyd, of Maryland.

The administration and the guardianship were first granted to Cuthbert Fenwick, Gent., and later to John Dandy, a blacksmith. During the administration Dandy testified that when Nicholas Harvey went to Virginia, he left a gold ring and a parcel of lace with his servant, Henry Spink, but that he wished he had them with him in Virginia "to supply his wants".

The estate was undoubtedly dissipated until the arrival of George Beckwith, Gent. in the Province, when in 1657 he championed the cause of the orphan and subsequently married her. He and the heiress of St. Joseph lived on the manor in a style excelled by few of the colonial planters and begot several children. All the girls married well and left many descendants.

The original manor house of Nicholas Harvey was undoubtedly small and compact, but it was the son-in-law, George Beckwith, Esq., who gained seigniory upon his marriage to the Harvey heiress and who constructed the manor house in the grand English manner which reputedly stood until

1880.* The Beckwiths of the next generation or two sought plantations in newer portions of the Province and early in the 18th century had alienated virtually their entire manorial holdings on the Patuxent.

According to the tax list of 1798, the manor house was possessed by James Hopewell and consisted of a main portion of 34 by 30 feet, with a one-story frame appendix on one side. The kitchen which was probably detached from the main structure was 28 by 11 feet, with several other detached dependencies. At the time of the fire it was owned by John H. Waters, Esq. An edition of the St. Mary's Beacon, April 15, 1880, stated that the house "took fire on Sunday morning about 8 o'clock and was entirely destroyed with two other buildings. The dwelling was of brick and was one of the oldest buildings in the county, its construction dating back to colonial times".

Sources: 1. Archives, vol. 3, p. 87; 2. Liber ABH, folio 102; 3. Archives, vol. 1, p. 168; 4. Archives, vol. 1, p. 175; 5. Archives, vol. 4, p. 166; 6. Archives, vol. 4, p. 230; 7. Archives, vol. 4, p. 294; 8. Md. Hist. Mag., vol. 7, p. 174.

* For description of the floor plan and the contents of each room, see Newman's "Seigniory in Early Maryland", pp. 44-49.

JEROME HAWLEY, ESQ.

Third in importance of the Adventurers connected with the Settlement of Maryland was Jerome Hawley, Esq., of Brentford, County Middlesex, Joint Commissioner with Captain Thomas Cornwalys, and certainly the most colourful and most unpredictable councilor of the group. He was reputed to be one of the heaviest investors in the enterprise and was likewise the heaviest loser. He was definitely one of the learned and fashionable Roman Catholic Gentlemen on the voyage, being the son of James Hawley, Esq., and born in the year 1590. He was also brother to Henry Hawley, Governor of the Barbadoes, and to William Hawley, one-time Deputy Governor of the same isles, later of Carolina and Maryland, so the Hawley family, including Gabriel, was quite interested and active in the settlement of the English plantations.

As a young man he seemed to have become somewhat involved in the web of the dissolute and alluring consort of the Earl of Somerset who conspired to poison the poet Sir Thomas Overbury, Knt. Among the British State papers, pertaining to the celebrated case, there is an order to the commissioners of King James, dated November 25, 1615, directing that "Jerome son of James Hawley now close prisoner in the Gate House be released on conditions of his not going farther than his father's house at Brentford".*

* Sir Thomas Overbury, who was infatuated with Sir Robert Kerr, Knt., became his adviser in affairs of the heart as well as politics. James I created Kerr the Earl of Somerset elevating him to a position beyond his education and ability. In the meantime Frances, daughter of Thomas Howard, 1st Earl of Suffolk, was then married to the Earl of Essex. Viscount Rochester involved himself in a liaison with the Countess and Overbury encouraged the intrigue and actually composed many of the poems and

After the accession of Charles I, Jerome Hawley was a member of the royal court and was one of the "sewers" or superintendent of the banquets and entertainments of the Queen Consort, Henrietta Maria, daughter of Henry IV of France.

Prior to his sailing on the Ark there is evidence that Lord Baltimore granted him at least two manorial holdings "St. Jerome", of 6000 acres, and "St. Helen", of unknown acreage. His consort who was his second wife came to Maryland, but there is no evidence of her accompanying him on the Ark in 1633. He lived on his townland in St. Mary's Hundred which he gave the name of "St. Peter" which was undoubtedly the most pretentious house in the Province. There were at least three white servants at his Maryland seat at the time of his death in 1638.†

Conflict perhaps provoked by difference of opinion and temperament between him and Governor Calvert in the matters of affairs of state occurred soon after the landing. After Cornwalys and Clayborne clashed in that memorial naval battle off the Eastern Shore, Hawley sailed for England on the first passage possible to defend the cause of Baltimore. Arriving in London he appeared in person before the Privy Council during June 1635. He remained at home for about a year during which time he corroborated with John Lewger, Esq. in the preparation of "A Relation of Maryland; Together With a Map of the Countrey, The Conditions of Plantation, His Majesties Charter to the Lord Balteimore, translated into English, September the 8. Anno Dom 1635", with the objective of selling Maryland to prospective British settlers.

On June 27, 1636, he had an audience with the King regarding tobacco trade and in August he and Sir John Harvey, Knt., sailed in the "Black George" for Virginia, but owing to the leakage of the ship returned to

---

` letters with which Rochester sought the lady's favour. Frances after having tired of Rochester ultimately succeeded in divorcing her husband, the Earl of Essex. She then turned her attentions to Kerr who had recently been made the Earl of Somerset. Sir Thomas Overbury passionately entreated Kerr, the Earl of Somerset, to break with the divorced Countess, but she gained complete control of her lover and resented Overbury's interest and infatuation with her husband. Kerr, Earl of Somerset, knew that Overbury had in his possession information, which, if Overbury revealed, would ruin him. It was hinted that they had once intrigued to murder Henry, Prince of Wales, son of James I. Kerr decided to dispose of Overbury and the Countess neglected no opportunity of emphasizing Overbury's intractability. At one time she approached Sir Davy Wood to assassinate Overbury. However, Overbury was sent to the tower and the Countess placed Richard Weston as his personal attendant to mix his food with poisonous phials. Two years after the death of Overbury, Kerr and his countess were tried for his murder and imprisoned in the tower from 1615 to 1622. The countess pleaded guilty and was sentenced to death, but both were later pardoned. Jerome Hawley was involved in some manner with the murder but was apparently declared not an accessory to the plot. Ref: Green State Papers.

† John Cook, carpenter; Richard Hill, carpenter; and Anne Smithson, widow. Other possible servants, as wages were paid them, were Robert Percy, Edward Brent, Chr. Plunkett and Edmund Deering. One or more of those could have been servants brought by him in 1633. Ref: Archives, vol. 4, pp. 59, 100.

England. No further attempt was made to reach Virginia until August 1637, when he arrived in the "Friendship", perhaps with his wife, carrying a commission from the King as Treasurer of the Virginia Colony.

He died in Maryland during the summer of 1638, and Thomas Cornwalys, as the greatest alleged creditor, was named the administrator of the Maryland estate. Although he was the Treasurer of the Virginia Colony at the time of his death, he still maintained plantations with servants in Maryland. He had made his last will and testament shortly, before the sailing of the Ark and the Dove or on October 20, 1633, naming William Hawley, of Grossmont, Monmouthshire, Arthur Dodington, and Lewis Hele, his executors.

His widow, Eleanor, who had likewise been the widow of Thomas Courtney, Esq., survived, but ultimately returned to England where she remained until her death. He apparently left an only daughter as his heiress by his first marriage as proved by a letter from his brother, James Hawley, of Brentford, to his brother Captain William Hawley, dated July 30, 1649, by which it was shown that Jerome had owed a sum of money to his brother James "do herewith send you the copy of writing betwixt my brother Jerome deceased and myself from which will appear a large sum of money to be due me, from him, which by virtue of my power of attorney, to do authorize you to receive in my behalf. Upon the decease of my brother Jerome one Cornwallis did seize upon his estate, pretending that he was indebted unto him, but I am informed it was only a doutful pretence to defraud me. . . . You must pretend your own right as next heir to Jerome as well as my interest, for indeed there is only one daughter of his before you which is at Brabant, and mindeth not the same".*

On August 27, 1638, Eleanor Hawley, his widow, made a deposition before John Lewger, Esq., Secretary of the Province, that her husband made a bill of sale to have received of Mr. John Sims, of Foundsford, in Somersetshire, £400 and that the debt had been assigned to Thomas Cornwalys.[1]

Cornwalys filed an inventory of the personal estate in Maryland, appraised at £849/6/9, and with debts due the estate they brought the total value to £944/13/–. After all disbursements and obligations were met, including £5 for funeral charges, £3 to the tailor for mourning clothes, and £5 for Surgeon's bill, the accounts balanced.[2]

His brother, Captain William Hawley, Esq., removed from the Barbadoes to Maryland and settled on his brother's Manor of St. Jerome sometime before 1650. On March 24, 1652, he declared that his brother, Jerome, deceased, upon the perusal of the deeds upon record of Mr. James Hawley, had claims to 6000 acres of land in Maryland which had not been taken

---

* The statement in the Md. Hist. Mag. of June 1939, p. 179, that Clement Halley who died testate in St. Mary's Co. 1695/6, leaving two daughters as coheiresses was a grandson of Jerome Hawley, Esq., is therefore without truth.

up.[3] If these claims were for land rights for transporting settlers, it is apparent that a number were for redemptioners in 1633 whose names are not known.

On November 25, 1655, Sir William Courtney, of Newhouse, Wilts, Bart., stepson of Jerome Hawley, appointed an attorney "to entere upon all Such Mannors, Tenements, Lands and Grounds which of right doe belong to me in the County of Maryland beyond the seas which have happened and accured to me by the death of my mother, Mrs. Eleanor Hawley, and which are commonly distinguished and knowe by the Names of the Manors of St. Jerome's and St. Helen's or by whatsoever other Names the said mannors are called".[4]

In the lawsuit over St. Jerome's Manor after the death of Captain William Hawley, Esq., it was shown that a daughter of Jerome Hawley had filed a claim to the estate. She was undoubtedly the daughter of Brabant as expressed in the letter of her uncle, James Hawley, and as it was not entered in the name of her consort, she was apparently a spinster in that year.

Sources: 1. *Archives*, vol. 2, p. 45; 2. *Ibid.*, vol. 4, pp. 100-101; 3. *Ibid.*, vol. 10, p. 250; 4. *Ibid.*, vol. 10, p. 444.

THOMAS HEATH

Thomas Heath was one of the transportees of Father White in 1633 whose land rights he assigned to Ferdinand Pulton. He witnessed the last will and testament of William Smith on September 22, 1635, but no further record can be found for him. He did not attend the 1637/8 General Assembly or is there any mention of his estate among the testamentary proceedings of the early courts.

Sources: Liber ABH, folio 65; Wills, Liber 1, folio 1.

CAPTAIN JOHN HILL

Captain John Hill is another Gentleman of Fashion of which nothing further is known other than his name being printed in the "A Relation of Maryland".

JOHN HILL

John Hill [Hilles] was one of the transportees of Father White in 1634. He had completed his service by the Assembly of 1637/8, for he personally attended a session on February 26, 1637/8.[1] In May 1638, he served on the jury of the local court, but by August 29, John Halfhead declared him a fugitive and demanded 690 lbs. tob. of his crop.[2] He had probably gone over to Virginia, and later events substantiates this belief. On February 21, 1638/9, he was back in Maryland and voted for David Wickliff to represent St. George's Hundred—though his mark is stated to be Richard Hill.[3] His assessment for expenditures of the Province in 1642 was 32 lbs. tob. He was probably the John Hilles (sic), of Westmoreland County, Virginia, who in 1656 was a contingent heir in the last will and testament of Thomas Boys, with his fellow Adventurer, Major John Hallowes.[4] Contemporary with him in Maryland was a John Hill who was a settler on Kent.

Sources: 1. Archives, vol. 1, p. 13; 2. Archives, vol. 4, pp. 33, 46; 3. Archives, vol. 1, p. 30; 4. Westmoreland Wills, Liber 1, folio 51.

JOHN HILLIARD

John Hilliard was transported by Father White in 1633 who assigned his land rights to Thomas Copley, Esq. He was literate, once stated in court that he wrote a letter by the direction of James Cauther, and was often called upon to appraise estates. At the convening of the Assembly of January 1637/8, as a planter of St. Mary's Hundred, Francis Rabnett held his proxy, but on March 3, 1637/8, he attended the Assembly in person.

As a resident of St. Michael's Hundred on December 11, 1642, he contracted to serve John Hollis [Hallowes] one year for 1100 lbs. tob.[*] On December 1, 1643, he complained of the injury sustained by John Hollis, late of Virginia, Carpenter, so he probably served in the capacity of a joiner or woodworker. On September 17, 1649, he witnessed the instrument by which Edward Hill granted power of attorney to John Hollis, and on February 1, 1661/2, he witnessed an assignment of Richard Smith to Thomas Gerard, Lord of St. Clement's Manor.

He ultimately became overseer for William Bromhall, of Calvert and Kent Counties, who died testate about 1660, making William Parratt and William Turner trustees of his estate. At the Prerogative Court on April 9, 1663, William Turner presented a petition stating that John Hilliard, the overseer of the servants of William Bromhall "hath clandestinely runne away out of this Province, as yor Pet^r carryed away in the Inventory and Appraisement of the Estate".

He had a life span of at least 27 years in the Province, but no marriage or any children have definitely been proved. If he begot a family, they no doubt accompanied him when he left the Province.[†]

Sources: Liber 1, folio 166, Land Office; Archives, vol. 4, pp. 225, 513; vol. 47, p. 214; Test. Proc. Liber 1d, folio 77, Hall of Records.

[*] While re-indenture was an exception in Maryland, this is evidence of its occurrence.

[†] Later Hilliards are found in Somerset Co., when in 1671/2 Thomas Hilliard son of John Hilliard was the sole heir in the will of George Evans, inheriting several plantations. Ref: Wills, Liber 1, folio 50; Liber 2, folio 410.

RICHARD HILLS

Richard Hills came in under the patronage of Governor Calvert in 1633. If he performed personal services, he had completed his indentureship by February 21, 1638/9, and was a planter in St. Georges Hundred. At times he was styled both Planter and Carpenter. He had been employed in some capacity by Jerome Hawley before his death, as he received £9 and 2 suits of clothes for wages at the settlement of the estate.[1]

In St. George's Hundred he voted for David Wickliff to represent that hundred at the General Assembly of February 1638/9[2]. On July 23, 1641, for the ensuing assembly he and others of St. George's Hundred elected George Pye, Esq. in place of Francis Gray.[3] At the Assembly of March 22, 1641/2, when all manhood suffrage was represented, he entrusted his proxy to John Worthy.[4]

Governor Calvert assigned him 50 acres of land which he made a claim for on August 6, 1641.[5] On December 14, following, a provincial warrant was issued for that amount which was surveyed and patented on October 23, 1642, as follows:[6] "Laid out for Richard Hills a parcel of land near Newtowne Marsh and bound on the south with the said Marsh on the East with the land of William Thompson on the East with a meriden line drawn from the head of the Hollow called Dixon's Hollow North in the woods for the length of 100 perches on the North with a parallel line drawn from the end of the former line West unto the land of William Thompson containing 50 acres".

On November 20, 1647, he received 40 lbs. tob. from the estate of Robert Tuttley. At the death of John Longworth, the court granted him letters of administration upon the estate. In 1649/50, it was recorded at the Provincial Court that Robert Edward claimed from Richard Hills, the administrator of the estate of John Longworth, 200 lbs. tob. plus 4 bbls. of corn.[7]

On June 29, 1649, he "sold and given possession of my plantacon in Maryland unto Richard Browne". It was witnessed by John Hallowes and William Withers. He made his mark as RH.[8] The scrivener wrote "Rich: Hilles".

On October 12, 1650, Richard Browne acknowledged a judgment to George Manners for 600 lbs. tob., formerly due by bill to Richard Hills, dated June 29, 1649, and assigned by the said Hills to George Manners.[9]

He was not listed among the landed proprietors found in Liber O, the first extant rent roll for the Province. With the common name of Richard Hill or Hills, it is difficult to place the Adventurer after 1650, as a Richard Hills was transported in 1670, and six Richard Hill (without s) were entered as land rights prior to 1679. So it would be risky to state that the Richard Hill who died in 1686 intestate with only 2 beds and furniture, 3 servants' beds and coverings, a Bible, and one servant-woman was the Adventurer of 1633. Then about 1650 a Richard Hill appeared in Anne Arundel County.

Sources: 1. Archives, vol. 4, p. 59; 2. Archives, vol. 1, p. 30; 3. Archives, vol. 1, p. 104; 4. Archives, vol. 1, p. 118; 5. Liber 1, folio 118, Land Office; 6. Liber ABH, folio 97, Land Office; 7. Archives, vol. 4, p. 95; 8. Md. Hist. Mag., vol. 7, p. 388; 9. Archives, vol. 10, p. 38.

JAMES HOCKLEY

James Hockley was transported into the Province by Governor Leonard Calvert who on April 3, 1640, demanded 100 acres of "Land due for Transporting into the Province one able man Servant called James Hoskly in the year 1633". Thereupon he assigned his rights to Peter Draper. The name of James Hockley or Hoskly does not appear on any of the early records, so he apparently died shortly after landing or returned to England.

BENJAMIN HODGES

Benjamin Hodges, a servant to John Sanders, was transported by him in 1633, but shortly before Sanders' death he assigned his land rights to Ferdinand Pulton. No further references to him are available. He did not attend the early assemblies, did not receive a land grant, or did he figure in any of the proceedings, of the Prerogative or Provincial Courts. No will, inventory or administration of his estate are on record. The only inference which may be drawn is of his returning to England or dying before 1638 without estate and issue.*

* Several members of a later Hodges family of Maryland believe themselves descended from a Benjamin Hodges, Gent., who came on the Ark and the Dove, and he is listed as such in the Constitution of the Ark and Dove Society, therefore, giving the servant the status of the county gentry. Inasmuch as 17 land rights were claimed prior to 1687 for settlers bearing the name of Hodges and the first reference to a Hodges in the prerogative court proceedings is a Robert of 1665, the claims of the family of their descent from the Adventurer are apparently not very well founded.

JOHN HOLDERN

John Holdern [Heldern, Holdene] was one of the servants of Captain Thomas Cornwalys who made the crossing in 1633. By August 1642, he had completed his service, for in that month he was assessed 30 lbs. tob. for the administration of St. Mary's Hundred.[1] At the General Assembly convened on September 5, 1642, he gave his proxy to his former master, Captain Thomas Cornwalys.[2] For the expedition which began on September 21, and completed on October 13, 1642, he received 75 lbs. tob. under the accounts due Captain Cornwalys and paid to his attorney, Cuthbert Fenwick.[3] No further reference can be found for him in Maryland.

Sources: 1. Archives, vol. 1, p. 142; 2. Archives, vol. 1, p. 167; 3. Archives, vol. 3, p. 119.

HENRY JAMES

Henry James was one of the transportees of the two Wintour brothers, and settled first in St. Mary's Hundred where he was domiciled as a freeholder at the General Assembly of January 1637. He empowered Thomas Morris to act as his proxy in 1641, and at the 1642 assembly he was fined 23 lbs. tob. for his non-appearance. He maintained a tenancy on Governor Leonard Calvert's Manor of St. Gabriel, where he died testate and without issue in 1646.

His last will and testament was dated April 27, 1645, and probated on September 23, 1646. He devised his house and plantation to Thomas Yewell and certain personalty to Thomas Allen for the use of his unnamed goddaughter. The residuary estate was bequeathed to Robert Sedgrave.[1]

His plantation was a leasehold on St. Gabriel's Manor, when on January 14, 1646/7, it was reported that there was an arrear of manorial rent. It was therefore decreed that his estate and several other tenants who were likewise in arrear "to Shew Cause why the said Land should not Escheat to the Lord of the Manor as aforesaid according to the Law and Custome of England in Such Case".[2]

Sources: 1. Wills, Liber 1, folio 33; 2. Archives, vol. 10, p. 93.

MARY JENNINGS

Mary Jennings was one of the few identified maidens on the Ark and was brought in as a servant of Father White, for whom land-rights were claimed in 1650. She was probably one of the "young women" who was nearly drowned in the act of washing the padre's linen shortly after the landing at St. Clement's Island. No further record is available, if she did not succumb to an early death, she probably married one of the yeomen and thus her identity became obliterated.

Sources: Liber 1, folios 19, 166, Land Office; Archives, vol. 3, p. 258.

JOSIAS, SERVANT

Josias, a servant of Captain Thomas Cornwalys, was drowned during the early days of the settlement. When Cornwalys in 1641 entered his land-rights for 12 persons, including himself, he gave the names of only ten Adventurers whom he brought-in in 1633. The name of Josias, the servant, was not on the list, so it is assumed that he was the eleventh transportee.

Sources: Warrants, Liber 1, folio 26; Liber 4, folio 623.

JOHN KNOWLES

John Knowles was one of the two lay members of the Society of Jesus whom Father White transported to Maryland. He died of fever September 24, 1637. Ref: Calvert Papers, reprinted in Fund Publication no. 7, pp. 117, 126.

LIEUTENANT WILLIAM LEWIS

As to whether William Lewis was one of the Adventurers in 1633, again circumstantial evidence plays its intriguing part. He was the early Steward or Chamberlain to the Jesuits and in charge of their redemptioners, and an ardent Roman Catholic. It is known that a complete list of the servants brought in by Father White is not extant, and some years later William

Lewis claimed his 50 acres for time of service.* In a letter to Lord Baltimore on April 3, 1638, Father White speaking of the Second Assembly stated that "William Lewis who is our overseer . . . had more Proxis than all the rest".[1]

The first mention of him in the archives was on the opening day of the General Assembly of January 25, 1637/8, when he appeared as a freeholder with a number of proxies.[2] On November 2, 1638, when he declared his intentions to marry Ursula Gifford, he swore that he was not "procontracted to any other woman than Ursula Gifford and no Impediment of consanqunity". He signed the statement.[3] Inasmuch as after 1640, he was styled Lieutenant William Lewis, it is apparent that he was one of the early officers of the Provincial Militia of the Province.

He probably left St. Mary's with Governor Calvert and was in exile when Ingle and Clayborne rode rough shod over the Province, but returned with his wife in 1646. At this time he claimed 100 acres for his and his wife's service in the Province, but he neglected to state the time or nature of the service performed which would lead one to believe that it was his service in the very early days to Father White and the Jesuits. He also proved his rights to 200 acres for his and his wife's emigration in 1646, and also rights for transporting six servants and one which he had purchased of Mr. Hatton, His Lordship's Secretary. Furthermore, he proved rights for 2000 acres which had been assigned him by Nathaniel Pope, then of Appomattacks, Gent., which had been assigned to Pope by Mrs. Stratton "at her going for England".[4]

In 1654 Lord Baltimore granted him a manor with court privileges of 3000 acres in Nanjemoy Hundred which was called "Lewis Neck Manor" but officially patented under the name of Rice Manor. He enjoyed his prerogatives but a short time, because he was one of the Loyalists, while fighting under the standard of the Lord Proprietary, at the battle of the Severn, who was condemned and shot in cold blood by the insurgent Puritans to whom Lord Baltimore had given asylum after they were chased out of Virginia.[5]

There was apparently no issue, as his manor escheated to the Lord Proprietary and in 1675 was granted with full baronial fanfare to Thomas Wharton, Esq., who left a distinguished issue.

Sources: 1. Fund Pub. no. 28, p. 158; 2. Archives, vol. 1, p. 2; 3. Liber 1, folio 133; 4. Liber ABH, folio 23; 5. See letter of Verlinda Stone printed in Hall's Narratives of Early Maryland, p. 266.

* It was stated that Father White imported 26 servants, see Liber 1, folio 117, yet only 15 can be proved.

RICHARD LOE

Richard Loe was one of the servants transported by Thomas Cornwalys in 1633, but was a freeholder by the time of the Second General Assembly of 1637, being a planter of St. Michael's Hundred. He died prior to May 2, 1639, when John Medley was granted letters of administration upon his estate. The inventory of his estate indicated one of the planter's class which included a servant, James Moulins. His personal wardrobe was rather extensive for a settler of that day, and contained a sword, book, a dogge, and a henne with 5 chickens. The total appraisement was 2,158 lbs. tob. Ref: Archives of Maryland, vol. 1, pp. 15, 29; vol. 4, pp. 57, 74.

NOTE: The Richard Loe, who was an Adventurer on the Ark and the Dove, should not be confused with Richard Loe, Planter, who emigrated in 1640, and who proved landrights on August 6, 1641. Ref: Liber 1, folio 119, Land Office.

RICHARD LUSTEAD [LUSLICK]

Richard Lustead [Luslick] was transported by Father White who assigned his rights to 50 acres of land to Ferdinand Pulton.[1] His mark on several documents seem to indicate that he was unschooled. In 1637 he was domiciled in Mattapanient Hundred and was also a resident at the time of his death in 1642. He failed to negotiate any land grants, so apparently he maintained a freehold on one of the large manors then held by the Jesuits at Mattapanient.

At the opening of the General Assembly in January 1637/8, he trusted his proxy to his father-in-law, Richard Garnett, later changed to Gardiner, but within a few days he revoked or cancelled his proxy with Richard Garnett, and was admitted to the Assembly as a freeholder.[2] He was elected a burgess from Mattapanient Hundred for the Assembly of October 1640, which seemed to have departed from the heretofore custom of a gathering of all freemen of the Province.[3] At the 1641 Assembly Cuthbert Fenwick held his proxy and at the one of March 21, 1641/2, Thomas Greene was given that prerogative.

He married a sister of Luke Garnett [Gardiner] who was undoubtedly Elizabeth. She was brought into the Province by her father, Richard Garnett, in 1637 at the age of 19 years.[*] She predeceased her husband, for on August 3, 1642, letters of administration upon the estate of Richard Lustead were issued not to his widow, but to Captain Thomas Cornwalys.[4] The inventory of the personal estate was made by Cuthbert Fenwick and Richard Garnett. Among the items were eight books, one servant, laced handkerchiefs, night caps, and some paper pictures.[5]

On March 10, 1650/1, Luke Gardiner after Ingle's Rebellion claimed 50 acres of land "due to Richard Luslick, Servant to Mr. Copley, who married my sister, deceased".[6] It is evident that no issue survived, inasmuch as the brother-in-law claimed the land-rights rather than the son and heir or the co-heiresses, and there is no record of the heir assigning rights to his uncle. Having been a retainer of Thomas Copley and having married into a Roman Catholic family, it can be concluded that he was of that faith.

Sources: 1. Liber ABH, folio 65; Archives, vol. 1, p. 28; 2. Archives, vol. 1, pp. 4, 11; 3. Archives, vol. 1, p. 89; 4. Archives, vol. 4, p. 71; 5. Archives, vol. 4, p. 94; 6. Warrants, Liber 1, folio 167.

* The late Mrs. Hodges concluded that he married Julian Gardiner another sister, but Julian was only 6 years old when her father transported her in 1637, and therefore was not more than 11 years of age at the death of Richard Lusthead.

JOHN MARLBURGH

John Marlburgh was one of the redemptioners brought in by John Saunders in 1633. It was not until the Assembly of 1642 that he was accorded the rights of a freeholder with a seat in that body. At that time he was fined 23 lbs. tob. for his non-attendance, but ultimately gave his proxy to Thomas Cornwalys. No record of any land grant is on record. In 1643 he was assessed 35 lbs. tob. for the welfare of St. Mary's County. No further reference can be found for him after that date.

Sources: Archives, vol. 3, p. 138.

CHRISTOPHER MARTIN, TAILOR

Christopher Martin became attached to the retinue of Captain Cornwalys in 1634, but we know not whether it occurred while the Ark and Dove were lying in the James River or whether Captain Cornwalys transported him from Virginia after the initial settlement. He was trained in the art of tailoring, so the clothes of the gentlemen during that early period were fashioned after his design and moulded with his needle.[1] His period of indentureship was completed by January 1637/8, for he attended the assembly as a freeholder of St. Mary's Hundred, and was able to write his name.

He died intestate, with letters of administration being issued to his widow, Eleanor Martin, on October 8, 1641.[2] At that time William Hawkins and Joseph Edloe assumed the obligation jointly and severally to pay all debts whatsoever "due from the estate of Xpfer martin late of St. Maries tailor deceased intestate". On June 28, 1642, Joseph Edloe appeared as the administrator of the estate. The personalty, inventoried jointly with that of Joseph Edloe, Planter, was appraised by John Weyvill and William Hawkins at 4181 lbs. tob., including three swords, two of which were labeled old.[3] It was furthermore stated that "one halfe is the inventory of the goods & chattles of the said Xpfer Martin at his deceased". This joint inventory was unusual, unless Martin and Edloe maintained a business partnership, yet Edloe was styled planter and not tailor. Edloe was not deceased at that time, for he lived until 1666, dying intestate. No further record has been found for Eleanor Martin, the widow, nor any record of children.

Sources: 1. Archives, vol. 4, p. 26; 2. Archives, vol. 4, p. 66; 3. Archives, vol. 4, p. 93.

JOHN MEDCALFE, GENT.

Cecilius, Lord Baltimore, stated in 1635 that among the nearly twenty gentlemen of fashion who had sailed for his Province was one John Medcalfe, Gent. No references have been found for his receiving land under the Conditions of 1633, but he was seated in St. Mary's Hundred by January 25, 1637/8, when he failed to appear at the assembly of freeholders summoned at that time.

Some years later on September 16, [1650], he applied for land rights stating that he arrived in the Province with his servant fifteen years ago, as follows:[1]

"16 Sept. [1650]. Mr. John Metcalf demandeth Eight hundred Acres of Land for Transportation of himself and John Robinson his Servant into this Province in July last was 15 Yeares. Warr^t to lay out for John Metcalf Eight hundred Acres of Land at Chingemixon Neck on the north side of Potomock River ret pr Jan^{ry}".

As this would place his emigration in 1635, it would somehow dispute his arrival with the Adventurers on the Ark and the Dove and leaves much for mental conjecture. It is possible that he returned to England on one of the boats which landed in Maryland shortly after the initial voyage of the Ark and the Dove, or perhaps he inadvertently stated 15 years instead of 16, yet he specially mentioned the month of July. Then, there is that possibility of his crossing the river to Virginia and persuading a Virginian to indenture himself for certain economic advantages and thus he returned to Maryland in July 1635.

It does not seem likely that two John Medcalfes could have figured in the early settlement of the Province, and there is no record of the death of the Gentleman Adventurer to prove definitely that two early settlers bore identical names. Furthermore, he was the only John Metcalf whose name appears upon the list of early settlers or those who were granted land for their entry into the Province from 1633 to 1683.[2] He was undoubtedly the Mr. Medcalfe referred to by Secretary Lewger when writing to Lord Baltimore in 1638/9 "Nothing will be coming for Mr. Medcalfe to dispose of to Mr. Copley".[3]

He was a kinsman of Anthony Metcalf, Gent., for whom Lord Baltimore requested the issuance of a warrant for 1,000 acres of land in 1636,[4] and which was later assigned to him.[5]

"Cecilius granted to John Metcalf, Gent. and heirs 1000 acres within our said Province which was due unto his cousin Anthony Metcalf, Gent. for which he had a warrant from us which together with an assignment thereof from him to the said John Metcalf were as we are informed lost in the late Troubles there". Given at London 26 August 1651.

Virtually no references are available on Anthony Metcalf in the printed Maryland Archives, so some doubt exists whether he actually made a voyage to Maryland. On January 25, 1637/8, John Robinson, carpenter, was admitted to the Assembly as a freeholder, but he had been transported by Thomas Cornwalys, Esq. In March 1641/2, a John Robinson, barber, who may or may not be the former servant of John Metcalfe, was seated at an Assembly.

At the Assembly of January 1637/8, it was discovered that Metcalfe had assigned his proxy to Lieut. William Lewis, with whom he was closely associated in the early period. In 1638 they proved the nuncupative will of John Smithson. By 1642 Metcalfe had removed to the Isle of Kent undoubtedly through the entreaties of Governor Calvert who wished to displace the radical Puritan element which early controlled affairs on that island by his loyal subjects. He was back in St. Mary's within a few years, for in 1647 he witnessed the assignment of the pinnace, which William Smoot had purchased of Leonard Calvert, to John Price.[6]

He often represented various planters at court as their attorney as well as witnessed numerous legal documents which he no doubt wrote. Crouch, secretary to Cecilius, Lord Baltimore, writing on August 6, 1650, to Governor Stone recommended him or Lieut. William Lewis for High Sheriff of St. Mary's County, both of whom had unhesitatingly approached Lord Baltimore for the honour. Medcalfe, however, won the appointment on November 25, 1652.[7]

In April 1658, "John Mettcalfe . . . by the Potowmeke River" was due 600 lbs. tob. as a burgess for that district.[8] In 1660 he and Jeremiah Metcalfe were summoned to testify at the Provincial Court.* In November 1659 he and William Hynes were commissioned to appraise the estate of Edward Clarkson. In April 1662, the legislature voted 500 lbs. tob. for John Metcalfe, the door keeper of the Assembly.

Subsequent references to the Metcalfe family are rather fragmentary. No administration of his estate seems to be on record, and it is not believed that he was the John Metcalf who died intestate in 1706, with a personal estate appraised at £17/8/10. The inventory of the estate indicated a single man.[9]

George Madcalfe died intestate in St. Mary's County in 1702, leaving a widow, Elizabeth, who by 1707 had married Samuel Davis. In that year the latter was in possession of 200 acres of "Rocky Point" in New Town Hundred, St. Mary's County, by marrying "the Relict of Geo: Midcalf".[10]

Sources: 1. Liber ABH, folio 50, Land Office; 2. List of Early Settlers, Land Office; 3. Calvert papers, p. 201; 4. *Ibid.;* 5. Liber ABH, folio 206; 6. Archives of Maryland, vol. 3, p. 340; 7. *Ibid.,* vol. 3, pp. 282, 294; 8. *Ibid.,* vol. 1, p. 376; 9. Inventories & Accounts, Liber 26, folio 252; 10. St. Mary's Rent Rolls (Calvert papers), p. 28.

* No land rights were claimed for a Jeremiah Metcalf prior to 1683, so there is a possibility of a father-and-son relationship.

CHARLES MIDDLETON

Charles Middleton was transported by Governor Leonard Calvert who claimed land for his entry on August 13, 1641. No further record.

THOMAS MINNUS

Thomas Minnus, an Adventurer, was transported by Richard Gerard, Esq., whose rights to land were conveyed to Ferdinand Pulton. He received no land, according to the extant records, or did he demand a sitting at any of the early Assemblies. No references are found to the administration of his estate, so he was undoubtedly one of the early casualties.

ROGER MORGAN

Roger Morgan was transported into Maryland by Captain Cornwalys in 1633 as one of his servants, for whom he proved land-rights in 1641. No further record, however, exists for him in Maryland, so he apparently died before the Assembly of 1637/8, or removed elsewhere.

JOHN NEVILL

John Nevill bore one of the proudest names in all England, but his connection with the noble Nevills of the ducal line was rather remote, and many attempts have failed to prove any immediate kinship. He was one of the few settlers in the Province who was addressed "goodman", a prefix of civility applied to a member of the yeomanry or urban middle-class. Ultimately, he owned the title of gentleman, and was so styled in 1662.

The appellation "goodman" was applied when he sued Mr. Thomas Baker for malicious defamation of his wife, "Goodie" Nevill's character. The case makes vivid reading and demonstrates what course, frank and vulgar language was used by the pioneers in those days, but not without some humour. After several depositions before the court in session Goody Nevill's name was cleared and Baker asked forgiveness on bended knees.[1] Later in court Goody Nevill stated that "she doath absoluly go in feare of her life of Thomas Baker".

John Nevill was transported by Leonard Calvert, Esq., apparently under the technicality of a servant.[2] He did not attend the December-January 1637 Assembly, or were any summons issued for his non-appearance. This condition can perhaps be occasioned by his being under age or had not fulfilled his freedom rights. It was not until March 14, 1637/8, that he appeared in St. Mary's and "claymed voice as freeman & was admitted".[3]

His early seat seemed to have been in St. Michael's Hundred. He and Christopher Carnell possessed a plantation on Popular Hill Creek called "Thomas Peteet" which they leased to Richard Bennett, the Puritan agitator, for the yearly rent of one bushel of corn or two shillings. The land so leased adjoined the dwelling-plantation of John Nevill. Subsequently, he pushed westward and was seated in Port Tobacco Hundred, Charles County at the time of his death.

He was an Anglican by faith and by occupation a mariner, being so styled at court on February 12, 1637/8. He was unable to write, yet there is admiration, for his son and heir was able to sign his name.

In 1644 he swore in court that in 1642 "Anne now wife of Ellis Beach" contracted with him to carry her to Elisabeth River in Virginia in a boat of Colonel Trafford and to compensate him with "stockins & shoes & other clothes to give him content". He carried Ann and Ellis Beach to Mr.

Mottram's in York and would have carried them on to Elisabeth River, but no provisions were made for victuals. It was necessary for him "to use all moral diligence to get passage back to Maryland . . . it was near three weeks more before he returned . . . that he made no profit that time of his labour. Christopher Carnell testified that he was present when the agreement was made.

He was out of the Province for a time, perhaps under contract as a mariner, and returned bringing with him a wife, Bridget Thorsley. On November 14, 1649, he applied to the Surveyor General for 200 acres of land by right of his own transportation and that of his wife in 1646. Accordingly, 400 acres of land were issued to him under the name of "Nevill's Cross".[4]

By 1651 Bridget was deceased, and he had married secondly Joan [Johanna] Porter. On January 29, 1652/3, he demanded 400 acres of land which had been assigned him by George Askwith and 100 acres more "for the transportation of Joan Porter now my wife in 1651 and whom I bought of Thomas Doynes".[5]

It was Joanna, as Goodie Nevill, who was brought to bed of a daughter about 1658 which was the occasion of the defamation suit. Later as Goodie Nevill she had a regular female hair-pulling contest with Goodie Rod at which time Goodie Rod yelled murder which brought several gentlemen to the scene. Goodie Rod seemed to have received the worst of the contest, for she was "hit in the chops" and was "Crying and torne or scratch about the throat and face and bled".[6]

Before the battle of the two housewives, Goodie Nevill made a trip to the homeland, for at court held in the Province in October 1656, Emperor Smith sued John Nevill for "Physick and Chirurgery" which he had administered to his wife. Nevill denied in court that his wife "never had any Such things of the said Smith", but inasmuch as at that time the wife of John Nevill was in England, both parties agreed to refer the case "till the said Nevill's wife returne out of England".

It was no doubt during the absence of his wife that John Nevill became a victim of the seductive charms of Susan Atcheson, the wife of James Atcheson, who accused him of adulterous relations on May 15, 1657. On November 4, 1657, the court found them both guilty and ordered 20 lashes upon the bare back and that John Nevill paid all court charges. John Nevill apparently had many friends in the county, for a number of petitions were presented at court, to impose a fine rather than the whipping and that they would pay a fine of 500 lbs. tob. in his behalf. No petitions were offered for the woman who apparently received no sympathy from her neighbors.[7]

Before 1659 John Nevill settled in Port Tobacco Hundred, for on November 3, of that year, he "commanded" John Jarbo and Mary his wife to hold to their bargain and convey to him 300 acres of land at Portoback (sic.).[8] In the same year he and eleven other freeholders were commissioned to appraise the estate of Captain Lewis, deceased, at Nanjemoy. Among Lewis' land holdings was Rice Manor of 3000 acres on which Lewis held lordship.

At a court held in Charles County in February 1662/3, John Nevill, Gent., made a deed of gift to his son-in-law, John Lambert, and his wife of certain livestock for a period of four years, and that in 1666 the stock and the increase were to be divided equally between the said John Lambert and William Nevill, the son of John. At the same time he assigned several servants to his son-in-law and certain bills due him.[9]

In October 1663, Henry Hudson assigned to John Nevill all goods, chests or truckes in the dwelling house of the said Nevill, but Hudson was to enjoy the use of the goods until a certain debt due Nevill was paid. John Lambert and William Nevill witnessed the transaction. The goods were subsequently attached by "Mr. John Nevill" at the following January court.[10]

In August 1664, Robert Slye, Esq., deeded a mare and her filly to John Nevill which occurred a few months before his death, for his last will and testament was dated January 14, 1664/5, and probated at court on February 4, following.

He devised his wife, Joanna, the real and personal property formerly bestowed by deed of gift, and to his son, William, the dwelling-plantation. To his daughter, Ellen Lambert, he bequeathed personalty.[11] The original administration bond of his son for 80,000 lbs. tob. is on file at Annapolis showing the signatures of William Price, Thomas Payne and Charles Calvert.

Only two children were named in his will. The girl born to Joanna in 1658 was probably Rachell who later married Michael Ashford.

Children of John Nevill

1. William Nevill.
2. Elleanor Nevill married John Lambert.
3. Rachel Nevill married Michael Ashford.

On March 24, 1664/5, his personal estate was appraised at 51,153 lbs. tob. by Francis Pope and Capt. Robert Troope. Among the chattels were one silver bowl, two white maid-servants, one white man-servant, one white boy-servant and three Negro slaves. Also 13 silver spoons, two silver items and a parcel of books.[12]

After his death Walter Story, Merchant of London, sued the estate for various items sold to him and not satisfied, among which was "one new Ring and setting a stone in another", also nine gallons of sacke, five gallons of brandy, and a pair of woman's shoes.[13]

On June 24, 1665, Johanna Nevill, widow, for 5,000 lbs. tob. purchased "Moore's Ditch" from Henry Moore and Elizabeth his wife, of Charles County, lying on the east side of Zachia Swamp, as laid out for 500 acres and patented to the said Henry Moore. In some manner the administration of the estate of John Nevill fell to William Price, inasmuch as on the preceding day John Lambert who declared himself as one of the partners in the administration of the estate of John Nevill, deceased, confirmed all accounts of William Price. The instrument was witnessed by Thomas Hussey and William Nevill.[14]

In July 1665, his widow, Johanna Nevill, deeded the "fillie foale" which had been acquired from Robert Slye to John Lambert for the use of Lambert's son John. The gift was witnessed by William Price and William Nevill.[15]

By August 13, 1666, the widow had married Thomas Hussey, Gent., for on that day William Nevill, Thomas Hussey and Joanna his wife conveyed to Thomas Wentworth for 10,600 lbs. tob. the land on the north side of the Piscataway known as "Heller's Palme", of 150 acres, as sold to the said Thomas Wentworth by John Nevill, deceased, but yet not acknowledged by reason of his untimely death. William Nevill and Thomas Hussey signed the deed of conveyance, while Johanna made her initial IH.[16]

Although she was formerly addressed as "Goodie Nevill", her second husband was Thomas Hussey, son of the Rev. John Hussey, of Harby, Lincolnshire, with title of "Gent." and one-time merchant and magistrate of Charles County. She was either his second or third wife, and while his daughters and co-heiresses have generally been stated to be issue of a previous marriage, a recent document would indicate that they were daughters by his wife, Johannah.*

Sources: 1. Archives, vol. 53, pp. 231-234, 432; 2. Liber ABH, folio 98; 3. Archives, vol. 1, p. 16; 4. Liber ABH, folio 27; 5. Liber ABH, folio 241; 6. Archives, vol. 53, pp. 380-382; 7. Chas. Co. Crt Records, Liber 3, folios 3, 222, 279, 348, 350; 8. Archives, vol. 65, p. 679; 9. *Ibid.*, vol. 53, p. 329; 10. *Ibid.*, vol. 53, p. 501; 11. Wills, Liber 1, folio 222; 12. Test. Proc. Liber 1E, folio 154; 13. Archives, vol. 53, p. 60; 14. Chas. Co. Deeds, Liber C, folio 1; 15. Archives, vol. 60, p. 63; 16. Chas. Co. Deeds, Liber C, folio 61.

* Thomas Hussey, of Maryland, Gent. and Johannah his wife deeded on Nov. 13, 1677 to Rachell Ashford, natural [legitimate daughter of the body] daughter of Johannah and wife of Michael Ashford, of Charles County, Carpenter, for love and affections "Moore's Ditch" in Charles County on the west side of Zachia Swamp adjoining the land of George Goodrick and Robert Goodrick. For want of issue after the death of Rachell Ashford, then "ye said Thomas Hussey & Johannah his wife do by these presents grant ye said land to Mary Hussey and Elizabeth Hussey *their* natural daughters equally and for want of such issue then ye said Thomas Hussey and Johanna his wife unto ye heirs of Her ye said Johannah sister Margaret wife of Francis Pope, of Charles County, deceased". Ref: Chas. Co. Deeds, Liber G, folio 72.

RICHARD NEVITT

Casual writers on early Maryland have incorrectly transcribed Richard Nevitt as Richard Nevill [Nevell], but careful study discloses that Nevitt and Nevill were the family names of two distinct personages on the Ark and were progenitors of two separate and unrelated families in Southern

Maryland. It is admitted that owing to the illegibility of the early 17th century script or poor penmanship, Richard Nevitt does appear in the public records as Richard Nevill, but studying both families, one will readily agree that they were two separate entities and both left descendants. Knevett is the usual English orthography and it was frequently used in the early Maryland records.

Of the social position of Richard Nevitt, it may be said that he was above the average of the Adventurers on the two vessels. Generally he made his signature with a large R, but there were occasions when his name was written by him. He was frequently commissioned by the court to appraise estates, and he eventually became a landed proprietor of considerable portions. Apparently before leaving England he had been a retainer in one of the great Catholic houses of the county. The family is an armorial one and appears in the visitations of the 15th and 16th century as Knevet, Knyvett, and the like. Members of the family have been raised to the peerage and the baronetage.

The fact that he had been a retainer in one of the Roman Catholic houses is perhaps correct, for he was brought over as one of the servants of the unfortunate John Saunders, Esq., who assigned his charges and land rights to Ferdinand Pulton, the Jesuit. The early association of him with the Catholic gentlemen would indicate a profession of that faith, and the early members intermarried with the Jarboes and the Dants, but most of the succeeding generations worshipped in the Anglican Church.

His period of indentureship was perhaps about five years, for he was not accorded a voice in the Second General Assembly of 1637/8, unless he was under age. When he acquired the privilege of a freeholder, he settled in St. George's Hundred, where he voted for David Wickliff as burgess to the Assembly called for February-March 1638/9.[1]

At that time he was perhaps a tenant on one of the proprietary manors early established in St. George's Hundred, for there is no record of his holding land until 1641. Inasmuch as he was in 1639 one of the debtors to the estate of Justinian Snow, Lord of Snow Hill Manor, it may indicate that he was one of the freeholders on that manor.

In 1641 he was still domiciled in St. George's Hundred, when he voted for the burgess to represent that district, and in March 1641/2, when all freeholders were summoned to the General Assembly, he gave his proxy to John Worthy. But in September 1642, for his non-appearance at the Assembly and his failure to send a proxy he was duly fined, but soon gave his proxy to William Broughe.*

In 1642 he was granted the power of attorney by one of his fellow planters to appear at the Provincial Court and answer in his name, and he occasionally served on juries.

* Up to this point his name had been printed in Archives vol. 1 as Nevill, but in this instance he appears in print as Nevett for the first time.

By 1641 a creek had been named after him which is indicative of his being an original settler in that locale. On August 25, 1641, he demanded 50 acres of land by assignment from Randall Revell and another 50 acres by assignment from John Medley.† Thereupon the Surveyor General stated on December 10, following, that he had laid out for Richard Nevett 100 acres of land "bounded on the south by a branch of Pacocomoc Creek called Medley's Branch, then into the woods . . . till it intercepts a parallel drawn from a branch in Nevett's Creek called Richard's Branch on the north . . . on the east with a creek falling into the Potomac River called Nevett's Creek".[2] This land fell into the then-newly organized St. Clement's Hundred or New Towne Hundred, in that day the western frontier of the young settlement.

This plantation is placed in the vicinity of Bretton Bay and was undoubtedly the 100 acres at Nevitt's Creek which were willed by William Tettershall of Bretton Bay in 1670, and was likewise the "Rachoon Point" of 100 acres on the east side of Bretton's Bay taken up by Richard Nevett which were willed by Stephen Gough in 1700 to his son Stephen Jr.[3]

On October 8, 1647, Robert Clarke, the Surveyor General, reported that he laid out for Richard Nevett 100 acres on Britain's Bay.[4] Likewise on May 14, 1651, Clarke surveyed for him, styled Richard Nevett, Planter, 300 acres on the north side of the Patuxent River near a creek called Hampton Creek. This plantation later fell into Calvert County.[5] It was due him by assignment of 100 acres from Richard Brown "according to His Lordship's Conditions of Plantation of August 8, 1636". At a subsequent rent roll, it was styled "Nevitt", a free hould.[6]

At a court held on February 8, 1649/50, he received a warrant for additional 100 acres of land which was probably not the grant which he received on October 20, 1653, for a parcel of land on Bretton Bay. The latter tract he assigned to William Stiles and it figured in 1679 during the inquisition over the estate of Robert Sheale.[7]

In 1648 Richard Nevitt appeared at court and stated that he had captured "fowre Patuxent Indians" whom he caught "felloniously killing & carrying away certaine hoggs", and wished to appear in behalf of himself and other inhabitants against "the divers intollerable iniuries suffered from time to time by the neighbouring Indians in stealing & dryving away their whole stocks of swine & in robbing & pillaging their howses much to their undoeing". A trial was held in which the four Indians declared their innocence and as Nevitt had no witnesses, the jury rendered a verdict of not guilty.[8]

Like all planters both high and low, he was frequently sued at the Provincial Court for various sums of tobacco. On January 2, 1646/7, at

---

† At this point one must reconcile the fact that in 1641 Randall Revell, then of Accomac County, claimed land rights for transporting his servant, Richard Nevill (sic) which rights Revell assigned to his former servant in the same year. The copies from the earlier books record distinctly "11". Ref: ABH, folio 79, Land Office.

the suppression of Ingle's Rebellion, he with a number of both Catholics and Anglicans swore fealty to the Lord Proprietary.

He was active in the militia company of his Hundred and held the rank of sergeant, the title which he was addressed at court in February 1650/1. On October 20, 1653, a land patent was recorded "in consideration that Sergt Richard Nevitt of our said Province hath 100 acres upon or near Britton Bay where he now lives by virtue of an order or grant in 1647 . . . a parcel on Britton Bay on the west side of Nevett's Branch to St. Ann's Creek south by a marsh called Nevitt's Marsh . . . containing 100 acres to be held of the Manor of West St. Maries . . . for the payment of 2 shillings or a bushel of corne at the Feast of the Nativity.[9]

Other plantations of which he was seized and on which he remitted quit rents were "Rocky Point", a freehold of 200 acres, due to Walter Pakes who assigned his patent to Richard Nevitt and "Red Budd Thickett", of 100 acres, surveyed for Walter Pake and sold to William Styles.[10]

At an early quit-rent roll he remitted rents on "Nevit's Hould" of 100 acres in New Towne Hundred which lay between the land of William Styles called "Nevitt's St. Anne's" and the land then held by John Hammond "due to Sergt Richard Nevitt by order made 1647".[11] He was also seized of 300 acres of "Freehould" which was surveyed for him on May 14, 1651, by assignment from Richard Ware and Richard Browne.[12]

He married presumably in or after 1639, a servant brought in by John Lewger Sr. Some years later or on October 14, 1651, John Lewger Jr. proved rights due him as the son and heir of his father for "rights of my father, Anne now the wife of Richard Nevitte . . . and Anne Goldsborough now the wife of John Shirtcliff who were transported 12 years since".[13]

The number of children blessed by this union is not known, but there was a Richard Jr., of age in 1666, and John, who was born in 1641, was perhaps the son and heir. No will or administration of his estate is on record.

Sources: 1. Archives, vol. 1, p. 30; 2. Liber 1, folio 120, Liber ABH, folio 98, Land Office; 3. Wills, Liber 11, folio 61; 4. Liber ABH, folio 3, Land Office; 5. Liber ABH, folio 171; 6. Rent Roll, Liber O, folio 48, Land Office; 7. Archives, vol. 51, pp. 273-274; 8. Archives, vol. 4, p. 409; 9. Liber ABH, folio 349, Land Office; 10. Rent Roll, Liber O, folios 27-28; 11. Rent Roll, Liber O, folio 23; 12. Rent Roll, Liber O, folio 48; 13. Liber ABH, folio 150.

JOHN NORTON ELDER AND YOUNGER

Captain Thomas Cornwalys imported from Virginia, apparently when the Ark tarried in Virginia waters before sailing up the Chesapeake, four servants among whom were John Norton the Elder and John Norton the Younger.[1] While it is assumed that they were father and son, yet no proof has been found to substantiate the belief. At the General Assembly of 1637/8, only one without the appellation of Elder or Younger was of freeman status and was then a planter of St. Mary's Hundred. Secretary John Lewger, Esq. held his proxy.[2]

By February 1638/9, he was a planter of St. Michael's Hundred and voted for James Cauther and John Price to represent that hundred at the elected Assembly of that year. In 1642 his tobacco assessment for public expenditures of the Province was 23 lbs.[3]

Although he was sometimes styled a Planter, he was also a sawyer, and in 1638 he refused for some reason to deliver 1000 ft. of sawn boards to Thomas Copley of the Jesuits. In September 1642, he was amerced 20 lbs. tob. for his failure to attend the Assembly, but he immediately assigned his rights to Captain Cornwalys.[4] In 1643 Leonard Calvert sued him for 2½ lbs. corn as rent due of his tenancy on one of Calvert's manors, and in 1644 he was likewise sued by Marks Phaypo.[5]

About this time the plundering period began with Ingle and his insurgents and the name of John Norton is missing from the records. After an interval of eleven years, John Norton appeared at court in 1655 and registered his cattle marks.*

Shortly afterwards or in 1657 the wife of John Norton "was abroad" and during her absence, one Jane Pauldin, a servant, made some slanderous allegations against him. While the allegations may not have been so magnificent, they were extremely interesting.[6] His wife was Elizabeth or Bess Norton and was addressed as Goody Norton during the depositions relative to the maid-servant, Jane Pauldin. As Norton was referred to as the Old Man, he was apparently the Elder.

The further history of this family from Maryland records is too fragmentary to be traced with any precision or completeness, as it is believed that if there were any descendants, they remained for a generation or two landless.

Sources: 1. Liber ABH, folio 244, Land Office; 2. Archives, vol. 1, p. 3; 3. Archives, vol. 1, pp. 28, 145; 4. Archives, vol. 1, pp. 170, 176; 5. Archives, vol. 4, pp. 202, 286; 6. Archives, vol. 10, p. 516; vol. 41, pp. 14-18.

* There are reasons to believe that he was the one who came with the Adventurers, for no land rights for a John Norton were claimed until 1687.

ROBERT PIKE

Governor Leonard Calvert in 1641 entered rights for the transporting of Robert Pike in 1633, but no further record is available on him in the Province. He apparently died early or returned to England. Ref: Liber ABH, folio 98; Liber 1, folio 121.

BLACK AND WHITE JOHN PRICES

Two Adventurers bearing the name of John Price were transported on the Ark, both by the Wintour brothers, one being styled "white" John Price and the other "black" John Price. Circumstances and knowledge of conditions of the times refute the oft repeated statement that the Black John Price was a Negro. The only Negroes of that period outside of Africa were slaves or bondsmen and in the 17th and 18th centuries Negro slaves were without a family name, as decreed by law and custom. It is therefore believed that one was of a light complexion and the other of a dark complexion, thus being styled as "white" and "black" for differentiation.

To follow out the careers of these two Adventurers in Maryland has been difficult, and no further reference has been found in the Archives of Maryland to identify these men other than the claims of Ferdinando Pulton in 1639 for land rights by assignment from the Wintour brothers.

At the opening day of the General Assembly of January 25, 1637/8, a "John Price of St. Maries hundred planter" appeared and was given the right of a seat.[1] Following out the career of this John Price, it proves definitely that he was the later Captain John Price and then Colonel John Price who emigrated in 1636 as the following will show:[2]

"Capt John Price came and demanded 100 Acres of Land for Transporting One Able Man Servant Vizt Richard Brown in this Province in the year 1637 and 200 acres more for 2 other Able Men Servants Vizt Thomas Jackson and William Hardidge Transported by him into this Province in the year 1636 and 100 More for Transporting one other Man Servant vizt Edward Williams in the Year 1644 and 100 acres for Transporting himself into this Province about 11 years Since".

The month and day of the foregoing instrument is December 20, but the year is not noted, but from circumstances of nearby entries, it is believed to be the year 1648.

The question therefore arises whether this John Price is one of the two who was transported by the Wintours and had returned to England or another part of the British possessions in America and reentered in or about 1636 transporting two servants. It is known that at least two of the Adventurers on the Ark returned to England and brought back their families, but their names were of a certain character that no doubts existed as to identity. In this instance one is dealing with the extremely common name of John Price, and it will always leave some doubt in the mind of the genealogist whether the John Prices, the two Adventurers, succumbed to an early death in the Province, or whether one returned to England and emigrated in 1636 and ultimately distinguished himself in the military affairs of the Province and was appointed a member of His Lordship's Council.

In 1648 John Price deposed to be aged 40, so he was born in or about 1608 and was in his late twenties when he emigrated in 1636. He signed his name and there are no other known instances of a John Price making his mark to indicate that there may have been two contemporary John Prices.

On February 18, 1638/9, he was domiciled in St. Michael's Hundred and was elected with James Cauther by the freemen to the first elected General Assembly held in the Province.[3] In 1642 he was assessed 46 lbs. tob. for the accounts of the Province, and at the same Assembly his proxy was held by Captain Thomas Cornwalys. In the expedition against the Sesquihanowes Indians, commanded by Captain Henry Fleete in 1644, Fleete was given instructions by John Lewger, Secretary of the Province, to consult with several named men in all matters of importance, among whom was John Price, Planter.[4]

On January 20, 1647/8, Captain John Price appeared at the General Assembly holding eight proxies from St. George's Hundred.[5] Four days later he assigned his proxies to Mr. William Thompson. In 1648 he was appointed to the Upper House by the Lord Proprietary,[6] but soon lost his seat when the Puritans took over. In that year he was styled "Muster Maister" of the Province.

His name was totally absent from the activities of the Province during the Puritan usurpation, thus denoting his alignment with the Proprietary Party. Upon the restoration of legitimate power by the Calverts, or on January 12, 1659/60, Cecilius, Lord Baltimore, appointed "our dear friend & Councellor Coll John Price" to the Upper House.[7]

On June 17, 1647, he was the Captain of the Fort at St. Inigoes and stated that there was a great need of corn for the maintenance of the soldiers. In the same year he was one of the appraisers of the personal estate of Governor Leonard Calvert.

He attended a session of the Council in December 1660. On February 10, 1660/1, he drew up his last will and testament which was probated on March 11, 1660/1, in St. Mary's County by William Wilkinson, Thomas Dent, and William Hatton.[8] He left a step-son and an only child, Anne Price, a minor at the time of his death.

Sources: 1. Archives, vol. 1, p. 3; 2. Liber ABH, folio 10, Land Office; 3. Archives, vol. 1, pp. 29, 32; 4. Archives, vol. 3, p. 150; 5. Archives, vol. 1, p. 214; 6. Archives, vol. 3, pp. 211, 213; 7. Archives, vol. 1, p. 382; 8. Wills, Liber 1, folio 141.

LODOVICK PRICE

Lodovick Price was transported by Governor Leonard Calvert for whom he claimed land-rights in August 1641. No further record. He did not attend the early Assemblies, and his name does not figure among the early records of the probate court.

FRANCIS RABNETT

Francis Rabnett [Rabnot] was among the Adventurers in 1633, having been transported at the cost of the two Wintours.[1] He conformed to the teachings of the Roman Catholic Church, as is evident by his arrest in Virginia during 1635 for the statement that it was lawful and meritorious to kill a heretic king.[2] In 1635 he appraised the estate of William Smith,

Gent. He was literate, signing his name on all occasions, and the fact that he voiced his personal beliefs indicated a thoughtful, if not tactful mind and judgment.

He attended the General Assembly of January 1637/8, as a freeman of St. Mary's Hundred, at which time he held the proxies of several of his fellow planters. He removed to the Isle of Kent with Giles Brent and several others who had come in 1633, and as a resident of that hundred in February 1639/40, he witnessed and signed an agreement made by John Smith, of Crayford, Planter, to place the property of Smith's daughter, Katherine, under the trusteeship of William Brainthwaite, Gent.

He was domiciled on Kent in 1642 and 1643, and in that former year he was assessed 32 lbs. tob. His last record was on July 18, 1643, when Giles Brent sued him for 1,300 lbs. tob. No administration of his estate is on record, and so far as it is known he left no descendants in Maryland.

Sources: 1. Liber ABH, folio 66; Liber 1, folio 38; 2. Neil's Terra Mariae, p. 72; 3. Archives, vol. 4, pp. 16, 17, 211.

JOHN ROBINSON, CARPENTER

John Robinson, Carpenter, was brought-in by Captain Thomas Cornwalys, but he had completed his indentureship by the Second Assembly of January 1637/8, when he was admitted as a freeholder.[1] In the same month at Mattapanient he was on the panel at the inquest for the death of John Briant.[2]

His early domicile was in St. Mary's Hundred, when he voted for burgesses to represent that hundred in the 1638 Assembly.[3] In the same year he received 20 lbs. tob. from the estate of William Smith. By March 1639/40, he had removed to St. Clement's Hundred and was commissioned the first High Constable for that hundred.[4] He attended the Assembly of March 1641/2, but at the session of September 1642, he was fined 30 lbs. tob. for his non-attendance.

He was alive in December 1642, when he paid his tobacco assessment, but was deceased by December 1, 1643, when Richard Wright appeared as the administrator of his estate. John Hollis at that time was alleged to owe the estate tobacco, beaver, salt, corn, and powder.[5]

The estate was unsettled as late as 1644 when John Worthy demanded of Richard Wright 514 lbs. tob. due him as one of the creditors of the estate. There is no record of any heirs, and inasmuch as no wife was granted letters of administration, it is assumed that he left no descendants in the Province. He should not be confused with John Robinson, Barber-Chirurgeon, who was a contemporary.

Sources: 1. Archives, vol. 1, p. 4; 2. Archives, vol. 4, p. 9; 3. Archives, vol. 1, p. 29; 4. Archives, vol. 3, p. 89; 5. Archives, vol. 4, pp. 214-215.

Mr. Francis Rogers

When Ferdinand Pulton made claims for land rights in 1639 by assignment from Father White, he entered the name of Mr. Rogers, and in 1650 we have his name as Mr. ffrancis Rogers, when Copley made a second claim. With the title "Mr.", we have evidence of the entry of a member of the county gentry, but unfortunately no further mention of him can be found among the Maryland archives.

William Saire, Esq.

William Saire, Esq., was mentioned as one of the Gentlemen of Fashion who had gone to the Maryland Plantations. No record of any transportees brought in by him or assignment has come to light, or does his name figure in any of the correspondence with Lord Baltimore. He either succumbed to an early death in the Province or did not find the country to his liking, so returned on the Ark.

Stephen Sammon

Stephen Sammon [Sammion, Salmon, Salman] was transported as a servant of Captain Thomas Cornwalys, for whom he claimed land rights in 1640/41. He was apparently quite young at the time, inasmuch as he does not seem to have completed his service until 1643 or thereabouts. At that time he was either assessed 50 lbs. tob. or received that amount for a campaign against the Susquehannock Indians.[1] There is no record of his attending the General Assemblies or delegating a proxy prior to his death which may lend a thought to the fact that he was not of British or Irish descent. On January 2, 1646/7, he was among the forty or more who took the Oath of Fealty after Ingle's Rebellion.[2] During the plundering years one of his steers was killed by Mr. Fenwick who offered to replace it, as testified in 1647/8 by Edmund Smith.[3]

There is definite proof of his marriage, for on November 14, 16—, Walter Gest gave his receipt to Walter Pakes for 200 lbs. tob. for the use of Steeven Salman (*sic*) as compensation for the "service done him [Salman] and his wife eight months and three days gatherine corne".[4]

In 1648 he served on jury duty, and on November 9, 1650, as Stephen Salmon he was impanelled on a jury in the suit of Levin Bufkin, Esq., vs Robert Brooke, Esq. He was deceased by December 2, 1651, for at a session of the Provincial Court on that day, it was shown that Walter Peake [Pakes], the administrator of the estate of Stephen Salmon, was sued by William Stone, Esq.[5] On January 22, 1652/3, the estate was also sued by Robert Brooke, Esq., who stated that he sold a cow with calf and a heifer with calf to Steven Samson and had received all but 600 lbs. tob. of the selling price.

The Christian name of his wife has not come down to posterity or is it known how many children were born and survived the union. There is proof, however, of a son, Thomas, as on November 1, 1659, Thomas Diniard, a Roman Catholic, who drew up his will on that day and naming no heirs of his body, bequeathed a legacy to "Thomas Salmon son of Stephen Salmon".[6] Whenever only one son is proved, question always arises whether there were daughters whose names do not appear on record, but who actually lived, married, and left issue.

Thomas Salmon, the son, followed the trade of a cooper and was perhaps attached to the Jesuit mission at Newtowne or dwelt nearby. He was a land owner, for he sold the tract "Poole" to John Herd, and possessed "Rochester", a plantation of 200 acres at his death. He died without issue in 1695, and after devising "Rochester" to John and Justinian Greenwell, sons of James Greenwell, he bequeathed legacies to four Roman Catholic priests.[7] His personal estate was small, being appraised at £2/19/8. No kinsmen approved the inventory, but James Greenwell and John Fancy signed as the creditors.[8]

NOTE: A Thomas Salmon, Merchant, died intestate in 1675, county not stated, who possessed a personal estate appraised at 114,375 lbs. tob. Ref: Inv. & Accts, Liber 2, folio 160, Hall of Records, Annapolis.

Sources: 1. Archives of Maryland, vol. 3, p. 138; 2. Archives, vol. 3, p. 174; 3. Archives, vol. 4, p. 362; 4. Archives, vol. 10, p. 374; 5. Archives, vol. 10, p. 113; 6. Wills, Liber 1, folio 82; 7. Wills, Liber 7, folio 134; 8. Inv. & Accts, Liber 10, folio 475.

JOHN SAUNDERS, ESQ.

John Saunders, Esq., one of the Gentlemen of Fashion, was a business partner of Captain Thomas Cornwalys, and with him was one of the co-owners of the pinnace Dove. He died in 1634 within a year of the settlement, as proved by the statement of Captain Cornwalys in 1653.[1] He transported at least ten servants. Before his death he assigned five of them to Ferdinand Pulton and five to Captain Cornwalys. When the latter made applications in 1640 for land rights, he failed to record their names, thus we are deprived of the identity of five additional Adventurers. However, when Pulton applied in 1639, as an assignee of Mr. Saunders he named his five, that is, Benjamin Hodges, John Elbin, Richard Cole, Richard Nevill [Nevitt], and John Marlborough.

Before his death he executed his last will and testament making Captain Cornwalys his executor, but no copy of the instrument has been found among the Maryland records. On February 12, 1638/9, before the Governor and Council, Captain Thomas Cornwalys exhibited the inventory and an administration account and gave several "discharges" under the hand of Richard Gerard, Thomas White, and Roger Walton. Jerome Hawley at the same time exhibited an assignment of a "legacie" by Valentine Saunders, brother and heir to James Saunders, and also requested of Thomas Cornwalys one-eighth portion of the Dove and the profits thereof due to John Saunders. Cornwalys, however, had already disbursed against the account of Valentine Saunders a sufficient sum to cover the legacy, so it was not possible for Jerome Hawley to expect any further discharges.[2] Valentine Saunders who acquired his brother's share of the Dove apparently was never in Maryland.

Sources: 1. Liber ABH, folio 244, Land Office; 2. Archives, vol. 4, p. 14.

ROBERT SHERLEY

Robert Sherley [Shirley] was brought in as a servant of Father Andrew White and for whom Thomas Copley alias Father Fisher claimed land-rights in 1639 and again in 1650. His attendance was not noted at any of the early assemblies or have any further references been found for him in Maryland records.

THOMAS SLATHAM

Thomas Slatham came into Maryland in 1633 at the expense of Father White who assigned his land rights to Ferdinando Pulton. He was alive on September 22, 1635, when he witnessed the last will and testament of William Smith, Gent. He was probably one of the early mortalities, as he was not summoned to the Assembly of 1637.

ROBERT SMITH, PLANTER

There are reasons to believe and sufficient circumstantial evidence to accept that Robert Smith who later settled in Talbot County was one of the Adventurers on the Ark and the Dove. He was a freeman of St. Mary's Hundred by January 1637/8, when he gave his proxy to Francis Rabnet, but he later spoke of his having performed service in the Province. Inasmuch as the indentureship of the men and boys on the Ark and the Dove was for three or four years, it would indicate that he had just completed his service in 1637 and was accorded the rights of a freeholder. If he were not an Adventurer on that memorable voyage, then he apparently came in the second ship during December 1634.

On November 3, 1638, he declared his intentions of marrying Rose Gilbert, the widow of Richard Gilbert, Planter. By his timely marriage with the widow, he was rewarded, for he acquired by law all the rights and interests which his wife held in the estate of her late husband, which formed the nucleus of the 600-acre plantation acquired by Gilbert on the Eastern Shore.

He was apparently not interested in civic and political affairs, for there is no record of his exercising his privilege of attending the General Assemblies. As mentioned above, Francis Rabnet held his proxy at the 1637/8 Assembly, in 1641 Thomas Baldridge, and in 1642 Captain Thomas Cornwalys. During his domicile in St. Mary's County his plantation lay first in St. Mary's Hundred which undoubtedly consisted of a few hundred acres on one of the private or public manors. Later he held a leasehold on

Governor Calvert's Manor of Trinity, when in 1646 his rent of 6 bbls. or corn and 12 capons for 100 acres was in arrears.[1]

In 1642 Captain Cornwalys sued him, Thomas Yewell and Steven Thomas for trespass upon "St. Jerome's Manor" and the shooting of game in violation of the ancient English game laws. The manor had been granted to Jerome Hawley, Esq., but Captain Cornwalys was in possession as the executor of the estate.

At a court held in 1643 he and others were summoned to show cause why they had failed to contribute to the maintenance of the garrison at Fort Conquest on Palmer's Island, according to their written agreement.[3]

While he swore fealty to Governor Calvert as Lord of Trinity Manor and was subject to the laws of the manor, he himself maintained a staff of servants. One of his labourers was William Stephenson who sued him for 500 lbs. tob. and 3 bbls. of corn as his annual wages. Stephenson was deceased by March 1652, when Robert Smith demanded 200 lbs. tob. from Humphrey Attwicks, the administrator of Stephenson's estate.

It has been mentioned elsewhere that in 1654 he gave a heifer to Elizabeth, the wife of William Asbiston, whom he styled as daughter. On this occasion Robert Smith made his mark, while William Asbiston wrote his name.

At a court held at St. Mary's on November 6, 1651, Rose Smith, his wife, deposed to be 42 years of age and appeared as a witness in the "domestic relation" affair of Robert Holt whose wife had threatened to murder him. Goodie Smith stated that she was at the house of Robert Holt, when Goodie Holt unburdened herself to her. Goodie Holt stated, "She were as good kill him as live as She did". Thereupon, Rose Smith cautioned her of the penalty of hanging to which she replied "Then there was an end of two". The husband and wife apparently separated and at a visit paid Rose Smith at her house, she advised "Dorothy Holt" to return to her husband again telling her "What a Covenant She made at their marriage that thereby She could not with Safe Conscience go from her husband". Thereupon, the troubled wife replied "That her heart was soe hardened against him that She would never darken his door again".[6]

Rose Smith was furthermore a member of the all-woman jury in 1656 which tried Judith Catchpole for the murder of her new-born child. She was living as late as 1658 when she, her husband Robert Smith, and William Ashbiston were summoned to testify at court.[7]

Goodie Smith also knew the art of mid-wifery and officiated at the delivery of a premature boy of Goodie Brooke whose husband, Francis Brooke, was apparently no saint. The birth was prematurely brought on by the brutal beating of his wife with a pair of tongs. Elizabeth Claxton testified that when the child was delivered, it was all bruised and that Rose Smith lectured him, but he established an alibi and stated that his wife fell out of a peach tree. Under the duress of her husband, the distressed wife agreed, but Brooke was ultimately tried of "Suspition of Murther" and convicted. Rose Smith signed her name at court on this occasion.[8]

On February 28, 1649/50, some 17 years after his arrival in the Province, Robert Smith demanded his first land grant. He requested 50 acres "for his service to the Lordship," 100 acres for Thomas Thomas brought in by Mr. Pasmore 15 years since, 300 acres in right of Rose his wife formerly the wife of Richard Gilbert being for the transportation of the said Gilbert, his wife, and Elizabeth and Grace his children, and 100 acres by assignment from Walter Waterling. The latter 100 acres were for the freedom of the said Waterling and 50 acres for a maid servant.[9] Accordingly, 550 acres of land were ordered to be laid out for Robert Smith on the Patuxent.

Apparently, the Patuxent plantation was never actually patented, for in 1659 Robert Smith was granted 600 acres of land on the east side of the Chesapeake Bay on St. Michael's River and Morgan's Creek in the name of "Smeath" . . . "due to him by marrying Rose the relict of Richard Gilbert . . . the land being due to the said Richard Gilbert for transporting himself and the said Rose, Grace and Elizabeth, her daughters, Walter Waterling and Thomas Thomas his servants.[10] Then another conflicting record shows that "Smeath" was granted to Robert Smith for transporting himself, Elizabeth his daughter, Richard Gilbert, Thomas Thomas, Thomas Wills and Patrick Frizzel his servants. This was in the year 1666 or thereabouts, so it was apparently a reaffirmation or confirmation.[11]

The several warrants contradict themselves, but the first approach in 1649 when Robert Smith declared 50 acres due him for service is undoubtedly the more authentic. Ultimately, he settled at "Smeath" on St. Michael's River which eventually fell into Talbot County.

In 1660 Robert Smith, who made his mark, and his wife Rose writing her name, gave Elizabeth Brooke, the daughter of Francis Brooke "one Grisell Sow with pigg", as witnessed by David Seely and Marke King, though it was not recorded at court until 1664.[12] On June 15, 1669, Robert Smith had the age of his servant, John Riding, adjudged at court.[13]

There is a reference in 1649 to a calf given to "one of the said Smith's children" by John Hilliard, thereby establishing proof that he had more than one child.[14] His will is rather ambiguous, naming only one child, one grandchild, and devising land to several King orphans. The instrument, dated May 4, 1671, was probated in Talbot County on December 19, following, by Thomas Jackson and Edward Tomlins.[15]

> To grandchild Mary Waterlin livestock.
> To Ann Walters daughter of Christopher Walters, decd., livestock.
> To Elizabeth King daughter of Mark King, decd., livestock.
> "Plantation whereon I now live to Robert King the oldest son of said Mark King and as much land joining to it, as will make 200 acres".
> To Robert Walters the plantation "which his father Chr: Walters decd live upon with that parcel of land that I formerly did marke out for to belong to it".

To daughter Ann Emory that plantation "whereon she now liveth during her naturall life and after her decease I give it and all that land" to John Kinge the younger son of said Marke Kinge.

Residue of land was to be divided into three parts and given to the following as they came of age—Robert Walters, John King and James Symonds son of Thomas.

In no instance did he name the land; they were evidently various farms on "Smeath". His name does not appear upon the deed index of neither Kent nor Talbot Counties as a grantor or grantee.

William Coursey and Tristam Thomas were appointed executors, but it seems as if William Coursey was the one to officiate. At a court held in Talbot County on November 9, 1672, Mr. William Coursey, the administrator of Robert Smith, acknowledged judgment for a cow and calf due Mary King.[16] And on September 16, 1673, it was shown that the estate left Ann Walters by Robert Smith was in the hands of Mr. William Coursey, that is, 3 cows, 1 steer 3 yrs. old, 1 cow calf, 1 steer calf, and 1073 lbs. tob.[17]

On September 16, 1673, the court ordered that Ann Walters have a cow paid her out and from her father's Christopher Walter's estate, being a debt due to Arthur Emory from the said estate and given to the said Ann Walters by the said Arthur Emory.[18]

Genealogically, the will and administration of the estate of Robert Smith leaves much to be desired. He named a daughter, Anne, but his devises of land to King and Walters orphans lend some belief that they could be his grandchildren. Traditionally, land was devised to blood kinsmen, and the landed estate of Robert Smith was not so extensive that he could afford to enrich others beside his daughter. Furthermore, his daughter Ann Emory was to enjoy only a life interest and at her death it was to revert to John King. Marke King and Christopher Walters so far as records indicate were landless and were tenants or lived upon the plantation of Robert Smith. By their dwelling on "Smeath", it may add stronger evidence to the belief that King and Walters had married his daughters and that he was providing for his orphan grandchildren. Both Marke King and Christopher Walters named sons Robert.

The following are placed as the children of Robert Smith, though Anne is the only one with definite proof:

1. Anne Smith married Arthur Emory.
2. . . . . Smith married Marke King.*
3. . . . . Smith married Christopher Walters.†

---

* Marke King came into the Province as one of the men-servants of Robert Brooke, Esq., in 1650, and seemed to have received no land grants. Ref: Archives, vol. 3, p. 256. He, however, signed his name when he witnessed the gift of Robert Smith and Rose his wife to Elizabeth Brooke, daughter of Francis. He was a tenant upon the estate of Robert Smith, but died intestate leaving minor children. In 1669 Arthur Emory was guardian to his orphans—Robert, Mary, Elizabeth, and John. Ref.:

Thomas Smith

No further reference has been found for Thomas Smith, the transportee of the two Wintours, whose land-rights they assigned to Father White. He attended none of the early General Assemblies and all references in the archives relative to a Thomas Smith for the early period can definitely be placed as those of the unfortunate Thomas Smith, Esq. who lost his head for alleged piracy and not paying homage to Lord Baltimore or his representatives.

William Smith, Gent.

William Smith, whose probated will of September 22, 1635, was the first on record officially in the Province, proves of special interest. At the beginning he stated that it was "made in Augusta Carolina at St. Maries in maryland anno 1635". Thomas Heath and Thomas Slatham, two servants of Father White, who came on the Ark, were the witnesses. He was a devout Roman Catholic stating in his will "I professe that I die a member of the Catholique Church out of wch there is no salvation", and consequently bequeathed a legacy to the Church. His wife, Anne, was made the executrix and the residuary heir, naming no children.

His personal estate, appraised at £135/18/6, was affluent for so early a period of Maryland's history, with a man-servant 2½ years to serve, and various amounts of tobacco owed him by John Hilliard, John Bryant, and Thomas Allen. Among the desperate debts due the estate were 21 lbs. of beaver, one-fourth of which was due from Mr. [Richard] Gerard and Richard Duke.

His widow, who made her mark, filed the inventory and an account

Archives, vol. 54, pp. 527, 567, 578. No formal administration of his estate is on file at Annnapolis.

† Christopher Walters likewise lived upon the plantation of Robert Smith, but was deceased by March 1669/70, when his estate was sued. Ref: Archives, vol. 54, pp. 458-459. On October 25, 1651, Christopher Walter, aged 12 or 13 swore at court that he was present when Thomas Lisle fell out of the tree on John Halfhead's plantation on the Patuxent, his being a servant to Halfhead at that time. Ref: Archives, vol. 10, p. 154. On January 8, 1669/70, the administration of the estate of Christopher Walters was granted to Francis Staunton, of London, Agent, with Robert Smith to appraise the estate. Ref: Test. Proc., Liber 3, folio 336. His orphan, Ann Walters, was placed under the guardianship of Arthur Emory who in 1671 petitioned court of Talbot County for 600 lbs. tob. out of the estate of Christopher Walters for board and schooling of his ward Ann. Ref: Archives, vol. 54, p. 497.

Sources: Archives, vol. 10, p. 93; 2. *Ibid.*, vol. 4, pp. 167-174; 3. *Ibid.*, vol. 4, p. 230; 4. *Ibid.*, vol. 10, pp. 10, 94, 250; 5. *Ibid.*, vol. 2, pp. 514-515; 6. *Ibid.*, vol. 2, pp. 109-110; 7. *Ibid.*, vol. 41, pp. 129, 157; 8. *Ibid.*, vol. 2, pp. 464-465; 9. Patents, Liber ABH, folio 37; Liber 2, folio 606, Land Office; 10. *Ibid.*, Liber 4, folio 220; 11. *Ibid.*, Liber 10, folio 281; 12. Archives, vol. 49, p. 303; 13. *Ibid.*, vol. 54, p. 439; 14. *Ibid.*, vol. 4, p. 525; 15. Wills, Liber 1, folio 466; 16. Archives, vol. 54, p. 540; 17. *Ibid.*, vol. 54, p. 576; 18. *Ibid.*, vol. 54, p. 577.

about October 1638. After three years of her husband's decease, she was still faithful to his memory, as she was recorded as Anne Smith. No further record is available to ascertain if she found an early grave or succumbed to the entreaties of some lonely planter.

William Smith is placed as the Adventurer on the Ark who assigned his land rights to Thomas Greene, Esq. No land rights, so far as it is known, were claimed for his wife or widow.

SMITH

When Ferdinando Poulton applied for land-rights in 1639, mostly by rights of assignment, he claimed land for "A Smith lost by the way". Smith could have been the family name of the Adventurer, then he could have been a blacksmith, for in those days the latter was frequently referred to as a "smith". Ref: Liber ABH, folio 65-66.

ANNE SMITHSON-NORMAN

Although definite proof is lacking, circumstances lead to the belief that Anne _____, a maid-servant brought-in by Jerome Hawley, Esq., and who later married John Smithson came with the first Adventurers. There is no extant list of the transportees of Jerome Hawley, and no servant, unless approved by her master, could contract marriage during her indentureship which under ordinary circumstances lasted about three or four years.

Anne, the maid-servant, married John Smithson who most likely emigrated in 1635, although from the poorly written script it could be taken for 1633. At the opening of the Second General Assembly of January 1637/8, John Smithson, of St. Mary's Hundred, gave his proxy to William Lewis, the overseer of the Jesuits' plantations, although he appeared in person at the session of March 12, 1637/8.[1]

John Smithson died before August 27, 1638, before he had filed claims for his 100 acres of land by rights of emigration. Lying very sick, John Medcalfe, Gent. asked him how should he dispose of his estate, to which he replied, "All that ever I have (meaning in this Province) or shall have coming out of England I freely give to my wife". William Lewis visited him the day before his death and Smithson complained that he was leaving his wife a poor widow, "All that I have I leave her and if I had more she should enjoy it".[2]

Under the oaths of John Medcalfe and William Lewis, his nuncupative will was accepted by the Judge of the Prerogative Court and probated as of August 28, 1638. His widow, Anne Smithson, thus became the sole legatee.[3]

Jerome Hawley died in 1638, and at that time Anne Smithson, his one-time servant, had not received all of her freedom dues. Therefore, if Anne had served Hawley the statutory four years, it would place her contract for indentureship before 1634 which is circumstantial evidence of her coming with the first settlers. By January 3, 1639/40, Anne was still a widow and received her 3 bbl. of corn from the estate of Jerome Hawley—due all indentured maid-servants at the expiration of their service.[4] In 1641 she had a claim of 45 lbs. tob. against three Irishmen, namely, Bryan Kelley, Baltasar Codd, and Cornelius O'Sullivan.[5]

After several years of widowhood, she married John Norman who had come in as a redemptioner of Captain Thomas Cornwalys.* On October 30, 1649, he made the following claims:[6]

> "John Norman demands 100 acres of Land which was due to John Smithson dec for transporting himself into this Province in the year 1635 [1633] the said Norman having intermarried the said Smithson's widd° & 50 acres in his own Rt as Servt to Capt. Cornwallis and 50 acres more in the Rt of his wife who was Servt to Capt. Hawley in this Prov."

From the above declaration, it is implied that his wife, Anne, was still alive, but by 1654, she was deceased and he had married one of the maid-servants brought-in by Robert Brooke, Esq., whose time he had bought from her master.[7]

> "Nov. 9, 1654. John Norman Demandeth one hundred acres of land for the Transportation of his Wife into this Province anno 1650 whose time of Service he bought of Robt Brook, Esq."

A warrant was therefore issued in his name for 100 acres of land. In June 1652, Robert Brooke gave his receipt to John Norman and John Mansfeeld for 2000 lbs. tob., so apparently all or part of the tobacco was for the release of Brooke's maid-servant.

From the death bed declaration of John Smithson in 1638, there is no evidence that he was leaving an heir by his wife, Anne, but there is a possibility that there was one, inasmuch as Anne Browne was styled a daughter-in-law [step-daughter] to John Norman.

On October 30, 1649, John Norman had the gift of a heifer with its marks registered at court for his daughter, Mary Norman, the heifer having been given her by Walter Beane.[8] Inasmuch as he had not married his second wife by that date, it stands to reason that this daughter was an issue of Anne. No further record was found for a possible marriage for this daughter, Mary.

The inventory of the estate of William Thompson, taken January 31, 1649/50, showed that the deceased owed "a cow calfe to John Norman's daughter-in-law & a barrell of Corne", and the notation also appeared in the final account rendered the court in 1658.[9]

---

* The year of John Norman's transportation is unknown, but he was apparently a freeholder by Apr. 10, 1638, when the Judge of Probate ordered Jerome Hawley to bring him into court. He was certainly a freeholder on Feb. 19, 1638/9, when he voted for a burgess to represent St. Mary's Hundred. Ref: Archives, vol. 1, p. 29; vol. 4, p. 29.

John Norman later became a tenant on St. Clement's Manor where he died in 1656. On June 17, of that year, administration of his estate was granted to his widow, Agnes Norman.[10] At a court held in 1658 the cattle mark of Agnes Norman was registered "wch was the mark of her father John Norman".[11]

Later a law suit developed over a cow and her increase which had belonged to John Norman's daughter-in-law. At court in 1656, William Bretton swore that "about five or Sixe yeares agoe a Cowe Calf was delivered by Capt. Wm Evens to one John Norman for the use of a young Girle which Norman was father in Law to the Said Girle and the Sd Norman bringing the Calf in this Deponents boate his own Son and one Cladrueny Maze being alsoe in the boate and arriving at this Deponents Landing the Said Norman Called divers amongst whom was this Deponent telling them all there present that he marked that Cow Calfe for the use of his daughter in Law".[12]

At a session of the Provincial Court held at the Governor's House in Wicomico River in 1658, it was shown that Clodeneus Mace on August 10, 1657, deposed that Capt. William Evans "delivered to John Norman (he being there actually present) for the sole use of the sd Normans Daughter in Law, Anne Browne, wch Calfe after a yeare or two growing had a calfe att Mr. Brettons, Afterwards leaving that his plantation att Mr. Brittons he carryed tht cow & her encrease to the head of the Bay St. Clements. Afterwards againe he removed to Longworth's Point in Mr. Gerards Mannor where he dyed".

Bartholomew Phillips made virtually the same statement as Mace, whereas Agnes Norman, the relict of John Norman, swore that when she was "newly marryed to the sd Norman shee asked him whose That heifer was wch is now in dispute betwixt Mr. Gerrard and Capt. Evans Hee made answere that it was his Daughters, Anne Browne".*

At court barons held on St. Clement's Manor in 1659 and 1660 John Norman is listed as a freeholder.[13] The only logical conclusion is that the freeholder on the manor in those years was the son of John Norman, the Emigrant, and this John Norman being of the age to be credited as a freeholder, therefore, making him a son of Ann Smithson-Norman or in 1659 being about 18 years of age.†

---

* When John Norman bought the services of the maid-servant [Agnes Neale] from Robert Brooke, she was definitely unmarried and without issue, and inasmuch as Robert Brooke did not arrive until 1649, the daughter-in-law of John Norman could not be the daughter-in-law [daughter of Agnes his last wife], so it is reasonable to assume that the daughter-in-law was the married daughter of his departed wife, Anne Smithson, unless she was the daughter of another wife of John Norman of which we have no knowledge.

† The John Norman, of Charles County, who in 1662 swore to be 28 years of age, therefore, born about 1634, could hardly be the son of John Norman Sr. who died on St. Clement's Manor, if so, there is another marriage for John Norman Sr. and the Norman of Charles County could not be the son of Anne Smithson-Norman. See, Archives, vol. 53, pp. 16, 203.

John Norman, of St. Clements Manor in 1659 and 1660 was no doubt the one who on November 25, 1661, witnessed the will of Christopher Carnell, of St. Mary's County. Land-rights were claimed in 1663 for a John Norman who can not be John Norman, the subject of this biography.

Analyzing genealogically the foregoing, one arrives at something like the following:

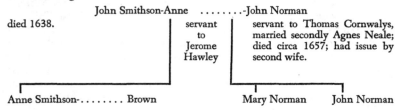

John Smithson-Anne ....-John Norman
died 1638.

servant to Jerome Hawley

servant to Thomas Cornwalys, married secondly Agnes Neale; died circa 1657; had issue by second wife.

Anne Smithson-........ Brown   Mary Norman   John Norman

Sources: 1. Archives, vol. 1, pp. 3, 14; 2. Archives, vol. 4, pp. 45-46; 3. Wills, Liber 1, folio 2; 4. Archives, vol. 4, p. 59; 5. Archives, vol. 4, p. 67; 6. Patents, Liber ABH, folio 24; 7. Patents, Liber ABH, folio 402; 8. Archives, vol. 4, p. 508; 9. Archives, vol. 41, p. 102; 10. Archives, vol. 10, p. 45; 11. Archives, vol. 41, p. 183; 12. Archives, vol. 10, p. 465; 13. Archives, vol. 53, pp. 627, 699.

MATHIAS SOUSA

When Ferdinando Pulton demanded land rights in 1639 for a number of transportees which had been assigned him by Father White, among the names was "Mathias Sousa a Motlato".[1] Likewise in 1650 when Thomas Copley demanded land rights by assignment from Father White as having brought in a number of Adventurers in 1633 among them was the name of Mathias Zause. The name has all the flavour of a Portuguese or Spanish basic blood stream, and inasmuch as it is a well known and proved fact that the Portuguese women integrated with the Negroes from the Portuguese Colonies in the 16th and 17th centuries, it can readily be understood why he was listed as a mulatto.*

Sousa apparently served Father White according to his contract of indentureship, and when Father White assigned his land rights to Ferdinando Pulton, the latter used him as a skipper on a small vessel and permitted him to trade with the Indians and perhaps other inhabitants in nearby Virginia.[2] In 1639 he owed the estate of Justinian Snow, and by that time he had apparently worked out his servitude.

At the Assembly called on March 23, 1641/2, he, recorded as Matt

---

* Benjamin H. Hartogensis (1865-1939), a 2d generation American of Dutch-Jewish origin, writing in his "Studies in the History of Maryland" attempts to prove that he was a Portuguese Jewish aristocrat and referred to him as Mathias de Sousa. According to his dark complexion, he was therefore listed as a mulatto. Hartogensis furthermore makes many unreliable claims in his arguments to prove that Sousa was the first Jew to settle in Maryland, but was forced to conceal his origin and faith on account of religious prejudice.

das Sousa, appeared as a freeholder and was not denied a seat. There is however no record of his attending at any other time.[3]

After serving Father White and perhaps Father Fisher, there is a record of his indenturing himself to John Lewger, the Secretary of the Province, for four months, a cause by which John Lewger had to result to the courts to force him to fulfill his contract. The court decided in favour of John Lewger, and in 1642 Sousa was ordered "to fulfill his indentureship".[4] In the same year John Hollis sued him for a debt of 500 lbs. tob. and the High Sheriff of St. Mary's County was ordered to seize the "person of Mathias de Sousa".[5] No further record exists for him in the Province, and inasmuch as there was a price on his head, he undoubtedly skipped on one of the trading vessels. Anyhow no further record of him can be found in Maryland.

NOTE: Mathias Sousa is not believed to be Mathias de Costa who emigrated to Maryland in 1664 with his wife, Elizabeth, and who held the Manor of Wiske. Their daughter and sole-heiress, Elizabeth, married Thomas Williams, of St. Mary's County. Ref: Warrants, Liber 8, folio 127; Provincial Court Liber TL no. 2, folios 761, 726, Land Office, Annapolis.

Sources: 1. Liber ABH, folios 65-66; 2. Archives, vol. 4, p. 138; 3. Archives, vol. 1, p. 120; 4. Archives, vol. 4, p. 138; 5. Archives, vol. 4, p. 155.

ROBERT SYMPSON

Robert Sympson, His Lordship's Surveyor, came in as a servant of Father White. The latter assigned his services to Ferdinando Pulton who claimed land rights in 1639.[1] Cecilius, Lord Baltimore, in his instructions to his brother, Leonard Calvert, and the two Commissioners, Jerome Hawley and Thomas Cornwalys, stated "That as soone as conveniently they cann they cause his L[opps] surveyor Robert Simpson to survay out such a proportion of Land doth in and about the intended towne as likewise wth in the Countrey adioyning as whilbe necessary to be assigned to the present adventurers, and that they assigne every adventurer his proportion of Land bothin and about the intended towne".[2]

It can be assumed that Robert Sympson made the earliest surveys of town lands in the vicinity of St. Mary's City and also the out-settlements at Mattapanient, but no further record is available on his life and activities in the Province. He did not attend the 1637 General Assembly, so he apparently was among the early mortalities or returned to England.

Sources: 1. Liber ABH, folio 65; Archives, vol. 3, p. 258; 2. Calvert Papers, Md. Hist. Soc., reprinted in Funds Publication no. 28, p. 138.

RICHARD THOMPSON

Richard Thompson was one of the many transportees of Father White in 1633, but beyond the fact that Father White was entitled to 50 acres of land by right of his transportation nothing further is known. He should not be confused with Richard Thompson, of the Isle of Kent, Gent., who attended the Assembly of 1637, who was associated with William Clayborne, and who was granted seigniorial rights on Popeley Island in the Bay.

WILLIAM THOMPSON, GENT.

There are circumstances which lead the genealogist to believe that William Thompson, Gent., who left a distinguished issue was on the Ark with the first Adventurers, but perhaps as a redemptioner of one of the Gentlemen of Fashion. No record has been found for his claiming land rights for either his emigration, or service or any one claiming rights for his transportation. He was certainly married by 1637 or 1638, and in religion followed the teachings of the Church of Rome.

He was not among those who were summoned to the General Assembly of 1637, perhaps not having completed his service, but at the Assembly of March 1641/2, he gave his proxy to Thomas Greene, Gent. In 1643 he was assessed 35 lbs. tob. for defraying the charges of St. Mary's County.[1] At subsequent Assemblies he generally authorized a proxy, but in January 1647/8, he attended in person and held the proxy of Captain John Price. At first he was seated in St. Michael's Hundred, but later his dwelling-plantation was in New Towne Hundred.

Some libelous statements were transmitted to Cecilius, Lord Baltimore, by persons unknown regarding his conduct during the Plundering Time or Ingle's Rebellion of 1645. The councilors and burgesses later disavowed them under their signatures, stating that they were "made out of hatred and spleen" and that "your Honour hath not a more faithful and cordial friend in the whole Province". On January 2, 1646/7, he swore fealty to Lord Baltimore which was given by a number of the planters who remained in Maryland during the rebellion.[2]

In January 1646/7, he proved land rights for 250 acres, 50 of which were for the service of his wife unnamed. One hundred acres were assigned him by Governor Calvert which could have been a gift for services and the other 100 acres he was entitled to as the executor of the estate of Robert Tulley who died testate. After his death his son and heir, William, received a grant for 100 acres which was due his father which could have been his rights under the 1648 Conditions of land grants as one of the original settlers.

His widow was Anne who was probably not the mother of his son and heir William, if so, they were married before 1640. In June 1647, Robert Tuttley, of New Towne, by his will bequeathed legacies to "Mr. Thomson and his children", and appointed William Thomson as the executor.[3]

In April 1648, as "Mr. Willm Tompson", he was appointed High Sheriff of St. Mary's County and subscribed to the oath accordingly.[4]

In his last will and testament he styled himself as William Thompson of New Towne, dating the instrument as of January 8, 1649/50. He made his wife, Anne, the sole legatee and executrix and thus failed to name a single child.[5] After his death some question occurred over the landed estate, thereupon his widow gave power of attorney to Lieutenant William Evans, whom she later married. Robert Robins deposed that he saw William Thompson sign and seal the will and made an acknowledgement of his plantation. Ralph Crouch, Gent., a Jesuit, deposed that he wrote the instrument and that William Thompson was of "sound and perfect understanding and memory" and that he made an acknowledgement under his hand touching upon his land.

Proved children of William Thompson

1. Andrew Thompson.
2. William Thompson, married thrice.*

Sources: 1. Archives, vol. 3, p. 138; 2. *Ibid.*, p. 174; 3. Wills, Liber 1, folio 10; 4. Archives, vol. 4, p. 379; 5. Wills, Liber 1, folio 21.

* For his descendants, see, The Maryland Semmes and Kindred Families, by Newman.

JAMES THORNTON

Mr. Copley claimed at one time that he brought James Thornton and others into the Province during 1633,[1] but later under the name of Ferdinando Pulton when he filed claims for a number of land rights, he stated that the several persons were by assignment. Among the several claims was the name of James Thornton,[2] but stating at that time that he was transported in 1635. During the hearings against William Lewis over prohibiting servants of the Jesuits from reading non-Catholic literature, James Thornton said that it was the intentions of the Protestants at the chapel to secure all signatures and send them to the Governor and Council of Virginia.[3] No further references have been found among the early records.

Sources: 1. Liber 1, folios 19-20; 2. Liber 1, folio 37; 3. Archives, vol. 4, p. 38.

CYPRIAN THOROWGOOD, GENT.

Although Cyprian Thorowgood was not listed among the Gentlemen of Rank and Fashion by Lord Baltimore, he was certainly a member of the county gentry and had had the benefit of English schools. He was styled "Mr." and "Gent." in all early records. It is assumed that he was from the same tree that Adam Thorowgood, of Virginia, sprang and was thus entitled to all the armorial trappings of that family which had its origin in Hertfordshire. He financed his own passage, for on October 18, 1641, he demanded 100 acres of land for transporting himself into the Province which accordingly was under the first Conditions of Plantation and another factor in accepting that he was among the original Adventurers of 1633.*

* Among my notes is a statement without the source noted that Cyprian Thoroughgood, Gent., declared in 1638 that he had performed 3½ years of service to Jerome Hawley, Esq. If so, it would place his indentureship in or about 1633 or the time that the Adventurers left England. The statement, if it could be verified, would prove definitely that he sailed on the Ark from Cowes. His alleged service, however, and his application for land-rights somewhat contradict one another.

He became one of the early traders of the Province, and was the first member of the Calvert colony to explore the Chesapeake Bay. Father White in his journal says, "Mr. Thorowgood who drives trade with the Indians".[1]

On April 24, 1634, just one month after the landing on St. Clement's Island, with seven men he explored the Chesapeake as far as the head of the bay and made a written report, the original of which is deposited in the Maryland Room of the Pratt Library, Baltimore. Unfortunately, the seven men were not named, for, with their names, we might have proof of other Adventurers who sailed on the Ark and the Dove or at least had proof that they were alive on that date.

He begins his journal with "Upon ye 24 of Aprill 1634 we sett saile from the mouth of Patuxan a riever about seven miles from St. Maries to place where our Colonie is seated a traveling in a small pinnace with 7 men to Susquehannah". It took them 32 days to make the trip and the first island they inspected and reported on the availability of harbors and settlements were Popeley Island some few miles South of the Isle of Kent. He then entered what later proved to be hostile territory, the Isle of Kent, and stated that it was "seated to the South and West". He described the bays, rivers, and inlets of Kent then under Captain Clayborne, of Virginia. After Kent they landed on an "island called Hookers and about one mile from Kent and about two miles long".

At Palmer's Island he found a boat belonging to Clayborne and about 40 men inhabitants, and spoke of the great beauty of the Island. The best land, however, was at the northern-most end. About two miles above Palmer's Island he found an island which contained an Indian town and excellent prospects for harbors. They arrived back at St. Mary's on 25 (15) May.

For service rendered the Province he was personally granted by Charles, Lord Baltimore, a warrant for 300 acres of land which is expressed in a letter to Governor Calvert, as follows:[2]

> "Dear Brother: Whereas we are informed that Cyprian Thoroughgood hath done unto us and the Colony good Service Especially in the business of Pocomoke now have therefore thought fitt at his request and for his better Encouragement to give him three hundred Acres of Land which is to be Assigned him in such place as you shall think fitt These are therefore to Authorize you that forthwith upon the Receipt hereof You pass a Grant of such freehold under the Great Seal of that our Province to him and his heires forever reserving such rent and Dutys as are Expressed for the like proportion and for so doing this shall be your Warrant Given under our hand and Seal at London in the Realm of England the 22d May 1637. C. Baltemore".

He attended the assembly of 1637/8, and was early domiciled in St. Michael's Hundred.[3]

In 1642 he was High Sheriff of St. Mary's County and in that year he was excused from attending the Assembly, but gave his proxy to Captain Thomas Cornwalys.[4]

On April 10, 1643, he acknowledged a debt to Randall Revell of "no more than 120 lbs. tob." The last reference which can be found for him was on April 13, 1643, when he assigned his warrant for 300 acres personally given him by Cecilius, Lord Baltimore, to his brother-in-law Joseph Edlow. "Do assign over this Grant of Land with all my right to it unto my well beloved Brother-in-law Joseph Edlow. Wittness my hand this present April 13, 1643". It was signed as Cyprian Thorowgood and witnessed by Robert Fornham.[5]

No record can be found of any probate of his estate—though we know that Robert Ingle destroyed many records upon his Puritan raid on Maryland in 1645. Cyprian Thorowgood most likely returned to England or settled elsewhere, and no issue has been proved from Maryland records.

Sources: 1. Fund's Publication, Md. Hist. Soc., no. 30, p. 44; 2. Liber ABH, folio 56, Land Office, Annapolis; 3. Archives, vol. 1, pp. 12, 29; 4. Archives, vol. 1, p. 128; vol. 7, p. 150; 5. Liber ABH, folio 56, Land Office.

John Tomson

John Tomson was one of the men or servants brought in by Father White.[1] He was certainly the John Tomkins (*sic*) who with Sergeant Vaughan was captured in 1635 near Palmer's Island by Thomas Smith and held for a time as a prisoner at Clayborne's stronghold on Kent.[2] No further early record can be found for a John Tomkins.[*] It is not believed that he was the John Thompson who was on Kent in 1638/9,[†] but he was most likely the John Thompson who in 1641 was a voter in St. Clement's Hundred.[3] In 1642 his proxy was held by John Worthy and in the same year he was levied 30 lbs. tob. for provincial expenditures. As John Tomson, William Broughe held his proxy at the September 1642 session of the Assembly.

He was indebted to Giles Brent in 1643 for 1000 lbs. tob. and the same year the estate of John Robinson owed him 547 lbs. tob. for wages.[4] The indebtedness apparently was for a pair of shoes and a one-half peck of salt which John Tomson had sold to John Robinson.

After law and order were established when Governor Calvert recovered the Province for his brother by the expulsion of the Puritan raiders, John Thompson was among those who remained in Maryland and on January 2, 1646/7, swore fealty to the Lord Proprietary.[5]

He died testate and without issue about May 1649, having made his will on February 19, 1648/9, and signing it as Jo: Tompson. He asked God to be merciful and forgive his sins. His plantation which was probably

[*] Perhaps incorrectly transcripted from old script.

[†] In 1642 there was a John Thompson on Kent and another in St. Mary's. Archives, vol. 1, pp. 143, 145.

a leasehold on a proprietary manor was devised to George Ackrick and his wife, and the old coat and "this shirt I have on" to Cloues Mace.[6] His estate, however, was not negligible for that day, as his house and plantation were appraised at 400 lbs. tob. There were books, a rug, and 5 barrels of corn.[7]

Sources: 1. Liber 1, folio 20, Land Office; 2. Fund Pub. no. 28, folio 187; 3. Archives, vol. 1, pp. 30, 105; 4. *Ibid.*, vol. 4, pp. 209, 213, 285; 5. *Ibid.*, vol. 3, p. 174; 6. *Ibid.*, vol. 4, p. 337; 7. *Ibid.*, vol. 4, p. 499.

CAPTAIN ROBERT VAUGHAN, GENT.

Although Captain Robert Vaughan has never been definitely listed as an Adventurer on the Ark and the Dove, all evidence points to the fact of his being one of the Anglican gentry who made that historic voyage. He was absolutely in Maryland on July 10, 1634, only five months after the landing of the two vessels, when he witnessed the last will and testament of George Calvert, Esq. And it is known that no other vessels from England had arrived at so early a date with a second contingent of settlers—the second not coming until December 1634.

There is a possibility of his crossing over from Virginia, but he was held in too much esteem by Governor Leonard Calvert to have been a refugee from that Colony. Then, the fact that he did not profess the same faith as the Roman Catholic overlords, but at the same time was held in great confidence by the Governor may indicate long associations and friendship before the Maryland settlement. Furthermore, no extant records have been found of his being first in Virginia.

By 1637 he was seated in St. George's Hundred, being its High Constable and the Sergeant of the Trained Band, and in that capacity he attended the Second General Assembly in St. Mary's City beginning January 25, 1637/8, at which time he was entrusted with several proxies of his fellow planters from St. George's.

In 1638 he assisted Governor Calvert in the reduction of the Isle of Kent to Maryland sovereignty, and some years later or at the Provincial Court of 1687 he swore that "in 1637 or thereabouts when he was a servant* to the Rt. Honble the Lord Propr of this Province and then under the Commander of Leonard Calvert, Esq., that he went with the Governor to reduce the Island of Kent under the Governor, and at that time caused Thomas Smith to be put to death, and after he was executed the Governor caused him to seize his estate for the use of the Lord Proprietary, but afterwards the Governor came to him to deliver the estate to Jane Smyth,

---

* The word servant is believed to signify serving under or a public servant rather than an indentured servant. In 1637 he was Constable and attended the Assembly. If he had been a redemptioner in 1637/8 at the submission of Kent, he would have been barred from civil office and would have been unable to attend the Assembly as a freeholder.

the Relict of the said Thomas Smith, for the use of her two young female children".[1]

In the early summer of 1638, as Sergeant Vaughan, he subdued Palmer's Island at the head of the Chesapeake in the name of the Lord Proprietary and made an inventory of all servants and goods there belonging to William Clayborne, and also a complete return of the livestock killed and the goods delivered to Mr. Lewger and others.[2]

By the next Assembly of February-March 1638/9, he had removed to the Isle of Kent and in that year voted for Christopher Thomas as a delegate from that hundred. He was back, however, on the Western Shore by September 1640, when as Lieutenant Robert Vaughan he was elected a burgess from St. Clement's Hundred.[3] He attended the August session of 1641, but some misunderstanding arose. It was his belief that he had been duly elected to represent St. Clement's Hundred, but it later developed that Thomas Gerard, Esq., had received a greater number of votes.

In 1642 Lord Baltimore commissioned him the Commander of Kent which gave him supreme authority on that once rebellious isle.[4] At the Assembly of July-August 1642, he with Richard Thompson, Lord of Thompson's Manor, represented the islanders. At this time he was also addressed as "Lieutenant of our Ile and County of Kent".

In 1647 after Ingle's Rebellion, Governor Calvert authorized him to commission all such officers for military service as he saw fit and empowered him to attach the property of all rebels remaining on the Isle who refused to take the oath of fealty.[5] At the Assembly of January 1647/8, he was addressed as Captain Robert Vaughan and held 26 proxies for the inhabitants of Kent.[6]

Thomas Greene, Esq., coming into power as governor upon the death of Leonard Calvert revoked his commission as Commander as of November 11, 1648, and accused him of arrogance and uttering "divers reviling scoffing speeches against the person of the said Governor and his authority".[7] He made his peace with Governor Greene, however, at court on December 9, was pardoned, and restored to all honours including the commandership of the Isle two days later.[8]

After Captain William Stone assumed the governorship "Robert Vaughan, Gent." was appointed on August 12, 1648, Commander of Kent by Cecilius, Lord Proprietary, "whereas we have found you [Vaughan] very faithful and well deserving of us upon the Occasion and insurrection and Rebellion in our said Province of Maryland Begun and Fomented by that Notorious and ungrateful Villain Richard Ingle and his Complices" commissioned him therefore Commander of the Isle of Kent.[9]

The General Assembly of 1650 was the first which afforded him to assume his seat in the Upper Chamber and the first in which the Puritan bigots appeared from Providence on the Severn. At this Assembly, he was allowed 2,250 lbs. tob. for "boate and hands".

During the Puritan supremacy he disappeared from the provincial scene and gave his attention solely to local affairs on Kent. In 1652 he took the Oath to the Commonwealth, perhaps for political expediency, but in that year the inhabitants of Kent who were mostly of Puritan sympathy complained against him, whereby the Council under Richard Bennett, an avowed Puritan fire-eater, summoned him to appear before that body.[10] On December 18, 1652, however, Governor Stone reaffirmed his commission as Commander of Kent.[11]

While being one of the ablest men associated with the formative days of the Province, he apparently was possessed with much impetuosity accompanied by quick temper who spoke his mind freely, or perhaps he was not too sympathetic to the manner in which the Puritans were dispersing justice. In 1652 he was fined 600 lbs. tob. for insulting the county court of Kent by using "Most opprobious epithets, neding his fist over the heades of the judges and swearing at the clerk as he sat at table". His letter of humble apology, dated April 1, 1653, addressed to the magistrate bespoke of the "grief and sorrow which I have sustained, and do sustain, through my great oversight, caused by my infirmity, committed in court, in using very unfitting language which I can confess, I am very sorry for". The letter of many words printed in full in Archives of Maryland, vol. 54, p. 16, indicates a gentleman well schooled in letters, with excellent background and training in England.

During the Commonwealth 1649-1658 in Maryland, except for the Assembly of 1650, Captain Robert Vaughan disappeared from the law-making body of the Puritans and it was not until 1658 when proprietary rule was restored that he appeared as a Gentleman Justice of the Quorum for Kent, receiving his commission from Josias Fendall, the first governor after the Puritan usurpation.[12] He seems to have held the honour of magistrate until his death in 1669. The last record of his attending court was on November 24, 1668.[13]

On October 9, 1640, Captain Vaughan demanded 50 acres of land due him by "Conditions of Services from his Lordship" which were assigned three days later to George Pye, Esq. On August 20, 1650, "Parson's Point", of 500 acres was surveyed for him on Kent Isle, and also another 1000-acre plantation now in Queen Anne's County. In 1658 he was granted 300 acres lying on the west side of Longford Bay which he called "Kimbolton" and which was named after a parish in Herefordshire, probably his native shire. In the same year he received an additional patent of 300 acres which lay on the east side of Longford's Bay, naming it "Ruerdon". A rent roll shows that William Coxe, late of the Isle of Kent, Gent., was granted 1,000 acres on a neck of land called "Coxe's Neck", beginning at the head of Flunt Point Creek which were to be held of the Manor of Crayford, and which had been assigned to Captain Robert Vaughan, Gent., the said Vaughan receiving confirmation on May 29, 1668.[14]

He married probably about the year 1653, for Charles, the eldest son, was born November 30, 1655. However, his daughter, Mary, and ultimately his sole-heiress may have been the elder of Charles. A third child, William, was born.

He died intestate in 1668. At a court held in Kent on January 26, 1668/9, Mrs. Mary Vaughan was styled the Relict of Captain Robert Vaughan.[15] Her administration bond in the amount of 40,000 lbs. tob., dated February 20, 1668/9, is now on file at Annapolis and shows her X mark, and the signatures of the witnesses Thomas Ingram, Morgan Williams, and Tobias Wells. Besides her name and that of Thomas Ingram may be seen wax seals displaying the facade of a cathedral, but not believed to be armorial.[16]

His personal estate was appraised at 46,112 lbs. tob. by Arthur Wright and Tobias Wells, listing a servant, library valued at 300 lbs. tob., currency, silver plate, two small rings, and wearing apparel—the latter being valued at 2000 lbs. tob.

His widow, Mary, married secondly Thomas Ingram who by his will, dated September 13, 1669, probated July 27, 1671, bequeathed her all property belonging to the estate of her deceased husband, Captain Robert Vaughan. To his step-son, William Vaughan, he devised land at Choptank and currency in the hands of Anthony Ingram, of London, brother to the testator, and provided that said William Vaughan was to be of age at 21.[17]

Sources: 1. Archives, vol. 57, p. 248; 2. *Ibid.*, vol. 3, pp. 76-77; 3. *Ibid.*, vol. 1, p. 89; 4. *Ibid.*, vol. 3, p. 127; 5. *Ibid.*, vol. 3, p. 183; 6. *Ibid.*, vol. 1, *p.* 214; 7. *Ibid.*, vol. 4, p. 439; 8. *Ibid.*, vol. 4, p. 459; vol. 3, p. 197; 9. *Ibid.*, vol. 3, p. 216; 10. *Ibid.*, vol. 3, p. 277; 11. *Ibid.*, vol. 3, p. 290; 12. *Ibid.*, vol. 54, pp. 130, 197; 13. *Ibid.*, vol. 54, p. 250; 14. Patents, Liber 11, folio 459, Land Office; 15. Archives, vol. 54, p. 253; 16. Test. Papers, Box 1, folder 11, Hall of Records; 17. Wills, Liber 1, folio 408.

ROGER WALTER

In 1641 Captain Thomas Cornwalys demanded land rights for bringing-in his servant, Roger Walter, in 1633. He did not attend the General Assembly called for all freemen in 1637/8, or are there any further references to him.

JOHN WARD

John Ward was one of the retainers of Richard Gerard, Esq., whose land rights were assigned to Ferdinando Poulton, but no further record is available. He failed to attend the early Assemblies, so he either succumbed to an early death in the Province or removed elsewhere.

NOTE: The John Ward who afterwards figured in the annals of Southern Maryland was another colonist who emigrated in 1647. See, Liber ABH, folio 48.

JOHN WELLS

No land-rights were claimed for John Wells either as an emigrant or a transportee, but he witnessed the last will and testament of George

Calvert, Esq. on July 10, 1634, less than four months after the arrival of the Adventurers in Maryland. No further references, however, can be found for him among the early archives.

FATHER ANDREW WHITE, S.J.

Andrew White who transported a number of indentured Adventurers on the Ark and the Dove, was born in London in 1579, and received his early education in the English College at Douai, France. He was ordained a secular priest of the Roman Catholic Church about 1605, and returned to England where he began to conduct missionary work or proselyting among the English people. As it was then unlawful to hold public services, other than the Established Church, and his violation of State laws, he was tried and imprisoned with other offenders. He was condemned to perpetual banishment and upon his release in 1606, he sought refuge at St. John's Louvain, where he entered as a Jesuit novitiate, with admission to the society in 1607. Although banished from England, five years later he was sent by the Order as a missionary priest where he laboured for some time. Between 1612 and 1632 apparently very little is known of his wanderings, but it is known that he spent some time teaching in Portugal, Spain and Belgium.

In 1632 he became secretary to George, Lord Baltimore, and thus his interest in Maryland developed. It was not a newly formed relationship, for in later years in writing to Cecilius, 2d Lord, he mentioned a letter written to him by his father, George, from Avalon. Father White is credited with the writing of "An Account of The Colony of The Lord Baron of Baltimore, 1633", and his two journals describing the voyage of the Adventurers to Maryland are two well known documents on that historic voyage.

Upon landing on St. Clement's Island on March 25, 1634, Father White with his assistants celebrated the first Roman Catholic Mass on Maryland soil. He established a mission at Mattapanient on the Patuxent, and it is quite possible that for a brief period he actually exercised manorial rights until such rights were contested by law.

His lengthy letters to Lord Baltimore which must have required hours to compose and carefully preserved for many years in the Calvert family gave a remarkable insight into conditions during the first few years. Besides Father Altham who found an early death in Maryland and two lay brothers, he was joined about 1637 by his kinsman, Thomas Copley, S.J., and to whom he assigned a number of land rights. In 1638/9 in writing to Lord Baltimore he spoke of a defect in hearing.

When Ingle and his Puritans invaded and ravished Maryland in 1644, Fathers White and Copley were transported by the Puritan rebels to England for trial, but was ultimately acquitted with a second banishment from England. About 68 years of age at that time he went to Belgium and then the Netherlands, but he never returned to his work in Maryland. He was permitted, however, to return to England in 1655, and became the chaplain of a family in Hampshire in whose home he died on June 6, 1656.

EVAN WILKINS

Evan Wilkins was transported by Leonard Calvert, Esq., as a servant, but no further record is available other than the mention of his name as a land-right.

FREDERICK AND EDWARD WINTOUR, ESQ.

Frederick Wintour [Winter] and his brother, Edward, both sons of Lady Anne, according to Lord Baltimore, and of Sir John Winter,* according to Captain Thomas Young, were other Roman Catholic gentlemen of rank to enter Maryland in 1633, but unfortunately both brothers failed to leave any posterity in the New World. They were undoubtedly kinsmen of Captain Robert Wintour, the commander of the Ark.

On July 13, 1634, Captain Thomas Young, uncle of George Evelyn, Lord of Evelynton Manor, writing from Jamestown to Sir Toby Matthew, relative to a recent trip he made to Maryland spoke of going in company with "two very young gentlemen of my Lord's Colony (whereof one was a younger brother of my Lord's the other of Sir John Winter's), with fair words finding them in a jovial humor".[1]

In June Governor Calvert had sent his brother, George Calvert, and Frederick Wintour to the Patuxent to confer with the Chief of the Patuxent, William Clayborne, and other Virginians.

The two brothers transported seven Adventurers to the Province, namely, Richard Duke, Henry James, Thomas Charenton, Thomas Smith, Francis Robnot, White John Price and Black John Price, whose land rights they assigned to Ferdinand Pulton, Gent. The two brothers either died in Maryland without issue or returned to England before the 2d Assembly held in St. Mary's City from January-March 1637/8. No record of any administration of their estates is extant among the archives.

Sources: Fund Publication.

* A John Winter was knighted at Belvoir in Aug. 1624; by Lord Baltimore referring to "Lady Anne", it would indicate that she was either the wife of a peer or a daughter of a peer who retained her own rank, though, married to a commoner. Under ordinary circumstances the wife of a knight would have been addressed as Lady Wintour.

CAPTAIN ROBERT WINTOUR, ESQ.

Captain Robert Wintour who brought the Ark so safely to Maryland was its gallant commander. John Coke writing to Admiral Pennington on October 19, 1633, stated that Captain Wintour had charge of the Ark of London with men for Lord Baltimore's new plantation in or about New England.[1] What relationship existed between him and the two youths of the same name on the adventure, it is not known, but Captain Wintour enjoyed the same social status and was, like them, a friend of the Calverts.

While it would seem that he was trained in seamanship and a naval career had been mapped out for him, he evidently found the pioneer life in the New World and the climate of Maryland so stimulating that he made a snap decision to return.[2]

> "Came into the Provinxe 12 July 1637 Capt. Robert Wintour who transported Richard Brown, Arth Webb, John Speed, Bartholomew Philipps, Thomas White, ... Morgan, and George Tailor a boy aged 15 years".

Captain Wintour surrounded himself with many luxuries of his English home that could conveniently be brought over, for his dwelling contained a small library, printed pictures and a "picture", presumably a painted portrait.

While there is no record of any proprietary grants or manors or plantations, owing to the invaluable loss of the early records, he was seated in St. George's Hundred in all the splendour and conveniences that the young Province could offer. No land rights were claimed for his retainers, yet he brought a retinue into the Province. On April 8, 1638, he agreed to let Captain George Evelyn five of his servants, especially Speed and Browne, for 10 days at the rate of 10 lbs. tob. per day for each servant.

He was among the first Adventurers to cross the river and to establish his plantation in what became St. George's Hundred, and was commissioned its first magistrate. He was early accorded a seat on the Council and sat in that capacity at the Second Assembly of January 1637/8. At the session of January 29, he was reported ill and "could not pass the river". He however was restored to health and was able to cross the river for the session of February 8, 1637/8.

On March 31, 1638, Leonard Calvert by orders of Cecilius issued the following: "whereas the west side of St. George's River is now planted by severall inhabitants and is thought fitt to be erected into a hundred by the name of St. George Hundred" commissioned Captain Wintour to be the Justice of the Peace and authorized him to appoint some able and sufficient freeman within his hundred to act as High Constable ". . . give full power and authority to doe and exequute all such acts and power within the said hundred as unto the highe constable of a hundred in England doe or may belong".[3]

On April 25, 1638, while in Virginia Governor Calvert writing to his brother, the Baron, stated "Capt Wintour remembereth his service to you. I left him well in Maryland". He was deceased, however, by September 7, following, when the inventory of his personal estate was filed at court. The estate was appraised by James Baldridge and Thomas Hebden, showing among other property seven men-servants, gold ring, two swords, silver belt and as already mentioned books and pictures. The total appraisement was 9000 lbs. tob. John Lewger was granted letters of administration, and in his account filed with the court showed 197 lbs. tob. earmarked for funeral expenses.[4]

On September 8, 1638, Thomas Hebden deposed that on April 11 last, he was at the house of Captain Wintour and heard Wintour discharge Edward Parker and William Nausin from all obligations, declaring that he had received from the mother of Edward Parker certain goods in England which he was obliged by the promise to free the said Edward from the ordinary conditions of apprenticeship at his arrival in this country. And for the said Nausin, he declared that he brought him over not as a servant but to keep him company and to breed him up at school.[5]

No record can be found of his heirs-at-law and who held his landed estate after his death. While no statements have been found for his religious faith, he was in all probability a member of the Roman Catholic Church.

Sources: 1. Archives, vol. 2, p. 23; 2. Patents, Liber 1, folio 18; 3. Archives, vol. 3, p. 70; 4. Archives, vol. 4; 5. Archives, vol. 4, p. 47.

ROBERT WISEMAN, ESQ.

Of the "very near twenty gentleman of fashion", few had better lineage than Robert [Henry] Wiseman, Esq., though he lived quietly at his Maryland seat and for some unknown reason took little or no interest in civil or military affairs.* He was a member of the Roman Catholic Gentry, but no references can be found for his wife among the extant early records of Maryland.

His early domicile was in St. Mary's Hundred, when on January 25, 1637/8, he failed to attend the General Assembly, but entrusted his proxy to Lieut. William Lewis.[1] It was shortly afterwards that he assigned some property, for Secretary Lewger writing in January 1638/9, to Lord Baltimore implied that Robert Wiseman had assigned certain property and that His Lordship was accountable only to "Wiseman's assignes".[2]

By February 14, 1638/9, he was seated in Mattapanient Hundred, the

* Although the list published in "A Relation of Maryland" prints his name as "Henry Wiseman, son to Sir Thomas Wiseman, Knt", all evidence indicates that his name was inadvertently written Henry instead of Robert, similar to the printing of the Christian name of Thomas Greene, Esq. as Henry. One Henry Wiseman is listed as a freeholder in 1641/2, when he attended the Assembly, but it is the first and only references to a Henry. Ref: Archives, vol. 1, pp. 118, 120. Robert Wiseman appeared for the first extant Assembly in 1637. No further reference to Henry Wiseman is found, and no land-rights were proved for or by a Henry Wiseman. Furthermore, the name of Robert Wiseman is missing from the March 1641/2 Assembly, thus affording no proof that there were two freeholders by the name of Wiseman in that year. It is possible that inadvertency again occurred and the name should have been Robert. It is also significant to note that no son by the name of Henry is listed for Sir Thomas Wiseman, of Canfield, Essex, Knt. who died in 1624, but a son Robert appears as his son in the Visitation. Ref: Harleian Soc. Pub., vol. 13, pp. 129-130.

first outpost of the infant settlement at St. Mary's and manifested not only a pioneer spirit but, other than the Jesuits who founded the Mattapanient Mission, he was the cultural layman of that hundred. On the above date he and others chose Henry Bishop as their burgess to the General Assembly, and of the inhabitants in that hundred he was the only literate voter.[8]

In 1642 he was granted license to kill wild swine, and in August 1642 "Mr. Wiseman" was assessed 60 lbs. tob. for the welfare of the Province.[4] In December 1642, he received 20 lbs. tob. from the estate of his neighbor, John Machin, late of Mattapanient, deceased.

He served on the jury of the Provincial Court in 1643, and during the same year as Robert Wiseman, Gent., he was summoned with others to give evidence for His Lordship against Richard Ingle, Mariner, the leader of the Puritan rebellion which bears his name and who was responsible for the destruction of many early records of the Province.

By January 12, 1643/4, he had removed from Mattapanient Hundred on the Patuxent and settled on the Potomac for "William Hardige demandeth of Mr Robert Wiseman, Gent. 900 lbs. tob. due for the price of his [Hardige] half share of the house and plantation upon St. Paul's foreland alias Wiseman's Point sold to the said Robert Wiseman by the phf".[5] Wiseman's Point afterwards became known as Chancelor's Point by which it is called today.

On January 9, 1648/9, Cuthbert Fenwick sued him for 1,000 lbs. tob., and on March 9, 1648/9, Ralph Beane sued him for 637 lbs. tob.

He died sometime before April 16, 1650, when the following deposition was made by his former servant, Joseph Edlowe, who paradoxically was his greatest creditor.[6]

> "The Deposition of Joseph Celowe *sic* sworn & Examined the 16th day of aprill anno Dmo 1650 Saith as followeth: vizt. That about a weeke before this death Mr. Robert Wiseman late of St. Maries in the Province of Maryland Decd upon this dept request providing him to be a man not likely to live long that he would make some settlement & deposition of his Estate or to that Effect, Desired him his Dept to take that Estate which he the said Wiseman had unto his possession & to manage it the best way he could for the satisfaction of his the said Wiseman debts & if any over plus remained he desired it should be employed & disposed of to the best for the use for his sonne John Wiseman or words to that Effect & he this Dept further deposeth that he doth not know that the said Mr. Wiseman made any further or other Disposition of his Estate before his Death then what is before rehearsed & further this Dept stands bound for the said Mr. Wiseman and other wise he conceives himself to be one of the greatest creditors of the said Mr. Wiseman who was heretofore this Dept Master".

It was sworn before Thomas Hatton, and on June 5, 1650, letters of administration were issued to Joseph Edlowe. It was the beginning of the Commonwealth in Maryland when the Dissenters overthrew the Proprietary Government and as confusion ensued, no inventory or administration accounts on the estate are available. Joseph Edlowe had completed his service to Robert Wiseman by January 1637/8, when he was admitted to the General Assembly as a freeholder.

From the foregoing deposition, only one heir is proved. No Wiseman other than John appeared in the next generation in Maryland, so it is apparent that there were no other sons, but it is not beyond the realm of reality to imagine that he left some daughters. John Wiseman, the son and heir, married Catherine, one of the daughters of Francis Miles, Gent., and it is noteworthy that Sir Thomas Wiseman, Knt. had married a daughter of Robert Miles, of Sutton, Suffolk. Dying in 1704, John Wiseman left two sons and two daughters. His issue left many descendants bearing the names of Greenwell, Manning, Leigh, van Rishwick, etc.

In 1656 it is of interest that Captain Thomas Cornwalys claimed land-rights for 18 transportees among whom was Robert Wiseman who was presumably a kinsman of Madam Cornwalys who came in at the same time. No further record can be found for him, so probably he returned to England with the Cornwalys family.

Sources: 1. Archives, vol. 1, p. 3; 2. Calvert papers no. 195; 3. Archives, vol. 1, p. 116; 4. Archives, vol. 1, p. 143; 5. Archives, vol. 4, p. 223; 6. Wills, Liber 1, folio 24.

PART III

DESCENDANTS OF CAPTAIN ROBERT VAUGHAN

Captain Robert Vaughan died in 1668, leaving three children—Charles, William, and Mary who eventually became the sole-heiress. At a court held in Kent County on January 26, 1668/9, Mrs. Mary Vaughan was styled the Relict of Captain Robert Vaughan.[1] Her administration bond, dated February 20, 1668/9, now on file at Annapolis, bears her mark. It was in the value of 40,000 lbs. tob. and was witnessed by Tobias Wells, Morgan Williams, and Thomas Ingram. The latter soon married the widow. Besides her name and that of Thomas Ingram may be seen wax seals displaying the facade of a cathedral.[2]

In 1672 Charles Vaughan, aged 17, son of Robert Vaughan, late of Kent County, Gent., deceased, in court selected Jonathan Sebrey, of Talbot County, Gent., as his guardian. This occasion was shortly after the death of his step-father, Thomas Ingram. At the same time, William Vaughan, aged 16, the other son of Captain Vaughan, made selection of Robert Dunn, of Kent County, Gent.[3] Both of these sons died intestate and ultimately left no heirs, so consequently their sister, Mary, became the sole heiress to the estate.

Mary Vaughan became the second wife of James Ringgold, the son of Thomas Ringgold, the latter an agitating Puritan who was unwelcome in Virginia, so settled in Maryland where he was granted religious freedom.

Sources: 1. Archives of Maryland, vol. 54, p. 253; 2. Testamentary Papers, Box 1, folder 11, Hall of Records; 3. Provincial Court, Liber JJ, folio 386.

CHARLES VAUGHAN
1655-16—

Charles Vaughan, the son and heir of Captain Robert Vaughan, was born November 30, 1655. He was not named in the will of his step-father in 1669, but in the "4th yr of Charles the Lord Proprietary" he deeded to Han Hanson, of Kent, for 6500 lbs. tob. "Kimbolton", of 300 acres, on the north shore of the Chester River and on the west side of Langford Bay and near the mouth of the North West Branch called Broad Neck Branch.[1] He was probably the Charles Vaughan who died intestate in Talbot, when his estate was inventoried at £98/8/– on May 23, 1685.[2]

Sources: 1. Kent Deeds, Liber A, folio 459; 2. Inv. & Accts., Liber 8, folio 443.

WILLIAM VAUGHAN
16—-1684

William Vaughan, the second son of Captain Vaughan, was under age at the death of his step-father, Major Thomas Ingram, in 1669. Apparently after his mother married Jeremiah Eaton, the court placed him under the guardianship of Robert Dun.

At the Provincial Court in 1675, Robert Dunn, of Kent, Gent., "guardian of William Vaughan one of the ophants of Robert Vaughan, deceased" petitioned the court that although he had been made the guardian and the court ordered the delivery of the ward's estate to him, Jeremiah Eaton who married the mother of the orphan detained in his possession 10,000 lbs. tob. bequeathed him as a legacy by Major Ingram, deceased, and also four head of cattle which were left him by his father. At a later session of the same year, it was shown that Mr. Eaton had promised to pay the 10,000 lbs. tob. to Mr. Robert Dunn, the guardian to the orphan of Captain Vaughan.[1]

Jeremy Eaton, his step-father, died the next year, or 1676 and devised him 400 acres of land in Baltimore County, making his wife, Mary Eaton, the executrix. He also left in trust 550 acres of land for the first Protestant minister and his successors who should reside in Kent County.[2]

William Vaughan married Elizabeth _____ and died testate in Kent County in 1684. He devised his unnamed daughter "Parson's Point" of 200 acres, and certain legacies to an unnamed son at the age of 14. The residue of the estate was to be divided equally between his wife and two children—all unnamed. James Ringgold who is placed as his brother-in-law was made the overseer of the estate.[3]

The original administration bond on his estate is extant, dated November 21, 1684, with Thomas Smyth and Mathew Miller as the sureties for the widow, Elizabeth Vaughan.[4] His personal estate was appraised at £104/15/8, which included a woman-servant 9 months to serve, an "Inke horne" and a silver seale.[5] When his widow filed an account on October 17, 1688, she was the wife of Richard Jones.[6]

It is quite evident that the children of William Vaughan and Elizabeth died without issue. The plantation "Parson's Point" which was devised to the unnamed daughter in 1684 was later possessed by the heirs of Mary (Vaughan) Ringgold. At the rent-roll of about 1705 "Parson's Point" which had been surveyed for Captain Robert Vaughan was "Posst by Dr. Tho: Godmont in rt the heirs of James Ringold".[7] No conveyance to James Ringgold for a valuable consideration has been found, therefore, it is obvious that title reverted to the orphans' aunt, Mary (Vaughan) Ringgold, or to her son and heir, James.

Sources: 1. Archives, vol. 65, pp. 178, 590; 2. Wills, Liber 10, folio 64; 3. Wills, Liber 4, folio 64; 4. Box 1, folder 64; 5. Inv. & Accts., Liber 8, folio 382; 6. Inv. & Accts., Liber 10, folio 181; 7. Calvert Papers (Queen Anne's Co.), folio 148, Md. Hist. Soc.

MARY (VAUGHAN) RINGGOLD
16__-16__

Mary Vaughan, the only daughter of Captain Robert Vaughan, became the second wife of Major James Ringgold, of Kent Isle, and the mother of his younger children. Major Ringgold was the son of Thomas, the Emigrant, and after holding numerous offices of state, he died testate in 1686.

The following are placed as the issue of Mary Vaughan.

1. James Ringgold, heir apparent to the Vaughan estates. *q.v.*
2. William Ringgold, died 1754.
3. John Ringgold.
4. Charles Ringgold, the youngest son.

Major Ringgold devised his son, James, the dwelling-plantation provided that his [testator] son, Thomas, an issue of the first marriage, refused to give up 300 acres of the northern portion of 600 acres of land which Thomas' grandfather, Thomas Ringgold, had given him. In the event, however, that his son, James, by reason of being the eldest son of the "now only daughter of Captain Robert Vaughan, dec'd", should inherit the landed estate of the said Vaughan, then Major Ringgold devised his son, Thomas, the entire tract of 600 acres together with the dwelling-plantation.[1]

James was to be of age at the death of his father, so his estimated birth can be about 1670. William, John and Charles were all styled minors, so it is evident that all four sons were the issue of his last wife, Mary Vaughan. He furthermore provided that Thomas, who was definitely the son and heir, and unmarried at the time was to "live with my deare wife" and the remainder of the children were to live "with their deare mother whilst they be of age or marry".

The widow of Major Ringgold was bequeathed her third of the personal estate, and a life interest in the dwelling-plantation. She and Colonel Henry Coursey were to administer jointly the estate.

As Mary Spears, the widow rendered an account upon the estate on October 8, 1694, when she reported a balance of £437/18/8. To the Rev. Mr. Lillingston, 400 lbs. tob. were paid for the funeral sermon, and since the death of Major Ringgold 6 bbl. of brandy, valued at £9 and 1360 gallons of cider, valued at £23/13/– had been processed on the estate.

Sources: 1. Wills, Liber 4, folio 232; 2. Inv. & Accts., Liber 13a, folio 213.

JAMES RINGGOLD
1670-1705

James Ringgold, the eldest son of Major James Ringgold by his second wife, Mary Vaughan, maintained his seat on the Isle of Kent, and married Mary, the daughter of Moses Harris, of Talbott.

Children of James and Mary (Harris) Ringgold

1. Moses Ringgold, *d.s.p.*
2. Mary Ringgold.
3. James Ringgold, died testate 1740.

He died testate in 1704/5, naming his wife, Mary, and his three children—Moses, Mary, and James who were placed under the guardianship of their mother during minority.[1]

The widow soon married Thomas Goodman [Godman]. They filed an account upon the estate on February 28, 1711/2, and accounted for £59/5/2 paid to Robert and Rebecca Morgan, the orphans of Herbert Morgan.[2] Her father, Moses Harris, died testate in Talbot in 1712/3, and mentioned his two Ringgold grandchildren by his daughter Mary, wife of Thomas Godman.[3]

Sources: 1. Wills, Liber 3, folio 660; 2. Inv. & Accts., Liber 33a, folio 202; 3. Wills, Liber 13, folio 455.

DESCENDANTS OF RICHARD GILBERT

When Richard Gilbert returned to England for his wife and two daughters, Grace and Elizabeth, he brought with them upon his return voyage a redemptioner, Walter Waterling, who had acquired his freedom by 1642. Sufficient evidence leads to the fact that Grace, the daughter, married Walter Waterling, her father's former protege. It is known that her widowed mother married secondly Robert Smith, but when Smith referred to his granddaughter, Mary Waterling, in 1671, circumstances led to the conclusion that he was actually referring to a step-granddaughter. The fact that the Christian name of Grace is found in the Waterling family and as other evidence and circumstances unfold in the history of the Smith, Gilbert, and Waterling families, they lend further substance to the conclusion that Grace Gilbert married Walter Waterling.

Waterling was assessed for the maintenance of the Province in 1642 at which time he had completed his term of indentureship.[1] He was born about 1608, being aged 40 in February 1647/8, so he was a matured man or about 29 years of age upon his entry into the Province. He was often commissioned to appraise estates, but was unlettered. At the 1642 Assembly he and Robert Smith gave their proxies to Thomas Baldridge and at another time he assigned his proxy to Thomas Cornwalys.[2]

At court in February 1647/8, he testified that in 1644 he had in his house one hogshead of tobacco belonging to Mr. Fenwick which the accomplices of Richard Ingle carried away while he was absent from home.[3] At the Assembly of January 1647/8, he personally attended and held two proxies.[4] On March 2, 1647/8, he received 80 lbs. tob. by vote of the Assembly for bringing "intelligence touching the Susquehannows".[5]

On February 28, 1649/50, when Robert Smith claimed 50 acres of land for Waterling's service by marrying the widow of Richard Gilbert, Smith also had the following recorded:[6]

> "I Walter Waterling do give Robert Smith Gratis as his own 100 acres of Land, 50 acres for my freedom and 50 for a maid servant."
>
> Walter X Waterling.
>
> Witnessed by William Asbeston.

On February 13, 1650/1, Andrew Painter, of London, Mariner, agreed to sell him a man-servant. In the same year he and William Marshall were security for the redeeming of the children of Thomas Allen who had been captured by the Indians.[7]

On June 8, 1654, he leased from Thomas Cornwalys all that neck of land being a part of the Long Neck within the Manor of Cornwalys' Cross for "1 bbl of Good Indian Corne containing five bushels and three goo fatt hens or Capons at the Manor House called the Crosse" upon the Feast of the Nativity.[8]

In no record has the given name of his wife been found. He gave land rights "gratis" to Robert Smith and the latter named Mary Waterling as a granddaughter in his will. If Waterling had married a blood daughter of Robert Smith, he was fully 45 years of age at the time of marriage, for Waterling was born about 1608, and Robert Smith did not marry until November 1638. As remarked previously, all circumstances lead to the belief that his wife was Grace Gilbert.

Children of Walter and Grace (Gilbert) Waterling

1. Mary Waterling.
2. Grace Waterling married John Barnes. *q.v.*
3. Patience Waterling.

His will was dated August 30, 1672, and probated in St. Mary's County on September 14, following, by William Asbeston and Henry Smith.[9]

> To daughter Mary Walterlyn (sic) 15,000 lbs. tob., 4,000 lbs. tob. in 1673 in case she marries this present year, if not, to pay the year after she married and the rest of 15,000 lbs. in 7 years.
> To two grandchildren Grace Barnes and Elizabeth Barnes the youngest mare and her increase.
> To Mary Walterlyn bed and furniture.
> To Grace and Patience my other two daughters all personal estate equally.
> To daughter Patience 4,000 lbs. tob.
> Executor—Son John Barnes.

Sources: 1. Archives, vol. 3, pp. 120, 123; 2. Archives, vol. 1, pp. 117, 176; 3. Archives, vol. 10, p. 370; 4. Archives, vol. 1, p. 214; 5. Archives, vol. 1, p. 231; 6. Liber ABH, folio 37, Land Office; 7. Archives, vol. 10, p. 50; 8. Archives, vol. 41, pp. 487-8; 9. Wills, Liber 1, folio 502; Inv. & Accts., Liber 1, folio 134, Hall of Records.

ELIZABETH (GILBERT) ASBESTON[2]

16__-16__

Elizabeth, the daughter of Richard Gilbert, was raised under the roof of her step-father, Robert Smith, and circumstances again play its part in the assumption of her marriage to William Asbeston [Osbaldston, Asberstone]. In January 1654/5, Robert Smith made a deed of gift of a red-pied heifer to his "daughter Elizabeth Asbeston" and her children and "her husband which is at present . . . and if her husband dye before her the Said Cattle Shall be divided into three parts and my daughter to have one share and the children two share". William Asbeston, her husband, gave his receipt and signed his name.[1]

A tie-in, therefore, exists with Robert Smith who married the widow of Richard Gilbert, and the existing proof that Gilbert had a daughter Elizabeth. As language relative to kinship was loosely employed in those days, the believed relationship was certainly that of step-daughter.

William Asbeston was born about 1625, deposing in 1667 as being aged 43. He gave service to Thomas Allen, and after the death of Allen, he petitioned the court in 1648 for his freedom, inasmuch as he had served his master, Thomas Allen, seven years by agreement. At that time John Hatch, the administrator of the estate of Thomas Allen, admitted that the "Pet^r hath accomplished his service".[2]

In 1658, he, Robert Smith and Rose Smith were summoned to the Provincial Court to testify in behalf of John Biscoe who was being sued by Nicholas Kaytin, and in the same year he, Rose Smith and Jane Chambers received another court summons.[3]

As William Asbeston, aged 33 years or thereabout, he stated at a session of the Provincial Court in 1658 that about 16 years ago he heard Mr. Leonard Calvert force a lease of 300 acres upon Thomas Orley and Isaack Edwards of which "they would have had but 50". He furthermore stated that he was a servant at that time to Thomas Orley and that the said Orley sold him to Thomas Allen and also half of the land. Asbeston was therefore in the province in 1642, being at that time about 17 years of age.[4]

On August 7, 1661, he recorded his cattle mark at court. On February 19, 1667/8, he gave bond to Fobbe Roberts, Merchant, to pay him 1,952 lbs. tob. "to be paid at my Dwelling house in St. Michael's hundred at or upon the tenth of November next".[5]

In August 1651, he leased 50 acres of land called "Asbeston Oake" on the east side of St. George's River in Trinity Manor to Marke Blomfeild for one shilling yearly rent, and in 1673 a reference was made to the land of William Assbiston at the lower end of the town in St. Mary's.[6]

Children of William and Elizabeth (Gilbert) Asbeston

1. Winifred Asbeston, left legacy 1675 by godmother Elizabeth Moy.
2. Mary Asbeston.
3. Isabella Asbeston.
4. Rebecca Asbeston married _____ [Green].
5. William Asbeston, born 1660. *q.v.*

The will of William Asbeston was dated December 12, 1680, and probated in St. Mary's County on February 11, 1681/2, by Richard Burgis, Edward Chester, and Richard Jones.[7]

Son William the dwelling-plantation, bed furniture, and livestock.
Daughter Winifred bed and livestock.
Youngest daughters Isabella and Rebecca the other bed equally, and livestock.
Daughter Mary livestock.
Son William to be under the guardianship of Jonathan Bisto until 21 years, and son to work for his guardian until 18 years of age; if son died without issue, then the estate to be divided among his three sisters.

On August 21, 1682, Richard Attwood, of St. Mary's, the executor of the will of William Asbeston, late of St. Mary's, accounted for the value of the personal estate appraised at 1,380 lbs. tob. He reported the following:[8]

> Cow and "half a mare" left by the will to Winifred Asbeston, a daughter; also 1,000 lbs. tob. due from the estate, a legacy "to ye Winifred left unto her by legacy by her Godmother".
> Two cows due from decd's estate to Mary Asbeston.
> Two cows due from the decd's estate to Isabella Asbeston his daughter.
> Two cows due from the decd's estate to Rebecca Asbeston his daughter.
> Two cows due from the decd's estate to William Asbeston.

The above legacies delivered to the heirs amounted to 13,674 lbs. tob., leaving a balance of 2,706 lbs. tob. due to the estate. An additional account filed on September 11, 1686, by Richard Attwood showed a legacy of £18/5/– paid to Rebecca Asbiston.[9]

Sources: 1. Archives, vol. 10, pp. 514-5; 2. Archives, vol. 4, p. 447; 3. Archives, vol. 41, pp. 129, 157; 4. Archives, vol. 41, p. 181; 5. Archives, vol. 57, p. 280; 6. Archives, vol. 57, pp. 228, 401-2; 7. Wills, Liber 2, folio 167; 8. Inv. & Accts., Liber 7c, folio 230; 9. Inv. & Accts., Liber 9, folio 88.

WILLIAM ASBESTON[3]
1660-1737

William Asbeston, the only son and heir of William and Elizabeth (Gilbert) Asbeston, was born in or about 1660, according to his deposition in 1721. Before the Court of Chancery in 1721, he swore that he was 51 years of age and that about 30 years ago he was told by Solomon Jones and Joseph Edloe that a house stood on St. Mary's Hill, the ruins of which were then visible.[1] His wife was Mary _____.

Children of William and Mary Asbeston

1. Samuel Asbeston, heir in will of John Askins 1697.
2. Rachal Asbeston married William Thomas.
3. Elizabeth Asbeston.

On August 2, 1718, he filed an account with the court on the estate of John Greene, late of St. Mary's County. After various obligations were settled, a balance of £9/2/– remained, but no heirs were mentioned.[2]

His will under the name of William Asbestone was dated February 8, 1736/7, and proved in St. Mary's County on May 7, 1737, by William Price, Charles Rawlins, and Thomas Price.[3]

> To daughter Rachell, wife of William Thomas, and her heirs "Asbestone Oak" in Smith's Neck now in the possession of Thomas Plummer.
> To William Thomas all right and title of all other land, and in the event that he recovered the land at his own cost, then he to give testator's daughter Elizabeth one-half, she dying without issue then to revert to daughter Rachel Thomas.
> To daughter Elizabeth two-thirds of the residue estate and she dying during minority, said legacy to be divided between wife Mary and daughter Rachel.
> Executrix—Wife Mary.

The inventory of the personal estate was made on July 25, 1737, and appraised at £29/15/3. Charles Smith and Rachel Thomas approved as the next of kin, whereas John Smith and John Hicks approved as the creditors. The widow and executrix, Mary Asbeston, filed the papers at court on September 24, 1737.[4] She filed an account on March 28, 1738, when she accounted for legacies paid to Rachel Thomas and also to Mary Thomas. Her sureties were Joseph Kirke and Joseph FitzJeffery.[5]

By February 3, 1741/2, the widow had married Robert Jackson when they both filed an additional account showing a check paid to Rachel Thomas.

Sources: 1. Chancery, Liber PL, folio 661; 2. Adm. Accts., Liber 1, folio 198; 3. Wills, Liber 21, folio 774; 4. Inventories, Liber 22, folio 409; 5. Administration, Liber 16, folio 88; 6. Administration, Liber 18, folio 533.

GRACE (WATERLING) BARNES[3]

16__-17__

Grace Waterling, daughter of Walter and Grace (Gilbert) Waterling, was born in St. Mary's County, and married John Barnes. Her two daughters, Grace and Elizabeth, were made heirs in the will of their grandfather, Walter Waterling, in 1672, and her husband was named as the executor of the estate.

In 1674 the Lord Proprietary instituted action against John Barnes as the administrator of the estate of Walter Waterling, inasmuch as Waterling and Garrett Vansweargen had been the sureties for Major Edward Fitzherbert and Caleb Baker, the executors of the estate of William Hattost, of Bristol, England. An audit of the estate was ordered.[1]

On July 26, 1676, John Barnes, of St. Mary's County, Planter, granted power of attorney to his wife, Grace Barnes, to sue for all money and tobacco due him. He signed the instrument in the presence of Edward Brotherton and George Fiddler who made their marks.[2] In 1677 he was sued by James Collins.

On July 29, 1678, still a resident of St. Mary's County, he offered bond for John Harris in the amount of 3,000 lbs. tob. and likewise for James Mills to the value of 10,000 lbs. tob.[3]

Sometime after 1678, he removed to Dorchester County where he died intestate. In August 1695, the administration bond on his estate was issued to his widow, Grace Barnes, with Cornelius Johnson and Thomas Harvy as her sureties.[4] The inventory of his personal estate, valued at £24/10/6, was appraised by John Minifee and John Harman.

By November 30, 1696, his widow had married William Lawyer, of Dorchester, when they filed an account upon the estate of John Barnes.[5]

The inventory of the estate of William Lawyer, appraised at £29/8/6, was made in Dorchester County on September 28, 1703. No administration accounts have been found.[6]

Further research may prove that the Barnes family living in Dorchester County after 1695 are descendants of John Barnes and his wife, Grace. A John Barnes died intestate in Dorchester County about 1706, when Hannah Barnes was granted letters of administration.[7]

Sources: 1. Archives, vol. 65, p. 441; 2. Archives, vol. 66, p. 204; 3. Archives, vol. 51, pp. 224, 230; 4. Test. Pro., Liber 16, folio 78; 5. Test. Pro., Liber 16, folio 206; Inv. & Accts., Liber 14, folio 67; 6. Wills, Liber 3, folio 139; 7. Test. Pro., Liber 19c, folio 18.

DESCENDANTS OF CUTHBERT FENWICK, GENT.

As soon as Cuthbert Fenwick completed his service under Captain Thomas Cornwalys, he assumed his place among the major gentry of the Province and thereafter was given the title of Gent. In 1640 he transported to Maryland at his own expense six servants and in the next year he brought in five servants, for which he was granted baronial rights on a 2000-acre manor which was called "Fenwick" but which he also referred to as the Manor of St. Cuthbert. Consequently, soon after his period of indentureship, he had established himself on a manorial estate with at least 11 retainers. Transportation of other servants followed and at his death his landed estate was stocked with retainers and slaves of three races— white, black, and red.

Sometime in the early forties he married his first wife whose even Christian name has not come down to posterity. Four children are proved at the issue of this union. On September 29, 1649, he registered his cattle mark at court and at the same time registered the marks of his children— Thomas, Cuthbert, Ignatius, and Teresa.[1]

About this time he had married his second wife, Jane Eltonhead, the widow of Robert Moryson, of Virginia. On August 1, 1649, he entered into a pre-nuptial agreement for "the unfayned love & affection tht I beare unto Mrs. Jane Moryson late Wife of Robert Moryson of the County of Kecoughtan in the Province (sic) of Virginia, gentn, deceased. And easpecially in Consideration of Matrimony intended presently (by gods grace) to be solemnized betweene the sd Cuthbert & the sd Jane".[2]

He therefore placed in trust with William Eltonhead and Robert Clarke, both styled Gentlemen, certain slaves, livestock, one-half of the household goods in his mansion at the time of his death, all jewels and wearing apparel of the said Jane, and the said trust was to descend to all heirs lawfully begotten between him and Jane. The property, however, was to remain in the possession of him during his life, but in the event that no issue resulted from the union, then at his death his betrothed wife Jane was to inherit all property so placed in trust.

Jane Eltonhead was born about 1633 presumably in Lancashire. Her father, Richard Eltonhead, had been born in 1611, and at a young age married Anne, daughter of Richard Massey, of Ruxton, Lancashire.*

---

* Six Eltonhead sisters married Virginia gentlemen, yet it is not known how and when these Eltonhead maidens arrived in Virginia. It is possible that the marriage of several may have occurred in England, but at least one was solemnized in Virginia. The other five daughters of Richard Eltonhead who came to Virginia were: Martha who became the second wife of Edwin Conway; Agatha who married Ralph Wormeley; Elinor who married Edward Brocas; Alice who married Rowland Burnham and William Henry Corbin; and Katherine who married Thomas Mears.

Richard Eltonhead was in turn the son of Richard Eltonhead, Gent., who was born in 1582, and who married Anne, daughter of Edward Sutton, of Rushton Spencer, Staffordshire. It was he, the grandfather of Jane (Eltonhead) Moryson-Fenwick, who at his estate Ormeskeite, on September 23, 1664, recorded his paternal ancestry back seven generations to one Henri Eltonhedde de Eltonhead, the manuscript being now in the British museum.

William Eltonhead, the brother-in-law of Cuthbert Fenwick, had been granted in 1648 letters patent to the Manor of Little Eltonhead of 2,000 acres on the south bank of the Patuxent River then in the County of Calvert, but later to fall into St. Mary's when the boundary of Old St. Mary's County was extended to the Patuxent. An uncle, Edward Eltonhead, Esq., was granted in 1652 Great Eltonhead Manor of 5,000 acres in Calvert County proper, and was also given a warrant for another manorial grant of 10,000 acres which he requested his nephew, William, to put through the proper channels. The seizure of power by the Puritans and the employment of the firing squad at the battle of the Severn in 1655, in which William Eltonhead with other conservatives was one of the first victims, precluded the formal survey and patent.

While the sisters of Madam Fenwick married into the Anglican gentry of Virginia and it is assumed that she was born into the Established Church of England, there is no question about her acceptance of the Church of Rome. In her will she made a contingency that one-half of her personal estate was to revert to the Roman Catholic Church.

Children of Cuthbert Fenwick

1. Thomas Fenwick, predeceased his father.
2. Cuthbert Fenwick, married and left issue.
3. Ignatius Fenwick.
4. Teresa Fenwick.
5. Robert Fenwick, extant 1676.
6. Richard Fenwick married twice and left issue.
7. John Fenwick, *d.s.p.* testate 1720.

He was quite ill when he drew up his last will and testament on March 6, 1654/5, for he made his mark to which a seal was affixed.[3]

> To his wife Jane the land lying westward of the Deep Branch of St. Cuthbert's Neck to "bee att her disposing".
>
> To his children Cuthbert, Ignatius, Robert, Richard and John all the remainder of the land "only sd Cuthbert is to have a hund: acres more then the Rest: & his Plantacon to bee uppon St. Cuthberts & to bee Lord of the Mannor, & the yearely Rent to be payd to Cuthbert ffenwicke, his Brothers paying their proportion".
>
> To wife the house and plantation and the children were to remain with her until coming of age.
>
> To Teresa, Cuthbert, and Ignatius the future increase of a certain mare.
>
> To Mr. Starkey and Mr. Fitzherbert [priests] legacies of tobacco.

He spoke of his debts and those owing to him "in my writings att home", which indicated that he was not at his mansion house at the writing of the instrument. He furthermore referred to tobacco and corn which were "oweing unto Brother Eltonhead for servants".

The appraisement of his personal estate was not made until after January 12, 1656/7, so it is not known whether he recovered from his illness or that the change in the government accorded by the Puritan Revolution delayed the taking of the inventory. A copy of the inventory, however, has not been located among the archives.

His widow executed her will on November 24, 1660, it being probated on December 12, 1660, by John Wright, John Turner, and Edmund Scott.[4]

> To sons Robert, Richard and John all land equally including the home plantation "Little Fenwick" and "Monsieur's Plantation" division to be made when eldest son Robert attained age of 18. No stock on the plantation was to be sold until Cuthbert Fenwick attained 21.
> To Teresa Fenwick personalty at age of 16.
> To son-in-law Cuthbert Fenwick livestock for his seat of land.
> To son-in-law Ignatius Fenwick personalty.
> To servants white, Indian and Negro personalty.
> Cuthbert Fenwick and Ignatius Fenwick were to be the guardians of their minor brothers and sister, and in the event of the death of her three sons, Robert, Richard and John under age, their land was to pass to Cuthbert, Ignatius and Teresa, and one-half of the personal estate to the Roman Catholic Church and the residue among the children of sisters Conaway and Mears.
> Overseers—Cuthbert Fenwick, William Mill, and John Bogue.

The value of her personal estate was not totaled, but among the assets were two servant men, one servant boy, three maid-servants, a Negro man and a boy.

By 1663 the partition of St. Cuthbert's Manor had been made among the brothers, but Cuthbert petitioned the court stating that the jury which fixed the boundaries "through unskillfullness or inadvertensy" had not allotted to him the full one hundred acres over and above his brothers according to the terms of his father's will.[5]

On July 12, 1663, Cuthbert Fenwick 2d inheriting the trust which his father held in St. Inigoe's Manor, of 2000 acres, and St. George's Island, of 1000 acres, released all claims which he maintained to Henry Warren his heirs and assigns forever. Thus the title to the manors passed to Henry Warren, Gent., a member of the Jesuits.[6]

During the same year the question of the ownership of a mare came before the court when Cuthbert Fenwick, Gent., identified the mare "wch his mother sold to Mr. Clarke". His brother uterine, Ignatius, also styled Gent. made the same statement.[7]

Sources: 1. Archives, vol. 4, p. 509; 2. Archives, vol. 41, p. 261; 3. Archives, vol. 41, p. 262; 4. Wills, Liber 1, folio 114; 5. Archives, vol. 49, p. 131; 6. Archives, vol. 57, p. 13; 7. Archives, vol. 49, p. 61.

CUTHBERT FENWICK 2D
164–1676

Cuthbert Fenwick, the second but first surviving son of Cuthbert, Gent., and his first wife, was born on St. Cuthbert's Manor and succeeded to the lordship at the death of his father in 1654. Being a minor he was placed under the guardianship of his step-mother, but he had not attained full majority at her death in 1660.

His marriage occurred perhaps early in the sixteen-seventies, but his wife predeceased him and neither her Christian nor family name has been proved. Only one issue is known, that of a daughter, Anne, who married and left a number of descendants.

He died intestate. The inventory of his personal estate was filed at court on January 16, 1676/7, and appraised at 13,103 lbs. tob. Among the items were two gold rings and a silver Jack cup.[1] Although no servants were listed, he maintained several, inasmuch as at an account filed by his brother german, Richard Fenwick, who was named the administrator, he accounted for 6 barrels of "indian corne made by deceased's servants" since the inventory, valued at 600 lbs. tob. The account also showed 756 lbs. tob. paid to John Darnall, who as it was later discovered, was a tenant on the manor. The estate, however, was overpaid by 556 lbs. tob.[2]

Before his death, however, he assigned a portion of "Fenwick Manor" to his brother, Richard, inasmuch as on July 10, 1677, according to Provincial Court, Liber 1676-1699, folio 49, Richard Fenwick, of Calvert County, Planter, conveyed to John Darnall, of the said County, Gent., for a consideration of 20,000 lbs. tob. a portion of "Fenwick Manor" on the southwest side of the Patuxent River and containing 400 acres more or less "lately made over to the said Richard Fenwick by his late brother Cuthbert Fenwick".

Anne Fenwick, the sole heiress, was born in or about 1671, being aged 45 in 1716. She was placed under the guardianship of her half-uncle, Judge Richard Fenwick, who leased portions of her manor for his ward's benefit. She married John Sawell [Sewell] and secondly Adam Head, and had issue by both husbands.

John Sawell died intestate. On March 8, 1708/9, Adam Head, who had married the relict and administratrix of John Sawell, late of St. Mary's County, deceased, filed an additional account upon the estate and accounted for a balance from the last account of £131/16/7. After various disbursements, a balance of £87/2/11 remained for the heirs.[3]

In 1707, according to the Rent Roll, the entire manor of 2000 acres was held by "Adam Head by his Marrying ye Relict of John Sewell". The leasees on the manor, however, were not listed.

Fenwick or St. Cuthbert's Manor passed through various owners or leasees, and about 1715 John Tawney who had acquired a portion petitioned the court of chancery to establish certain boundaries. On February

2, 1715/6, a number of depositions were taken which threw much light on the transactions of the manor and also proved that Richard Fenwick, as heretofore stated, by past genealogists, was not the only child of Cuthbert Fenwick Sr., to have left issue.[4]

Ann Head, aged 45 years, declared that sometime during her minority "her uncle & guardian Mr. Richard Fenwick did lease the Land now in possession of Mr. Tawny (then belonging to her) to Mr. John Darnall & that ye said Darnall did occupy the same some years as Tenant to her said uncle & Guardian (as this Depont has been often informed) and further this Depont saith not".

Her husband, Adam Head, aged 40, swore that "Mr. Richd Fenwick late deceased (who had been Guardian to this Depont now wife Ann Head) did show this Depont the head of a branch" where stood a cedar post which was the dividing line "between the Land formerly in ye sd Fenwick's and Colonel Low's possession".

Martin Yates, aged 49, swore that "as a servant to Mr. Henry Darnall and about 29 years or since he (this Depont) did work upon a piece of land now in possession of Mr. John Tawney . . . his master had leased of Mr. Richd Fenwick as Guardian to his Neece now called Mrs. Ann Head".

Simon Gerling, aged 50, had once been a servant to Mr. John Gittings, and swore that a certain bound tree during his time of service to Mr. Gittings was the boundary "between his master and the land of Mr. Fenwick, formerly in possession of Coll Henry Lowe". He furthermore declared that "whilst Mr. Richard Fenwick was a Magistrate he happended to be in his company" and that Fenwick pointed out the dividing line between the possession of Mr. John Darnall and Mr. John Tawney.

Peter Joy, aged 50, swore that the land then in possession of Mr. John Tawney "was in the hands of John Sawell's [when] he gave this Depont Leave to tend some ground in the neck between the two branches".

Lewis Hasler, aged 65, stated that he was in company with Mr. Fenwick and he enquired of Fenwick how far the land of Mr. John Darnall (since Coll Henry Lowe) then Cuthbert Fenwick's possession, and Mr. Fenwick pointed to a certain cedar post which was the same one mentioned by Mr. Adam Head.

Nicholas Cooper, of St. Mary's County, aged 42 years, stated that 26 years ago he was servant to Mr. Michael Tawney and he dwelt on a tract of land formerly in tenure of John and Ann Sawell "now in possession of Mr. John Tawney". Paul Peacock who was the overseer to Michael Tawney said that he had asked of "one John Sawell who held at that time part of the same tract" to fense a cold spring which was the boundary between Mr. Tawney and Mr. Sawell.

John Hall, aged 50 years, also made a deposition relative to the dividing line and the cedar post.

John Sawell, the son and heir, settled in the Barbadoes and died there testate. His last will and testament, written on August 20, 1715, devised his brother, Cuthbert Sawell, of St. Mary's County, Province of Maryland, all land belonging to him in Fenwick Manor, and to his sister, Mary Green, of Charles County, he devised "Cuthbert's Fortune" and "Additional to Cuthbert's Fortune". The residuary estate "in this island and elsewhere" was willed to his sister and brother, whom he named as executors. No mention was made of his mother who was alive at that time nor to his sisters uterine.

Five names were signed to the will, and on September 13, 1721, John Brown, one of the five, appeared in Maryland before Judge Thomas Bordley and swore that he was present when John Sawell, of the Barbadoes, wrote his last will and testament and that he saw the other four sign their names accordingly. The will was probated, but before the final settlement citations were issued to Mary Green several times to show cause why a final settlement could not be made.[4a]

Cuthbert Sewell, son of John and Ann (Fenwick) Sewell, died testate and without issue. His will, dated January 31, 1723/4, was probated in St. Mary's County, on March 7, 1723/4.[5]

> To his sister Mary Green and her heirs all his interest in "Fenwick Manor", "Cudbirt's Fortune" and "Addition to Cudbirt's Fortune".
> To his sisters Priscilla Head and Elizabeth Herbert and his father-in-law, Adam Head, certain personalty, some of which was due from Mrs. Grace Brooke.
> To his sister Mary Green residuary estate.
> Executor—Brother Leonard Green.

His personal estate included an old holster, pistol, and a sword—the latter always the symbol of a gentleman. His inventory was approved by Adam Head, William Thompson, John Medley, and Robert Hutchins, but no division or notation was made between kinsmen and creditors.

Ann (Fenwick) Sewell-Head drew up her will on May 22, 1727, presumably with the permission of her spouse, Adam Head, inasmuch as she devised him the tract "Prevention" during life and at his decease to her two daughters, Elizabeth Herbert and Priscilla Head, equally. In the event of the death of Priscilla without issue, then her portion was to revert to her sister, Elizabeth, and her heirs. The will was proved in St. Mary's County on June 7, 1727.[6]

The administration or settlement of the estate of Adam Head Sr. can not be located. Although neither the will of Cuthbert Sewell nor Ann Head mentioned an Adam Head Jr., yet there was a son, Adam, who died intestate leaving four minor children.

The inventory of the personal estate of Adam Head was taken in St. Mary's on June 22, 1739, and approved by Francis Herbert, Elizabeth Herbert, and Priscilla Head. No debts were recorded of the intestate, by Ann Head, the administratrix.[7]

The final settlement was rendered the court on March 14, 1742, with assets of £83/9/8. After disbursements, the balance was divided as follows: one-third to the widow, Ann Head, and the remainder to the four children—Cuthbert, Jane, Anne, and Sarah Head.[8]

Children of John and Anne (Fenwick) Sawell
1. John Sawell, *d.s.p.* in the Barbadoes betw. 1715-1721.
2. Mary Sawell married Leonard Green, of Francis.*
3. Cuthbert Sawell, *d.s.p.* 1724.

Children of Adam and Anne (Fenwick) Head
1. Elizabeth Head married Francis Herbert. *q.v.*
2. Priscilla Head, unmarried in 1739.
3. Adam Head married Anne _____; estate distributed in St. Mary's Co., 1742. Issue: Cuthbert; Jane; Ann; Sarah.

Sources: 1. Inv. & Accts., Liber 3, folio 42; 2. Inv. & Accts., Liber 4, folio 515; 3. Inv. & Accts., Liber 29, folio 102; 4. Chancery, Liber PL no. 3, folios 237-239; 4a. Original Wills, Box S, folder 25; 5. Wills, Liber 18, folio 235; 6. Wills, Liber 19, folio 200; 7. Inventories, Liber 24, folio 377.

* For descendants, see, Newman's "The Maryland Semmes and Kindred Families".

ELIZABETH HEAD HERBERT
17__-1759

Elizabeth Head, the daughter of Adam Head by his wife Anne Fenwick, was born undoubtedly on Fenwick Manor, and before January 31, 1723/4, she married Francis Herbert, son of William and Elinor Herbert [Harbert]. By the will of his maternal grandfather, James Pattison, of St. Mary's County, he received in 1698 a plantation on "St. Jerome's Plain".

Children of Francis and Elizabeth (Head) Herbert
1. Cuthbert Herbert.
2. Mary Herbert.
3. Jane Herbert married _____ Fenwick.
4. Elizabeth Herbert married William Spalding, of John.
5. William Herbert.
6. Michael Herbert.
7. Francis Herbert, youngest son.
8. Priscilla Herbert.
9. _____.

At the remarriage of the widow of their uncle, Mark Herbert, who died testate in 1739, the children of Francis Herbert inherited the greater portion of their uncle's estate, according to the terms of his will.[2]

Francis Herbert died testate in St. Mary's County. His will, dated November 13, 1734, was probated on December 24, 1734, by George Leigh, John Dossey, and Richard Thomson.[3]

To wife Elizabeth Negroes and other personalty.
To son Francis a portion of "St. Jerome's Plains" which was unsold; Negroes.
Executor was to sell the plantation on the Patuxent and out of the proceeds the widow was to have 5000 lbs. tob. and the remainder was to be divided equally among his four children—Michael, William, Priscilla, and Mary Herbert.
The residuary estate was to be divided equally among his wife and nine unnamed children.

His personal estate was appraised at £253/7/9 and the inventory was filed at court on April 14, 1755, by his widow and executrix, Elizabeth Herbert. Cuthbert Herbert and Michael Herbert approved as the kinsmen, while William Spalding and William Herbert approved as the greatest creditors.[4]

An account filed on February 14, 1756, by the widow showed land rents paid to Arnold Lewis and also 300 lbs. tob. paid to Cuthbert Herbert as part of his inheritance. A balance of £182/12/9 remained for the heirs.[5]

An additional account filed by the widow on August 21, 1757, showed disbursements to Priscilla Herbert, Michael Herbert, William Herbert, Mary Herbert, and William Spalding in right of his wife Elizabeth, due them from the estate of their uncle, Mark Herbert.[6] George Fenwick Jr. and Cuthbert Fenwick were the sureties.

The widow died testate in St. Mary's County. Her will, dated April 20, 1759, was proved at court on May 6, 1759, by Elizabeth Milburn and Thomas Lowe.[7]

> To youngest son Francis a legacy and Negroes at the age of 21, if he died before majority then his legacies were to be divided among Priscilla, Mary, Michael and William.
>
> To daughters Priscilla and Mary use of certain Negroes during their single lives.
>
> To son Cuthbert, daughters Jane Fenwick and Elizabeth Spalding 10 shillings each.
>
> Residue of estate to be divided equally among children—Priscilla, Mary, Francis, William, and Michael.
>
> Dwelling-plantation to sons William and Francis during the term of the lease.
>
> Son William was to be guardian to his brother, Francis.

Her personal estate was appraised at £130/19/4, according to the inventory of June 1760. Cuthbert Herbert and Elizabeth Spalding approved as the kinsmen, while William Spalding and Bennett Spalding approved as the creditors.[8]

Sources: 1. Wills, Liber 6, folio 85; 2. Wills, Liber 22, folio 101; 3. Wills, Liber 29, folio 293; 4. Inventories, Liber 60, folio 217; 5. Administrations, Liber 39, folio 62; 6. Administrations, Liber 41, folio 185; 7. Wills, Liber 30, folio 687; 8. Inventories, Liber 69, folio 123.

DESCENDANTS OF RICHARD NEVITT

John Nevitt, born 1641, was undoubtedly the son and heir of his father, Richard Nevitt and Anne his wife. In June 1652, he was given by his godmother, Frances the wife of Walter Peake, a cow calf and her increase, but his mother was to have the use of the animal until he attained the age of 16 years.

In 1665 he patented "Nevitt's Desire", of 200 acres, 50 acres were for the transporting of his wife, Elizabeth, and 150 acres were by assignment from Robert Page who brought in three persons. The plantation lay in the woods and adjoined the land laid out for Edward Swann and John Compton.*

On March 25, 1683/4, John Nevit and William Medley were sureties in the amount of 60,000 lbs. tob. for the administrator of the estate of William Coale, late of St. Mary's County. Likewise, on March 10, 1697/8, John Nevitte and John Brown were sureties for Charles Daught, the administrator of William Medley, and also for Elizabeth Kertly, the administratrix of her deceased husband. In June 1698, he and John Brown were sureties for Ann Jarboe, the executrix of Peter Jarboe, late of St. Mary's County.[1]

At the death of his daughter, Ann Jarboe, the relict and executrix of Peter Jarboe, he assumed the administration of the estate. In June 1698, styled John Nevitt, of Newtown, he filed an account stating "soon after her and her child dyed in which said Estate [remained] in the possession of the said John Nevitt". He was allowed a payment of 600 lbs. tob. paid "from the said Deceased to my Son John Nevitt as by receipt appears", and also a disbursement of 440 lbs. tob. paid to Brother [of the deceased] Henry Jarboe.[2]

Question arose over the boundary of the dwelling-plantation of Richard Vowles, whereas on September 28, 1711, several depositions were taken. John Nevitt, aged 70, therefore born about 1641, swore that the bound tree on St. Clement's Bay which was then "wasted into the bay" was the bound of Richard Vowles' dwelling-plantation called "Redbudd Thickett" and the other "Rocky Point", the two tracts having "formerly belonged to one Richard Nevett the deponent's father". Elizabeth Gough, aged about 28, formerly the wife of George Medcalf, who owned land on the east side of the bay made virtually the same deposition.[3]

On January 8, 1713/4, John Nevitte and William Johnson were sureties

---

* In 1707 this plantation was held by Walter Beane for Ebsworth Beane. Ref: Rent Roll (St. M.-Chas.) Liber 7-8, folio 298, Land Office.

for David Evans, the administrator of James Williams, late of St. Mary's County.[4]

An undated rent-roll, prior to 1715, states that "Rocky Point", of 200 acres was surveyed for Walter Pake, assigned to Richard Knevett, and was possessed at the time of the rent taking by Samuel Davis who married the Relict of George Medcalf. The Calvert papers, however, state that on May 11, 1715, John Nevitt Sr. sold all 200 acres to William Maria Farthing and James Wheatley. It is not known how Nevitt repossessed the tract.[5]

He was extant in 1724, when he approved the valuation of the personal estate of his deceased brother.

Children of John Nevitt

1. Ann Nevitt married Henry Jarboe; line extinct.
2. John Nevitt, extant 1699.
3. [Millescent Nevett], witnessed 1693 will of Andrew Wheatley.
4. [Francis Nevitt] married Elinor ——————. *q.v.*

Sources: 1. Testamentary Proceedings, Liber 13, folio 103; Liber 17, folios 66-67, 156; 2. Inventories & Accounts, Liber 19½B, folio 120; 3. Chancery, Liber 2, folio 751; 4. Testamentary Proceedings, Liber 22, folio 324; 5. Rent Rolls 7-8 (St. M. Co.), folio 30, Land Office; St. M. Co. Rent Rolls, Calvert Papers, folio 28, Md. Hist. Soc., Balto.

RICHARD NEVITT*

16—-1724

Richard Nevitt Jr., was summoned to the Provincial Court in 1666 as a witness by the demands of Raymond Staplefort through the Sheriff of Calvert County.[1] He is consequently placed as the son of Richard Nevitt and his wife. He removed to Charles County, but no record is extant to show whether he bought or sold land in that county. On August 11, 1674, the court of Charles County issued a writ against him [Richard Nevett] by the demands of William Gwither.[2] On February 13, 1717/8, he and William Benson were sureties for Thomas Rookwood, the executor of Edward Rookwood.[3]

He died intestate. On August 6, 1724, letters of administration were issued to Mary Nevitt with John Gardner and John Ward as her sureties with bond of £200. His estate was appraised on September 3, 1724, by John Beale and Mark Mackferson at £79/2/1. Among the items were one Negro woman and eight books, as approved by "John Neavill (*sic*) brother of the deceased". Mary Nevitt filed an account with the court on August 16, 1725, when she accounted for a balance of £105/3/2. After various

* In the printed or transcribed records the last two consonants of his name frequently appear as ll. John Nevell did not name a son, Richard, in his will, and then there is proof in 1724 that John and Richard Nevitt [Neavill] were brothers.

disbursements a balance of £50/17/7 remained, but no distribution to the heirs was recorded.[4]

Sources: 1. Archives, vol. 57, p. 99; 2. Archives, vol. 60, p. 574; 3. Testamentary Proceedings, Liber 23, folio 179; 4. Inventories, Liber 2, folio 155; Chas. Co. Adm. Accts., 1708-1738, folio 281.

FRANCIS NEVITT
16__-1724

Francis Nevitt, placed as the son of John Nevitt and his wife, was born in St. Mary's County where he continued to live until his death. In 1717 he witnessed the will of Edward Spinke, of St. Mary's County. His wife was Elinor, who was styled as "Cozen Elinor Nevet" in the will of William Dant, of St. Mary's County, in 1714.[1]

Children of Francis and Elinor Nevitt
1. Elizabeth Nevitt.
2. Mary Nevitt.

His will, dated February 20, 1723/4, was probated in St. Mary's County, on March 17, following, by Charles Dafft, Mathew Dafft, and Ezekiel Pain.[2]

To daughters Elizabeth and Mary at marriage personalty.
To Lewis Moor and John Farr personalty.
To wife Elinor the residue of the estate and to be executrix, but in the event of her death, then John Mills and James Thompson.

The personal estate was appraised at £108/7/4. His wife apparently died soon afterwards, for on August 4, 1725, James Mills and James Thompson filed an account, and a second one on August 3, 1726, showing a balance of £69/11/10.[3]

Sources: 1. Wills, Liber 14, folio 221; 2. Wills, Liber 18, folio 238; 3. Adm. Accts., Liber 7, folios 96, 512.

NICHOLAS NEVITT
16__-1711

Nicholas Nevitt who died intestate in St. Mary's County in 1711, presumably fits into this family history. Robert Tunnihill was appointed the administrator of his estate which was appraised at only £13/12/-. At an account on July 15, 1711, 98 lbs. tob. were paid to Nich° Nevitt which would indicate that there was a son and namesake of the testator, if not a son, certainly a close kinsman. Ref: Inventories and Accounts, Liber 32c, folio 96, Hall of Records, Annapolis.

DESCENDANTS OF RICHARD DUKE

The two children whom Richard Duke referred to in 1653 must be accepted by inference rather than documentary proof. There are the facts and circumstances of his being out of the Province for about five years, then the statement that he was bringing his wife and two children into Maryland. There is no record of his wife and children coming into the Province through the medium of land rights, but it apparently occurred during the Puritan control when many records were lost or not even kept. In 1681 Mary Duke a *feme sole* patented land in her own rights. Furthermore, one of the sons in 1665 gave his age as 32 years, making his birth about 1633, so it is evident that Richard Duke, the Adventurer, was married before sailing on the Ark and had left behind a family.

On December 19, 1681, a plantation of 100 acres called "Mary Duke's Doom" was surveyed for Mary Duke on the north side of the Patuxent River in the woods. This land was later held by James Duke, with the implications that he inherited from Mary Duke.[1]

Richard Duke in January 1665/6, made oath that he was aged 32 years or thereabouts and signing his name declared that certain livestock had been delivered to Mr. Groome.[2]

On February 10, 1686/7, a tract of 30 acres was surveyed for James Duke on the north side of Island Creek in Calvert County next to the land of David Hellen, as due him by assignment from Edward Batson.[3]

It is therefore apparent that there were a *feme sole* and two planters all bearing the family name of Duke domiciled on the right or north bank of the Patuxent River in Calvert County, who fit perfectly into the genealogical pattern as the wife and two children whom Richard Duke, the Adventurer, declared his intentions of bringing into the Province in 1653.

Issue of Richard and Mary Duke

1. Richard Duke, born circa 1633.
2. James Duke. *q.v.*

Sources: Rent Rolls (Calvert) no. 3, folio 26, Land Office; 2. Archives, vol. 57, pp. 319-320; 3. Liber NS no. B, folio 547, Land Office.

JAMES DUKE[2]
16__-17__

James Duke inherited the plantation "Mary Duke Doom" in Calvert County which Mary Duke, a *feme sole*, had patented in 1681. The family for a number of generations thereafter became identified with Calvert

County, and neither he nor Richard Duke Jr. made claim to the early patent of Richard Duke, the Adventurer, on the Wicomico in Charles County. The rent rolls show that this plantation called "Duke", of 100 acres, had escheat to the Lord Proprietary and that it had been included in the resurvey on "Peer".

In 1684 and 1685 James Duke served on the Provincial Grand Jury. On February 10, 1686/7, he was granted 30 acres of land on the north side of Island Creek, adjoining the land of David Hellen which he called "Mary's Widdower".[1] On December 31, 1689, he signed as a Loyal Protestant Subject of William and Mary and expressed hopes that Their Majesties would protect him as well as others from the rebels who had "taken up Armes and have taken into Custody the Magazine of Armes and Ammunition". James Duke was without question a member of the Proprietary Party and disavowed the revolution led by Nehemiah Blakistone, John Coode, Ninian Beall and others.[2]

It is believed that it was he rather than his son, James, who married before March 31, 1685, Mary Dawkins. On that date, John Dawkins, a planter of Calvert County, bequeathed a legacy to his daughter, Mary, the wife of James Duke.[3]

On July 24, 1694, he patented "Shirt Come Off", of 22 acres, on the east side of the Patuxent. At the rent roll of 1707 or thereabouts this plantation was possessed by him.

In 1709 he and James Duke Jr. witnessed the will of John Houldsworth, of Calvert County, Gent.,[4] which therefore implies father and son, as no other Duke family or branch was domiciled at that time in Calvert County.

No formal administration of his estate is extant. The 1707 rent roll for Calvert County indicates only one James Duke as a land owner, so it was probably he who remitted quit rents on "Shirt Come Off" and "Rich Level" which adjoined the land of John Dawkins and Robert Ambrose, rather than James Duke Jr. In 1712 he was bondsman for Elizabeth Holdsworth which is the last reference which can be identified.[4] One son has been proved, but there is always that possible question of daughters.

Sources: 1. Rent Rolls, Calvert Co., Liber 3, folio 33; 2. Archives, vol. 8, p. 110; 3. Wills, Liber 4, folio 86; 4. Testamentary Proceedings, Liber 22, folio 174.

JAMES DUKE[3]
16—-1731

James Duke, son and heir of James, was born in or about the year 1670, inasmuch as he had a son who was aged 46 in 1737.[1] He was either living on his father's plantation in 1707 or on land belonging to his father-in-law, for he was seemingly not a land owner in 1707 according to the extant rent roll. "Mary's Widdower" which had been patented by his father had been alienated by the family and was possessed by Darby Henly. A wife was mentioned in his last will and testament, but no letters of administration were granted to her at the probation, so it is not known whether she refused to act or died shortly after her husband. As a consequence, her Christian name has not been found among source records.

No public service has been placed. He executed his will on November 10, 1731, it being probated in Calvert County on December 21, following, by Grace Hambleton, William Dawkins, and John Dorrumple.[2]

> To son James whom he named as executor, tract whereon he lived being part of "Brooke Place Manor" bought of Robert Brooke, decd.
> To granddaughter Martha the dwelling-plantation "Rich Levell" during life, at her decease to pass to grandson Benjamin.
> To grandson Samuel the plantation "Shirt Come Off" where his father Samuel Rowland then lived.
> To daughter Martha Gray and son Andrew Duke one shilling.
> To daughter Catherine Beal 20 shillings
> To wife one-third of the estate as the law directed.

The personal estate was appraised at £80/3/11, including two Negro slaves. William Gray and Samuel Rowland approved the valuation, while James Somerville and Benjamin Johns signed as the greatest creditors. The papers were filed at court on November 25, 1732, by James Duke, the executor.[3]

Children of James Duke

1. James Duke, born 1691, died 1754.*
2. Andrew Duke.
3. [Mary] Duke married Samuel Rowland.
4. Martha Duke married William Gray.
5. Catherine Duke married _____ Beall.

Sources: 1. Liber IR no. 4, folio 25, Hall of Records; 2. Wills, Liber 20, folio 364; 3. Inventories, Liber 16, folio 625.

* His will, dated Feb. 6, 1754, probated Calvert Co. Mar. 20, 1754, named his sons, James, John, Leonard, Basil, Andrew, and Benjamin; and his daughters Martha Mackall and Mary Hellen. His dwelling-plantation was a portion of "Brooke Place Manor", and he operated a water mill at the head of Battel Creek. His personal estate was appraised at £1023/13/–, and John Duke and Catherine Rigby approved the valuation at court on Aug. 21, 1754. Ref: Wills, Liber 29, folio 106; Inventories, Liber 58, folio 234.

DESCENDANTS OF WILLIAM EDWIN

William Edwin, the younger son of William Edwin, and presumably an issue of the second wife, Margarite, settled in Kent County, where on August 6, 1689, he received a grant for 240 acres which was called "Edwin's Addition", lying on the east side of Swann Creek and adjoining the land of John Blackistone.[1]

After January 29, 1674/5, but before January 24, 1684/5, he married Mary Ricaud, the daughter of Benjamin Ricaud, and the sister of the half-blood of Christopher Hall. The latter dated his will January 29, 1674/5, and named his mother, Elizabeth Ricaud, and his sisters Sarah, Elizabeth, and Mary Ricaud. The instrument, however, was not probated in Kent County until July 7, 1678.[2] Benjamin Richaud (*sic*) drew up his last will and testament on January 24, 1684/5, and among other bequests named his daughter, Mary Edwin, and his wife, Elizabeth Richaud.[3]

Issue of William and Mary (Ricaud) Edwin
1. William Edwin.

The will of William Edwin, of Kent County, was dated October 30, 1716, and witnessed by William Deane and Tamer Hodges, with date of probate missing.

To brother, Michael Edwin, and his heirs 100 acres, being one-half of "Cra Tree Neck" near Swann Creek.

To wife, Mary, whom he appointed executrix, the dwelling-plantation during life, then to son William and his heirs; and he to inherit residue of land at 18 years.

The administration bond of the widow was dated January 30, 1716/7, in the amount of £1000, with Michael Byrne and Thomas Gidions as her sureties.[4] On November 6, 1718, an account was filed on his estate by Thomas Ricaud and Mary his wife,[5] the widow having apparently married a kinsman.

Sources: 1. Patents, Liber C no. 3, folio 495; Land Office; 2. Wills, Liber 9, folio 99; 3. Wills, Liber 4, folio 80; 4. Testamentary Proceedings, Liber 23, folio 121; 5. Testamentary Proceedings, Liber 23, folio 269.

MICHAEL EDWIN
16__-17__

Michael Edwin was named as the "eldest son" of his father, William Edwin, of St. William, St. Mary's County. After his father's death in 1663, he settled in Kent County on the Eastern Shore. The parental plantation passed out of the family and by 1695, it was held by Daniel Bell who had it resurveyed into 114 acres. By the will of his brother, William Edwin II, in 1716, he was devised 100 acres of his brother's patent on Swan Creek and made the contingent heir in the event that his (William) son, William III, died without issue.

On March 31, 1720, Michael Edwin, of Kent County, Planter, conveyed to Ralph Page, of the same county, for 3200 lbs. tob. and £7 a tract of land in Kent County on Swan Creek containing 100 acres, being a portion of "Edwin's Addition", with improvements. He made his mark, but no wife waived dower.

On February 8, 1721/2, he conveyed to William Bradsha, of Kent County, for 12,600 lbs. tob. "Edwin's Addition", of 171 acres, lying in Kent County on Swan Creek and adjoining the land formerly belonging to John Blakistone. The deed was witnessed by John Emory and Edward Scott Jr., before Thomas Ringgold and Marmaduke Tilden, two Justices of the Peace for Kent County.

Inasmuch as the acreage for "Edwin's Addition" was 240 acres, and Michael Edwin deeded 100 acres as received by the will of his brother, and then in 1721 conveyed an additional 171 acres, it looks as if William Edwin III died without issue and Michael Edwin became heir to his nephew's estate.

No further record of Michael Edwin can be found in Maryland. By his conveying his landed estate, it is possible that he was preparing to settle elsewhere.

DESCENDANTS OF ROBERT WISEMAN, ESQ.

John Wiseman, son and heir of Robert Wiseman, Esq., and his wife, of Wiseman's Point, was certainly a minor at the death of his father in 1650, if not, he was approaching middle age at the time of his marriage. Like his father, he dwelt quietly upon his plantation and took no interest in either civil or military affairs.

He married Catherine Miles, presumably a woman his junior in years, for at his death in 1704, both being grandparents, the widow married secondly and from all circumstances begot at least one child. His wife was the daughter of Francis Miles, who on February 4, 1674/5, proved his rights to 250 acres of land, 100 acres being for his "own and Katherine his wife's time of Service performed in the province and 150 acres the remainder for Transporting John his son, Katherine and Prudence his daughter into this Province to Inhabit".[1] The will of Francis Miles, his father-in-law, was proved in St. Mary's County on September 23, 1700, by Cornelius Manning and Mary Manning (identified as his granddaughter and her husband). He bequeathed personalty to his daughter Catherine Wiseman, and to his grandson, Robert son of John Wiseman, he devised a remainder in the plantation "Back Acres" in the event that Francis Miles, another grandson, to whom it was willed, died without issue.[2]

Children of John and Katherine (Miles) Wiseman

1. John Wiseman, *d.s.p.*
2. Mary Wiseman, married Cornelius Manning. *q.v.*
3. Robert Wiseman. *q.v.*
4. Catherine Wiseman, married John Greenwell. *q.v.*

The will of John Wiseman was written on December 6, 1703, being proved on July 13, 1704, in St. Mary's County, by Thomas Courtney, George Mason, Gilbert Robinson, and C. Butler. He devised his dwelling-plantation and one-half of the land purchased from Hugh Hopewell to his son and heir, John, with the residue of the purchased realty to his younger son Robert. One hundred acres of land near Accomak Valley on the Patuxent Main Road were devised to his daughter Mary and her husband Cornelius Manning. The residuary estate was bequeathed to his wife, Catherine, during her widowhood, but in the event of her marriage then only her dower rights. He appointed his son-in-law, Cornelius Manning, the overseer.[3]

The personal estate, appraised on August 12, 1704, manifested a value of £182/10/10, quite affluent for that era, including four slaves and a number of books.[4] Before September 20, 1705, the widow married secondly

Richard Shurley (Shirley) who with his wife rendered an account upon the estate as late as July 20, 1720, showing the delivery of a Negro, mare, and gun to John Wiseman, the eldest son; £61/6/5 to Robert Wiseman as share of his brother's estate and the like amount as share of his father's estate; and £61/6/5 to John Greenwell for Katherine Wiseman his wife's part of her father's estate.[5]

John Wiseman, son and heir, died without issue. His will, dated January 26, 1716/7, was admitted to probate in St. Mary's County on April 18, 1716/7, by Nicholas Richardson, Francis Miles, and Mary Miles. He appointed his "father" Richard Shirley executor and bequeathed him and his mother, Katherine Shirley, certain personalty. Other bequests were made to his brothers Robert Wiseman and Richard Shirley, his sister Catherine Wiseman, and his cousin Francis Miles.[6]

The inventory of the personal estate was appraised on July 9, 1716, at £41/16/6, listing a Negro slave, silver buckles, pistols, sword, belt, etc. . . . Robert Wiseman and Katherine Greenwell approved as the next of kin.[7]

Madam Katherine Wiseman-Shirley predeceased her second husband, thereupon he married Sarah _____, and died in 1737. His will, dated April 16, 1737, was admitted to probate in St. Mary's County on July 15, 1737, by Robert Greenwell, Thomas Norris, and John Brion. His dwelling-plantation (unnamed) of 100 acres was to be sold by his wife with the advice of Robert Greenwell. To his son, Richard Shirley, he devised the land on the east side of Westone Branch that emptied into the head of St. Mary's River. The residuary estate was willed to his wife.[8]

The personal estate, appraised at £99/19/4, in January 1737/8, included among other items several books and portraits. Richard Shirley, son and heir, was the sole kinsman signing. At that time Sarah, the relict and executrix, had married John Diall. A subsequent account by them showed assets of £110/1/10, and after various disbursements a balance of £95/9/1 remained for the heirs. William Aisquith and Francis Hilton were the sureties.[9]

Richard Shirley Jr. died intestate in 1747, when his personal estate was appraised on July 15, 1747, at £33/5/6, with Grace Shirley as the administratrix. John Wiseman Greenwell and John Wiseman signed as the next of kin, with Benjamin Salley and Charles Greenwell as the greatest creditors.[10]

Sources: 1. Liber 18, folio 169, Land Office; 2. Wills, Liber 6, folio 375; 3. *Ibid.*, Liber 3, folio 242; 4. Inv. & Accts., Liber WB no. 3, folio 589; 5. *Ibid.*, Liber 25, folio 52; Adm. Accts., Liber 3, folio 71; 6. Wills, Liber 14, folio 238; 7. Inv. & Accts., Liber 37a, folio 164; 8. Wills, Liber; 9. Administration Accounts, Liber 17, folio 111.

MARY (WISEMAN) MANNING[3]

Mary Wiseman, daughter to John Wiseman and Catherine his wife, was born in St. Mary's County. Before December 6, 1703, she married

Cornelius Manning, of Hatton, and became the mother of his three children. She predeceased her husband sometime before June 17, 1719, when he was married to Mary, the relict and administratrix of George Simeon. Cornelius Manning was a prosperous merchant, leaving a comfortable estate at his death.

Children of Cornelius and Mary (Wiseman) Manning

1. Cornelius Manning.
2. Mary Manning married John Miles [Mills].
3. Ann Manning.

Cornelius Manning was granted letters of administration upon the estate of John Manning, and filed an account on May 17, 1718, showing a balance of £207/14/6.[1] On June 17, 1719, it was divided among the children of the deceased, namely, Mark, Mary, and John Manning.[2]

Having married the widow of George Simeon, his account was passed by the court of June 17, 1719, displaying a balance of £172/12/–, and a disbursement of "fees Expanded by this Acct and Mary his wife late Ex of George Simeon late deceased as sold vizt being in defence of ye Dec'd Estate agt Wm Vaughan and Eliz ux".[3]

His second marriage was brief, for before his death in 1721, he had married Elizabeth _____ who survived and afterwards married William Combs.

The will of Cornelius Manning was dated April 10, 1721, and proved in St. Mary's County on August 15, 1721, by Archball Johnstone, Mary Johnstone, Rodolph Simon, and William Johnson.[4] He devised his son, Cornelius, the plantation in Porkhall Neck, whereon Henry Nowell lately dwelt, then in the possession of Dr. Johnson, also "Manning's Hold" in Smith's Neck and the tract adjoining Calvert's Creek purchased from George Parker.

His two daughters, Mary Miles and Ann Manning, were devised the residue of Porkhall Neck, but if either died without issue then to the survivor. His wife, Elizabeth, was devised the dwelling-plantation "Hatton" during life, provided that she lived thereon, otherwise John Miles was to take over the plantation until his son Cornelius arrived at 21. His wife was to have one-third of the residuary personal estate, remaining two-thirds to be divided among his three children. His daughter, Ann, was placed in care of her "Grandmother Shurley", but if she refused to take her, then to her Sister Miles until she attained 16 years or marriage. Cornelius was placed under the guardianship of John Miles until 21 years of age.

John Manning, the son of John Manning, deceased, presumably his nephew, was devised "Riggs" or "Cornelius' Swampt", but if he died without issue it was to revert to the testate's estate. Personalty was bequeathed to William, son of Edward Morgan, and George Thurald. He appointed his wife Elizabeth and John Miles the executors.

Appraisement of his estate was made on October 14, 1721, showing numerous articles of merchandise. It included personalty at the home plantation at Smith's Neck, and also the plantation at Porkhall Neck. The total value was £444/13/10, with William Maria Farthing and James White signing as the creditors, and Mary Morgan and Mary Simes as the kinswomen. It was filed at court on December 8, 1721, by the executors Elizabeth Manning and John Miles.[5]

The account of "William Combs and Elizabeth his wife and John Miles executors of Cornelius Manning" recorded an inventory of £444/3/10, and with other assets the estate was brought up to £482/2/2½. Five Negroes appraised at £117 were assigned to Mary Margarett Tant for the orphans of John and Mary Manning. On March 18, 1723/4, a balance of only £7/15/7½ remained for the heirs.[6]

Sources: 1. Administration Accounts, Liber 1, folio 49; 2. *Ibid.*, Liber 2, folios 50, 136; 3. *Ibid.*, Liber 2, folios 27, 43, 50; Test. Proc., Liber 23, folios 67, 80, 199; 4. Wills, Liber 17, folio 6; 5. Inventories, Liber 6, folio 238.

ROBERT WISEMAN[3]

16___-1737

Robert Wiseman, second but only surviving son of John Wiseman and Catherine Miles his wife, ultimately inherited the entire landed estate of the family. His wife was Elizabeth, daughter of William Heard, of St. Mary's County.

Children of Robert and Elizabeth (Heard) Wiseman

1. John Wiseman.
2. Edward Wiseman.
3. Richard Wiseman.
4. Mary Wiseman married Joseph Leigh.
5. Ann Wiseman married _____ van Rishwick.
6. Elizabeth Wiseman married David Downie.
7. William Wiseman, apparently died without issue.

He died intestate in St. Mary's County sometime before August 15, 1737, when his personal estate was inventoried and appraised at £373/12/–, including 11 Negro slaves and books among other personalty, with debts owing to the estate of 4,580 lbs. tob. Richard Shirley and John Wiseman signed as the kinsmen, with Abraham Barnes and Richard Hopewell as the creditors. An additional inventory was filed by Elizabeth Wiseman, the administratrix, on December 22, 1737, showing a Negro woman valued at £30.[1]

The final account was rendered the court on May 23, 1738, by Elizabeth Wiseman, with Francis Hopewell and Mark Heard as her sureties. The balance or £396/6/3 was distributed to the widow and the following orphans of the deceased—John, Edward, William, Richard, Mary, Ann, and Elizabeth.[2]

The last will and testament of his widow, Elizabeth Wiseman, was proved at court in St. Mary's County on February 20, 1743/4, by Mary

Kough and Henrietta Heard. Negroes were willed to the following: son John Wiseman; daughter Ann van Rishwick during life then to the testatrix' grandchildren Monica and Wilford van Rishwick; son Richard Wiseman; grandson Robert Wiseman of Richard; daughter Elizabeth Downie; and granddaughter Peggy Leigh. The residuary estate was to be divided among the following children—John Wiseman, Richard Wiseman, Mary Leigh, Ann van Rishwick, and Elizabeth Downie.[3]

The inventory of the personal estate, including 8 Negroes, was appraised on January 26, 1763, at £296/14/–, by George Aisquith and Joseph Hopewell. John Wiseman and David Downie signed as the kinsmen, while William Kilgour and Hugh Hopewell signed as the creditors. The final account and distribution were made on October 30, 1765, when £273/8/7 were divided among the following heirs: John Wiseman, Ann van Rishwick, Richard Wiseman, Robert Wiseman of Richard, Elizabeth Downie, Peggy Leighe, and Mary Leighe. Jeremiah Rhodes and Mark Heard were sureties for the administrator, Richard Wiseman.[4]

Sources: 1. Inventories, Liber 22, folio 407; Liber 23, folio 24; 2. Administration Accounts, Liber 16, folio 295; 3. Wills, Liber 31, folio 863; 4. Inventories, Liber 82, folio 201; Balances, Liber 4, folio 147.

CATHERINE (WISEMAN) GREENWELL[3]
16__-17__

Catherine Wiseman, daughter to John and Catherine (Miles) Wiseman, married before August 12, 1704, John Greenwell, son of James, of "Pileswood Lane", St. Mary's County. He was named as son and heir in the will of his father in 1709, probated in 1714, and made the guardian of the younger children in the event of the death or remarry of Grace Greenwell, the testator's widow.[1]

Children of John and Catherine (Wiseman) Greenwell
1. John Wiseman Greenwell.
2. John Basil Greenwell.
3. James Greenwell.
4. Joshua Greenwell, *d.s.p.* test. 1750.
5. John Baptist Greenwell.
6. Susanna Greenwell.
7. Anne Lettice Greenwell.

His last will and testament, dated December 22, 1739, was probated in St. Mary's on July 15, 1741, by Thomas Norris Jr., John Norris, and Thomas Norris. To his sons, John, John Basil, and James, he devised "Pilese Woodland", and to his son, Joshua, the plantation "Last Shift", and to his son John Baptist 100 acres of "Rochester". "I leave all my sons at age for themselves at the age of 18 years and the Negro woman Hannah and her increase to be equally Divided amongst my Surviving children when my youngest child arrives to be 18". His wife, Catherine, was named as sole executrix.[2]

The personal estate was inventoried on August 21, 1741, with a value of £218/15/6, with John Greenwell and John Wiseman Greenwell signing as the next of kin, and John Manning and James Gough as the greatest creditors. The relict, Catherine Greenwell, filed the papers on September 5, 1741.[3] Before February 1, 1742/3, the widow had married John Manley who with him filed an account showing a balance of £224/12/6 which was to be distributed according to law. John Manning, of Newton Neck, and Cornelius Manning were sureties.[4]

Joshua Greenwell, the unmarried son, died testate in 1750, bequeathing his brother, Basil Greenwell, his saddle and wearing apparel, and to his two sisters, Susanna Greenwell and Ann Lettice Greenwell he devised "Last Shift", of 100 acres. His nephew, James Manning, received his box, and the residue of the estate was willed to his brother, John Greenwell, whom he named as executor. The witnesses were James Pike and John Manning.[5]

Sources: 1. Wills, Liber 18, folio 725; 2. Wills, Liber 22, folio 368; 3. Inventories, Liber 26, folio 333; 4. Adm. Accts., Liber 19, folio 368; 5. Wills, Liber 27, folio 326.

DESCENDANTS OF JOSEPH EDLOWE SR.

Joseph Edlowe Jr. in his petition for his freedom dues from John Walton, the greatest creditor and administrator of his father's estate, spoke of his father's children, but proof of only two has been found.

On December 9, 1665, Barnaby Edlowe and Joseph Edlowe, both of Calvert County, leased to John Halfhead, Planter, of the same county, for 3000 lbs. tob. 100 acres of land which adjoined the plantation of the said John Halfhead. Both Edlowes made their marks and delivery was made by turf and twig in the presence of John Powick and John Wiseman. Barnaby Edlowe died shortly thereafter, for on January 4, 1665/6, John Wiseman swore in court that before the death of Barnaby Edlowe he was present at the delivery of the land to Halfhead.[1]

The seat of Joseph Edlowe Jr. was on the south side of the Patuxent, then in Calvert County. He died testate in 1666, presumably a widower, leaving two sons.

By his will, dated July 3, 1666, and probated on August 30, same year, he devised his sons, Joseph and John, his entire estate real and personal equally. He appointed William Lucas and Thomas Wright the overseers, at which time the instrument was witnessed by George Walker and Jane Wright.[2] The personal estate was appraised in that year.

Children of Joseph Edlowe Jr.

1. Joseph Edlowe married Jane _____. *q.v.*
2. John Edlowe, died intestate circa 1676, no issue proved.

Thomas Wright, of St. Jerome's Manor, the overseer of the estate, died testate in 1673, and bequeathed a legacy to Joseph Edlowe 3d.[3]

Sources: 1. Archives, vol. 49, pp. 568-9; 2. Wills, Liber 1, folio 265; 3. Wills, Liber 1, folio 553.

JOSEPH EDLOWE 3D
16__-1700

Joseph Edlowe, son of Joseph Edlowe and his wife, was of sufficient age in 1674 to purchase from John Anderson and Eleanor his wife, of Somerset County, for 3000 lbs. tob. "Timber Neck" on the north side of the Patuxent River.[1]

After his father's death he instituted action against John Halfhead over the lease which his father and uncle had given John Halfhead, so finally in 1675 John Halfhead Jr. and Jane his wife settled their differences over "Halfhead's Hallow" or Susquahannough Point, with Joseph Edlowe the "son and heir of Joseph Edlowe, deceased".[2]

In 1674/5 he received 250 lbs. tob. for conveying dispatches from the Governor to certain military officers.[3] For his services in the Nanticoke Indian War he was paid 140 lbs. tob. by vote of the legislature in November 1678.[4]

William Cane dying testate in 1675/6 willed to Jean Edlowe, the daughter of Joseph and Jean Edlowe, his entire estate real and personal in the event that his son, William Cane, did not come into the Province. In the event of the death of his son and Jean Edlowe, then the entire estate was to revert to Joseph Edlowe, whom he appointed executor.[5]

Proved Children of Joseph and Jean Edlowe

1. Jean Edlowe married John Noble.
2. Edward Edlowe, *d.s.p.* 1711.

By the will of Edward Mulins, dated January 20, 1684/5, he bequeathed legacies to Jane Edlowe and to Edward Edlowe* whom he called godson.[6] In 1688 the Assembly voted to lay out a town between the plantation of Joseph Edlowe on the south side of the Patuxent and Abingdon Creek.[7]

He died intestate. On May 23, 1700, the inventory of his personal estate was made and appraised at £247/3/10, including a gold ring, four men-servants, one woman-servant, one Negro wench, and several books.

His son, Edward, died testate and without issue. His will, dated April 21, 1711, and probated in St. Mary's County, on June 14, following, was entered in the records as Edward Enloes.[8]

> To niece Henrietta Jane Noble and her heirs, daughter of brother John Noble and sister Jane his wife, the dwelling-plantation "Susquehannock Point" and the "Addition".
> To John Noble and his heirs son of the afsd John and Jane Noble, 400 acres of "Edloes Hope" also "Edloes Lott" in Dorchester Co.
> To John and Jane Noble personalty.
> To servant Robert Potter personalty.
> Executor—Barnaby Anctill.

It was witnessed by John Lewis, Ann Lewis, and Henry Horn. The inventory was made on June 19, 1711, and appraised at £80/11/4. Among the items were one gun, one sword, pair of pistols, and one servant boy. Barnaby Anktill, the executor, filed an account on June 2, 1712, showing a balance of £57/13/–.[9]

Sources: 1. Archives, vol. 65, p. 306; 2. Archives, vol. 65, p. 132; 3. Archives, vol. 2, p. 469; 4. Archives, vol. 7, p. 103; 5. Wills, Liber 2, folio 386; 6. Wills, Liber 4, folio 81; 7. Archives, vol. 13, p. 197; 8. Wills, Liber 13, folio 216; 9. Inv. & Accts., Liber 33a, folios 46, 224.

  * Incorrectly transcribed as Enloe in Baldwin's Calendar of Wills.

DESCENDANTS OF JOHN NEVILL

William Nevill [Neville] was the only son named in the last will and testament of his father, John Nevill, in 1665. It is estimated that his birth occurred about 1645, and he would therefore be the son of Bridget Thorsley, the first wife. At a court held in 1662, John Nevill recorded a deed of gift of one cow to his son William.[1] By the next year William Nevill was witnessing various court instruments which indicated that he had at least attained the age of 16 or 18 years.

The will of his father was probated in 1665, and at a court held in Charles County on June 12, 1666, he demanded a summons be issued to Mr. William Price and John Lamber (sic) to deliver him his estate then in their possession. On August 14, same year, he proved to the court that he had reached his majority and requested that he make choice of a freeholder to receive his estate. The court assented and Samuel Cressy was named to receive the orphan's estate. On October 10, 1666, he gave his receipt to John Lambert and William Price for his inheritance.[2]

On August 17, 1666, styled William Neville, of Portobacco, he conveyed to Thomas Mathews, Gent., for 3000 lbs. tob. "Huckle Berry Swamp", as laid out for 300 acres, adjoining the land of Thomas Baker, with barns, stables, and other improvements. The body of the deed referred to Joane as the "wife of the said William Nevill". He was addressed as "Mr.".[3] In the same year he gave bond to William Allen and John Munn for the conveyance of 150 acres of land.

On June 8, 1669, William Allen and John Munn sold the land located on the High Cliffs of the Potomac about Cedar Point, which they had purchased from William Neville, to Richard Bennett, stating in the deed that it had been granted to John Jarbo who assigned to John Neville, deceased, and which became the inheritance of William Neville, the son and heir[4].

On the same day, John Munn deeded to William Neville for 2700 lbs. tob. land formerly laid out for Thomas Cotes, of Charles County, on the south side of the Piscataway River and on a branch of the Mattawoman. At a court in 1674, John Munn swore that he witnessed the delivery of a mare to Edmond Lindsey by William Neville.

After 1674 the references to William Neville are rather fragmentary, but it is possible that he was in and out of the Province as a mariner. In 1697 Thomas Davis, taylor, of Charles County, under oath swore that William Neville "doth keepe & Entertaine another man's wife by force & against ye peace of our Sovereigne Lord ye King". At the September court of that year William Neville appeared and swore that the woman was his lawful wife. He presented a certificate from Salem [Massachusetts] dated October 28, 1694, as follows:

> "This may satisfy whom it may concerne that William Neville & Sarah Noble is lawfully marryed by me according to ye Laws of our Country. Given under my hand ye Day & yeare above written. witnessed by:"

(signed) Tho: Hartshorne

Wm Fraford
Richard Whitman
Mary Whitman

At the same time Jane Browike signed a statement that she had received full satisfaction from all claims from the said Nevill as by deed 28 March 1695, and that she "acquit discharge ye sd Wm Nevill from any pretense of marriage & will never trouble nor any way molest ye sd Nevill During his natural life".[6] If the subject of this marriage were William Neville, the son and heir of John, he was fully 50 or more years of age.

In 1700 William and Thomas Neville appeared in court records, so there is a question whether William and Thomas are father and son or two brothers. At court on December 12, 1700, William Neville and Thomas Neville, of Charles County, were accused of carrying away at Mattawoman one spotted barrow hog valued at 400 lbs. tob. belonging to Matthews Sanders. They were represented by their attorney, Joshua Cecil, but were declared guilty by a jury of seventeen and given "one hour in the pillory" and at the whipping post each one was to receive 10 lashes on the bare back and to pay the four-fold value of the hog which was appraised at 300 lbs. tob.[7]

Sources: 1. Archives, vol. 53, p. 214; 2. Archives, vol. 60, pp. 22, 31-32, 55; 3. Archives, vol. 60, pp. 69-72; 4. Archives, vol. 60, p. 196; 5. Archives, vol. 60, p. 202; 6. Chas. Co. Deeds, Liber V no. 1, folios 210, 243; 7. Chas. Co. Crt Records, Liber Y, folio 123.

RACHEL NEVILLE ASHFORD

Rachel Neville, daughter of John Neville and Joan Porter his wife, married Michael Ashford, of Charles County, sometime before November 13, 1677, when her mother and the latter's second husband, Thomas Hussey, Gent., deeded them "Moore's Ditch".[1] Michael Ashford was a carpenter and planter of Nanjemoy Hundred, and on June 13, 1670, he had witnessed a deed of Thomas Hussey and Joan his wife.[2] In 1671 a reference was made to the estate of Michael Ashford whose wife was Deborah, so it was possible that they were the parents of younger Michael.[3]

Michael Ashford became involved in several lawsuits. It seemed as if he was out of the Province for a time, whereby his estate was placed in the hands of his step-father-in-law, Thomas Hussey, especially on November 11, 1673, when the court ordered the attachment of his goods to the value of 9000 lbs. tob.[4]

About 1680 Michael Ashford, addressed as Captain, was surety with Francis Wyne for Thomas Marshall, the administrator of the estate of Samuel Raspin, late of Charles County. By 1683 Francis Wyne was deceased and his widow had married Henry Hawkins. Hawkins consequently became the joint-surety with Ashford, but at court Hawkins declared that Ashford had gone to Virginia.[5]

When he assigned "Moore's Ditch" to his father-in-law, Thomas Hussey, Gent., on June 10, 1691, he was styled Michael Ashford, of Charles County, Carpenter. The consideration was 35,000 lbs. tob. and the plantation lay on the west side of Zachia Swamp adjoining the land of George and Robert Goodrick.[6] This could have been a mortgage or only a portion of the plantation, for on March 10, 1714/5, he sold to Ignatius Luckett, of Charles County, Planter, "Moore's Ditch" for 7000 lbs. tob.[7]

On April 14, 1726, being of Stafford County, Virginia, he conveyed to John Smallwood, of Portobacco Creek, for 600 lbs. tob. "Totsal", lying on the south side of Potomac River.[8]

The loss of many records of Stafford County prevents greater knowledge of the activities of Michael Ashford and his immediate descendants. The last will and testament of a Michael Ashford was probated in Prince William County, Virginia, in 1734.

Sources: 1. Charles Co. Deeds, Liber G, folio 72; 2. Archives, vol. 60, p. 272; 3. Archives, vol. 60, p. 561; 4. Archives, vol. 60, pp. 509-510; 5. Testamentary Proc., Libers 12a, folio 120; 13, folios 87, 109; 6. Charles Co. Deeds, Liber R, folio 297; 7. Charles Co. Deeds, Liber F no. 2, folio 61; 8. Charles Co. Deeds, Liber L no. 2, folio 264.

ELEANOR NEVILLE LAMBERT
16__-167_

By 1662 John Lambert had married Eleanor Neville, the daughter of John Neville, Mariner, and his wife, as the birth of a son was recorded at court in 1663/4. Furthermore, John Neville by his will of February 14, 1664/5, named his daughter, Ellen Lambert and his son John Lambert. Lambert furthermore administered on the estate of his father-in-law. The births and parentage of four children are proved by the court records of Charles County.[1]

Children of John and Eleanor (Neville) Lambert

1. John Lambert, born Feb. 5, 1663/4.*
2. Eleanor Lambert, born Jan. 1667/8, married John Allen. *q.v.*
3. William Lambert, born Feb. 27, 1669/70. *q.v.*
4. Samuel Lambert, born Mar. 16, 1671/2.

———

* He is placed as the John Lambert, of Nanjemoy, who died testate and without issue in 1693/4, when he bequeathed legacies to his two god-daughters, Elizabeth daughter of John Gawley and Prudence daughter of Nicholas Cooper, and also a legacy to Janey Smoot—the residue of his estate to his two friends, Thomas Michell of Portobacco and William Dent of Nanjemoy, whom he named as executors. His estate was appraised at £86/18/6, and his executor, William Dent, accounted for 10 gallons of Rum served at the funeral. Ref: Wills, Liber 2a, folio 126; Inv. & Accts., Liber 13b, folio 57.

On November 12, 1666, John Lambert conveyed realty to Richard True, of Nanjemoy Creek, at which time his wife, Eleanor, waived dower rights. On January 8, 1666/7, John Lambert, of Charles County, bought 100 acres of land on the westernmost branch of Nanjemoy Creek from Richard True. On March 12, 1666/7, he bought of Roger Dickinson for 7000 lbs. tob. 100 acres of land on the north side of Potomac River in a creek called Nanjemoy which had been granted originally to Edmund Linsey.[2]

On March 10, 1667/8, John Lambert conveyed to John Godshall for the consideration of a servant named Thomas Porch the tract "Hogge Quarter", of 100 acres, adjoining Poynton Manor in Charles County, the said tract having been patented by Lambert.[3]

On November 5, 1670, he assigned to his wife, Ellen Lambert and her heirs, in consideration of the property received from his wife's father, John Nevill, deceased, 150 acres of land which he, the said John Lambert, bought of Richard True, and also 100 acres of his present dwelling-plantation and much livestock. The conveyance was witnessed by Luke Greene and John Godshall.[4]

On January 10, 1670/1, Ellenor Lambert with the consent of her husband made a deed of gift of a young heifer[5] to Mary Cosleton, the daughter of Robert.

On March 8, 1672/3, John Lambert bought of Thomas Alanson, of Charles County, "Simpson's Supply" which adjoined the manor [Christian Temple] of the said Alanson. Luke Greene and Robert Cossellton witnessed the assignment.[6] On March 8, 1674/5, he bought realty of Clement Theobald, of Charles County, which Theobald had at one time sold to Thomas Cocker and which the latter had re-sold to Theobald. It lay on Portobacco Creek.[7]

His wife, Eleanor, died sometime after the birth of her fourth child, and her husband married secondly Sarah Barker. In 1675 John Lambert, of Charles County, in consideration of a marriage "by God's grace soon to be contracted between the said John Lambert and Sarah Barker, daughter of John Barker of ye County" deeded to his betrothed wife a tract of land on Mattawoman Creek being one-half of "Simpson's Supply" and also a portion of a tract formerly belonging to Gerard Browne, of 100 acres.[8]

On January 9, 1692/3, John Lambert, of Charles County, who styled himself as cooper, deeded to John Allan [Allen] and Ellinor his wife for natural love and affections which he held for his daughter, Eleanor, the wife of John Allan, 100 acres of land on the north side of the Potomac River and on the east side of the Avon River formerly called Nanjemoy River and beginning at the land formerly surveyed for William Boarman.[9]

At a session of the court held in Charles County on August 3, 1703, "John Lambert an Ancient & Decripped Person Petitions ye Court to be Exempted from paying Taxes", thereupon the court decreed that he be "levied free".[10]

In June 1714, John Lambeth (*sic*), of Charles County, conveyed to John Shakerly, of the same county, for 1200 lbs. tob. a portion of an unnamed tract taken up by Major William Boarman on the western branch of Nanjemoy Creek. Sarah Lambeth, wife, waived all dower rights.[11]

No last will and testament is on file with the Prerogative Court, but he was deceased by November 14, 1717, when a deed cited a conveyance made by "John Lambeth the Elder in his life time".[12] On September 29, 1726, his grandson and heir-at-law, John Lambert, settled the estate.

Sources: 1. Archives of Maryland, vol. 60, pp. 603-604; 2. Chas. Co. Deeds, Liber C no. 1, folios 114, 136; 3. Archives of Maryland, vol. 60, p. 147; 4. Archives of Maryland, vol. 60, p. 278; 5. Archives of Maryland, vol. 60, p. 312; 6. Archives of Maryland, vol. 60, p. 452; 7. Charles Co. Deeds, Liber F, folio 82; 8. Charles Co. Deeds, Liber F, folio 182; 9. Charles Co. Deeds, Liber D no. 2, folio 35; 10. Charles Co. Deeds, Liber A no. 2, folio 250; 11. Charles Co. Deeds, Liber F no. 2, folio 40; 12. Charles Co. Deeds, Liber H no. 2, folio 131.

ELEANOR LAMBERT ALLEN[3]
16__-171_

Eleanor Lambert, daughter of John and Eleanor (Neville) Lambert, married John Allen, of Nanjemoy Hundred, Charles County. In 1693 his father-in-law deeded him and his wife 100 acres of land on the Avon River.

Eleanor was deceased by 1716, when John Allen had married secondly Katherine _____, but there is proof of one son born to her and her husband, John Allen, that is, James Allen, the son and heir.

On February 18, 1716/7, John Allen, of Charles County, Planter, conveyed to Joseph Harrison, son of Richard Harrison, Gent., for 3000 lbs. tob. the plantation "Conveniency" which "I [John Allen] had in Marriage with ye daughter of John Lambert, deceased", consisting of 36 acres. Katherine Allen, wife, waived all dower rights.[1]

On November 14, 1717, John Lambeth (*sic*), presumably the grandson and heir of John Lambert Sr. conveyed to Joseph Harrison, son of Robert, Gent., whereas John Lamberth the Elder in his lifetime gave on January 10, 1692/3, for natural love and affections to John Allen and Eleanor his wife and to the heirs of the said Eleanor born of her body 100 acres on Nanjemoy Creek adjoining to the land formerly laid out for William Boarman. At the same time he deeded 36 acres of "Conveniency". Sarah Lambeth, wife of John, waived all dower rights.[2]

On November 16, 1717, Joseph Harrison ye son of Richard Harrison, of Charles County, Gent., deeded to John Allen and James Allen, the latter the eldest son and heir of "ye said John Allen by Ellinore his wife", inasmuch as a certain Edmund Lyndsey formerly of Charles County was granted on August 16, 1658, land on the north side of the Potomac River on the eastern side of a branch of the Creek called Nanjemoy Creek, now the Avon River, adjoining the land laid out for William Boarman, of 100 acres, and which on February 10, 1662/3, the said Lyndsey assigned to William Allen, and the said William Allen assigned to Roger Dickeson, and on March 12, 1686/7, said Roger Dickeson assigned to John Lambert. Furthermore, the said John Lambert conveyed on August 13, 1692, the land in question for natural love and affections which he had for his daughter, Eleanor Allen, by his wife Ellen, the former then being the wife of John Allen. Then, John Allen and James Allen "eldest surviving son of John Allen by his wife Ellianore" for 5000 lbs. tob. deeded the land to Joseph Harrison. John Allen made his mark to the deed of conveyance, while his son, James Allen, wrote his name. No wives waived dower.[3]

On February 2, 1718/9, John Allen, of Charles County, Planter, conveyed to William Maconchie, of the said county, for 4000 lbs. tob. "Adventure", formerly surveyed for Owen Jones, late of said county, deceased. The said Jones on September 4, 1669, assigned to Edward Knight, likewise then deceased, and the said Knight on January 2, 1670/1, conveyed to Nicholas Reade, who on June 13, 1693, had assigned to John Allen, the said grantor. It lay in the woods above the Avon River. Catherine Allen, wife, waived all dower rights.[4]

Apparently at this date or sometime thereafter John Allen had alienated his entire landed estate, for on March 10, 1724/5, he leased from Mathew Stone a farm for ten years with a stipulated annual rent.[5]

Sources: 1. Chas. Co. Deeds, Liber H no. 2, folio 2; 2. Chas. Co. Deeds, Liber H no. 2, folio 131; 3. Chas. Co. Deeds, Liber H no. 2, folio 135; 4. Chas. Co. Deeds, Liber H no. 2, folio 219; 5. Chas. Co. Deeds, Liber L no. 2, folio 235.

WILLIAM LAMBERT[3]
1670-1700

William Lambert, son of John Lambert and Eleanor Nevill his wife, was born February 27, 1669/70, in Nanjemoy Hundred. On March 1, 1680/1, Lewis Jones, for natural love and affections, but no relationship stated, made a deed of gift to "William Lambert the son of John Lambert" of land on the west side of Portobacco Creek, but in the event that he died before the age of 21 years or without lawful issue then to his sister, Elinor Lambert.[1]

He married Mary, the eldest child of John and Coniey [Conyer] Clarke, of Charles County. On October 4, 1698, Anne Clarke, the orphan of John Clarke, by the consent of her mother, Coniey Clarke, was placed by the court of Charles County to serve her brother-in-law, William Lambert, and her sister his wife until the age of 16 years.[2]

William Lambert died intestate in Charles County in 1700, when his widow, Mary Lambert, was granted letters of administration. The inventory of his personal estate was made on June 4, 1700, and appraised at £8/19/18 or 2156 lbs. tob. John Barker and John Allen approved as the kinsmen.[3] His widow and administratrix, Mary Lambert, filed an account on August

29, 1700, accounting for the value of the personal estate, but no mention was made of the heirs.[4]

Various genealogical indicators and the fact that John Lambert Jr. died without issue and testate in 1693, and that no further record exists for Samuel Lambert, the third son of John Lambert Sr., it is therefore concluded that John Lambert Jr. of the next generation was the son of William Lambert, and at a young age was adding to his landed estate.

Sources: 1. Chas. Co. Deeds, Liber I no. 1, folio 78; 2. Chas. Co. Deeds, Liber V no. 1; 3. Inv. & Accts., Liber 20, folio 27; 4. Inv. & Accts., Liber 22, folio 19.

JOHN LAMBERT[4]
16__-1726

John Lambert, son of William and Mary (Clarke) Lambert, was born in Nanjemoy Hundred, and as the eldest son inherited the entire landed estate of his father as well as that of his grandfather whose estate he settled on September 29, 1726, certainly several years after the death of John Lambert Sr. On that date he filed an account as "John Lambeth administrator of John Lambeth Sr., late of Charles County", showing a balance of £5/10/6.[1] He seemed to have adopted Lambeth as the spelling of the family name.

He married twice. His first wife was Sarah _____ and his second one Mary _____, who survived him.

On May 4, 1708, as John Lambeth Jr., he purchased of John Bearfoot, of Charles County, for 500 lbs. tob. a tract of 150 acres which lay on the west side of Portobacco Creek and which adjoined the land of Francis Wyne called "Simpson's Delight" and which extended to a bound tree of John Robinson's land then in possession of Mr. Wyne.[2]

On June 6, 1709, he purchased from his kinsman, John Allan, for 9000 lbs. tob. a portion of a 160-acre tract formerly belonging to Clement Theobald, lying on the west side of Port Tobacco Creek and containing 80 acres. Eleanor Allan joined her husband in the conveyance, both making their marks.[3]

On November 14, 1717, he conveyed to Joseph Harrison, son of Robert, Gent., 100 acres of land on Nanjemoy Creek adjoining the land formerly surveyed for William Boarman and also 36 acres of "Conveniency" which a certain John Lambeth the Elder in his lifetime gave on January 10, 1692/3, for natural love and affections to John Allen and Eleanor his wife and to the heirs of the said Eleanor born of her body. His wife, Sarah Lambeth, waived all dower rights.[4]

In 1708 he had petitioned the court for a resurvey of his plantation "Haberadventure", of 150 acres.* On June 10, 1724, as John Lambeth,

* The plantation "Haber Adventure" was made famous by Thomas Stone, one of the Signers of the Declaration of Independence. He constructed his dwelling house there which is now one of the show places of Charles County. Some members of the Stone family insist that "Haber Adventure" was an original grant to the Stone family, though proof can be produced to the contrary which they refuse to accept.

of Charles County, Planter, he sold "Habberadventure" near the head of Portobacco Creek and adjoining the land of John Robinson now in the possession of the heirs of Francis Wine called "Sympson's Delight" to Robert Hanson, Gent. for 2000 lbs. tob. Sarah Lambeth, wife, waived all dower rights.[5]

He closed the estate of his grandfather on September 29, 1726, but died intestate shortly afterwards, inasmuch as the inventory of his personalty was made on January 22, 1726/7, by Mathew Barnes and Francis Adams. The estate included a servant-man, Evan Mackoonald, and four beds with furniture, thus revealing several members in his immediate household. John Clarke and John Clarke Jr. approved as both kinsmen and creditors.[6]

His widow, Mary, lost no time in acquiring an additional husband, for at the time the inventory of his estate was filed at court on January 22, 1726/7, she was Mary Tippett, the wife of Philip Tippett.[7]

Sources: 1. Administration Accounts, Liber 8, folio 80; 2. Charles Co. Deeds, Liber C no. 2, folio 107; 3. Charles Co. Deeds, Liber C no. 2, folio 138; 4. Charles Co. Deeds, Liber H no. 2, folio 131; 5. Charles Co. Deeds, Liber Y no. 1, folio 210, L no. 2, folio 147; 6. Inventories, Liber 11, folio 864; 7. *Ibid.*

Note: Contemporary with John Lambert Jr. was a Thomas Lambert who in 1699 was sued by Nicholas Leigh for trespass. If he were of this family, he was too old to be a brother of John Lambeth Jr., so was probably the youngest son of John Lambert Sr. whose birth was not recorded at court. Thomas was married by 1701, when he was having trouble with his wife, and in 1718 he sued Thomas Allen. Ref: Chas. Co. Deeds, Liber X no. 1, folio 366; Y no. 1, folio 210; I no. 2, folio 190.

DESCENDANTS OF WILLIAM BROWN

William Brown, the Adventurer of 1633, left two children as proved by his will. Mary, his daughter, who was an heir of her godfather, John Thimbleby, married Thomas Kerbley [Kirtly], a planter of St. Mary's County. She died about 1675, leaving an infant, William, who died soon afterwards.

On November 8, 1675, at the dwelling of Thomas Kertley on Bretton Bay an inquisition was taken over the landed estate of John Thimbleby, deceased. It was stated that John Thimbleby and William Brown were in possession of 150 acres of land adjoining the plantations of John Medley and John Shirtcliffe. Furthermore, that on November 10, year forgotten, William Brown and Margaret Brown his wife, assigned their interest in writing to John Thimbleby. The latter made his will in 1659, died without issue, and left his landed estate to his goddaughter, Mary Brown. William Brown possessed the land in the right of his daughter until his death in 1665, leaving John Warren and Edward Clarke guardians of his daughter. The guardians possessed the land until Mary's marriage to Thomas Kertley. They thus possessed the land until about 8 months ago, when Mary Kertley died leaving an infant, William, who died on the last day of September last. It was therefore adjudged by the Provincial Court that the 150 acres "Escheated unto his Lord the Lord Proprietary for want of heyre".[1]

The Rent Roll for New Town Hundred shows that "Honest Tom's Inheritance" had been surveyed for John Timbleby and William Brown. Brown released his half to Thimbleby who died without heirs "whereby the same became escheat and was after granted to Thomas Kirtly".

John Brown, the son and heir of William Brown the Adventurer, continued to live in the vicinity of Bretton Bay. He and his brother-in-law, Thomas Kerbey witnessed the will of Thomas Sallmon of New Town in 1695. Thomas Kertely remarried and died intestate in 1697, thereupon, John Brown became one of the sureties for the widow, Elizabeth Kertley.[2] Likewise, the same year, John Brown and John Nevitte were sureties for William Medley, of Bretton Bay. He, John Brown, witnessed the will of Peter Jarboe in 1698 and offered bond for the widow, Anne (Nevitte) Jarboe.[3]

John Brown apparently found his bride from among the eligible maidens of Bretton Bay, but she apparently predeceased him, as she was not mentioned in his will—dated August 29, 1701, and witnessed by Richard Newman, Thomas Cooper, and Joseph Chantry.[4] He began his will, thus,

"According to the Computacon of the Church of England, I John Brown of St. Mary's County". It was probated on February 24, 1701/2, by Thomas Cooper and Edward Spink.

> To daughter Jane livestock, best feather bed, one ring, and pair of new blankets.
>
> To son John the dwelling-plantation "Brown's Purchase" on the east side of Brittain Bay, to be the executor, and the residuary estate.

NOTE: "Brown's Purchase" was apparently a name he personally gave to his plantation, as it is not listed as an official grant from His Lordship's Land Office, and therefore not entered on the 1707 tax list.

Sources: 1. Archives, vol. 66, pp. 5-8; 2. Test. Proc., Liber 17, folio 67; 3. Wills, Liber 7, folio 373; Test. Proc., Liber 17, folio 156; 4. Wills, Liber 11, folio 177.

DESCENDANTS OF MAJOR JOHN HALLOWES, GENT.

John Hallowes, Jr., apparently died young and without issue, inasmuch as there is no further record after his transportation from Maryland to Virginia. His sister, Restituta, eventually became his sole heiress. She married John Whetsone [Whitston], a Virginia planter, whose land grants adjoined those of her father. John Whetstone died testate in Westmoreland County, his will being probated at court on July 27, 1670. He devised his entire estate to his wife, his son John Whitson, and daughter Restitute Whitson.[1] Ref: Fothergill's Wills, Westmoreland County.

RESTITUTA (WHETSTONE) STEELE-MANLEY
16__-1688

Restituta Whetstone, daughter and eventually sole heiress of John and Restituta (Hallowes) Whetstone, was born in Northumberland County, Virginia, and married first Matthew Steele, the son and heir of Thomas Steele, of Virginia. After the death of her husband, she married about 1679 John Manley [Manly], and had two sons—William and John. As the Widow Manley, she made her last will and testament on January 30, 1687/8, and devised her estate to her three sons, Thomas Steele, William Manley and John Manley, but it was to remain in the hands of her executors until the sons attained the age 16 years.

Thomas Steele, son and heir, died intestate without issue about the time he reached the age of 21 years. At his death his half-brother and heir-at-law, William Manley, born June 1686, entered upon the land of his maternal ancestor and had seizin. By 1712 William Manley had married Penelope Higgins, the daughter of John Higgins and the sister to the wife of John Elliott.

In the meantime Samuel Hallowes "nephew to Major John Hallowes late of Rachedale, County Palatine of Lancaster, England, who died in Virginia beyond the seas" instituted action in the Virginia courts for possession of 2400 acres of land which his uncle died seized of in Westmoreland County, Virginia. The nephew declared himself to be the son and heir of Matthew Hallowes, who was the eldest brother to Major John Hallowes, of Virginia.

The reply to the lawsuit by the American descendants stated that Restituta, the daughter of Major Hallowes, married one Whiston and by him had Restituta, her daughter and heiress, who married Thomas Steele and had issue, Thomas Steele, eldest son and heir. Afterward she married _____ Manley and had issue two sons, John and William Manley.

Being a widow the said Restituta made her will on January 30, 1687, leaving her estate to her three sons. Thomas Steele died when he had almost attained the age of 21 and without issue, after whose death John Manley entered into possession of the landed estate and left issue. The case was sent from Virginia to Sir Robert Raymond, Knt., who rendered the opinion. For further information, see Virginia Colonial Decisions, by Robert T. Barton, and also Tyler's Magazine, vol. 1, p. 66.

WILLIAM MANLEY

17__-1716

William Manley, the son of John and Restituta (Whetston) Manley, was born in Westmoreland County, Virginia. He married Penelope Higgins, the daughter of John Higgins and the sister to the wife of John Elliott.

Children of William and Penelope (Higgins) Manley

1. Penelope Manley.
2. Jemina Manley.
3. John Manley. *q.v.*

On January 13, 1711/2, William Manley, of Copley Parish, Westmoreland County, conveyed to George Eskridge and John Sturman, of the same parish, for five shillings a tract of land of 1600 acres "which was granted to John Hallows by patent 13 January 1650" on Carramon (sic) Creek and extending up the Potomac River.[1] At the same time it was shown that William Manley was in possession of 2430 acres in Copley Parish which had been granted on September 24, 1667, to John Whitstone who by his last will and testament entailed the land on Restituta, the mother of the said William Manley. The latter requested the docking of the entail in order to sell the land.

At a court held in Westmoreland County on September 30, 1713, Penelope Manley, wife of William Manley, waived all dower interests on the 1600 acres of land to George Eskridge.[2]

On March 10, 1712/3, William Manley, of Copley Parish, assigned to the Hon. Robert Carter, of Lancaster, Esq., for five shillings the land lying at the head of Nominy River, adjoining to Colonel Allerton's mill or 2430 acres which had first been taken up by "John Whittson, grandfather by the mother's side of the said William Manly . . . William Manly the heir-at-law of John Whittston". The consideration was £800.[3]

His last will and testament was dated May 30, 1716, and probated in Westmoreland County on November 26, 1716.[4]

> To wife Penelope, daughters Jemina and Penelope and son John Manley all Negroes.
> Wife to have tuition of the children during widowhood.
> Residue equally to wife and children.
> Executors—Wife, Samuel Pope and John Elliott.

Sources: 1. Westmoreland Deeds & Wills, Liber 5, folio 104; 2. *Ibid.*, folio 230; 3. *Ibid.*, folios 128-133; 4. *Ibid.*, Liber 6, folio 43.

JOHN MANLY
17__-1734

John Manly, the son and heir of William and Penelope (Higgins) Manly, established his seat in Prince William County, but the destruction of the early records of that county precludes any great amount of genealogical data, but he died before November 20, 1734, intestate. Richard Osborn, Gent., was apparently the administrator, as at the filing of the inventory of the personal estate on the aforementioned date, ". . . that part of the Personal Estate Belonging to John Manly in the hands of Richard Osborn, Gent., as appeared by the Inventory of his deceased ffathers Estate to be his Due in manner as above". The signatures to the instrument were Thomas Lewis, John Minor, and John Sturman.

There were perhaps other issue, but the son and heir John was the only one so proved during this research.

Source: Pr. Wm. Co. Wills, Liber C, folio 21.

JOHN MANLY, GENT.
17__-1751

John Manly, the son and heir of his father, John Manly, who died in Prince William County in 1734, became a planter of Fairfax County. Perhaps his land was in that portion of Prince William County which became a part of the newly created County of Fairfax in 1742.

On May 11, 1744, of Truro Parish, Fairfax County, he bought of Thomas Marshall and Elizabeth his wife, of Prince Georges County, Maryland, Gent., for £200 land on the upper side of Doeg's Creek, being the land which Thomas Marshall had purchased of William Spencer and which had been granted to Nicholas Spencer, the grandfather of the said William Spencer. The witnesses were John Minor, Daniel French and George Harrison.[1]

On May 14, 1744, styled, John Manly, Gent., he purchased from George Harrison, of Truro Parish, Gent., for £80 a tract of 100 acres on upper Doeg's Creek beginning at the land which George Harrison and Martha his wife had purchased of William Spencer, the heir of his grandfather, Nicholas Spencer.[2]

At one time John Manly and Sarah his wife sold realty to Thomas Marshall, inasmuch as on February 17, 1745, Zaphaniah Wade, Gent. and Valinda his wife, of Truro Parish, conveyed to John Hamilton, Gent., of Overwharton Parish, Stafford County, 150 acres of land along Beaver Dam and Raccoon Branch which had been sold by Zaphaniah Wade to John Manly and by John Manly and Sarah his wife to Thomas Marshall and by Thomas Marshall to Zaphaniah Wade.[3]

On August 29, 1746, he conveyed to Daniel French Jr., of Truro Parish, 68 acres of land being a portion of a larger tract granted to Nicholas

Spencer, Esq., deceased, and by his grandson, William Spencer, sold to George Harrison by deeds of lease and release dated May 24, 1739.[4]

Children of John and Sarah Manley

1. Penelope Manley married Daniel French.
2. Sarah Manley.
3. Harrison Manley married Margaret Barrey. *q.v.*
4. John Manley.

His last will and testament was dated December 26, 1745, and probated in Fairfax County on June 25, 1751.[5]

Negroes equally among children—Penelope, Sarah, Harrison, and John Manley.

Executors—Brother Anthony Russell, cousin John West, and wife Sarah Manley.

The inventory of the personal estate was filed at court on March 28, 1750, showing an appraisement of £321/14/10.[6] Division of the Negroes was made on April 5, 1754, as follows: Mrs. Manly her third 4 Negroes; Harrison Manly 3 Negroes; Mr. French his part, 3 Negroes; and Mary Manly 4 Negroes.[7]

Sources: 1. Fairfax Deeds, Liber A, folio 170; 2. *Ibid.*, folios 173, 180; 3. *Ibid.*, folio 530; 4. *Ibid.*, Liber B, folio 161; 5. Wills, Liber A, folio 551.

HARRISON MANLEY
17__-1774

Harrison Manley, son of John Manley and Sarah his wife, was born presumably in that portion of Prince William County which in 1731 became Fairfax County. His wife was Margaret Barrey, the daughter of Edward Barrey, of Fairfax County.

Children of Harrison and Margaret (Barrey) Manley

1. John Manley, son and heir.
2. Sarah Manley.
3. Mary Manley.
4. Penelope Manley.

On June 16, 1772, Harrison Manley and Margaret his wife, and Samuel Tillet and Anne his wife, all of Fairfax County, conveyed to Moses Simpson, of the same county, for a consideration of £90 two-thirds of an undivided moiety of a certain tract of land in Fairfax County containing 450 acres, being the land which Mr. Edward Barrey, deceased, in his lifetime bought of Captain Francis Aubrey's executors and by his last will and testament devised to his son, John Barrey, and his daughter, Mary Barrey. No division had been made of the property, and the son, John Barrey, died without issue before he attained the age of 21 years, therefore, his share of the tract descended to his sisters, Margaret, Anne and Mary as coheiresses.[1]

Harrison Manley drew up his last will and testament on December 8,

1773, in the presence of Penelope French, William Rumney and Mary Manley.[2]

> To wife Margaret the entire use of the estate during widowhood but if she remarried, the estate was to be divided equally among the widow and four children—John, Sarah, Mary and Penelope.
>
> Executor was empowered to sell any portion of the estate and purchase land for the benefit of his widow and children; his children were to be educated and maintained; the suit against Hon. Philip Ludwell Lee was to be revived, if considered proper.
>
> Executors—Wife and brothers William Triplett and Thomas Triplett and friend Lund Washington.

On September 15, 1783, Sarah Triplett, widow of Thomas Triplett, deceased, who was one of the executors of Harrison Manley, deceased, late of Fairfax County, filed an account with the court. She accounted for the payment of £15/16/3 for a pew in Pohick County, £2 to the account of Mrs. Sarah Manley, £2/2/– to Mrs. Margaret Manley for Colonel Washington's wheat, and a disbursement to Mr. Donaldson for the schooling of three children.[3]

The widow married Edward Sanford. On September 22, 1786, "William Triplett, Edward Sanford and Margaret his wife formerly the widow of Harrison Manley the only surviving executors of Harrison Manley" conveyed to George Washington, inasmuch as Harrison Manley ". . . did nominate and appoint his wife Margaret Manley now Margaret Sanford and part to these presents executrix and William Triplett, Lund Washington and Thomas Triplett executors and Thomas Triplett now deceased" for a consideration of £426 the said grantors deeded land within a certain patent granted to Nicholas Spencer and Colonel John Washington which a certain John Manley purchased of Thomas Marshall and his wife on May 11, 1744, and also the land purchased of George Harrison and Martha his wife on May 15, 1744, except 68 acres which were conveyed by the said John Manley and Sarah his wife to Daniel French on August 27, 1746.[4]

The estate was unsettled as late as December 1793, when William Triplett, the surviving executor, filed an account at court and reported a balance of £1409/3/6 due the legatees or the children unnamed of the deceased. The account was not recorded at court until July 1794.[5]

On February 17, 1794, John H. Manley acknowledged a conveyance to John S. Stone, but the recorded deed is missing.

Sources: 1. Fairfax Co. Deeds, Liber L, folio 51; 2. Wills, Liber C, folio 215; 3. Wills, Liber D, folio 409; 4. Deeds, Liber Q, folio 295; 5. Wills, Liber G, folios 6-9.

DESCENDANTS OF COLONEL JOHN PRICE, GENT.

Colonel John Price who may have been one who arrived in 1634 with the Wintours married late in life or after February 12, 1661/2, the widow of Thomas Bushell who made a nuncupative will in March 1653, bequeathing his estate to his wife and children—all unnamed.[1] She was later identified as Ann _____, but predeceased her husband leaving a sole heiress—Ann. Colonel Price in some manner was a kinsman of Owen James, of St. Mary's County, who died without issue in 1659, leaving him the residuary estate and making him the executor.

His will was probated in St. Mary's County on March 11, 1660/1, by the Rev. William Wilkinson, Thomas Dent and William Hatton. An abstract follows:

> To son-in-law Joseph Bullett [Bushell] land on Herring Creek.
> To Herbert Howman and William Styles personalty.
> To daughter Anne Price, executrix, and residuary legatee of estate real and personal at 18 years of age, but if she died under age one-half of estate to pass to said son-in-law Joseph Bushell.
> Residue of the estate was to establish a free school and in the event that the said Joseph and Anne died without issue or under age, all real estate to be used for establishing a free school.
> Overseers: William Hatton, Daniel Clocker, George Mankell and Thomas Dent.

Anne Price, the sole-heiress of Colonel John Price, married Richard Hatton, the son of Richard and Margaret Hatton. Richard Hatton Jr. established his plantation at Poplar Hill, and died testate; his will dated February 5, 1675, was probated February 14, 1675/6.[2] He left a widow and an only son, Richard Hatton III.

Sources: 1. Warrants, Liber 19, folio 375; Chan. Pro. Liber 2, folios 59, 66-70; 2. Wills, Liber 2, folio 403.

DESCENDANTS OF NICHOLAS HARVEY, ESQ.

Frances Harvey, the sole heiress of Nicholas Harvey, and in her own rights entitled to seigniory on St. Joseph's Manor, was left an orphan at a tender age and before her marriage with George Beckwith, Esq., she and her estate sustained various vicissitudes. She was born in or about 1641 in England and was not more than three years of age at her father's death in 1644.

She was apparently first placed under the guardianship of Cuthbert Fenwick, Esq., who was the executor of her father's estate, but later under John Dandy, blacksmith. By 1657 she had married George Beckwith, Esq., who retrieved his wife's valuable estate and her manorial inheritance from dissipation.

George Beckwith, who is believed to be of the squirarchy of that Yorkshire family, certainly his culture and style of life indicate such, entered the Province in 1648 as a retainer of Thomas Hatton, the Secretary of State for the Province.[1] In 1650 when the Puritans were usurping authority and complaining against the alleged autocracy of the Proprietary Government, the name of George Beckwith with others is on a petition to the Lord Proprietary as a loyal Protestant subject who had always enjoyed religious freedom under his sovereignty.[2]

After completing his apprenticeship with His Lordship's Secretary of State, he returned to England or visited another portion of England in America. He reentered the Province before 1657 and transported several fresh settlers for whom land rights were claimed.[3]

By October 3, 1657, he had married the Harvey heiress and petitioned the court on that day for the livestock due her then in the possession of her guardian, John Dandy, who at that time was a prisoner of the Province for the murder of one of his servants.[4]

He made another trip out of the Province and in 1669 demanded land rights for his return entry and five transported persons, among whom was Johannah Porter who later found a husband in John Nevill.

At St. Joseph's Manor on the Patuxent along with the occupation of a colonial planter, George Beckwith maintained an ordinary or inn as well as a ferry from the manor to Point Patience in Calvert County. His public service seemed to have been rather minor charges—one time coroner and another time overseer of the public roads. Both civil endeavours which in that day were looked upon with distinction.

While back in England, he died at London before April 19, 1676, the date of the death of his widow. Letters of administration on both estates were issued first to John Halls [Halles], the Steward of the Manor, but later to Cuthbert Fenwick, of St. Cuthbert's Manor, Esq. The inventory of his estate indicated life in the grand manner and few colonial plantations of that day could equal his in wealth.* There were 42 books "great and small" in the library and 22 additional ones in the Master's chamber, nine white indentured servants, and much livestock. The overseer of the manorial holdings was Alexander Younger. The inventory was taken room by room which gave the floor plan of the brick manor house. On an island in the Patuxent was a 50-foot frame dwelling.[5] The appraised value of the estate was 108,726 lbs. tob., with debts owing the estate of 24,994 lbs. tob. An additional inventory in 1676 reported a value of £516/2/9.

On November 18, 1676, at court John Halles, the Steward, accounted for various articles delivered to "the daughters and to the two sons". There were also "goods made into a suite for Charles and petticoats for the girls" and "to daughter Margaret one paire of childes boddies".[6] By 1677 John Halles had relinquished the administration and Thomas Banks, of Calvert County, Innholder, was the administrator. In that year he accounted for 573 lbs. tob. paid for clothing for Elizabeth one of the orphans and 439 lbs. tob. for clothing for Margaret another orphan.[7]

An account was rendered by Thomas Banks on April 28, 1679, when tobacco was earmarked for Charles Beckwith, the son and heir, and the like sums to "Every of ye Unmarryed sisters of ye said Charles, vizt, Barbara and Margaret Beckwith". Each orphan was entitled to an estate valued at 18,800 lbs. tob.[8]

Thomas Banks died intestate at which time he still retained certain property of the orphans. His widow, as Ann Dennis, on April 3, 1688, accounted for 41,136 lbs. tob. paid to Major Nicholas Sewell, the guardian of Charles Beckwith, and to Michael Taney, the husband of Margaret, one of the daughters of George Beckwith.

Children of George and Frances (Harvey) Beckwith

1. Charles Beckwith, son and heir, left issue.
2. [son] died a minor.
3. Mary Beckwith married John Miles.
4. Elizabeth Beckwith married Elias Nutall.
5. Barbara Beckwith married as his second wife Jacob Seth, of the Eastern Shore.
6. Margaret Beckwith married Michael Taney, Joakim Kirsted and George Gray.

Elizabeth Beckwith, probably one of the older children, married Elias Nutall between 1677 and 1679. Immediately upon marriage, Elias Nutall petitioned the court for the share of his wife's estate, and on July 29, 1679, Philip Calvert stated that Elias Nutall had received his share and

---

* For the complete inventory of his estate, see, Newman's *Seigniory in Early Maryland.*

that "security for the portion due to Charles, Margaret and Barbara Beckwith or otherwise to Committ them to ye said Elias or any other person".[9]

On February 9, 1679/80, Elias Nutall questioned the account of the estates of George and Frances Beckwith made by Thomas Banks, the administrator. On April 28, 1681, the Provincial Court ordered him to "clothe properly his servant Jones".[10] He received no land grants from His Lordship and no further record of either him or his wife can be found among the Maryland records after 1681.

A portion of the manor was sold before June 2, 1707, when Charles Beckwith, of St. Mary's County, petitioned for a resurvey of his portion of the manor which had not been alienated. At that time the Beckwith holdings were reputed to be about 1250 acres. The neighboring planters or lease-holders at that time were Mathew Lewis, Peter Pillon, the Widow King and the land held by George Mason as guardian to the orphans of Hugh Hopewell. During or after the resurvey George Plater 2d stated that his father who died in 1707 purchased from Charles Beckwith a portion of the manor.

John Rousby of the Patuxent River, Esq., swore that "he heard and verily believed that George Plater, late of the Patuxent, deceased, purchased from Charles Beckwith "St. Joseph's Manor alias Beckwith's Manor" for a consideration of £300. The purchase money was given to either Henry Darnell, Esq. or Charles Beckwith and that quit-rents had been duly paid.[11]

Sources: 1. Liber ABH, folio 125, Land Office; 2. Md. Hist. Mag., vol. 4, p. 63; 3. Liber 7, folio 81, Land Office; 4. Archives, vol. 10, p. 545; 5. Inventories & Accounts, Liber 2, folio 179, Hall of Records; 6. *Ibid.*, Liber 2, folio 343; 7. *Ibid.*, Liber 4, folios 175-180; 8. *Ibid.*, Liber 6, folios 47-59; 9. Testamentary Proceedings, Liber 11, folios 139, 193; 10. Liber WC, folio 421, Land Office; 11. Liber IL no. 8, folio 181, Land Office.

MARGARET (BECKWITH) TANEY-KIRSTED-GRAY
16__-1720

Margaret Beckwith, one of the younger daughters of George Beckwith and Frances his wife, was born at St. Joseph's Manor, and by April 3, 1688, had married Michael Taney, when he received a portion of his wife's estate from Anne Dennis, the administratrix of Thomas Banks who had been the administrator of George Beckwith.[1] She was his second wife, and so far only the unnamed daughter, placed as Margaret, in his will has been proved of her issue by him.

He drew up his last will and testament on May 19, 1692, which was duly probated in Calvert County on June 21, following, by James Duke, Joachim Kirstead, George Young and William Sturmy. He devised the dwelling-plantation to his wife, Margaret, during life in lieu of dower rights. After providing for his sons, Thomas, Michael and John and daughter Elizabeth, he bequeathed one half of the personal estate to his wife's "Youngest daughter born of her".[2]

The widow married shortly afterwards Dr. Joachim Kirsted who was present at the writing of her late husband's will. In 1689, Dr. Jockem Kested (sic) had been made the guardian of James Barber, of Calvert County, according to the will of his father, Numan Barber.[3]

Presumably before the marriage to the Widow Taney, John Bigger, of Calvert County, Gent., gave bond for Dr. Kirsted to the value of £700 with the understanding that the said Kirsted was to "pay to one Margaret Taney ye younger £200 and four good negroes on ye day of ye marriage to said Margaret or at the age of twenty-one . . . in the meantime to maintain suitable to her birth and degree as also to pay unto one Edward Miles £25 Sterling and one good negro when ye said Miles should arrive to ye age of 21". The matter was presented to the Court of Chancery on April 15, 1700, at which time it was shown that Joachim Kersted was deceased "leaving his wife Margaret formerly ye widow of Michael Taney administrator of his estate who is since married to one George Gray".[4]

George Gray died intestate in Calvert County. The inventory of his personal estate was filed at court during June 1715, and appraised at £343/16/10. Thomas Crabb approved as the greatest creditor and next of kin. Among the chattels were five Negro slaves, a parcel of old books, and a chest of doctor's instruments.[5] A subsequent account filed by his widow reported assets of £356/3/–, with tobacco paid to John Broome, High Sheriff of the county. The balance due the heirs was £344/2/–.[6]

The Widow Gray executed her will on November 29, 1719, it being probated in Calvert County on June 9, 1720. She styled herself as of the Patuxent River, and bequeathed her entire estate to her five children equally, but in the event that any died during minority, the survivors were to share equally. She named Colonel John Mackall and Thomas Howe as the overseers and appointed her son, John Gray, as the executor.[7]

Children of George and Margaret (Beckwith) Gray

1. John Gray.
2. George Gray.
3. Elizabeth Gray married William Meads [Meeds], of Queen Anne Co.
4. Ann Gray.
5. Jane Gray married Thomas Smith.

The appraised value of the personal estate of Margaret Gray was £372/2/6, including two gold rings and 500 gal. of cyder.[8]

An account filed by her son and executor, John Gray in Nov. 1728 indicated that the estate of his father had not been completely settled. He accounted for the balance of the estate of George Gray as £218/2/2, and after deducting that figure from the estate of Margaret Gray, it left the net estate of the latter valued at £177/7/5.

He accounted for the following disbursements:[9]

£63/3/4 to William Meads in right of his wife, Elizabeth, daughter of George and Margaret Gray.

£53 plus £25/6/9 to George Gray, son of the decedents.

£43/4/– plus £35/5/9 to Ann Gray, daughter of the decedents.

£53/18/6 to Thomas Smith who married Jane, a daughter of George and Margaret Gray.

"This Accountant Stands chargeth but not yet received the receipt of ye said William Meads living in Queen Anne's Co., which he humbly prays may be allowed £19."

"Of this Accountant's own part and portion of ye Said Estates he being another of ye sons and Representatives of said George and Margaret Gray ... £78/9/9."

Sources: 1. Inventories & Accounts, Liber 9, folio 476; 2. Wills, Liber 6, folio 3; 3. Wills, Liber 6, folio 51; 4. Chancery, Liber PC, folio 433, Land Office; 5. Inventories & Accounts, Liber 36B, folio 183; 6. *Ibid.*, Liber 37C, folio 119; 7. Wills, Liber 16, folio 50; 8. Inventories, Liber 4, folio 245; 9. Administration Accounts, Liber 9, folio 100.

DESCENDANTS OF
JAMES AND THOMAS BALDRIDGE, GENT.

William Baldridge, only son and heir of James and Dorothy Baldridge, was born in Maryland and about 1650 accompanied his parents to the Northern Neck of Virginia. His wife, was Elizabeth _____, who became the mother of his only son, Charles. His will, dated March 20, 1658/9, was probated in Westmoreland County on July 20, 1659. With minor tobacco legacies to Daniel Hutt and Edmond Lindsey, he devised his entire estate to his wife Elizabeth and son Charles. The next day after writing the instrument, he added a codicil, as follows: "William Baldridge being in good memory desire that there shall be given unto my brother Bainham his three children three cows which I nominate to Captain Pillman and had forgotten them in the will witness my hand this 21st of March 1658". He signed the document. Ref: Westmoreland Co. Wills, Liber 1, folio 93.

MADAM (BALDRIDGE) BAYNHAM
16__-16__

The Baldridge maiden who married Captain Alexander Baynham is generally given as Jane, although no source record as to her Christian name was found, so far as this research was conducted.* Her mother did not name her in her will, but did provide for her three Baynham grandchildren. It can be assumed therefore that she was deceased at that time, though it is not necessarily absolute. Her husband was certainly extant at the writing of his mother-in-law's will in 1662.

Alexander Baynham, also recorded as Banum, was in Maryland before 1642 at which time he was a retainer in the household of Thomas Baldridge. How and when he arrived in Maryland, the records of that province are somewhat baffling, but in 1642, as a servant of Thomas Baldridge, the latter received 75 lbs. tob. for the services of Alex: Banum.[1] In 1655 he deposed to be about 35 years of age, therefore, his birth occurred in or about the year 1620. By December 20, 1643, he had fulfilled his contract with Thomas Baldridge, inasmuch as a free man he witnessed a chattel deed of John Smith.[2] As three years was usually the period of indentureship, he apparently entered the Province about 1640. His marriage apparently occurred in Maryland and he was certainly senior to his wife.

---

* Some researchers claim that Alexander Baynham and Thomas Butler married the same daughter of James Baldridge, but evidence is rather conclusive that both sons-in-law of Mrs. Dorothy Baldridge were alive at the writing of her will.

He was a member of that exodus of Marylanders to the Northern Neck of Virginia about 1649 or so, when John Hallowes, John Tew, the Baldridges and others crossed the Potomac and settled in what was then Northumberland County.

On January 12, 1651/2, he witnessed a deed of conveyance in Northumberland County and soon became one of the outstanding subjects of the Colony in the matter of public service. On April 3, 1653, he was elected by the county court of Westmoreland to serve as High Sheriff for the ensuing year. The next day he was appointed by the Governor and Council a Justice of the Peace and a Captain of the Colonial Militia.[3]

On October 1, 1655, he deposed to be aged 35 and swore that he was in a boat with Mr. Hallowes and Mr. Turney when he heard Turney make several incriminating statements about Mrs. Hallowes.[4]

William Baldridge, son of James, by his will of 1659, bequeathed three cows to "brother Bainham" and his three children. When Madam Dorothy Baldridge executed her will on November 2, 1662, she named her three Baynham grandchildren and also her son-in-law.

He was likewise alive on March 18, 1662/3. On the aforementioned date, Alexander Baynham was granted 300 acres of land in Westmoreland County on Hollis [Hallowes] Creek, which had been acquired from William Wildey. The tract had been granted originally in 1652 to William Freeke who conveyed to Thomas Hawkins. Seth Foster who later settled on Maryland's Eastern Shore, acting as attorney for Hawkins, deeded the land to William Wildey.[5]

If Alexander Baynham left a last will and testament, it failed to survive the exigencies of time, but three daughters—Mary, Elizabeth, and Anne— are proved. Regrettably from a genealogist's point of view, no further history has been found to carry on to posterity a distinctive lineage through their father's service to Maryland and Virginia.

Sources: 1. Archives, vol. 3, p. 119; 2. *Ibid.*, vol. 4, p. 284; 3. Westmoreland Record Book 1653-59, folio 26; 4. *Ibid.*, folio 43; 5. Nugent's Cavaliers and Pioneers, folio 501.

MADAM (BALDRIDGE) BUTLER
16__-16__

Dorothy Baldridge, the widow of James Baldridge, in her will of November 2, 1662, named her son-in-law, Thomas Butler, the executor of her estate and at the same time bequeathed a legacy to Joshua, the son of Thomas Butler. It is assumed that "son-in-law" is defined as having married one of her daughters and that Joshua was consequently a grandson—however, Madam Baldridge failed to name a daughter Butler.

Thomas Butler was in Westmoreland County as early as September 25,

1654, when he filed his hog and cattle marks at court. It has been declared that he likewise was in Maryland before his settlement in Virginia.*

On March 23, 1664/5, Thomas Butler received 391 acres in Westmoreland County on the south side of Appomattock Creek which on the northeast was contiguous to the land of "Mr. Thomas Baldridge and James Baldridge" and northwest of the land "sometime" in the possession of Mr. Johnson and Mr. Alex. Benum.[1] On the same day he received another grant of 257 acres on Appomattox Creek beginning at a small branch issuing out of Hollis Creek. Ref: Nugent's Cavaliers and Pioneers, pp. 432, 447.

JAMES BALDRIDGE
16___-1664

James Baldridge, son and heir of Major Thomas Baldridge and his wife, married Elizabeth _____, and died leaving a minor son, William. He styled himself as of Appomattox Parish, Westmoreland County, when he executed his will on April 20, 1664. He bequeathed his wife, Elizabeth, and son William, equally his realty, but his wife was to have only one-third of the personal estate, and to be the guardian of her minor son. Ref: Westmoreland Co. Wills, Liber 1, folio 235.

---

* A Thomas Butler was a freeholder on the Isle of Kent in 1638, and in 1644 Richard Smith acknowledged a debt to him of 250 lbs. tob. Ref: Archives of Maryland, vol. 1; p. 31; vol. 4, p. 302. In 1650 Edward Thompson, the guardian of the orphans of a Thomas Butler, instituted legal action against Margaret Brent, the executrix of Leonard Calvert. He held a tenancy of 100 acres on St. Michael's Manor, St. Mary's Co., and was declared to be arrear in 3 years of rent, amounting to 6 bbl. of corn and 12 capons. Ref: Archives, vol. 10, pp. 26, 93.

APPENDIX

DOCUMENTED LIST OF THE ADVENTURERS ON THE ARK AND THE DOVE AND THOSE WHO WERE EARLY IDENTIFIED WITH THE SETTLEMENT

NOTE: Authorities to the following for the most part refer to the Patent books on file at the Land Office, Annapolis.

Adventurer	Mode of entry	Proof or remarks
John Alcome, Altham	Transported	Liber 1, folio 37; Liber ABH, folio 65.
Thomas Allen	do	Liber 1, folio 121.
William Andrews	do	do
John Ashmore	do	Liber 1, folio 121; Liber ABH, folio 98.
William Ashmore, Ashmead	do	Liber ABH, folios 65-66; Liber 1, folio 37.
James Baldridge, Gent.	————	No proof of entry
Thomas Baldridge, Gent.	————	do
James Barefoot, Gent.	Emigrated	Relation to Maryland; Fr. White's Journal.
John Baxter, Esq.	do	Relation to Maryland.
Ralph Beane, Bayne, Gent.	Transported	Liber 1, folio 121.
Thomas Beckwith	do	Liber ABH, folio 94.
Anan Benham, Bennan	do	Liber ABH, folio 6; Liber 1, folio 17.
Henry Bishop*	do	Liber 1, folio 37.
John Bolles, Bowles, Gent.	Emigrated	Calvert Papers; Fund Pub. no. 28, p. 136.
Richard Bradley	Transported	Liber 1, folio 121.
William Browne	do	Liber ABH, folio 94.
John Bryant	do	Liber ABH, folio 65-66.
Mathew Burrowes	do	Liber ABH, folio 94.

* Transcribed sometimes as Henry Briscoe.

Adventurer	*Mode of entry*	*Proof or remarks*
George Calvert, Esq.	Emigrated	Relation to Maryland.
Leonard Calvert, Esq.	do	do
Christopher Carnell	Transported	Liber ABH, folio 37.
Thomas Charington	do	Liber ABH, folio 65-66; Liber 1, folio 37.
Richard Cole	do	Liber ABH, folio 65.
John Cook	_____	Circumstantial evidence.
Thomas Cooper	Transported	Liber 1, folio 17.
Thomas Cornwalys, Esq.	Emigrated	Relation to Maryland.
Ann Cox, Gentlewoman.	do	Liber ABH, folio 12.
Edward Cranfield, Esq.	do	Relation to Maryland.
Thomas Dorrell, Esq.	do	do
Peter Draper, Gent.	Transported	Liber 1, folio 121.
Richard Duke, Gent.	do	Liber 1, folio 37; Liber ABH, folio 65-66.
Joseph Edlowe, Edloe	_____	Circumstantial evidence.
Richard Edwards	_____	Fund Pub. no. 35, p. 25.
Robert Edwards	Transported	Liber ABH, folio 66; Liber 1, folio 37.
William Edwin	do	Liber ABH, folio 66.
John Elbin	do	Liber ABH, folio 65.
Nicholas Fairfax, Esq.	Emigrated	Relation to Maryland.
Cuthbert Fenwick, Esq.	Transported	Liber ABH, folio 94.
William Fitter, Gent.	do	do
Henry Fleete, Gent.	_____	Fund Pub.
Lewis Fremand	Transported	Liber ABH, folio 65.
Richard Gerard, Esq.	Emigrated	Relation to Maryland.
Thomas Gervase, Esq.	do	Fund Pub. no. 7, pp. 116, 126.
Richard Gilbert	Transported	Liber 1, folio 121.
Stephen Gore	do	Liber ABH, folio 94.
Thomas Greene, Esq.	Emigrated	Relation to Maryland.
Thomas Grisgston	Transported	Liber 1, folio 37; liber ABH, folios 65-66.
John Halfhead	do	Liber 1, folio 121.

Adventurer	Mode of entry	Proof or remarks
John Hallowes, Gent.*	do	Liber 4, folio 623.
Nicholas Harvey, Gent.	do	Liber ABH, folio 65-66.
Jerome Hawley, Esq.	Emigrated	Relation to Maryland.
Thomas Heath	Transported	Liber ABH, folio 65.
Capt. John Hill, Gent.	Emigrated	Relation to Maryland.
John Hill	Transported	Liber ABH, folio 66.
John Hillard	do	Archives, vol. 3, p. 258.
Richard Hills	do	Liber ABH, folio 98; Liber 1, folio 121.
James Hockley	do	Liber ABH, folio 98; Liber 1, folio 121.
Benjamin Hodges	do	Liber ABH, folio 65-66; Liber 1, folio 37.
John Holderen	do	Liber 1, folio 26.
Henry James	do	Liber ABH, folio 66.
Mary Jennings	do	Archives, vol. 3, pp. 258-9.
John Knowles	do	Calvert Papers.
William Lewis, Gent.	do	Inference.
Richard Loe, Lee	do	Liber ABH, folio 94.
Richard Lustead	do	Liber ABH, folio 65; Liber 1, folio 37.
John Marlborough	do	Liber ABH, folio 65-66; Liber 1, folio 37.
Christopher Martin	do	Liber 4, folio 623.
John Medcalfe, Esq.	Emigrated	Relation to Maryland.
Charles Middleton	Transported	Liber ABH, folio 98; Liber 1, folio 121.
Thomas Minnus	do	Liber ABH, folio 66.
Roger Morgan	do	Liber 1, folio 26.
John Nevill	do	Liber 1, folio 121; Liber ABH, folio 98.
Richard Nevitt	do	Liber 1, folio 37; Liber ABH, folio 65.

* Appears sometimes as Hollis, Hallis.

Adventurer	*Mode of entry*	*Proof or remarks*
John Norton Jr.	do	Liber 4, folio 623.
John Norton Sr.	do	do
Robert Pike	do	Liber ABH, folio 98; Liber 1, folio 121.
John Price, black	do	Liber 1, folio 37; Liber ABH̄, folio 65.
John Price, white	do	Liber 1, folio 37; Liber ABH, folio 65.
Lodovick Price	do	Liber 1, folio 121.
Francis Rabnett	do	Liber ABH, folio 66; Liber 1, folio 37.
John Robinson	do	Liber ABH, folio 94.
Francis Rogers, Gent.	do	Liber 1, folio 37; Liber ABH, folios 65-66.
William Saire, Esq.	Emigrated	Relation to Maryland.
Stephen Sammion	Transported	Liber ABH, folios 35, 94.
John Sanders, Esq.	Emigrated	Relation to Maryland.
Robert Sherbys, Sherley	Transported	Liber ABH, folio 65.
Thomas Slathan	do	Archives, vol. 3, p. 258.
Madam Ann Smith, Gentlewoman.	Emigrated	Inference
Robert Smith	_____	do
Thomas Smith, Gent.	Transported	Liber ABH, folios 65-66.
William Smith	Emigrated	Inference
_____ Smith	Transported	Liber ABH, folios 65-66.
Anne Smithson	do	Inference
Mathias Sousa, mulatto	do	Liber ABH, folio 65.
Robert Sympson	do	Liber 1, folio 37.
Richard Thompson	do	Liber ABH, folio 65.
William Thompson, Gent.	_____	Inference
James Thornton	Transported	Liber 1, folios 19-20.
Cyprian Thorowgood, Gent.	_____	Inference
John Tomkins [Tomson]	_____	Liber 1, folio 20.
Robert Vaughan, Gent.	_____	Inference

Adventurer	Mode of entry	Proof or remarks
Roger Walter	Transported	Liber 1, folio 26.
John Ward	do	Liber ABH, folio 65-66.
John Wells	———	Inference
Andrew White, Gent.	Emigrated	Liber 1, folio 37; Liber ABH, folios 65-66.
Evan Wilkins	Transported	Liber ABH, folio 98.
Edward Wintour, Gent.	Emigrated	Relation to Maryland.
Frederick Wintour, Esq.	do	do
Robert Wintour, Esq.	do	do
Robert Wiseman, Esq.	do	do
Josias ———	Transported	Liber 1, folio 26.
Sam ———	do	Liber ABH, folio 94.
Francisco, mulatto	do	Liber 1, folio 37.
James ———	do	Archives, vol. 3, p. 258.

The Crew

John Boulter. Purser and steward of the Ark. He had been a citizen and skinner of St. Botolph Algate, London, and was about 40 years of age at the time of his sailing with the Adventurers. He had lived three years in London and previously had spent 12 years in the East Indies. Ref: Sherwood's American Colonists.

John Curke. Helper on the Dove.

John Games. On the Dove.

Richard Kenton. Boatswain on the Dove.

Samuel Lawson. Mate on the Dove.

Richard Orchard. Master of the Dove.

Nicholas Perrie. Helper on the Dove.

——— Warreloe. Mate on the Dove.

REPRINTS OF DOCUMENTS WHICH PROVE MORE THAN FIFTY PASSENGERS ON THE ARK AND THE DOVE

The Names of the Gentlemen Adventurers that are gone in Person to this Plantation*

Mr. Leonard Calvert, the governor, His Lordships brother.

Mr. George Calvert, his Lordships brother.

Mr. Jerome Hawley, Esq., Commissioner.

Mr. Thomas Cornewallis, Esq., Commissioner.

Mr. Richard Gerard, son to Sir Thomas Gerard Knight and Baronet.

Mr. Edward Wintour, sonne of the Lady Anne Wintour.

Mr. Frederick Wintour, sonne of the Lady Anne Wintour.

Mr. Henry Wiseman, sonne to Sir Thomas Wiseman, Knt.

Mr. John Saunders.

Mr. Edward Cranfield.

Mr. Henry Greene.

Mr. Nicholas Fairfax.

Mr. John Baxter.

Mr. Thomas Dorrell.

Captaine John Hill.

Mr. John Medcalfe.

Mr. William Saire.

NOTE: It is now known that at least two discrepancies occurred in the Christian names—it was Thomas Greene instead of Henry, and Robert Wiseman instead of Henry.

TRANSPORTEES OF LEONARD CALVERT, ESQ.

13 August 1641. Leonard Calvert demanded 6,000 acres of land due by Conditions of first plantation for transporting 15 able men into the

---

* A Relation of Maryland, see, reprint in Hall's Narratives of Early Maryland, p. 101.

Province in the year 1633, and likewise 100 acres of Townland for the said title vizt: *

Peter Draper	Thomas Allen	Ralph Beane
Robert Pike	Charles Middleton	Evan Wilkins
James Hockley	John Halfhead	Richard Hills
Richard Gilbert	Richard Bradley	John Nevill
John Ashmore	William Andrews	Lodovick Price

* In this document the record does not refer to them as servants.

Laid out for Leonard Calvert, Esq., a parcell of Townland lyeing nearest together about the ffort and commonly called Governor's ffield bounding on the West with St. George's River on the North with St. Maries Bay on the East with the Mill brooke to the distance of about 47 perches above the place where the Mill now standeth where the ffreehold of St. Peters and the Chappell Land meet in one Angle. And on the south with the said Chappell Land by a right line drawn Westerly from the said angle unto St. George's River where the rail formerly began containing one hundred acres or thereabouts.

Ref: Liber 1, folio 121, Land Office, Annapolis.

Transportees of Father Andrew White

August 16, 1650. The names of certain persons transported into Maryland in right of whom Thomas Copley Esq. demandeth Land.

Transported Anno 1633.

Mr. Andrew White	Henry Bishop	Jo: Hilliard
Mr. Jo: Altam	Richd Lusted	Mathias Zause
Tho Slatham	Tho Heath	ffra Moloto
Robert Simpson	W. Ashmore	Lewis ffreman
Mary Jennings	Robt Sherley	James killed at Mattapanie

Transported ano 1634.

Mr ffrancis Rogers	Richard (sic) Harvey
John Hill	Xpofer Carnoll

John Bryant

Thomas Copley, Esq. entered rights for 20,000 acres due him over and besides what is already entered.

August 25, 1650. That the names lately delivered to the Secretary's Office by Thomas Copley, Esq. were servants of Andrew White, Esq. and that he had other servants whose names I [Thomas Greene] do not know for which there is undoubtedly rights to 8,000 acres due to Mr. White and his successors upon the first adventure into Maryland and that it is believe that other rights were due for adventurers brought into the Province upon latter conditions, and I doe avouch first and last the Gent abovesaid transported at least 60 persons into this Province.

(signed) Thomas Greene.

Ref: Proceedings of the Council, printed in Archives of Maryland, vol. 3, pp. 258-259.

TRANSPORTEES OF THOMAS CORNWALLYS, ESQ.

12 February 1640/1. Thomas Cornwallys, Esq. Demandeth four thousand acres due by first Conditions of Plantation for Transporting into the Province in the year 1633 ten Able Manservants that is to say:

Thomas Beckwith	Sam that was brought from St. Xtopher
Matthew Burraws	John Robinson, Carpenter
Cuthbert Fenwick	William Brown
Richd Loe	Stephen Gore
William Fitter	Stephen Sammion

Ref: Liber ABH, folio 94, Land Office, Annapolis.

[Undated] Memoriall of rights Entred by Capt Cornwallis — 1633 Thomas Cornewallis transported himself and Eleven Servants into Maryland which is 12 for which is due to Mannors of 4000 acres and 400 acres of Town Land for 10 and 400 acres for the 20 odd persons in all 4800.

Given me by Mr. John Saunders 5 Servants and their rights 2200— Bought John Hollowes, Cuthbert fenwicke, Christopher Martin, John Norton Senr and Jen^r in all 5 that year for which is due 2200 in all 9200.

Ref: Liber 4, folio 623, Land Office, Annapolis.

1 Feb. 1652/3. Anno Dom 1634 Transported in the Ark myself and twelve Servants. By my Partner Mr. John Sanders who dyeing gave me that year five Servants . . . Brought the same year and Exported from Virginia four Servants Vizt Cuthbert ffenwick, Christopher Martin, John Norton Senr, John Norton Jenr . . . So in all that year Two and Twenty persons for which I was by Conditions of plantation then sett forth by the Lord Baltemore to have for every five persons a Manor of Two Thousand Acres and one hundred Acres of Town Land And for the Odd persons two Hundred Acres Each. So there is due unto me upon the first Year's Account Eight Thousand Eight Hundred Acres.

Ann Dom 1635. Transported into this province Zachary Mottershead, Walter Waterling, John Cage, Robert Nicholls, Frances Vanenden for whom is due according to the First Conditions Two Thousand one Hundred Acres.

Ref: Liber ABH, folio 244, Land Office, Annapolis.

7 March 1641. Thomas Cornwaleys, Esq. Demandeth 2,000 Acres of Land by first conditions of ye Plantation for transporting into the Province five able men Servants in the year 1633.

John Hallowes	Roger Walter	And Josias that was drowned thereafter
John Holdern	Roger Morgan	

Ref: Liber 1, folio 26, Land Office, Annapolis.

LAND RIGHTS ASSIGNED TO FERDINANDO PULTON

9 Oct. 1639. Mr. Ferdinando Pulton Demandeth Land Due by Condtions of plantation under these Devall Titles following that is to say for men brought in by the Severall persons whose Assignee the Said Ferdinando Pulton is and for Men brought in in his own right.

As Assignee of Mr. Andrew White brought into the Province Anno 1633.

Mr. Andrew White	Lewis Freemond
Mr. John Alcome	Richard Thompson
Thomas Statham	Mathias Sousa, a Molato.
Robert Simpson	Richard Lusthead
Henry Briscoe*	William Ashmead†
Thomas Heath	Robert Sherbys

As Assignee of Mr. John Sanders Anno 1633.

Benjamin Hodges	Richard Cole
John Elbin	Richard Nevill (*sic*)

John Marlburgh

As Assignee of Mr. Richard Gerrard.

Thomas Minns	Robert Edwards
Thomas Grogson	John Ward

William Edwin

As Assignee of Messrs Edward & Frederick Wintour Ano Eod.

black John Price	Thomas Smith
white John Price	Richd Duke
Francis Robnot	Henry James

Thomas Charinton

---

* Incorrect transcription from the original, should be Henry Bishop. See original land claims of Father White in 1633, Archives, vol. 3, p. 258.

† Should be William Ashmore.

Anno 1634.

Mr. _____ Rogers	Nicholas Harvey
John Hill	Christopher Carnot
John Briant	A Smith lost by the way

Ref: Liber ABH, folios 65-66, Land Office, Annapolis.

LAND RIGHTS CLAIMED BY FERDINANDO PULTON

Mr. fferdinando Pulton demandeth the land due by Conditions of Plantations under these Several titles following that is to say for men brought in by Several persons whose assigne the said fferdinando Pultons and for men brought in in his own right.

As assigne of Mr Andrew White brought in to the Province anno 1633.

Mr Andrew White	Henry Bishop	Mathias Sousa, a molato
Mr John Altome	Thos Heath	Richard Lusthead
Thomas Slatham	Lewis ffremond	William Ashmore
Robert Simpson	Richard Thompson	Robert Sherley
	Anno 1634	
Mr Rogers	Nicholas Hervey	A Smith lost by the way
John Hill	Xpofer Carnoll	
John Briant		
	Anno 1635	
John Horwood	James Thornton	ffrancisco a molato

As assignee of Mr. John Sanders anno 1633

Benjamin Hodges	Richard Cole	John Marlburgh
John Elbin	Richard Nevell (sic)	

As assignee of Mr. Richard Gerrard ao cod

Thomas Munns	Robert Edwards	William Edwin
Thomas Grigston	John Ward	

As assigne of Mr Edward and ffrederick Wintour ao cod

black John Price	Thomas Smith	Henry James
White John Price	Richard Duke	Thomas Charinton
ffrancis Rabinett		

Ref: Liber 1, folio 37, Land Office, Annapolis.

16th August 1650

The names of certain persons transported into Maryland in right of whome Thomas Copley Esq. demandeth Land.

Transported Anno 1633

Mr Andrew White	Henry Bishop	Jo: Hilliard
M^r Jo: Altam	Richd Lusted	Mathias Zause
Tho Slatham	Tho Heath	ffra Moloto
Robert Simpson	Wm Ashmore	Lewis ffreman
Mary Jennings	Robt Sherley	James killed at Mattapanie—

Transported Ano 1634

M^r ffrancis Rogers	Richard Harvey*	John Bryant
John Hill	Xpofer Carnoll	

Ref: Archives of Maryland, vol. 3, pp. 258-259.

The following transportees of Leonard Calvert have been cited as coming in 1633, but a careful inspection of the script (though a copy from an earlier liber) states "since the year 1633" and not "in the year 1633".

17th ffebry 1641/2. Leonard Calvert, Esq., demandeth 5000 acres of land due by Conditions of Plantation for transporting 25 able men into the Province Since the year 1633.*

John ffridd a boy that he bought of Thomas Steg of Virginia ao 1637.	William Harrington
	Daniel an Irishman
Thomas Cooper	Avill Pinley
Richard Smith	Samuel Barrett
A boy called York sold to Thomas Bradneck	Edward Ebbs
A purblind youth sold to Mr. Brainthwt.	Thomas Mosse
One called Small sold to himself.	Six new hands [unnamed] brought out of Virginia this year
Thomas Ouley	
Sam Scovell	Thomas Oliver Smith
Nicholas Polhampton	
Matthew Rodan	
One that served the latter part of his time with Hales	

Ref: Patents, Liber 1, folio 27, Land Office.

---

* Should be Nicholas Harvey.

---

† Only 24 names were listed.

MEN WHO REMAINED WITH EDWARD WYNNE
THIS YEARE [1622]

NOTE: While the above caption is vague, it is certain that the following list were members of Sir George's colony at Ferryland in 1622.

Captain Powell

Nicholas Hoskins.

Robert Stoning.

Roger Fleshman, Chirurgion

Henry Dring, Husbandman

Owen Evans

Mary Russell

Sibell Dee, maide

Elizabeth Kerne ⎱ girls
Jane Jackson ⎰

Thomas Wilson ⎱ smith
John Prater ⎰

James Beuell, Stone-layer

Benjamin Hacker, Quarry-man

Henry Doke, Boats Master

William Sharpus, Tailor

Elizabeth Sharpus, his wife.

John Bayly

Ann Bayly, his wife

Widdow Bayly

Joseph Parsoer

Robert Row, Fishman

Philip Jane, Cooper

William Bond ⎱ Boats master
Peter Wotton ⎰

Ellia Hichson ⎱
Digory Fleshman ⎰ Boye
Richard Higgins

Nicholas Hinckson ⎱
Robert Bennett ⎰ Carpenter
William Hatch

Ref: A Discourse and Discovery of New Found Land, by Capt. Richard Whitbourne, printed London, 1622.

Index

CPSIA information can be obtained
at www.ICGtesting.com
Printed in the USA
LVHW081316030620
657308LV00019B/1789